# Financial Options

by
M. D. Fitzgerald

Euromoney Publications

Published by
Euromoney Publications Limited,
Nestor House, Playhouse Yard,
London EC4

ISBN 1 870031 55 5

Filmset by Eta Services (Typesetters) Ltd, Beccles, Suffolk
Printed in Great Britain by Page Bros (Norwich) Ltd.

# Contents

# List of exhibits

# Foreword

In hardly more than a decade, options markets the world over have seen explosive growth, expansion and diversification. Today, options on stocks, indexes, currencies and interest rates offer innovative ways of increasing and protecting capital and assets. Options continue to evolve as superior tools for the transfer and control of financial risk, for insurance, for protection, and for hedging.

Professor Fitzgerald's book is basic to understanding why options exist and why they have brought about the fastest growing financial markets of the 1980s. For investment managers, professional investors, traders and serious students and observers of the derivative markets, this publication will serve as a handbook, guide and advisor to the financial options markets.

In simple language, Professor Fitzgerald reviews and goes beyond the basics of options to deliver a truly comprehensive view of options products as well as developments in the options markets that are factual, timely and interesting. Particular attention is paid to the relationships between options and futures, between securities and commodities and among options markets in the United States, Europe and other parts of the world.

Professor Fitzgerald's book emphasizes the practical aspects of using options. Trading and hedging strategies available to market participants are presented not only as theories but as actual case studies that are explained and demonstrated. The latest concepts and practical applications of options pricing are reviewed. What has often seemed difficult becomes surprisingly easy to understand.

While there is a great deal of information to assimilate, it is presented in a brief, clear and logical sequence. Here, at last, is a book that should forever erase the use of the word 'arcane' in describing options and the options markets.

Howard A. Baker
Senior Vice President, Options
American Stock Exchange

December 1986

# Author's biography

Professor M. Desmond Fitzgerald BA(York), PhD(Manchester) is currently Group Chief Economist and Head of Planning for Alexanders Laing and Cruickshank Holdings Limited, the international securities division of Mercantile House Holdings. He is also Visiting Professor of Finance at the City University Business School.

Prior to his latest appointment he served as the Ernst and Whinney Professor of Finance at the University of Strathclyde. He has also taught at the City University Business School and the Graduate School of Business Administration, New York University, and headed the Economic Research Department of Chemical Bank in London. He has acted as a consultant to numerous major financial institutions including the London Stock Exchange and the London International Financial Futures Exchange, and served as Chairman of the London Maritime Investment Company, a specialist option trading firm.

He has published widely in academic and general journals and is the author of *Financial Futures*, published by Euromoney Publications in 1983. Two further books, one on Financial Regulation (with Roy Batchelor) and the other, a Directory of Financial Futures and Options Markets, will be published in 1987. His current interests include program trading systems, optimal bond hedging, medieval financial markets, and optimal strategies at games of chance.

# Preface

Since the opening of trading in stock options on the Chicago Board Options Exchange in 1973, the growth of trading in financial options worldwide – both over-the-counter and exchange traded – has been spectacular. Individual stock options have been followed by options on stock indices, options on short- and long-term fixed interest instruments, currency options, and options on physical commodities. Significant financial option exchanges have developed not only in the United States, but in the United Kingdom, Canada, The Netherlands, Australia and other centres throughout the world.

New techniques have been developed for trading, arbitrage and hedging with cash and options instruments, and a whole new range of concepts has arisen such as portfolio insurance, 90–10 portfolios, return enhancement programmes, and many others. The most recent volume figures, particularly in the United States, suggest that future expansion in options trading could be even greater than it has been over the last five to 10 years. It is already apparent that all participants in the financial markets need to know about these new instruments and how they can be integrated into their trading and investment strategies.

This book is designed to provide a wide-ranging coverage of all aspects of traded financial options, covering the general principles of options, including pricing, trading and hedging, and the individual characteristics and behaviour of the different types of options. All types of options are dealt with, from stock and stock index options to interest rate and currency options.

A great many individuals and institutions have helped me in the writing of this book. I would particularly like to thank my colleagues at City University and New York University for many discussions on options, and Jacques Pezier, ex of the Investor Intelligence Systems Corporation and now of Barclays de Zoete Wedd, for supplying the software largely used to construct graphs and tables for the book. My thanks also to the London International Financial Futures Exchange, and the London Stock Exchange, not only for permission to make use of course material, but also for the opportunity to be involved in their option training programmes on which I learnt a great deal about options. My gratitude is also due to Andrew Sutton of Price Waterhouse for kindly contributing the chapter on taxation and accounting aspects of options, and to Richard Ensor of Euromoney for putting up with such a slow author. Finally I can say that the book would never have been completed without the help and assistance of my secretary Patricia Baker, with her excellent typing and her willingness to put up with an author's eccentricities during the writing of this book.

M. Desmond Fitzgerald
December 1986

# Chapter 1

# The development of financial options markets

The history of options contracts on physical commodities is a long one. There is evidence of the use of option-related contracts in the ancient world, and among the medieval banks and financial institutions of Italy, Germany and other financial centres. Options on individual stocks were traded on semi-organized exchanges in Holland and the United Kingdom as early as the 17th century. The history of options trading has been characterized by scandals, defaults and other criminal activities. One of the reasons for this was the lack of an adequately organized exchange on which trading could take place, and adequate clearing and regulatory systems to ensure the maintenance of an orderly market and the efficient fulfilment of the option contracts.

Until the opening of the Chicago Board Options Exchange in 1973, options in both stocks and physical commodities were trading worldwide on an over-the-counter basis. The advantage of such a system is that, like the foreign exchange forward market, it allows buyers and sellers of options to define the conditions of the options precisely to suit their specific requirements. The disadvantage is that the specific nature of the contracts may hinder the development of adequate market liquidity, and that the absence of an organized clearing system may render the possibility of default significant.

The solution was to start trading standard options contracts on an organized exchange, with contract fulfilment guaranteed by an independent clearing organization. This was achieved with the commencement of stock option trading on the Chicago Board Options Exchange, and the founding of the Options Clearing Corporation to guarantee performance on all stock options contracts traded on US stock exchanges. The success of traded stock options contracts on the CBOE subsequently led to a vast expansion of options trading in the United States, both on additional exchanges such as the American Stock Exchange, the Philadelphia Stock Exchange, the Chicago Board of Trade and the Chicago Mercantile Exchange, and on many different underlying assets such as currencies, stock indices, and Treasury bonds. Exchange traded options markets also developed in Amsterdam, London, Sydney and Toronto.

Trading in financial options is one of the largest growth areas in the financial markets. The volume expansion and the proliferation of new traded options is staggering, and shows no signs of slowing down. In some cases, such as the Standard and Poor's 100 index option traded on the CBOE, the dollar value of option trading comfortably exceeds the cash value of trading in the underlying assets.

This chapter attempts to answer basic questions about the whys and wherefores of financial traded options, as a background to the more detailed chapters that follow.

## 1. What is an option contract?

An option contract is the right to buy or sell a specific quantity of an underlying asset at a specific price on or before a specific date in the future. The right to buy is called a *call* option and the right to sell is called a *put* option.

A typical physical commodity option might involve one investor selling to another the right to buy 50 tonnes of copper at a fixed price of £1,000 per tonne on September 30. On that date, if the buyer of the option chooses to exercise his option, he has the right to hand over £50,000 and take delivery of 50 tonnes of copper. If the option is exercised the seller of the option has the obligation to hand over 50 tonnes of copper in exchange for cash at a fixed price. The asymmetry of an option contract should be noted. For a buyer, the option involves a *right* which may be exercised or not according to the circumstances. For a seller, the option involves an *obligation* which must be fulfilled if the buyer so demands.

A *financial option* is an option to buy or sell an underlying financial instrument, which might be the spot or cash instrument or a financial futures contract.[1] For instance, a currency option traded on the London Stock Exchange calls for the option buyer to hand over dollars in exchange for £12,500 sterling at a fixed dollar-sterling exchange rate. If the specified rate was, say, $1.50, the call option buyer would have the right to hand over $18,750 to receive £12,500 sterling. If sterling at the time were trading spot $1.75, the right would be very valuable. The option buyer could hand over $18,750 and receive sterling worth $21,875 at the spot rate – giving a net value of $3,125 less the original cost of the option.

What are the important differences between traded options and over-the-counter options?

1. Traded financial options are traded on a centralized and regulated exchange.
2. Traded options contracts are highly standardized, with trading and delivery in specific months for specific quantities of a specifically defined product.
3. Fulfilment of traded options contracts is guaranteed by a margining and marking to market system operated by a centralized clearing house, which also organizes the physical delivery of the underlying assets and guarantees such delivery in the case of default by an option seller.
4. Most traded options can be exercised by the option buyer at any time before the expiration date of the option.
5. Traded options purchased can easily be sold in the market place to a third party.

All these features serve to create in many cases a highly liquid trading vehicle.

## 2. Types of options contracts traded

The first breakthrough in exchange traded options came with the start of trading in individual stock options in the United States in 1973. Individual stock options also trade in Amsterdam on the European Options Exchange, on the London Stock Exchange, on the Sydney Stock Exchange and on various Canadian exchanges. Since the original success of the individual stock options, however, the emphasis has shifted to options based on more complex financial instruments, with the two greatest single successes being the Standard and Poor's 100 index option traded on the Chicago Board Options Exchange, and the Treasury bond futures option traded on the Chicago Board of Trade. Other new products include currency options, sub-index options, Treasury bill and Eurodollar options, and commodity options. Below is a list of those financial options contracts which were actively traded in 1986.

### United States

| | |
|---|---|
| Stock options | Chicago Board Options Exchange, Chicago Stock Exchange, Pacific Stock Exchange, Philadelphia Stock Exchange, New York Stock Exchange, NASDAQ |
| Stock index options (cash) | Chicago Board Options Exchange, New York Stock Exchange, American Stock Exchange, Philadelphia Stock Exchange, NASDAQ |
| Stock index options (futures) | Chicago Mercantile Exchange, New York Futures Exchange, Kansas City Board of Trade |
| Sub-index options (cash) | American Stock Exchange, Philadelphia Stock Exchange, Pacific Stock Exchange |
| Interest rate options (cash) | Chicago Board Options Exchange (Treasury bond), American Stock Exchange (T-bond, T-note, T-bill, CD) |
| Interest rate options (futures) | Chicago Board of Trade (T-bond, T-note), Chicago Mercantile Exchange (T-bill, Eurodollar) |
| Currency options (cash) | Chicago Board Options Exchange, Philadelphia Stock Exchange |
| Currency options (futures) | Chicago Mercantile Exchange |

---

[1] For a full discussion of financial futures contracts, see M. D. Fitzgerald, *Financial Futures*, Euromoney Publications (1983).

**Europe**

| | |
|---|---|
| Stock options | London Stock Exchange, European Options Exchange (Amsterdam), Frankfurt Börse, Paris Bourse |
| Stock index options (cash) | London Stock Exchange, London International Financial Futures Exchange |
| Interest rate options | London Stock Exchange (short and long gilt cash), London International Financial Futures Exchange (futures – long gilt, Eurodollar, T-bond) |
| Currency options | European Options Exchange (cash), London Stock Exchange (cash), London International Financial Futures Exchange (futures) |

**Other regions**

| | |
|---|---|
| Stock options | Sydney Stock Exchange, Montreal Exchange, Toronto Stock Exchange, Vancouver Stock Exchange |
| Stock index options | Toronto Stock Exchange (cash), Montreal Exchange (cash), Sydney Futures Exchange (futures) |
| Interest rate options | Sydney Futures Exchange (90-day acceptances future, Treasury bond future, Eurodollar) |
| Currency options | Montreal Exchange (cash), Vancouver Exchange (cash), Sydney Futures Exchange (futures) |

The range of options contracts on financial instruments currently traded is very wide, and there is no sign of an end to the proliferation. The highly successful Chicago Exchanges are expected to increase their range of option products over the next few years, and the Far Eastern exchanges such as Hong Kong, Singapore and Tokyo will probably develop financial options trading.

## 3. Financial options trading volume

The current volume of financial options trading in the United States is beginning to dwarf the underlying cash markets. Exhibit 1.1 shows the volume of trading in the most successful futures options: the Chicago Mercantile Exchange S & P 500 index, and the Chicago Board of Trade long Treasury bond and note, plus the CME Eurodollar and currency contracts.

**Exhibit 1.1: Volume of trading in futures options in the United States**

| | *Annual volume* | | | |
|---|---|---|---|---|
| *Contract* | *1982* | *1983* | *1984* | *1985* |
| CBT T-bond | 51,965 | 1,022,376 | 6,636,209 | 11,901,116 |
| CBT T-note | — | — | — | 177,292 |
| CME S & P 500 | — | 157,863 | 672,884 | 1,090,068 |
| CME Eurodollar | — | — | — | 743,080 |
| CME currencies | — | — | 727,634 | 2,216,285 |

The Chicago Board of Trade Treasury bond option is by far the most successful of any futures option traded on any options exchange. The volume growth is continuing, with daily volume frequently over 300,000, representing T-bond face value of $30 billion.

Cash options trading, particularly in individual stock options, stock indices and currency options, has also shown extraordinary volume growth (see Exhibit 1.2).

Apart from the extraordinarily high daily volume figures, the interesting and continuing trend is the switch away from equity options to non-equity options, particularly on the Chicago Board Options Exchange. This reflects the rise of the S & P 100 index option, now the dominant option across all exchanges, which traded over 90 million contracts in 1985. The other rapid advance has been by currency options trading on the Philadelphia Stock Exchange.

Some volume statistics for non-US exchanges are shown in Exhibit 1.3.

## Exhibit 1.2: Volume of trading in cash options in the United States

| | *Average daily volume* | | |
| Contract | *1983* | *1984* | *1985* |
|---|---|---|---|
| AMEX equity | 43,194 | 130,536 | 143,140 |
| AMEX non-equity | 10,889 | 27,030 | 49,549 |
| CBOE equity | 303,953 | 231,754 | 228,154 |
| CBOE non-equity | 41,636 | 254,985 | 363,544 |
| NYSE equity | — | — | 1,119 |
| NYSE non-equity | — | 16,148 | 16,944 |
| PHLX equity | 65,678 | 63,071 | 47,755 |
| PHLX non-equity | 789 | 6,370 | 24,165 |
| PSE equity | 44,062 | 44,167 | 50,136 |
| PSE non-equity | — | 770 | 367 |

Abbreviations: AMEX, American Stock Exchange; CBOE, Chicago Board Options Exchange; PHLX, Philadelphia Stock Exchange; NYSE, New York Stock Exchange; PSE, Pacific Stock Exchange.

## Exhibit 1.3: Trading volume on non-US exchanges

### a. LIFFE options trading volume 1985–86

| | *Sterling* | | *Eurodollar* | |
| | *Volume* | *Open interest* | *Volume* | *Open interest* |
|---|---|---|---|---|
| June 1985 | 4,385 | 3,327 | 660 | 458 |
| July | 33,501 | 14,060 | 5,830 | 1,184 |
| August | 21,890 | 19,331 | 5,327 | 3,172 |
| September | 33,906 | 20,961 | 4,189 | 2,994 |
| October | 18,228 | 26,488 | 6,517 | 5,402 |
| November | 15,588 | 26,804 | 6,419 | 6,183 |
| December | 15,334 | 12,943 | 2,453 | 3,991 |
| January 1986 | 15,805 | 16,578 | 5,929 | 6,382 |

### b. London Stock Exchange options trading volume 1984–85 (quarterly)

| | *Sterling stocks* | *Dollar stocks* | *Currencies* | *Index* | *Gilts* |
|---|---|---|---|---|---|
| 1984(4) | 326,185 | 5,168 | 0 | 46,130 | 0 |
| 1985(1) | 523,187 | 5,289 | 0 | 56,067 | 19,235 |
| 1985(2) | 330,194 | 3,990 | 23,439 | 35,893 | 20,426 |
| 1985(3) | 366,532 | 5,326 | 43,847 | 43,011 | 29,975 |
| 1985(4) | 747,580 | 5,622 | 21,400 | 82,259 | 28,374 |

### c. Other exchanges' options trading volume 1984–85 (quarterly)

| *Exchange* | *Contract* | *1984* | *1985(1)* | *1985(2)* | *1985(3)* | *1985(4)* |
|---|---|---|---|---|---|---|
| Montreal | Canadian bond | 147,122 | 61,794 | 80,532 | 39,114 | 59,381 |
| | Currencies | 17,066 | 6,578 | 12,693 | 12,142 | 3,766 |
| | Gold | 181,151 | 51,985 | 32,586 | 43,021 | 28,234 |
| Toronto | Canadian bond | — | — | — | 952 | 5,337 |
| Sydney | 90-day bills | — | — | 1,212 | 5,335 | 5,365 |
| | All Ord. share index | — | — | 76 | 1,446 | 1,906 |
| | Treasury bond | — | — | — | — | 772 |
| | Currency | — | — | 168 | 442 | — |

Growth in financial options trading outside the United States, except in individual stock options, is modest, although the recently introduced gilt and Treasury bond options seem to be doing better. The next few years will show whether the non-US exchanges are able to rival the US exchanges in developing and trading liquid option contracts other than individual stock options.

## 4. Uses of financial options

The successful introduction of traded financial options indicates that they fulfil a real need in modern financial markets. The trading merits of options contracts are self-evident. Because options are inherently a right not an obligation, the maximum loss the option buyer can ever face is the original cost of the premium. Thus options allow the trader to act upon his forecasts for the underlying asset price, while limiting his total capital at risk to any desired level – something he cannot do when trading the underlying asset. In addition, as will be discussed later in the book, options allow the trader to speculate not just upon where the underlying asset price is going to move, but also upon how volatile the underlying asset price is going to be.

The limited risk nature of options allows a specific type of hedging. Suppose a portfolio manager owns GEC stock: he could fix a price at which he could guarantee to sell that stock at a subsequent date by purchasing a GEC put option. Such a purchase would insure the manager against a fall in the price of GEC for the payment of the option premium. If the GEC price rose, however, the manager would lose no more on the option position than the original put premium, and be able to reap some of the benefits of a further upward price movement. Some fund managers may find this a more favourable hedging strategy than simply selling the stock in the market.

Subsequent chapters in this book will discuss the many strategies that can be adopted with options. For instance, options may be written against underlying asset portfolios to enhance returns; complex arbitrage strategies may be implemented with combinations of put options, call options and the underlying asset; and complex option positions may be used to produce profit-loss profiles to suit any trader's price and volatility forecasts, no matter how precise.

The world's traded options markets provide a wealth of trading, hedging, arbitrage and investment opportunities to both the occasional and the sophisticated investor. The aim of this book is to explore the essential techniques for valuing option contracts and for designing successful trades, hedges and arbitrages.

# Chapter 2
# The basics of options

## 1. Introduction

An option contract is the right to buy or sell a specific quantity of a given asset at a specific price at or before a specific date in the future. As such it has certain important characteristics.

1. An option conveys upon the buyer a right not an obligation. Since it can be abandoned without further penalty, the maximum loss that the buyer faces is the original cost of the option.
2. By contrast if the buyer chooses to exercise his right to buy or sell the asset, the seller has an obligation to deliver or take delivery of the underlying asset. His potential loss is therefore unlimited.

Although a complete glossary of option terms is given in Appendix 1, some elementary terms are so frequently encountered that they are listed here.

### Options vocabulary

| | |
|---|---|
| Call option | The right to buy at a fixed price. |
| Put option | The right to sell at a fixed price. |
| Strike or exercise price | Fixed price at which the option may be exercised and the underlying asset bought or sold. |
| Premium | The price or cost of an option. |
| Maturity or expiration day | Final day on which an option can be exercised. |
| Exercise | To put into effect the right to buy or sell. |
| In-the-money | The option has exercise value, i.e. the exercise price lies below (in the case of a call) or above (in the case of a put) the prevailing price of the underlying asset. |
| At-the-money | The option exercise price approximately equals the prevailing price of the underlying asset. |
| Out-of-the-money | The option exercise price lies above (in the case of a call) or below (in the case of a put) the prevailing price of the underlying asset. |
| American option | The option can be exercised by the buyer at any time before maturity. |
| European option | The option can be exercised by the buyer only on the maturity day. |

The characteristic profits and losses of option contracts can be illustrated by considering a typical set of option prices. The table below illustrates call and put option premiums for British Petroleum stock options on 10 June 1986.

| | Calls | | | Puts | | | |
|---|---|---|---|---|---|---|---|
| Exercise price | July | Oct. | Jan. | July | Oct. | Jan. | |
| 500 | 78 | 90 | 100 | 2 | 8 | 10 | |
| 550 | 38 | 53 | 65 | 10 | 25 | 30 | Equity price = 569 |
| 600 | 10 | 25 | 38 | 40 | 50 | 55 | |

Although these prices are for a share traded on the London Stock Exchange, the options are representative of options traded worldwide. Each option on the London market calls for the purchase or sale of 1,000 shares of the underlying stock.[1] At any point in time various different exercise price options will be traded, as well as different maturities. As can be seen the BP options have specific exercise days in the months of July, October and January, i.e. a three-month cycle. Note also that the option premiums tend to be higher the more the option is in-the-money and the longer the option has to go to maturity.

Let us examine the profit and loss at expiration for buying and selling put and call options.

## Call option

The BP call option buyer has the right to buy 1,000 shares of BP at a fixed price. The buyer of a call has an unlimited profit potential if the BP stock price rises and a risk of loss limited to the premium.

The BP call option seller has the obligation to sell 1,000 shares of BP at a fixed price if the buyer exercises the option. While a call seller is exposed to unlimited risk if the BP price rises, he is assured of a fixed profit if the call remains unexercised.

The profit profile is shown in Exhibit 2.1a. The profit profile for the seller of the call is the exact opposite of the profit profile for the buyer of the call.

## Put option

The BP put buyer has the right to sell 1,000 BP shares at a fixed price. The buyer of a put has unlimited profit potential if the BP price falls and a risk of loss limited to the amount paid for the put. The BP put seller (or writer as he is often known) has the obligation to buy 1,000 shares at a fixed price if the buyer exercises the option. While a put seller is exposed to unlimited risk if the BP price falls, he is assured of a fixed profit if the put remains unexercised.

The profit profiles for the put buyer and seller are also shown in Exhibit 2.1b. Once again the buyer's and seller's profiles are exactly opposite.

## Options positions compared

It is also worth quickly comparing option profit profiles with a holding in the underlying stock. Exhibit 2.2 shows profits and losses for buying a BP 550 call, buying the stock at 568, and selling the 550 put. The long 550 call behaves like a long BP stock position with a guaranteed stop-loss order at an effective 512p, and an effective purchase price of 588p (20p above the current price of 568p). The short put position also behaves like a long BP stock position but with a guaranteed profit-taking order and an effective purchase price 28p below the current stock price.

Many different profit and loss profiles can be generated using combinations of put and call options and long and short asset positions. This is discussed in detail in Chapter 4 on trading techniques.

# 2. Different types of options

A full description of all the major traded options worldwide is given in Appendix 2. This section attempts to classify options into the major types, with illustrations drawn from all the major exchanges.

## a. Individual stock options

The basic characteristics of individual stock options have been demonstrated by the BP options discussed above. Individual stock options are traded on many stock exchanges and option exchanges worldwide. The largest exchanges in the United States are the Chicago Board Options Exchange, the American Stock Exchange, the Philadelphia Stock Exchange and the Pacific Stock Exchange. Part of a typical *Wall Street Journal* options page (in this case for 6 June 1986) is shown in Exhibit 2.3.[2] There are close similarities to the London BP options. Note the varying exercise prices.

---

[1] In the United States, the option is usually defined on 100 shares of stock, largely because the average stock price is significantly higher.

[2] In this, r = no option traded, s = no option offered.

# Exhibit 2.1: Profit profiles

### a. Call buying and selling

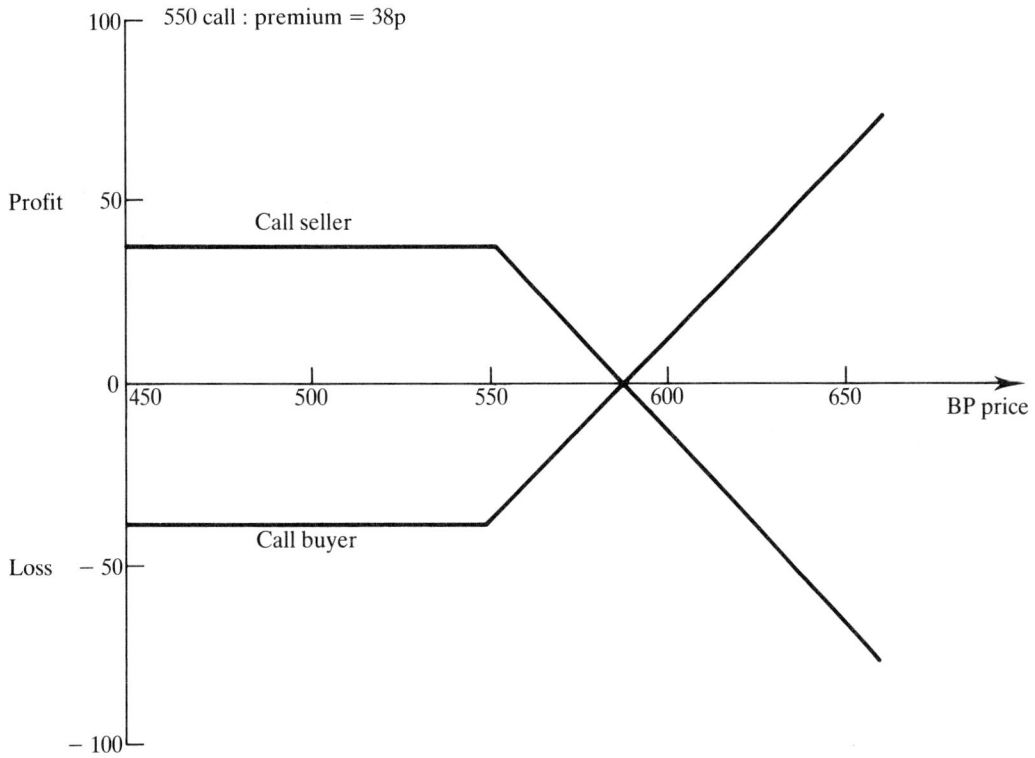

100 — 550 call : premium = 38p

Profit 50

Call seller

0
450       500       550       600       650       BP price

Call buyer

Loss — 50

— 100

### b. Put buying and selling

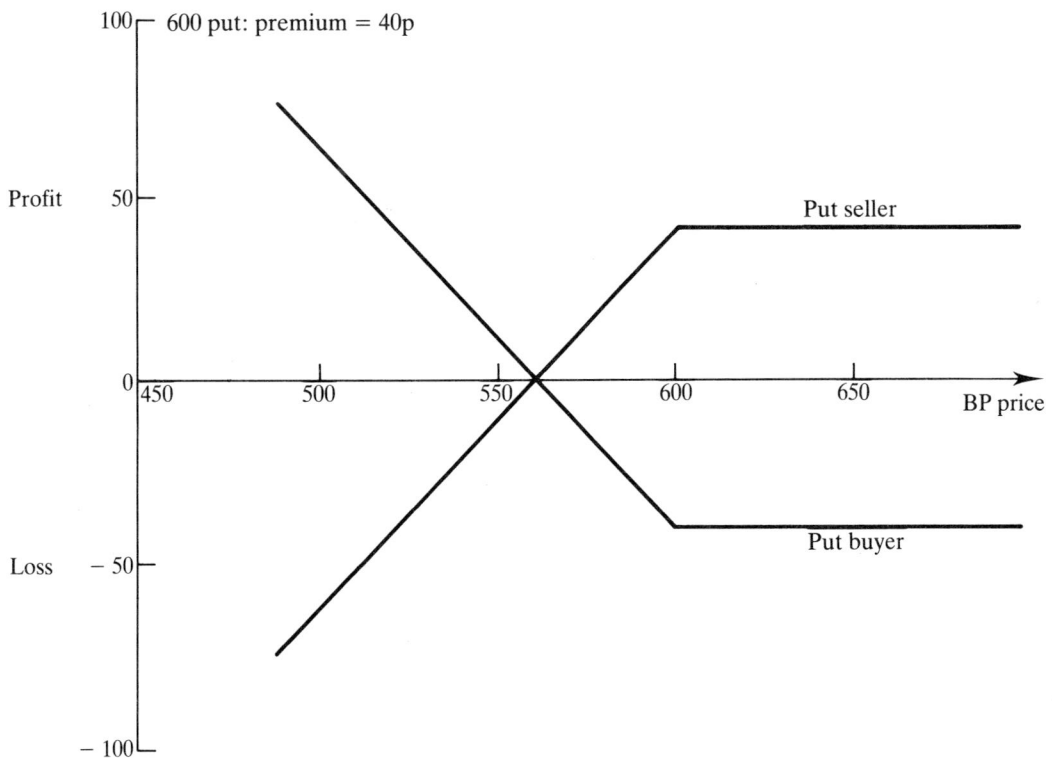

100 — 600 put: premium = 40p

Profit 50

Put seller

0
450       500       550       600       650       BP price

Put buyer

Loss — 50

— 100

**Exhibit 2.2: Comparative stock and option profiles**

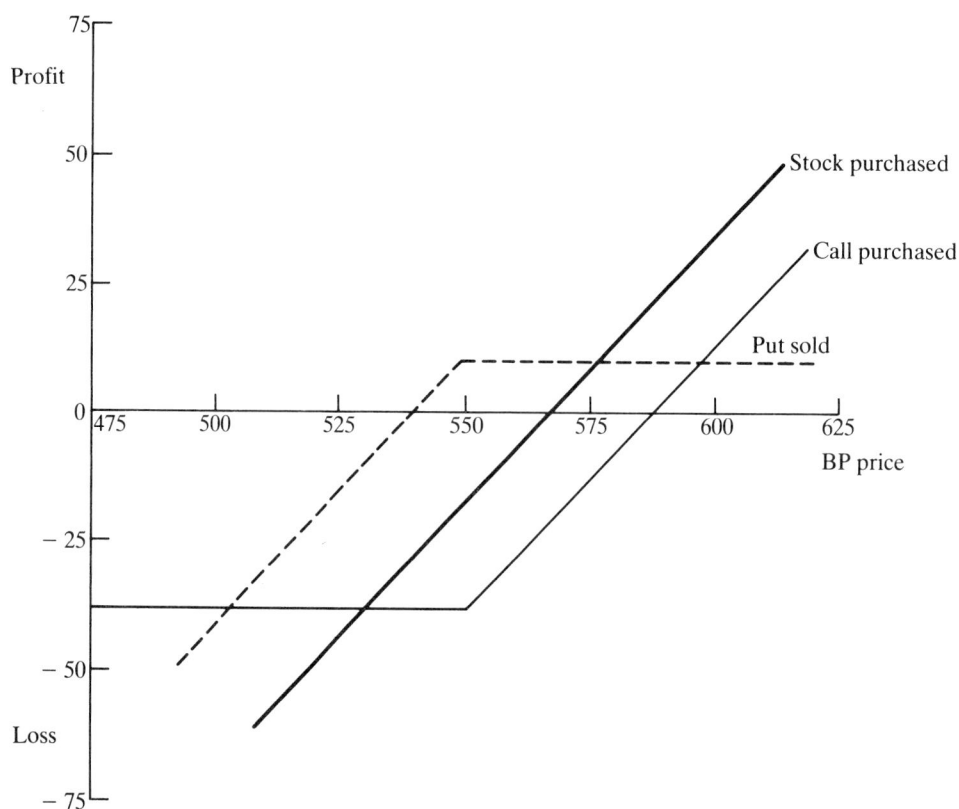

Exchanges attempt to trade a range of exercise prices around the current price of the stock, so that new exercise prices would be introduced if the stock price fell towards the bottom of the current exercise price range or if the stock price rose towards the top of the range.[3] This procedure can result, for more volatile stocks, in a large number of option exercise prices being quoted at any time. A case to note is the Upjohn Corporation on the CBOE, where 14 different exercise prices were quoted from $60 per share to $105 per share, with the current share price quoted at $97 per share. However, many of the exercise prices are either not traded or not offered during the trading day.

The American exchanges (like the UK ones) trade their options on a regular three-month expiration cycle, with a new option expiration date being introduced as one goes off the board. The daily figures for volume and open interest for the five US exchanges give an idea of their comparative size.

| Exchange | Total option volume (6 June 1986) | Total open interest (6 June 1986) |
|---|---|---|
| CBOE | 387,649 | 6,100,950 |
| American Stock Exchange | 163,946 | 3,562,741 |
| Pacific Stock Exchange | 44,257 | 1,206,617 |
| Philadelphia Stock Exchange | 48,290 | 1,263,771 |
| New York Stock Exchange | 9,633 | 189,057 |
| Total | 653,775 | 12,383,136 |

As each option is the right to buy or sell 100 shares, the volume of US stock option trading in a standard day becomes apparent.

---

[3] Different exchanges have different rules for the introduction of new exercise prices. Anyone wishing to trade options should check the precise procedure with the exchange concerned.

# Exhibit 2.3: Example of listed US options page, *The Wall Street Journal*

Source: *The Wall Street Journal.*

**CBOE**

| Option & Strike 3:00 p.m. price | | Calls-Last July | Oct | Jan | Puts-Last July | Oct | Jan |
|---|---|---|---|---|---|---|---|
| Alcoa | 40 | r | r | r | r | $1\frac{7}{8}$ | r |
| $41\frac{1}{2}$ | 45 | $\frac{3}{8}$ | $1\frac{1}{4}$ | r | r | r | r |
| $41\frac{1}{2}$ | 50 | r | $\frac{5}{8}$ | s | r | r | s |
| AmGenl | 45 | r | 1 | $1\frac{1}{4}$ | r | r | r |
| AGreet | 30 | $8\frac{1}{4}$ | r | r | r | r | r |
| AT&T | $22\frac{1}{2}$ | $2\frac{5}{16}$ | $2\frac{3}{4}$ | r | $\frac{1}{8}$ | $\frac{7}{16}$ | $\frac{5}{8}$ |
| $24\frac{3}{4}$ | 25 | $\frac{9}{16}$ | $1\frac{1}{8}$ | $1\frac{1}{16}$ | $\frac{3}{4}$ | $1\frac{1}{4}$ | r |
| $24\frac{3}{4}$ | 30 | $\frac{1}{16}$ | $\frac{3}{16}$ | $\frac{1}{2}$ | r | r | r |
| Apple | 40 | r | $3\frac{3}{4}$ | r | r | r | r |
| Avon | 30 | $3\frac{7}{8}$ | $4\frac{1}{4}$ | r | r | r | $1\frac{3}{8}$ |
| 33 | 35 | $\frac{3}{4}$ | $1\frac{7}{8}$ | r | 2 | r | $3\frac{3}{8}$ |
| 33 | 40 | $\frac{3}{16}$ | $\frac{5}{8}$ | $1\frac{1}{8}$ | r | r | r |
| BearSt | 30 | $5\frac{5}{8}$ | r | $7\frac{5}{8}$ | $\frac{1}{4}$ | r | r |
| $34\frac{3}{4}$ | 35 | 2 | $3\frac{1}{4}$ | $4\frac{3}{4}$ | 2 | r | r |
| $34\frac{3}{4}$ | 40 | $\frac{3}{8}$ | $1\frac{5}{8}$ | r | $5\frac{1}{8}$ | r | r |
| Beth S | 15 | $1\frac{5}{8}$ | r | r | $\frac{3}{8}$ | r | r |
| $16\frac{1}{4}$ | $17\frac{1}{2}$ | $\frac{7}{16}$ | $1\frac{1}{4}$ | r | r | r | $2\frac{1}{8}$ |
| $16\frac{1}{4}$ | 20 | $\frac{1}{8}$ | $\frac{1}{2}$ | $\frac{7}{8}$ | r | r | r |
| Burl N | 60 | r | $8\frac{5}{8}$ | r | r | r | r |
| $65\frac{5}{8}$ | 65 | $3\frac{1}{4}$ | r | r | r | 3 | r |
| $65\frac{5}{8}$ | 70 | 1 | r | r | r | r | r |
| $65\frac{5}{8}$ | 75 | $\frac{1}{4}$ | r | r | r | r | r |
| CIGNA | 60 | $3\frac{3}{4}$ | $5\frac{3}{4}$ | r | 1 | $2\frac{1}{8}$ | r |
| 63 | 65 | $1\frac{3}{8}$ | $3\frac{1}{2}$ | r | r | r | r |
| 63 | 70 | $\frac{5}{16}$ | $1\frac{1}{4}$ | r | r | r | r |
| Dryfus | 85 | r | r | r | $1\frac{1}{4}$ | r | r |
| $93\frac{3}{4}$ | 90 | $7\frac{1}{2}$ | r | r | $2\frac{1}{2}$ | r | r |
| $93\frac{3}{4}$ | 95 | r | r | $11\frac{1}{4}$ | r | r | r |
| $93\frac{3}{4}$ | 100 | $2\frac{3}{8}$ | $6\frac{1}{2}$ | r | r | r | r |
| Enron | 40 | r | $3\frac{1}{4}$ | r | r | r | r |
| $41\frac{7}{8}$ | 45 | $\frac{1}{2}$ | r | r | r | r | r |
| FstChi | 30 | r | r | r | r | $\frac{5}{8}$ | r |
| $34\frac{1}{8}$ | 35 | 1 | r | r | r | r | r |
| Fluor | 15 | r | r | r | $\frac{1}{16}$ | r | r |
| $17\frac{7}{8}$ | $17\frac{1}{2}$ | 1 | $1\frac{7}{8}$ | $2\frac{1}{8}$ | $1\frac{11}{16}$ | 1 | $1\frac{3}{8}$ |
| $17\frac{7}{8}$ | 20 | $\frac{5}{16}$ | $\frac{7}{8}$ | $1\frac{1}{2}$ | $2\frac{1}{4}$ | $2\frac{3}{4}$ | $2\frac{1}{2}$ |
| Gentch | $42\frac{1}{2}$ | r | $45\frac{3}{4}$ | s | r | r | s |
| $86\frac{3}{4}$ | 60 | 28 | r | s | r | r | s |
| $86\frac{3}{4}$ | 65 | 25 | r | s | $\frac{1}{4}$ | 1 | s |
| $86\frac{3}{4}$ | 70 | $18\frac{1}{2}$ | r | r | r | $1\frac{3}{4}$ | r |
| $86\frac{3}{4}$ | 75 | 15 | r | r | $1\frac{1}{4}$ | r | r |
| $86\frac{3}{4}$ | 80 | $9\frac{3}{4}$ | 15 | r | 2 | $4\frac{1}{2}$ | 3 |
| $86\frac{3}{4}$ | 85 | $6\frac{1}{4}$ | 12 | $14\frac{3}{4}$ | $3\frac{3}{8}$ | $6\frac{3}{4}$ | r |
| $86\frac{3}{4}$ | 90 | 4 | $8\frac{1}{4}$ | r | $6\frac{1}{2}$ | r | $11\frac{3}{4}$ |
| $86\frac{3}{4}$ | 95 | $2\frac{5}{8}$ | 7 | r | r | r | r |
| $86\frac{3}{4}$ | 100 | 2 | $5\frac{1}{2}$ | $8\frac{3}{4}$ | r | r | r |
| Gt Wst | 30 | $8\frac{7}{8}$ | r | s | r | r | s |
| $38\frac{1}{8}$ | 35 | $3\frac{5}{8}$ | r | r | $\frac{3}{8}$ | r | r |
| $38\frac{1}{2}$ | 40 | $1\frac{1}{4}$ | $2\frac{1}{2}$ | $3\frac{3}{8}$ | $2\frac{1}{2}$ | $3\frac{3}{4}$ | r |
| $38\frac{1}{8}$ | 45 | $\frac{5}{16}$ | 1 | r | 7 | 7 | r |
| In Min | 30 | r | r | r | $\frac{3}{4}$ | $1\frac{3}{4}$ | $2\frac{1}{4}$ |
| $31\frac{1}{4}$ | 35 | $\frac{1}{2}$ | r | r | r | r | r |
| $31\frac{1}{4}$ | 40 | r | r | $\frac{5}{8}$ | r | r | r |
| John J | 50 | 19 | $19\frac{3}{4}$ | s | r | r | s |
| $68\frac{1}{2}$ | 55 | 14 | r | s | r | r | s |
| $68\frac{1}{2}$ | 60 | $8\frac{3}{4}$ | r | r | $\frac{3}{16}$ | 1 | r |
| $68\frac{1}{2}$ | 65 | 5 | $6\frac{1}{2}$ | 8 | 1 | 2 | r |
| $68\frac{1}{2}$ | 70 | 2 | 4 | 5 | $2\frac{3}{4}$ | 4 | r |
| $68\frac{1}{2}$ | 75 | r | $2\frac{1}{8}$ | r | 3 | r | r |
| Kerr M | 25 | r | r | r | r | r | 1 |

**CBOE**

| Option & Strike 3:00 p.m. price | | Calls-Last July | Oct | Jan | Puts-Last July | Oct | Jan |
|---|---|---|---|---|---|---|---|
| $28\frac{3}{8}$ | 30 | r | $1\frac{1}{2}$ | r | r | $2\frac{1}{4}$ | 3 |
| $28\frac{3}{8}$ | 35 | $\frac{1}{16}$ | r | r | r | r | r |
| L S I | 15 | r | r | $1\frac{5}{8}$ | r | r | r |
| LizCla | 30 | $14\frac{1}{2}$ | r | s | r | r | s |
| $44\frac{3}{4}$ | 35 | $10\frac{1}{2}$ | r | r | $\frac{1}{8}$ | $\frac{3}{4}$ | r |
| $44\frac{3}{4}$ | $37\frac{1}{2}$ | r | r | s | $\frac{3}{8}$ | r | s |
| $44\frac{3}{4}$ | 40 | $5\frac{3}{4}$ | $8\frac{1}{4}$ | r | $\frac{1}{2}$ | $1\frac{5}{8}$ | r |
| $44\frac{3}{4}$ | 45 | $2\frac{5}{8}$ | $5\frac{5}{8}$ | 6 | 2 | r | r |
| $44\frac{3}{4}$ | 50 | $1\frac{1}{8}$ | $2\frac{7}{8}$ | $4\frac{1}{2}$ | r | r | r |
| Loral | 45 | $1\frac{1}{4}$ | $2\frac{5}{8}$ | r | r | r | r |
| M C I | $7\frac{1}{2}$ | 2 | $2\frac{1}{4}$ | r | r | r | r |
| $9\frac{3}{4}$ | 10 | $\frac{3}{8}$ | $\frac{7}{8}$ | $1\frac{3}{8}$ | $\frac{7}{8}$ | 1 | $1\frac{1}{4}$ |
| $9\frac{3}{4}$ | $12\frac{1}{2}$ | $\frac{1}{8}$ | $\frac{7}{16}$ | $\frac{9}{16}$ | r | r | r |
| $9\frac{3}{4}$ | 15 | $\frac{1}{16}$ | $\frac{3}{16}$ | s | r | r | s |
| Merck | 55 | $41\frac{3}{4}$ | s | s | r | s | s |
| $96\frac{1}{4}$ | $67\frac{1}{2}$ | r | r | s | r | $\frac{1}{16}$ | s |
| $96\frac{1}{4}$ | 70 | r | r | s | r | $\frac{1}{8}$ | s |
| $96\frac{1}{4}$ | 80 | r | r | s | $\frac{3}{16}$ | r | s |
| $96\frac{1}{4}$ | 85 | r | $14\frac{1}{4}$ | r | r | $1\frac{3}{8}$ | r |
| $96\frac{1}{4}$ | 90 | $8\frac{1}{2}$ | $10\frac{7}{8}$ | r | 1 | $2\frac{3}{4}$ | $3\frac{1}{4}$ |
| $96\frac{1}{4}$ | $92\frac{1}{2}$ | $6\frac{1}{4}$ | r | r | r | r | r |
| $96\frac{1}{4}$ | 95 | $4\frac{3}{4}$ | $7\frac{3}{4}$ | $10\frac{3}{4}$ | r | 4 | r |
| $96\frac{1}{4}$ | 100 | $2\frac{5}{8}$ | $5\frac{1}{2}$ | 7 | r | r | r |
| Monsan | 55 | r | r | r | r | r | 1 |
| $66\frac{1}{4}$ | 60 | r | $8\frac{3}{8}$ | r | r | r | r |
| $66\frac{1}{4}$ | 65 | 3 | r | 7 | $1\frac{1}{4}$ | $3\frac{3}{8}$ | 5 |
| $66\frac{1}{4}$ | 70 | r | $2\frac{3}{4}$ | r | r | r | r |
| N W A | 45 | r | r | r | $\frac{3}{8}$ | r | r |
| $52\frac{1}{2}$ | 55 | $\frac{7}{8}$ | r | r | r | r | r |
| PainW | 35 | $3\frac{7}{8}$ | r | r | $\frac{1}{2}$ | r | r |
| $37\frac{7}{8}$ | 40 | 1 | $2\frac{3}{8}$ | $3\frac{3}{8}$ | r | $3\frac{3}{4}$ | r |
| $37\frac{7}{8}$ | 45 | $\frac{3}{8}$ | $1\frac{1}{4}$ | r | r | r | r |
| Pennz | 45 | $5\frac{3}{4}$ | $7\frac{1}{4}$ | r | $\frac{3}{8}$ | r | $2\frac{1}{8}$ |
| $50\frac{1}{8}$ | 50 | $2\frac{1}{4}$ | 4 | 6 | r | r | 5 |
| $50\frac{1}{8}$ | 55 | $\frac{3}{4}$ | $2\frac{5}{8}$ | 4 | r | r | r |
| $50\frac{1}{8}$ | 60 | $\frac{3}{8}$ | $1\frac{1}{2}$ | s | r | $10\frac{5}{8}$ | s |
| $50\frac{1}{8}$ | 65 | $\frac{1}{4}$ | r | r | r | $15\frac{5}{8}$ | r |
| $50\frac{1}{8}$ | 70 | r | $\frac{5}{8}$ | r | r | r | r |
| $50\frac{1}{8}$ | 75 | $\frac{1}{8}$ | $\frac{1}{2}$ | s | r | r | s |
| Squibb | 85 | $13\frac{1}{4}$ | r | s | r | r | s |
| $96\frac{5}{8}$ | 90 | 9 | r | r | r | r | r |
| $96\frac{5}{8}$ | 95 | $5\frac{3}{8}$ | $8\frac{1}{2}$ | r | r | $5\frac{5}{8}$ | r |
| $96\frac{5}{8}$ | 100 | r | $5\frac{3}{4}$ | r | $4\frac{3}{4}$ | r | r |
| $96\frac{5}{8}$ | 105 | $1\frac{1}{4}$ | r | r | r | r | r |
| $96\frac{5}{8}$ | 110 | $\frac{3}{4}$ | r | r | r | r | r |
| Upjohn | 60 | 37 | s | s | r | s | s |
| 97 | $62\frac{1}{2}$ | r | 35 | s | r | r | s |
| 97 | 70 | $27\frac{1}{2}$ | 29 | s | r | r | s |
| 97 | $72\frac{1}{2}$ | $25\frac{1}{2}$ | r | s | r | r | s |
| 97 | 75 | r | r | r | $\frac{1}{4}$ | r | r |
| 97 | $77\frac{1}{2}$ | r | r | r | $\frac{1}{4}$ | r | r |
| 97 | 80 | r | $19\frac{1}{4}$ | r | r | r | $2\frac{11}{16}$ |
| 97 | $82\frac{1}{2}$ | 15 | r | r | $\frac{1}{2}$ | r | r |
| 97 | 85 | $13\frac{7}{8}$ | $15\frac{3}{4}$ | r | $\frac{3}{4}$ | r | $3\frac{3}{4}$ |
| 97 | $87\frac{1}{2}$ | $10\frac{3}{4}$ | r | r | $1\frac{1}{4}$ | r | r |
| 97 | 90 | $9\frac{1}{4}$ | $12\frac{1}{2}$ | r | $1\frac{5}{8}$ | $4\frac{1}{4}$ | r |
| 97 | 95 | $6\frac{1}{4}$ | $10\frac{1}{4}$ | $13\frac{1}{2}$ | $3\frac{1}{2}$ | $7\frac{1}{2}$ | r |
| 97 | 100 | 4 | 8 | r | 7 | $9\frac{1}{2}$ | r |
| 97 | 105 | $2\frac{3}{8}$ | 6 | r | r | r | r |

Apart from the United States, the largest individual stock option exchanges are London and Amsterdam, although the volume of trading can be in no way compared with the United States. Typical *Financial Times* pages for the European Options Exchange in Amsterdam and the London Stock Exchange are shown in Exhibit 2.4 and Exhibit 2.5.

The range of stocks is much smaller and volumes are much smaller.

## Exhibit 2.4: Example of European Options Exchange page, *Financial Times*

| Series | | Vol. | Last | Vol. | Last | Vol. | Last | Stock |
|--------|--------|------|------|------|------|------|------|-------|
| | | *June* | | *Sept.* | | *Dec.* | | |
| £/FL C | Fl.375 | 10 | 5.50 | 1 | 8A | — | — | Fl.380.64 |
| £/FL C | Fl.395 | — | — | — | — | 45 | 1 | ,, |
| £/FL P | Fl.370 | — | — | 12 | 4 | — | — | ,, |
| £/FL P | Fl.380 | — | — | 7 | 9.50 | — | — | ,, |
| $/FL C | Fl.240 | — | — | — | — | 10 | 13.50 | Fl.248.70 |
| $/FL C | Fl.245 | 15 | 5.50 | 9 | 9.30 | — | — | ,, |
| $/FL C | Fl.250 | 523 | 2.40 | 42 | 7 | — | — | ,, |
| $/FL C | Fl.255 | 505 | 0.70 | 176 | 5.20 | 4 | 7 | ,, |
| $/FL C | Fl.260 | 10 | 0.40 | 10 | 3.50 | 3 | 4.80 | ,, |
| $/FL C | Fl.265 | — | — | 85 | 2.30 | — | — | ,, |
| $/FL C | Fl.270 | 20 | 0.10 | 120 | 1.70 | 3 | 3.50 | ,, |
| $/FL C | Fl.275 | — | — | 15 | 0.90 | 1 | 2.80 | ,, |
| $/FL C | Fl.280 | — | — | 20 | 0.80 | — | — | ,, |
| $/FL P | Fl.240 | 72 | 0.30 | 77 | 4 | 1 | 7.30 | ,, |
| $/FL P | Fl.245 | 58 | 0.80 | 217 | 6.30 | — | — | ,, |
| $/FL P | Fl.250 | 630 | 3.20 | 44 | 8.50 | 11 | 12.20 | ,, |
| $/FL P | Fl.255 | 49 | 6.20 | 66 | 11 | 3 | 14.20 | ,, |
| $/FL P | Fl.260 | 56 | 11.70 | 16 | 15 | 3 | 18.50A | ,, |
| $/FL P | Fl.265 | 2 | 16.50 | 13 | 19.50 | 2 | 22 | ,, |
| | | *July* | | *Oct.* | | *Jan.* | | |
| ABN C | Fl.580 | 691 | 15.80 | 15 | 28.50 | — | — | Fl.577.00 |
| ABN P | Fl.540 | 106 | 2 | 34 | 6.50 | — | — | ,, |
| AEGN C | Fl.115 | 40 | 2.50 | 21 | 6 | — | — | Fl.110.20 |
| AEGN P | Fl.105 | 10 | 1.80 | 22 | 4.70 | — | — | ,, |
| AH C | Fl.85 | 67 | 4.80 | 8 | 8.90 | 10 | 9.50 | Fl.87.20 |
| AH P | Fl.80 | 3 | 1 | 12 | 2.20 | 25 | 4 | ,, |
| AKZO C | Fl.170 | 360 | 4.70 | 307 | 10.60 | 73 | 14.20 | Fl.167.50 |
| AKZO P | Fl.170 | 457 | 5.30 | 294 | 7.80 | 35 | 10 | ,, |
| AMEV C | Fl.85 | 10 | 1.60 | 52 | 4.20 | 26 | 5.50B | Fl.80.90 |
| AMEV P | Fl.75 | 7 | 1.20A | 55 | 2 | 5 | 3.50 | ,, |
| AMRO C | Fl.110 | 110 | 2.90 | 56 | 6.70 | 9 | 10 | Fl.106.80 |
| AMRO P | Fl.100 | 89 | 1 | 23 | 2.80 | 10 | 4 | ,, |
| GIST C | Fl.300 | 141 | 3.70 | 25 | 13 | — | — | Fl.285.50 |
| GIST P | Fl.280 | 24 | 4.30 | 81 | 10.50 | — | — | ,, |
| HEIN C | Fl.180 | 24 | 2.40 | 43 | 7 | — | — | Fl.170.50 |
| HEIN P | Fl.150.00 | 20 | 0.50 | 10 | 1.50 | — | — | ,, |
| HEO P | Fl.142.50 | 50 | 0.30 | — | — | — | — | ,, |
| HOOG C | Fl.100 | 257 | 13.80 | 84 | 16.50A | 7 | 22A | Fl.112.60 |
| HOOG P | Fl.115 | 116 | 5 | 19 | 7.50 | — | — | ,, |
| KLM C | Fl.50 | 392 | 2 | 56 | 3.90 | 15 | 5.50A | Fl.48.80 |
| KLM P | Fl.50 | 283 | 2.70 | 78 | 5 | 19 | 6 | ,, |
| NEDL C | Fl.180 | 282 | 4.90 | 162 | 11.50 | 10 | 14.50 | Fl.178 |
| NEDL P | Fl.180 | 180 | 7 | 15 | 11.50 | — | — | ,, |
| NATN C | Fl.95 | 80 | 0.60 | — | — | — | — | Fl.85.70 |
| NATN P | Fl.90 | 141 | 4.90 | 12 | 6.80 | 1 | 9.20 | ,, |
| PHIL C | Fl.60 | 99 | 0.60B | 530 | 2.80 | 336 | 3.80 | Fl.55 |
| PHIL P | Fl.55 | 273 | 1.30 | 160 | 2.80B | 348 | 3.80 | ,, |
| RD C | Fl.200 | 285 | 2.20 | 109 | 6.70 | 45 | 11.50 | Fl.193.50 |
| RD P | Fl.200 | 46 | 6.70 | 286 | 11.60 | 28 | 12 | ,, |
| UNIL C | Fl.500 | 35 | 3.40 | 93 | 12B | 25 | 22 | Fl.465 |
| UNIL P | Fl.460 | 95 | 7.50 | 74 | 15.10 | 2 | 19 | ,, |

Total volume in contracts: 24,130

| A = Ask | B = Bid | C = Call | P = Put |
|---------|---------|----------|---------|

Source: *Financial Times*.

# Exhibit 2.5: Example of London traded options page, *Financial Times*

| Option | | Calls July | Oct. | Jan. | Puts July | Oct. | Jan. |
|---|---|---|---|---|---|---|---|
| Allied Lyons | 330 | 20 | 33 | 45 | 17 | 23 | 33 |
| (*333) | 360 | 8 | 20 | 27 | 33 | 38 | 45 |
| B.P. | 500 | 75 | 87 | 98 | 2 | 7 | 10 |
| (*568) | 550 | 35 | 50 | 62 | 10 | 27 | 30 |
| | 600 | 9 | 23 | 35 | 40 | 50 | 55 |
| Cons. Gold | 420 | 42 | 55 | 65 | 5 | 17 | 27 |
| (*442) | 460 | 17 | 38 | 47 | 30 | 44 | 52 |
| | 500 | 7 | 20 | 27 | 70 | 74 | 78 |
| Courtaulds | 260 | 24 | 36 | 51 | 4 | 12 | 18 |
| (*278) | 280 | 13 | 25 | 35 | 15 | 20 | 26 |
| | 300 | 4 | 14 | 24 | 30 | 33 | 38 |
| | 330 | $1\frac{1}{2}$ | 7 | — | 56 | 57 | — |
| Com. Union | 300 | 12 | 23 | 27 | 14 | 18 | 21 |
| (*297) | 330 | 5 | 12 | 17 | 36 | 39 | 41 |
| | 360 | $1\frac{1}{2}$ | 6 | 12 | 65 | 67 | 71 |
| Cable & Wire | 600 | 80 | 100 | 125 | 7 | 15 | 25 |
| (*660) | 650 | 43 | 68 | 895 | 25 | 38 | 45 |
| | 700 | 15 | 40 | 68 | 60 | 70 | 80 |
| | 750 | 4 | 20 | 43 | 90 | 100 | 100 |
| Distillers | 550 | 125 | 150 | — | 1 | 3 | — |
| (*658) | 600 | 75 | 100 | — | 4 | 10 | — |
| | 650 | 28 | 75 | — | 12 | 25 | — |
| | 700 | 15 | 40 | — | 45 | 60 | — |
| G.E.C. | 180 | 30 | 38 | 46 | 3 | 7 | 9 |
| (*202) | 200 | 14 | 24 | 30 | 9 | 13 | 16 |
| | 220 | 5 | 13 | 20 | 24 | 28 | 30 |
| Grand Met. | 360 | — | — | 75 | — | — | 18 |
| (*393) | 382 | 28 | 47 | — | 8 | 22 | — |
| | 390 | — | — | 53 | — | — | 30 |
| | 420 | 12 | 25 | 40 | 33 | 38 | 47 |
| I.C.I. | 850 | 87 | 105 | 125 | 7 | 20 | 37 |
| (*919) | 900 | 47 | 67 | 92 | 22 | 37 | 52 |
| | 950 | 25 | 47 | 67 | 52 | 60 | 75 |
| | 1000 | 10 | 30 | — | 92 | 102 | — |
| Land Sec. | 280 | 42 | 51 | — | 1 | 4 | — |
| (*317) | 300 | 24 | 34 | 43 | 4 | 9 | 11 |
| | 330 | 7 | 13 | 24 | 17 | 22 | 24 |
| Marks & Spen. | 180 | 18 | 27 | 37 | $2\frac{1}{2}$ | 5 | 8 |
| (*192) | 200 | 6 | 17 | 25 | 10 | 15 | 19 |
| | 220 | $1\frac{1}{2}$ | 11 | 15 | 29 | 30 | 33 |
| Shell Trans. | 700 | 90 | 103 | 125 | 2 | 11 | 17 |
| (*778) | 750 | 48 | 70 | 85 | 9 | 27 | 33 |
| | 800 | 20 | 38 | 52 | 37 | 50 | 55 |
| Trafalgar House | 280 | 23 | 36 | 44 | 5 | 11 | 15 |
| (*292) | 300 | 11 | 24 | 34 | 14 | 20 | 26 |
| | 330 | 4 | 11 | 17 | 40 | 42 | 45 |

| Option | | Calls Aug. | Nov. | Mar. | Puts Aug. | Nov. | Mar. |
|---|---|---|---|---|---|---|---|
| Lonrho | 236 | 24 | 31 | — | 7 | 10 | — |
| (*246) | 240 | — | — | 38 | — | — | 17 |
| | 255 | 14 | 19 | — | 18 | 22 | — |
| | 260 | — | — | 26 | — | — | 30 |
| | 273 | 6 | 12 | — | 30 | 32 | — |

| Option | | Calls Aug. | Nov. | Feb. | Puts Aug. | Nov. | Feb. |
|---|---|---|---|---|---|---|---|
| Brit Aero | 500 | 40 | 55 | 68 | 23 | 30 | 40 |
| (*515) | 550 | 18 | 32 | 43 | 52 | 60 | 67 |
| | 600 | 6 | 15 | — | 92 | 97 | — |
| BAT Inds | 360 | 30 | 45 | 60 | 15 | 20 | 34 |
| (*370) | 390 | 15 | 30 | 38 | 30 | 35 | 48 |
| | 420 | 7 | 16 | — | 53 | 60 | — |
| | 460 | 4 | 7 | — | 93 | 98 | — |
| Barclays | 460 | 45 | 65 | 82 | 13 | 18 | 25 |
| (*477) | 500 | 25 | 42 | 57 | 35 | 40 | 45 |
| | 550 | 10 | 25 | 37 | 82 | 82 | 82 |
| Brit. Telecom. | 220 | 13 | 24 | 32 | 11 | 14 | 18 |
| (*222) | 240 | $6\frac{1}{2}$ | 11 | 22 | 25 | 28 | 34 |
| | 260 | 3 | 8 | 13 | 46 | 46 | 48 |
| Cadbury Schweppes | 160 | 17 | 24 | 25 | 7 | 11 | 13 |
| (*166) | 180 | 7 | 10 | 16 | 19 | 22 | 26 |
| Imperial Gr. | 300 | 58 | 67 | — | 1 | 5 | — |
| (*344) | 330 | 35 | 45 | — | 10 | 15 | — |

| Option | | Calls Aug. | Nov. | Feb. | Puts Aug. | Nov. | Feb. |
|---|---|---|---|---|---|---|---|
| | 360 | 17 | 25 | — | 22 | 25 | — |
| Ladbroke | 300 | 55 | 66 | 77 | 2 | 5 | 7 |
| (*349) | 330 | 30 | 43 | 56 | 7 | 11 | 16 |
| | 360 | 14 | 25 | 39 | 19 | 27 | 34 |
| LASMO | 110 | 14 | 22 | 30 | 9 | 13 | 17 |
| (*113) | 120 | 9 | 17 | 23 | 15 | 21 | 24 |
| | 130 | 6 | 14 | 18 | 27 | 30 | 37 |
| P. & O. | 460 | 73 | 87 | — | 3 | 7 | — |
| (*518) | 500 | 35 | 55 | 68 | 11 | 23 | 33 |
| | 550 | 15 | 30 | 43 | 42 | 48 | 58 |
| | 600 | 6 | 14 | — | 83 | 85 | — |
| Racal | 180 | 30 | 40 | — | 6 | 8 | — |
| (*198) | 200 | 17 | 28 | 38 | 13 | 15 | 18 |
| | 220 | 8 | 16 | 22 | 26 | 30 | 32 |
| R.T.Z. | 550 | 107 | 120 | — | 4 | 9 | — |
| (*642) | 600 | 67 | 80 | 102 | 10 | 20 | 30 |
| | 650 | 38 | 54 | 70 | 32 | 42 | 57 |
| | 700 | 16 | 35 | 48 | 67 | 74 | 87 |
| Vaal Reefs | 50 | 8 | 11 | $13\frac{1}{2}$ | 4 | 6 | 7 |
| (*$53) | 60 | 5 | $7\frac{1}{2}$ | $9\frac{1}{2}$ | 10 | 13 | 14 |
| | 70 | $2\frac{1}{2}$ | 5 | — | $18\frac{1}{2}$ | $20\frac{1}{2}$ | — |
| | 80 | $1\frac{1}{4}$ | $2\frac{1}{2}$ | — | 28 | $29\frac{1}{2}$ | — |
| | 90 | 1 | $1\frac{1}{2}$ | — | 38 | $39\frac{1}{2}$ | — |
| Tr. 11¾% 1991 | 108 | $2\frac{13}{16}$ | $3\frac{5}{16}$ | — | $0\frac{9}{16}$ | $1\frac{3}{16}$ | — |
| (*£110) | 110 | $1\frac{5}{8}$ | $2\frac{1}{8}$ | $2\frac{9}{16}$ | $1\frac{5}{16}$ | $1\frac{15}{16}$ | $2\frac{7}{16}$ |
| | 112 | $0\frac{11}{16}$ | $1\frac{1}{16}$ | $1\frac{3}{4}$ | 2 | 3 | $3\frac{7}{16}$ |
| Tr. 11¾% 03/07 | 116 | $4\frac{1}{2}$ | $5\frac{7}{8}$ | — | $1\frac{3}{8}$ | $2\frac{3}{4}$ | — |
| (*£119) | 118 | $3\frac{1}{4}$ | $4\frac{16}{32}$ | — | $2\frac{1}{16}$ | $3\frac{3}{8}$ | — |
| | 120 | $2\frac{1}{8}$ | $3\frac{3}{4}$ | $4\frac{5}{8}$ | $3\frac{1}{8}$ | 4 | 5 |
| | 122 | $1\frac{5}{8}$ | 3 | $3\frac{13}{16}$ | $4\frac{1}{8}$ | 5 | 6 |
| | 124 | $1\frac{1}{4}$ | $2\frac{5}{16}$ | — | $5\frac{7}{8}$ | $6\frac{1}{8}$ | — |
| | 126 | $0\frac{3}{4}$ | $1\frac{11}{16}$ | — | $7\frac{7}{8}$ | $7\frac{7}{8}$ | — |

| Option | | Calls June | Sep. | Dec. | Puts June | Sep. | Dec. |
|---|---|---|---|---|---|---|---|
| Beecham | 330 | 62 | 73 | 83 | 2 | 8 | 13 |
| (*390) | 360 | 35 | 53 | 63 | 4 | 18 | 23 |
| | 390 | 13 | 35 | 45 | 17 | 33 | 40 |
| | 420 | 4 | 22 | 33 | 40 | 47 | 53 |
| Boots | 240 | 10 | 22 | 36 | 5 | 11 | 13 |
| (*243) | 260 | $2\frac{1}{2}$ | 14 | 25 | 19 | 26 | 27 |
| | 280 | 1 | 9 | 16 | 38 | 40 | 42 |
| BTR | 280 | 30 | 40 | — | 2 | 7 | — |
| (*308) | 307 | 10 | 23 | 33 | 8 | 17 | 22 |
| | 333 | $1\frac{1}{2}$ | 10 | 20 | 30 | 33 | 37 |
| Bass | 750 | 38 | 70 | 95 | 4 | 28 | 35 |
| (*765) | 800 | 10 | 43 | 65 | 40 | 55 | 70 |
| | 850 | 1 | 25 | 40 | 90 | 95 | 100 |
| Blue Circle | 600 | 43 | 63 | 87 | 3 | 15 | 22 |
| (*636) | 650 | 12 | 33 | 52 | 23 | 40 | 50 |
| | 700 | 2 | 16 | 27 | 67 | 72 | 75 |
| De Beers | 600 | 40 | 80 | 100 | 8 | 45 | 65 |
| (*$6.20) | 650 | 10 | 50 | 70 | 40 | 75 | 90 |
| | 700 | 6 | 30 | 50 | 90 | 105 | 120 |
| | 750 | 3 | 20 | 30 | 140 | 150 | 160 |
| GKN | 300 | 50 | 61 | 70 | 1 | 5 | 8 |
| (*347) | 330 | 23 | 38 | 47 | 3 | 10 | 14 |
| | 360 | 4 | 19 | 29 | 14 | 21 | 26 |
| | 390 | 1 | 9 | 16 | 44 | 45 | 47 |
| Glaxo | 900 | 140 | 190 | 215 | 3 | 23 | 27 |
| (*1033) | 950 | 95 | 150 | 175 | 10 | 32 | 42 |
| | 1000 | 50 | 120 | 140 | 18 | 50 | 65 |
| | 1050 | 20 | 80 | 105 | 45 | 75 | 80 |
| Hanson | 150 | 20 | 29 | — | $1\frac{1}{2}$ | 5 | — |
| (*168) | 160 | | 23 | 30 | — | 8 | 10 |
| | 165 | 7 | — | — | 4 | — | — |
| | 180 | $1\frac{1}{2}$ | 13 | 19 | 14 | 18 | 19 |
| | 200 | $0\frac{1}{2}$ | 6 | 12 | 33 | 34 | 38 |
| Jaguar | 420 | 88 | 100 | 120 | 1 | 6 | 10 |
| (*500) | 460 | 48 | 68 | 93 | 2 | 11 | 17 |
| | 500 | 15 | 40 | 65 | 10 | 33 | 35 |
| | 550 | — | 18 | 37 | — | 52 | 55 |

# Exhibit 2.5: Example of London traded options page, *Financial Times* (*cont.*)

| Option | | Calls June | Calls Sep. | Calls Dec. | Puts June | Puts Sep. | Puts Dec. | Option | | Calls June | Calls July | Calls Aug. | Calls Sept. | Puts June | Puts July | Puts Aug. | Puts Sept. |
|---|---|---|---|---|---|---|---|---|---|---|---|---|---|---|---|---|---|
| Thorn EMI | 420 | 37 | 52 | 70 | 2 | 13 | 17 | FT-SE | 1525 | 63 | — | — | — | 4 | — | — | — |
| (*447) | 460 | 10 | 27 | 45 | 20 | 30 | 37 | Index | 1550 | 45 | 67 | 87 | — | 7 | 26 | 43 | — |
|  | 500 | 2 | 13 | 27 | 57 | 62 | 67 | (*1572) | 1575 | 32 | 55 | 80 | 100 | 20 | 35 | 52 | 60 |
|  | 550 | 2 | 6 | 15 | 107 | 110 | 112 |  | 1600 | 20 | 40 | 65 | 85 | 30 | 50 | 68 | 75 |
| Tesco | 300 | 45 | 58 | — | 1 | 3 | — |  | 1625 | 9 | 27 | 55 | 70 | 55 | 65 | 83 | 100 |
| (*340) | 330 | 18 | 35 | 45 | 3 | 9 | 13 |  | 1650 | 5 | 18 | 45 | — | 80 | 85 | 100 | — |
|  | 360 | 5 | 15 | 28 | 23 | 25 | 32 |  | 1675 | 3 | 12 | 30 | — | 103 | 110 | 120 | — |
|  | 390 | 2 | 8 | 15 | 50 | 52 | 55 |  | 1700 | 2 | 7 | — | — | 130 | 135 | — | — |

June 11, Total contracts 16,522.  Calls 9,275.  Puts 7,247
*Underlying security price.

Source: *Financial Times*.

## b. Stock index options

In addition to individual stock options, it is possible to trade options on stock indices. Such options can either be options on cash indices or options on stock option index futures.

A *cash index option* gives the buyer the right to buy or sell a specific stock index at a specific price. Because it is obviously impossible to physically deliver a stock index, any profits or losses at exercise are achieved by cash settlement rather than the physical delivery of the underlying asset.

### Example

An investor buys a CBOE Standard and Poor's 100 index call option with an exercise price of 225 for June expiration for a premium of $10\frac{3}{4}$. The current level of the index is 235.27.

The investor has purchased the right to buy the S & P 100 index at any time between the current date and June at a price of 225 for a premium of $10\frac{3}{4}$. Suppose the index rises to 260 and the option is exercised.

The S & P 100 index option is defined in $100 units. That is, an index value of 260 is equivalent to $260 \times \$100 = \$26,000$.

$$\text{Premium} = 10.75 \times \$100 = \$1,075$$
$$\text{Exercise price} = 225 \times \$100 = \$22,500$$
$$\text{Index level} = 260 \times \$100 = \$26,000$$

Hence the exercise value is $\$26,000 - \$22,500 = \$3,500$. If the option is exercised, the transaction is effectively terminated by the payment of $3,500 from the option seller to the option buyer. The net profit for the buyer is $3,500 minus the option premium of $1,075, or $2,425.

A typical newspaper page for index options is displayed in Exhibit 2.6. The first obvious difference between the CBOE S & P 100 index and the individual stock options is that the former are traded on a one-month rather than a three-month cycle, and options for June, July and August expiration are trading simultaneously. With the exception of the Chicago Mercantile Exchange, which trades S & P 500 futures options, all the other options displayed are cash options.

Two points are evident: first, there are many different index options available, and second, some index options are substantially more successful than others. Any trader contemplating trading the cash index options will have to explore carefully the characteristics of the underlying index on which a specific option trades. This will involve examining the number of stocks in the index, how the weights of each stock are determined (by market value weighting or equal weighting), how the index is constructed and other factors.

---

**Anyone trading index options should study carefully the characteristics and properties of the underlying index.**

---

The CME S & P 500 index is a so-called *futures option*, i.e. the option does not convey the right to buy or sell a physical asset but a futures contract written on that asset. To explain this, a short digression on futures contracts is needed.[4]

---

[4] This brief discussion of futures contracts is simply to describe fully a futures option. For a fuller discussion, see M. D. Fitzgerald, *Financial Futures*, Euromoney Publications (1983).

# Exhibit 2.6: Example of US options indexes page, *The Wall Street Journal*

## NASDAQ 100 INDEX

| Strike price | Calls—Last June | July | Aug | Puts—Last June | July | Aug |
|---|---|---|---|---|---|---|
| 310 | .... | .... | .... | $1\frac{3}{8}$ | .... | .... |
| 315 | $4\frac{1}{4}$ | .... | .... | $2\frac{3}{4}$ | .... | .... |
| 320 | $1\frac{3}{8}$ | .... | .... | $6$ | .... | .... |
| 325 | $\frac{7}{8}$ | .... | .... | $10\frac{7}{8}$ | .... | .... |

Total call volume 22.    Total call open int. 256.
Total put volume 78.    Total put open int. 279.
The index: High 317.42; Low 314.35; Close 316.21, −1.01

## LONDON STOCK EXCHANGE
## FT-SE 100 SHARE INDEX

| Strike price | Call—Settle June | July | Aug | Put—Settle June | July | Aug |
|---|---|---|---|---|---|---|
| 1525 | 78 | .... | .... | 3 | .... | .... |
| 1550 | 58 | 77 | 100 | 8 | 25 | 38 |
| 1575 | 42 | 65 | 85 | 18 | 32 | 50 |
| 1600 | 26 | 50 | 70 | 27 | 45 | 65 |
| 1625 | 13 | 32 | 58 | 44 | 62 | 80 |
| 1650 | 8 | 22 | 45 | 67 | 77 | 95 |
| 1675 | 3 | 13 | 38 | 92 | 97 | 118 |
| 1700 | 2 | 8 | .... | 115 | 115 | .... |
| 1750 | 1 | 4 | .... | 165 | 165 | .... |

Actual volume June 9:303; Calls:27; Puts:276
Open Interest June 9:9,975

## NYSE OPTIONS INDEX

| Strike Price | Calls—Last June | July | Aug | Puts—Last June | July | Aug |
|---|---|---|---|---|---|---|
| 125 | .... | .... | .... | .... | $\frac{3}{16}$ | $\frac{3}{8}$ |
| 130 | $7\frac{1}{4}$ | .... | .... | $\frac{1}{16}$ | $\frac{7}{16}$ | 1 |
| 135 | $3\frac{3}{8}$ | $4\frac{1}{2}$ | .... | $\frac{5}{8}$ | $1\frac{5}{8}$ | $2\frac{9}{16}$ |
| 140 | $\frac{9}{16}$ | $1\frac{15}{16}$ | 3 | $3\frac{5}{16}$ | $4\frac{1}{8}$ | $5\frac{1}{2}$ |
| 145 | $\frac{1}{16}$ | $\frac{11}{16}$ | $1\frac{5}{16}$ | 8 | $8\frac{1}{16}$ | 9 |
| 150 | .... | $\frac{1}{4}$ | $\frac{1}{16}$ | .... | .... | .... |

Total call volume 7,719.    Total call open int. 38,646.
Total put volume 7,690.    Total put open int. 37,792.
The index: High 137.98; Low 137.02; Close 137.70, −0.33.

## NYSE DOUBLE INDEX

| Strike price | Calls—Last June | July | Aug | Puts—Last June | July | Aug |
|---|---|---|---|---|---|---|
| 255 | .... | .... | .... | $\frac{1}{16}$ | .... | .... |
| 260 | .... | .... | .... | $\frac{1}{8}$ | $1\frac{1}{8}$ | .... |
| 265 | .... | .... | .... | $\frac{3}{8}$ | $1\frac{5}{8}$ | .... |
| 270 | $5\frac{3}{4}$ | $8\frac{1}{4}$ | $10\frac{1}{4}$ | $1\frac{1}{4}$ | $3\frac{9}{16}$ | .... |
| 275 | $3\frac{1}{16}$ | .... | .... | $3\frac{5}{16}$ | $5\frac{7}{8}$ | .... |
| 280 | $1\frac{1}{4}$ | .... | .... | $6\frac{3}{4}$ | .... | .... |
| 285 | $\frac{5}{16}$ | $2\frac{1}{4}$ | .... | .... | .... | .... |
| 290 | $\frac{1}{8}$ | .... | .... | .... | .... | .... |
| 295 | .... | $\frac{11}{16}$ | .... | .... | .... | .... |
| 300 | .... | $\frac{9}{16}$ | .... | .... | .... | .... |

Total call volume 677.    Total call open int. 8,531.
Total put volume 1,605.    Total put open int. 8,956.
The index: High 275.96; Low 274.04; Close 275.40, −0.66.

## NYSE BETA INDEX

| Strike price | Calls—Last June | July | Aug | Puts—Last June | July | Aug |
|---|---|---|---|---|---|---|
| 305 | .... | .... | .... | $\frac{1}{2}$ | $2\frac{7}{16}$ | 4 |
| 310 | $6\frac{5}{8}$ | .... | .... | $1\frac{7}{16}$ | $3\frac{3}{4}$ | 6 |
| 315 | $3\frac{3}{8}$ | .... | .... | $2\frac{7}{8}$ | .... | .... |
| 320 | $1\frac{7}{8}$ | $5\frac{3}{8}$ | $7\frac{5}{8}$ | $6\frac{1}{2}$ | $9\frac{1}{2}$ | .... |
| 325 | $\frac{13}{16}$ | $3\frac{7}{8}$ | .... | 10 | .... | .... |
| 330 | $\frac{7}{16}$ | $2\frac{3}{8}$ | $3\frac{3}{4}$ | 16 | .... | .... |
| 335 | .... | $1\frac{1}{4}$ | $3\frac{3}{8}$ | .... | .... | .... |
| 340 | $\frac{1}{16}$ | $\frac{7}{8}$ | .... | .... | .... | .... |

Total call volume 1,137.    Total call open int. 4,827.
Total put volume 2,538.    Total put open int. 4,158.
The index: High 317.30; Low 314.17; Close 315.76, −1.53.

## PACIFIC EXCHANGE
## TECHNOLOGY INDEX

| Strike price | Calls—Last June | July | Aug | Puts—Last June | July | Aug |
|---|---|---|---|---|---|---|
| 125 | .... | .... | $3\frac{1}{2}$ | .... | .... | .... |
| 130 | .... | .... | .... | .... | .... | $8\frac{1}{2}$ |

Total call volume 20.    Total call open int. 1,214.
Total put volume 20.    Total put open int. 1,093.
The index: High 122.79; Low 121.89; Close 122.76, −0.03.

## NEW YORK FUTURES EXCHANGE
## NYSE COMPOSITE INDEX (NYFE)
### $500 times premium

| Strike price | Calls—Settle June-c | Sept-c | Dec-c | Puts—Settle June-p | Sept-p | Dec-p |
|---|---|---|---|---|---|---|
| 134 | 3.80 | 7.25 | 9.40 | 0.35 | 2.75 | 3.85 |
| 136 | 2.35 | 6.05 | 8.20 | 0.90 | 3.55 | 4.65 |
| 138 | 1.25 | 4.95 | 7.15 | 1.80 | 4.50 | 5.55 |
| 140 | 0.60 | 4.05 | 6.20 | 3.15 | 5.45 | 6.55 |
| 142 | 0.25 | 3.25 | 5.30 | 4.80 | 6.65 | 7.60 |
| 144 | 0.10 | 2.55 | 4.55 | 6.50 | 7.95 | 8.80 |

Est. vol. 1,173, Mon vol. 518 calls, 499 puts.
Open interest Mon, 15,828 calls, 13,297 puts.

## CHICAGO MERCANTILE EXCHANGE
## S & P 500 STOCK INDEX (CME)
### $500 times premium

| Strike price | Calls—Settle June-c | Sept-c | Dec-c | Puts—Settle June-p | Sept-p | Dec-p |
|---|---|---|---|---|---|---|
| 230 | 9.50 | 14.45 | .... | 0.25 | 3.85 | .... |
| 235 | 5.30 | 11.25 | 15.10 | 1.00 | 5.60 | 7.65 |
| 240 | 2.25 | 8.60 | 10.45 | 2.95 | 7.75 | 9.80 |
| 245 | 0.75 | 6.40 | 10.15 | 6.45 | 10.45 | 12.25 |
| 250 | 0.25 | 4.70 | 8.20 | 10.90 | 15.65 | 15.10 |
| 255 | 0.05 | 3.40 | 6.55 | 15.70 | 17.20 | 18.25 |

Est. vol. 6,998; Mon.; vol. 4,009 calls; 3,817 puts.
Open interest Mon; 51,043 calls; 36,584 puts.

## PHILADELPHIA EXCHANGE
## GOLD/SILVER INDEX

| Strike price | Calls—Last June | July | Aug | Puts—Last June | July | Aug |
|---|---|---|---|---|---|---|
| 60 | .... | $6\frac{3}{4}$ | .... | $\frac{1}{16}$ | $\frac{1}{16}$ | $\frac{1}{2}$ |
| 65 | $4\frac{7}{8}$ | $5\frac{3}{4}$ | .... | $\frac{1}{8}$ | $\frac{13}{16}$ | $1\frac{7}{16}$ |
| 70 | $1\frac{1}{8}$ | $2\frac{3}{4}$ | .... | $1\frac{3}{8}$ | $2\frac{1}{2}$ | $3\frac{3}{8}$ |
| 75 | $\frac{3}{16}$ | $1\frac{1}{8}$ | .... | .... | .... | .... |
| 80 | $\frac{1}{16}$ | $\frac{3}{8}$ | .... | .... | .... | .... |

Total call volume 697.    Total call open int. 3,216.
Total put volume 189.    Total put open int. 2,582.
The index: High 70.45; Low 69.27; Close 69.73, −0.69.

## VALUE LINE INDEX OPTIONS

| Strike price | Calls—Last June | July | Aug | Puts—Last June | July | Aug |
|---|---|---|---|---|---|---|
| 230 | $9\frac{1}{2}$ | .... | .... | $\frac{1}{8}$ | 1 | .... |
| 235 | $5\frac{5}{8}$ | $6\frac{1}{4}$ | .... | $\frac{3}{4}$ | $2\frac{15}{16}$ | $3\frac{7}{8}$ |
| 240 | $2\frac{1}{8}$ | $3\frac{3}{4}$ | .... | $3\frac{1}{4}$ | $5\frac{1}{4}$ | .... |
| 245 | $\frac{3}{8}$ | $2\frac{7}{16}$ | .... | $7\frac{5}{8}$ | 9 | $9\frac{3}{8}$ |
| 250 | $\frac{1}{16}$ | $\frac{7}{8}$ | .... | $12\frac{1}{4}$ | $12\frac{1}{2}$ | .... |
| 255 | .... | .... | .... | $7\frac{3}{4}$ | .... | .... |
| 260 | .... | $\frac{3}{16}$ | .... | .... | .... | .... |

Total call volume 3,458.    Total call open int. 22,985.
Total put volume 2,395.    Total put open int. 31,553.
The index: High 240.64; Low 238.99; Close 239.83, −0.77.

**Exhibit 2.6: Example of US options indexes page, *The Wall Street Journal* (cont.)**

### NATIONAL O-T-C INDEX

| Strike price | Calls—Last June | July | Aug | Puts—Last June | July | Aug |
|---|---|---|---|---|---|---|
| 230 | $3\frac{1}{8}$ | .... | .... | .... | .... | .... |
| 235 | $\frac{7}{8}$ | .... | .... | .... | 5 | .... |
| 240 | .... | $2\frac{3}{4}$ | | .... | .... | .... |

Total call volume 66.   Total call open int. 665.
Total put volume 2.   Total put open int. 2,191.
The index: High 233.68; Low 230.93; Close 232.11, −1.57.

### CHICAGO BOARD S&P 100 INDEX

| Strike price | Calls—Last June | July | Aug | Puts—Last June | July | Aug |
|---|---|---|---|---|---|---|
| 200 | 29 | .... | .... | .... | .... | .... |
| 205 | $25\frac{1}{8}$ | .... | .... | $\frac{1}{16}$ | $\frac{1}{16}$ | $\frac{3}{8}$ |
| 210 | $18\frac{1}{4}$ | $19\frac{1}{2}$ | $20\frac{1}{2}$ | $\frac{1}{16}$ | $\frac{5}{16}$ | $\frac{3}{4}$ |
| 215 | $14\frac{1}{8}$ | $15\frac{1}{2}$ | $16\frac{1}{4}$ | $\frac{1}{16}$ | $\frac{5}{8}$ | $1\frac{7}{16}$ |

| Strike price | Calls—Last June | July | Aug | Puts—Last June | July | Aug |
|---|---|---|---|---|---|---|
| 220 | 10 | $11\frac{1}{4}$ | $12\frac{1}{8}$ | $\frac{3}{16}$ | $1\frac{3}{8}$ | $2\frac{1}{2}$ |
| 225 | $5\frac{1}{2}$ | $7\frac{5}{8}$ | $9\frac{1}{2}$ | $\frac{7}{8}$ | $2\frac{3}{4}$ | $4\frac{1}{4}$ |
| 230 | $2\frac{1}{4}$ | $4\frac{3}{4}$ | $6\frac{1}{2}$ | $2\frac{13}{16}$ | $4\frac{7}{8}$ | $6\frac{5}{8}$ |
| 235 | $\frac{11}{16}$ | $2\frac{15}{16}$ | $4\frac{3}{8}$ | $6\frac{3}{8}$ | 8 | $9\frac{1}{4}$ |
| 240 | $\frac{3}{16}$ | $1\frac{1}{2}$ | $2\frac{7}{8}$ | $10\frac{3}{4}$ | 12 | $12\frac{3}{4}$ |
| 245 | $\frac{1}{16}$ | $\frac{3}{4}$ | $1\frac{5}{8}$ | $16\frac{1}{4}$ | $16\frac{1}{2}$ | $18\frac{1}{8}$ |
| 250 | $\frac{1}{16}$ | $\frac{1}{4}$ | $\frac{7}{8}$ | $21\frac{1}{4}$ | 22 | $22\frac{1}{4}$ |

Total call volume 252,242.   Total call open int. 627,699.
Total put volume 247,998.   Total put open int. 732,346.
The index: High 230.70; Low 228.28; Close 229.99, +0.20.

### S&P 500 INDEX (NEW)

| Strike price | Calls—Last June | July | Sept | Puts—Last June | July | Sept |
|---|---|---|---|---|---|---|
| 220 | $\frac{1}{4}$ | .... | .... | .... | .... | .... |

Source: *The Wall Street Journal.*

A futures contract is simply the obligation to buy or sell a specific asset at a specific price at some future date. Thus, it might be an agreement to buy 50 tonnes of copper at $1,500 a tonne in December 1986. However, if no interim payments were made, a considerable credit risk could build up before December if copper prices moved violently. To avoid this, all traded futures contracts on organized exchanges use a margin system. Each party to a futures contract puts up an initial deposit called an *initial margin*. Every day the value of the contract is adjusted to be in line with the current price, and interim profits and losses are credited or debited. This process is known as *marking to market* and the aim is to keep the value of the margin account at a certain level, normally that of the original initial margin. The interim payments made as the futures price changes are called *variation margin*. Below is an example, using a copper future.

## Contract

December delivery 50 tonnes (Buyer)

| | | | | |
|---|---|---|---|---|
| Price | $1,500 | $1,550 | $1,475 | $1,500 |
| Required margin | $7,500 | $7,500 | $7,500 | $7,500 |
| Margin account | $7,500 | $10,000 | $6,250 | $8,750 |
| Variation margin | — | $2,500 (withdrawn) | ($1,250) (required to be deposited) | $1,250 (withdrawn) |

Given this marking to market process, an option on a stock index future is easily explained. The option gives the right to buy or sell a stock index future at a specific price. If the option is exercised, a futures position is set up for the buyer which is immediately marked to market.

### Example

An investor buys a CME S&P 500 index put option for June expiration exercise price 245; premium 3.60.
The price falls to 230 and the buyer exercises the put option. The buyer acquires a short S&P 500 futures position at an effective price of 245 which is immediately marked to market at 230.

$$\text{Margin account} = (245 - 230) \times \$500$$
$$= \$7,500$$
$$\text{Required margin} = \$6,000.00$$

So the buyer can withdraw $1,500 from the margin account. To obtain the remaining $6,000.00 he must buy an S&P 500 futures contract in the market to cancel his short position.

$$\text{Net profit} = \$7,500.00 - (3.60 \times \$500)$$
$$= \$5,700.00$$

One specific difference with most of the cash index options, as shown in the S & P 500 CME options in Exhibit 2.6, is that they trade on a regular three-month cycle of December, March, June and September in line with the delivery cycle for the underlying stock index futures contracts.

## c. Currency options

The basic characteristics of a currency option are no different to any other option. A currency option is the right to buy or sell a fixed quantity of one currency in exchange for a specific quantity of another currency in a ratio determined by a specific exchange rate at or before a specific date in the future. Once again the currency options can be classified as options on cash or options on currency futures.

### Example: Cash option

Buy a Philadelphia Stock Exchange September sterling call option with a strike price of $1.20 for a premium of 4.2¢.

You are buying the right between now and September to purchase £12,500 sterling for $15,000 (£12,500 × $1.20).

$$\text{Cost of right} = £12,500 \times \$0.042$$
$$= \$525$$

The exercise price for all options traded in the United States, and worldwide, is determined in units of foreign currency per dollar. Call and put options are defined in the following way.

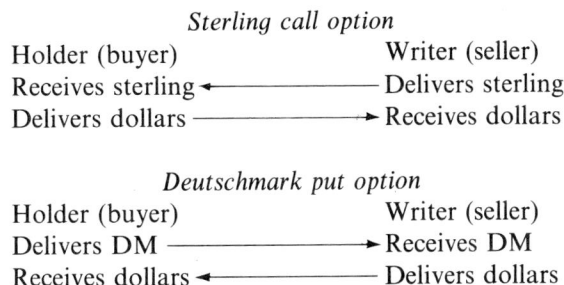

*Sterling call option*

| Holder (buyer) | Writer (seller) |
|---|---|
| Receives sterling ← | Delivers sterling |
| Delivers dollars → | Receives dollars |

*Deutschmark put option*

| Holder (buyer) | Writer (seller) |
|---|---|
| Delivers DM → | Receives DM |
| Receives dollars ← | Delivers dollars |

There are some exceptions to this, particularly on European exchanges. The trader should be careful to make sure, for example, whether a call option on a specific exchange is the right to exchange dollars for the currency or the currency for dollars. The vast majority of currency options traded are for dollars against currency, although there are a few exceptions such as the dollar/DM option traded on the London International Financial Futures Exchange and the sterling/florin option on the European Options Exchange.

Exhibit 2.7 shows the relevant currency options information from *The Wall Street Journal* for 5 June 1986. The cash currency options traded on the Philadelphia Stock Exchange, the London Stock Exchange and the Chicago Board Options Exchange trade on a monthly cycle, while the options on futures which trade on the CME follow the same quarterly expiration cycle as the underlying futures contracts. The sterling contract on LIFFE is an exception in that it is an option on cash currency but trades with a quarterly expiration cycle. The only other point to note for the cash options is that the trading unit for the CBOE and LIFFE currency options is always twice that traded in Philadelphia and London – £25,000 instead of £12,500 and so on. The CBOE options are European style options rather than American options, i.e. they cannot be exercised early, but only on the expiration day.

As with the stock index futures options discussed earlier, the CME currency options call for the setting up of a currency futures position at exercise rather than the delivery of cash currency. The currency futures is then marked to market, and the margin account of the client credited accordingly. To close the transaction, an opposite currency futures position is bought or sold. Futures options, however, may have some advantages over the cash options for the trader. At exercise of a cash option, the entire value of the currency position has to be exchanged which may necessitate access to and heavy use of foreign exchange lines. With the futures option, the transaction is carried out entirely in one currency and the sums involved are only the difference between the exercise price and the current currency futures price. This point will be discussed in the section on delivery procedures.

**EURODOLLAR (CME) $ million; pts. of 100%**

| Strike price | Calls—Settle | | | Puts—Settle | | |
|---|---|---|---|---|---|---|
| | June-c | Sept.-c | Dec.-c | June-p | Sept.-p | Dec.-p |
| 9225 | 0.62 | 0.60 | 0.62 | 0.004 | 0.18 | 0.39 |
| 9250 | 0.37 | 0.44 | 0.48 | 0.004 | 0.26 | 0.48 |
| 9275 | 0.16 | 0.30 | 0.36 | 0.04 | 0.37 | 0.60 |
| 9300 | 0.03 | 0.20 | 0.27 | 0.16 | 0.51 | 0.74 |
| 9325 | 0.01 | 0.12 | 0.18 | 0.39 | 0.68 | 0.89 |
| 9350 | 0.004 | 0.08 | 0.12 | 0.63 | 0.87 | 1.08 |

Est. vol. 5,180, Wed.; vol. 1,648 calls, 3,330 puts.
Open interest Wed.; 82,481 calls, 55,998 puts.

## CURRENCY FUTURES

| | Open | High | Low | Settle | Change | Lifetime High | Lifetime Low | Open Interest |
|---|---|---|---|---|---|---|---|---|

**BRITISH POUND (IMM)—25,000 pounds;**
**$ per pound**

| | Open | High | Low | Settle | Change | High | Low | Interest |
|---|---|---|---|---|---|---|---|---|
| June | 1.4860 | 1.5040 | 1.4845 | 1.4985 | +0.0135 | 1.5525 | 1.1530 | 24,453 |
| Sept | 1.4785 | 1.4950 | 1.4760 | 1.4895 | +0.0130 | 1.5430 | 1.3240 | 7,735 |
| Dec | 1.4680 | 1.4890 | 1.4680 | 1.4815 | +0.0125 | 1.5360 | 1.3250 | 480 |

Est vol 7,584; vol. Wed. 6,489; open int. 32,679, +255.

**CANADIAN DOLLAR (IMM)—100,000 dlrs.;**
**$ per Can $**

| | Open | High | Low | Settle | Change | High | Low | Interest |
|---|---|---|---|---|---|---|---|---|
| June | 0.7174 | 0.7185 | 0.7155 | 0.7165 | −0.0009 | 0.7360 | 0.6845 | 7,390 |
| Sept | 0.7144 | 0.7153 | 0.7125 | 0.7130 | −0.0011 | 0.7305 | 0.6809 | 4,748 |
| Dec | 0.7115 | 0.7115 | 0.7100 | 0.7096 | −0.0011 | 0.7285 | 0.6790 | 881 |
| Mar87 | 0.7072 | 0.7080 | 0.7068 | 0.7058 | −0.0014 | 0.7256 | 0.6770 | 297 |

Est. vol. 3,157; vol. Wed. 3,934; open int. 13,348, −352.

**JAPANESE YEN (IMM)—12.5 million yen;**
**$ per yen (0.00)**

| | Open | High | Low | Settle | Change | High | Low | Interest |
|---|---|---|---|---|---|---|---|---|
| June | 0.5861 | 0.5935 | 0.5859 | 0.5920 | +0.0069 | 0.6245 | 0.4220 | 30,260 |
| Sept | 0.5898 | 0.5977 | 0.5896 | 0.5958 | +0.0071 | 0.6280 | 0.4690 | 6,793 |
| Dec | 0.5938 | 0.6015 | 0.5938 | 0.6001 | +0.0073 | 0.6320 | 0.4720 | 844 |

Est. vol. 23,549; vol. Wed. 19,723; open int. 37,900, +781.

**SWISS FRANC (IMM)—125,000 francs;**
**$ per franc**

| | Open | High | Low | Settle | Change | High | Low | Interest |
|---|---|---|---|---|---|---|---|---|
| June | 0.5368 | 0.5443 | 0.5368 | 0.5436 | +0.0095 | 0.5580 | 0.4190 | 21,680 |
| Sept | 0.5405 | 0.5486 | 0.5402 | 0.5471 | +0.0098 | 0.5625 | 0.4790 | 8,189 |
| Dec | 0.5460 | 0.5510 | 0.5442 | 0.5510 | +0.0100 | 0.5660 | 0.4878 | 608 |

Est. vol. 24,477; vol. Wed. 19,987; open int. 30,484, −347.

**W. GERMAN MARK (IMM)—125,000 marks;**
**$ per mark**

| | Open | High | Low | Settle | Change | High | Low | Interest |
|---|---|---|---|---|---|---|---|---|
| June | 0.4428 | 0.4477 | 0.4428 | 0.4467 | +0.0057 | 0.4648 | 0.3335 | 48,564 |
| Sept | 0.4459 | 0.4506 | 0.4459 | 0.4496 | +0.0058 | 0.4675 | 0.3762 | 10,001 |
| Dec | 0.4497 | 0.4530 | 0.4490 | 0.4527 | +0.0059 | 0.4703 | 0.4090 | 323 |

Est. vol. 33,947; vol. Wed. 26,653; open int. 58,899, −745.

## CURRENCY OPTIONS
## PHILADELPHIA EXCHANGE

| Option & Underlying | Strike price | Calls—Last | | | Puts—Last | | |
|---|---|---|---|---|---|---|---|
| | | June | July | Sept | June | July | Sept |
| *12,500 British Pounds-cents per unit.* | | | | | | | |
| BPound | 145 | r | 4.80 | r | 0.30 | 0.90 | r |
| 149.94 | 150 | 1.25 | 2.45 | 3.70 | 1.30 | 2.95 | r |
| | 155 | 0.15 | r | 1.85 | r | r | r |
| *50,000 Canadian Dollars-cents per unit.* | | | | | | | |
| CDollar | 72 | 0.20 | 0.46 | 0.77 | r | r | r |
| 71.62 | 73 | r | r | 0.40 | r | r | r |
| *62,500 West German Marks-cents per unit.* | | | | | | | |
| DMark | 41 | r | r | r | 0.01 | r | r |
| 44.67 | 42 | r | 2.80 | r | 0.02 | 0.18 | 0.45 |
| 44.67 | 43 | 1.36 | 2.03 | 2.55 | 0.06 | 0.28 | 0.67 |
| 44.67 | 44 | 0.82 | 1.35 | 1.97 | 0.20 | 0.53 | 1.00 |
| 44.67 | 45 | 0.29 | 0.77 | 1.41 | 0.80 | 1.07 | 1.50 |
| 44.67 | 46 | 0.08 | 0.42 | 0.96 | r | r | r |
| 44.67 | 47 | 0.02 | 0.23 | 0.69 | r | r | r |
| | 48 | 0.01 | r | 0.47 | r | r | r |
| 44.67 | 49 | r | r | 0.33 | r | r | r |
| *125,000 French Francs-10th of a cent per unit.* | | | | | | | |

| Option & Underlying | Strike price | Calls—Last | | | Puts—Last | | |
|---|---|---|---|---|---|---|---|
| | | June | July | Sept | June | July | Sept |
| FFranc | 135 | r | r | r | 0.30 | r | r |
| 140.33 | 140 | r | 2.85 | r | r | r | r |
| 140.33 | 145 | r | r | 3.10 | r | r | r |
| *6,250,000 Japanese Yen-100ths of a cent per unit.* | | | | | | | |
| JYen | 52 | r | s | r | r | s | 0.13 |
| 59.14 | 54 | 5.08 | r | r | r | r | r |
| | 55 | r | r | r | r | r | 0.50 |
| 59.14 | 56 | r | r | r | 0.03 | 0.26 | r |
| 59.14 | 57 | 2.10 | r | r | 0.08 | r | 1.07 |
| 59.14 | 58 | 1.34 | r | 2.46 | 0.22 | 0.60 | 1.49 |
| 59.14 | 59 | 0.64 | 1.35 | 2.28 | 0.50 | 1.08 | 1.87 |
| 59.14 | 60 | 0.10 | 0.61 | 1.38 | r | r | r |
| 59.14 | 62 | r | 0.37 | 1.06 | r | 3.07 | r |
| 59.14 | 63 | r | 0.21 | 0.70 | r | r | r |
| 59.14 | 64 | r | r | 0.68 | r | r | r |
| 59.14 | 65 | r | r | 0.48 | r | r | r |
| *62,500 Swiss Francs-cents per unit.* | | | | | | | |
| SFranc | 45 | 8.60 | s | r | r | s | r |
| 54.26 | 49 | 4.70 | r | r | r | r | r |
| 54.26 | 50 | r | r | r | r | r | 0.39 |
| 54.26 | 51 | r | r | 3.88 | r | r | 0.52 |
| 54.26 | 52 | 1.75 | r | r | 0.05 | 0.38 | 0.77 |
| | 53 | 1.30 | r | r | 0.16 | r | r |
| 54.26 | 54 | 0.66 | r | 1.97 | 0.43 | 0.93 | 1.55 |
| 54.26 | 55 | 0.24 | 0.79 | 1.48 | 0.96 | r | r |
| 54.26 | 56 | 0.06 | 0.47 | r | r | r | r |
| 54.26 | 57 | r | r | 0.65 | r | r | r |
| 54.26 | 58 | r | r | 0.50 | r | r | r |

Total call vol. 9,808.     Call open int. 331,351.
Total put vol. 6,478.     Put open int. 268,601.
r—Not traded.     s—No option offered.
Last is premium (purchase price).

## LONDON STOCK EXCHANGE

| Strike price Sterling | Call—Settle | | | Put—Settle | | |
|---|---|---|---|---|---|---|
| | June | July | Aug | June | July | Aug |
| 145 | 400 | 495 | 575 | 30 | 145 | 255 |
| 150 | 100 | 215 | 315 | 220 | 375 | 495 |
| 155 | 15 | 80 | 155 | 655 | 750 | 840 |
| 160 | 5 | 25 | 75 | 1,180 | 1,190 | 1,250 |

Actual volume June 4:75; Calls:55; Puts:20.
Open interest June 4:9587.

## EUROPEAN CURRENCY UNIT VALUES

The value of one ECU in terms of other currencies as reported by the European Commission.

| Currency | Thu. | Prev. | Currency | Thu. | Prev. |
|---|---|---|---|---|---|
| Belg Fr. | 43.896 | 43.939 | D-Mark | 2.1498 | 2.1517 |
| Guilder | 2.4182 | 2.4206 | Pound Stg. | 0.6401 | 0.6365 |
| Dan Kr. | 7.9510 | 7.9536 | French Fr. | 6.8447 | 6.8515 |
| It Lira | 1473.1 | 1274.5 | Irish Pound | 0.7082 | 0.7077 |
| Gr Drachma | 134.56 | 135.16 | US Dollar | 0.9525 | 0.9469 |
| Swiss Fr. | 1.7758 | 1.7793 | Sp Peseta | 137.21 | 137.25 |
| Swed Kr. | 6.9031 | 6.8898 | Nor Kr. | 7.3095 | 7.2955 |
| Can Dlr. | 1.3256 | 1.3180 | Por Escudo | 144.78 | 144.21 |
| Aus Sch. | 15.121 | 15.107 | Fin-Mark | 4.9840 | 4.9667 |
| Yen | 162.69 | 162.24 | | | |

**BRITISH POUND (CME) 25,000 pounds;**
**cents per pound**

| Strike price | Calls—Settle | | | Puts—Settle | | |
|---|---|---|---|---|---|---|
| | June-c | Sept-c | Dec-c | June-p | Sept-p | Dec-p |
| 1450 | 4.85 | 6.35 | 7.35 | 0.004 | 2.50 | 4.30 |
| 1475 | 2.40 | 4.90 | 6.05 | 0.10 | 3.50 | 5.45 |
| 1500 | 0.55 | 3.70 | 4.95 | 0.65 | 4.75 | 6.70 |
| 1525 | 0.004 | 2.75 | 4.00 | 2.70 | 6.20 | 8.15 |
| 1550 | 0.004 | 2.00 | 3.25 | 5.15 | 7.90 | 9.75 |
| 1575 | 0.004 | 1.35 | 2.50 | 7.65 | 9.75 | 11.45 |

Est. vol. 2,610, Wed.; vol. 105 calls, 143 puts.
Open interest Wed.; 16,130 calls, 16,139 puts.

## Exhibit 2.7: Example of currency futures options page, *The Wall Street Journal* (*cont.*)

### W. GERMAN MARK (CME) 125,000 marks, cents per mark

| Strike price | June-C | Sept-c | Dec-c | June-p | Sept-p | Dec-p |
|---|---|---|---|---|---|---|
| | *Calls—Settle* | | | *Puts—Settle* | | |
| 43 | 1.67 | 2.54 | 3.16 | 0.0008 | 0.61 | 0.97 |
| 44 | 0.70 | 1.90 | 2.56 | 0.03 | 0.96 | 1.33 |
| 45 | 0.10 | 1.37 | 2.01 | 0.43 | 1.41 | 1.75 |
| 46 | 0.0008 | 0.98 | 1.57 | 1.33 | 2.00 | 2.28 |
| 47 | 0.0008 | 0.67 | 1.21 | 2.33 | 2.67 | 2.88 |
| 48 | 0.0008 | 0.45 | 0.92 | 3.33 | 3.43 | 3.56 |

Est. vol. 15,374, Wed.; vol. 3,787 calls, 3,547 puts.
Open interest Wed.; 75,102 calls, 66,171 puts.

### SWISS FRANC (CME) 125,000 francs; cents per franc

| Strike price | June-c | Sept-c | Dec-c | June-p | Sept-p | Dec-p |
|---|---|---|---|---|---|---|
| | *Calls—Settle* | | | *Puts—Settle* | | |
| 52 | 2.36 | 3.33 | 4.06 | 0.0008 | 0.65 | 1.07 |
| 53 | 1.37 | 2.65 | 3.41 | 0.01 | 0.95 | 1.38 |
| 54 | 0.47 | 2.05 | 2.83 | 0.12 | 1.34 | 1.76 |
| 55 | 0.06 | 1.55 | 2.34 | 0.71 | 1.83 | 2.24 |
| 56 | 0.0008 | 1.15 | 1.89 | 1.64 | 2.42 | 2.76 |
| 57 | 0.0008 | 0.84 | 1.53 | 2.64 | 3.08 | .... |

Est. vol. 5,111, Wed.; vol. 2,537 calls, 1,933 puts.
Open interest Wed.; 24,619 calls, 22,482 puts.

### JAPANESE YEN (CME) 12,500,000 yen, cents per

| Strike price | June-c | Sept-c | Dec-c | June-p | Sept-p | Dec-p |
|---|---|---|---|---|---|---|
| | *Calls—Settle* | | | *Puts—Settle* | | |
| 57 | 2.20 | 3.37 | 4.08 | 0.00 | 0.87 | 1.19 |
| 58 | 1.23 | 2.73 | 3.48 | 0.03 | 1.19 | 1.95 |
| 59 | 0.42 | 2.15 | 2.94 | 0.22 | 1.60 | .... |
| 60 | 0.05 | 1.67 | 2.47 | 0.85 | 2.10 | 2.41 |
| 61 | 0.01 | 1.29 | 1.99 | 1.81 | 2.70 | 2.95 |
| 62 | 0.00 | 0.99 | 1.65 | 2.80 | 3.36 | 3.60 |

Est. vol. 5,416, Wed.; vol. 4,199 calls, 2.102 puts.
Open interest Wed.; 26,776 calls, 26,227 puts.

### STERLING (LIFFE)—b-£25,000; cents per pound

| Strike price | June-c | Sept-c | Dec-c | June-p | Sept-p | Dec-p |
|---|---|---|---|---|---|---|
| | *Calls—Settle* | | | *Puts—Settle* | | |
| 145 | 4.09 | 6.18 | 7.28 | 0.32 | 3.30 | 5.07 |
| 150 | 0.99 | 3.69 | 4.92 | 2.22 | 5.81 | 7.71 |
| 155 | 0.09 | 2.02 | 3.17 | 6.32 | 9.14 | 10.96 |
| 160 | 0.00 | 1.01 | 1.95 | 11.23 | 13.13 | 14.74 |
| 165 | 0.00 | 0.46 | 1.15 | 16.23 | 17.58 | 18.94 |
| 170 | .... | .... | .... | .... | .... | .... |

Actual Vol. Thursday, 44 calls, 10 puts.
Open interest Wednesday; 3,934 calls, 5,701 puts.
  b-Option on physical sterling.

### EURODOLLAR (LIFFE) $1 million; pts. of 100%

| Strike price | June-c | Sept-c | Dec-c | June-p | Sept-p | Dec-p |
|---|---|---|---|---|---|---|
| | *Calls—Settle* | | | *Puts—Settle* | | |
| 9200 | 0.87 | 0.82 | 0.84 | 0.00 | 0.12 | 0.32 |
| 9250 | 0.38 | 0.46 | 0.54 | 0.01 | 0.26 | 0.52 |
| 9300 | 0.04 | 0.21 | 0.30 | 0.17 | 0.51 | 0.78 |
| 9350 | 0.00 | 0.07 | 0.15 | 0.63 | 0.87 | 1.13 |
| 9400 | 0.00 | 0.02 | 0.06 | 1.13 | 1.32 | 1.54 |
| 9450 | 0.00 | 0.00 | 0.02 | 1.63 | 1.80 | 2.00 |

Actual vol. Thursday, 117 calls, 0 puts.
Open interest Wednesday; 4,042 calls, 3,252 puts.

---

## WEDNESDAY'S MARKET DATA

The following Market Statistics for Wednesday, June 4, were unavailable at press time for yesterday's edition.

---

## FOREIGN EXCHANGE

### CURRENCY OPTIONS
### CHICAGO BOARD OPTIONS EXCHANGE

| Option & underlying | Strike price | June | July | Sept | June | July | Sept |
|---|---|---|---|---|---|---|---|
| | | *Calls—Last* | | | *Puts—Last* | | |
| 25,000 British Pounds-cents per unit. | | | | | | | |
| BPound | 150 | r | r | r | 2.40 | r | r |
| 100,000 Canadian Dollars-cents per unit. | | | | | | | |
| CDollar | 72 | r | 0.48 | r | 0.49 | 0.72 | r |
| 71.77 | 74 | r | 0.11 | r | r | r | r |
| 125,000 West German Marks-cents per unit. | | | | | | | |
| DMark | 43 | r | r | r | 0.16 | r | r |
| 44.04 | 44 | r | r | r | 0.49 | r | r |
| 44.04 | 45 | 0.12 | r | r | r | r | r |
| 44.04 | 46 | r | r | r | 2.08 | r | r |
| 12,500,000 Japanese Yen-100ths of a cent per unit. | | | | | | | |
| JYen | 55 | r | r | 4.25 | r | r | r |
| 58.45 | 56 | r | r | 3.55 | r | r | 0.76 |
| 58.45 | 57 | r | r | 2.95 | r | r | r |
| 58.45 | 58 | r | r | 2.45 | 0.45 | 0.98 | r |
| 58.45 | 59 | 0.43 | 1.06 | 1.73 | 0.98 | r | r |
| 58.45 | 60 | r | r | 1.40 | r | r | r |
| 58.45 | 61 | r | 0.40 | r | 2.60 | r | r |
| | 62 | r | r | 0.76 | r | r | r |
| 58.45 | 64 | r | 0.08 | r | r | r | r |
| 125,000 Swiss Francs-cents per unit. | | | | | | | |
| SFranc | 48 | r | r | r | r | r | 0.16 |
| 53.29 | 49 | r | r | r | r | r | 0.28 |
| 53.29 | 51 | r | r | r | r | r | 0.69 |
| 53.29 | 52 | r | r | r | 0.13 | r | 1.01 |
| 53.29 | 53 | r | r | r | 0.48 | 0.85 | 1.42 |
| | 56 | r | r | 0.79 | r | r | r |

Total call volume 504.    Total call open int. 27,618.
Total put volume 921.    Total put open int. 19,163.
r—Not traded.    s—No option offered.
Last is premium (purchase price).

---

Source: *The Wall Street Journal.*

### d. Interest rate options

Options on interest rates, or more correctly options on underlying fixed interest instruments, can be categorized along two axes: first, between short-term rates and long-term rates, and second, between cash options and options on futures.

#### (i) Short-term rates

The majority of short-term interest rate options are options on futures, with the major contracts being the Treasury bill and Eurodollar options on the Chicago Mercantile Exchange, and the Eurodollar option on the London International Financial Futures Exchange and Sydney Futures Exchange. The Eurodollar option is used as an example.

A Eurodollar futures contract fixes the effective interest rate for borrowing or lending three-month Eurodollar funds at a specific date in the future. On that date, unless the contract has been closed out previously, there is a cash settlement with final profits and losses being credited based on a final futures settlement price determined from the cash market. It is this final convergence of futures implied interest rates and cash rates which enables the hedger to fix the Eurodollar interest rate in advance.

**Example**

A borrower sells a September Eurodollar futures contract at a price of 90.00.

The borrower has fixed an effective Libor rate for the third Wednesday in September of 10.00% (i.e. 100.00 minus the futures price of 90.00 = 10.00%).[5]

Suppose Libor rises by the September delivery day to 12%; then the Eurodollar futures price will have fallen to 88.00.

The 200 basis points (2%) profit from the short futures position will exactly compensate for the 200 basis points rise in Libor to the borrower.

Because the three-month Eurodollar futures contract is based on $1 million units, each basis point price change represents a cash change of $25.

$$\text{Tick size} = \$1,000.000 \times 0.0001 \times \tfrac{3}{12}$$
$$= \$25.$$

The Eurodollar option then simply gives the right to buy or sell one of these futures contracts at a specific price.

**Example: Call option**

September 15 prices

December Eurodollar 90.00 call = 0.75
December Eurodollar future = 90.50

The investor who buys the call has bought the right between September 15 and December to buy a December Eurodollar futures contract at an effective price of 90.00.

$$\text{Cost of right} = \$1,875 \ (75 \text{ basis points} \times \$25)$$

Suppose by October 15, the December Eurodollar price has risen to 91.00. The investor decides to exercise. He buys a Eurodollar future at 90.00 and it is marked to market at 91.00.

$$\text{Margin account} = (91.00 - 90.00) \times 100 \times \$25$$
$$= \$2,500.00$$
$$\text{Net profit} = \$2,500.00 - \$1,875 = \$625.00$$

As before, to realize the profit on exercise, an opposite Eurodollar futures position needs to be bought or sold in the market.

The Treasury bill futures option on the CME works on exactly the same principle. Cash Treasury bill options are also traded on the American Stock Exchange but the trading volume is so small as to make them of little importance.

#### (ii) Long-term rates

Options on long-term fixed interest instruments such as Treasury notes and bonds in the United States, gilts and Treasury bonds in London, and long-term bonds in Sydney, Canada and Amsterdam have proved to be some of the most popular interest rate options. Once again the

---

[5] This is because short-term interest rate futures contracts are priced on an index basis. For the Eurodollar futures contract

$$\text{Futures price} = 100 - \text{three-month Libor.}$$

division is between cash and futures options. For the purpose of example, we will look at the gilt options traded on the London Stock Exchange and the Treasury bond futures options traded on the Chicago Board of Trade. Other cash and futures options have essentially the same characteristics as these two groups.

The London Stock Exchange short cash gilt option is a typical bond option. It calls for the physical delivery of £50,000 nominal of the Treasury $11\frac{3}{4}$ 1991. The table below gives the option information for 10 June 1986.

| Exercise price | Calls | | | Puts | | |
|---|---|---|---|---|---|---|
| | Aug. | Nov. | Dec. | Aug. | Nov. | Dec. |
| 108 | $3\frac{1}{2}$ | $3\frac{11}{16}$ | — | $\frac{3}{8}$ | $\frac{15}{16}$ | — |
| 110 | $1\frac{15}{16}$ | $2\frac{7}{16}$ | 3 | 1 | $1\frac{13}{16}$ | $2\frac{1}{4}$ |
| 112 | $\frac{13}{16}$ | $1\frac{7}{16}$ | 2 | $1\frac{3}{8}$ | $2\frac{5}{8}$ | 3 |

Gilt price = £111–00

The premium is per £100 nominal of the underlying instrument, with the option following a three month expiration cycle.

### Example
Buy a £110 August call at $1\frac{15}{16}$.

You are buying the right between now and August to hand over £55,000 + accrued interest and receive £50,000 nominal of the Treasury $11\frac{30}{4}\%$ 1991.

$$\text{Cost of right} = 500 \times £1\frac{15}{16} = £968.75$$

This is a cash option. Upon exercise, the trader has to come with £55,000 plus accrued interest and will then have to sell the cash gilt in the market to realize any profit. The seller of the option also needs to remember that if an option is exercised against him he will, if he does not already own the stock, have to be able to purchase £50,000 nominal of the gilt to deliver against the option. Thus the delivery process for cash gilt options can involve the temporary tying up of large amounts of cash funds.

The CBT Treasury bond futures option is like other futures options. It is written on the long-term Treasury bond future traded on the CBT, which is defined on a hypothetical 8% Treasury bond and where bonds of maturity of more than 15 years can be delivered.[6] The quotation for the Treasury bond future is dollars per $100 nominal of the bond ($100,000 units) and the option premiums are quoted in 64ths.

$$\tfrac{1}{32}\text{nd} = \$100,000 \times 0.0003125 = \$31.25$$

$$\tfrac{1}{64}\text{th} = \$100,000 \times 0.00015625 = \$15.625$$

The relevant data from *The Wall Street Journal* for 10 June 1986 are shown in Exhibit 2.8. The options trade the same January, March, June, September cycle as the underlying futures contracts.

### Example
Buy a September T-bond futures call option, exercise price 92, for a premium of 3–28.

The investor acquired the right to set up a long T-bond futures position at an effective price of 92–00.

$$\text{Cost of right} = 220/64\text{th}(3\text{–}28) \times \$15.625 = \$3,437.50$$

Suppose the September bond futures price rose to 96–00 and the investor exercised.

$$\text{Margin account} = (96\text{–}00 \text{ minus } 92\text{–}00) \times 32 \times \$31.25$$
$$= \$4,000.00$$
$$\text{Net profit} = \$562.50$$

There is an important difference between cash options and futures options. At exercise of a cash option, the trader has to come up with the full value of the underlying position; at the exercise of a futures option, only the difference between the exercise price and the market price is required.

---

[6] For a fuller description of Treasury bond futures, see Chapter 8 on interest rate options, and M. D. Fitzgerald, *Financial Futures*, Euromoney Publications (1983).

## Exhibit 2.8: Example of CBT Treasury issue options page, *The Wall Street Journal*

For notes and bonds, decimals in closing prices represent 32nds; 1.01 means $1\frac{1}{32}$. For bills, decimals in closing prices represent basis points; $25 per 0.01.

### Chicago Board Options Exchange

**US Treasury bond—$100,000 principal value**

| Underlying issue | Strike price | Calls—Last | | | Puts—Last | | |
|---|---|---|---|---|---|---|---|
| | | June | Sept | Dec | June | Sept | Dec |
| $9\frac{1}{4}$% due | 114 | .... | .... | .... | 1.16 | .... | .... |
| 2/2016 | 116 | .... | .... | .... | 3.10 | .... | .... |
| | 118 | .... | 1.27 | .... | .... | .... | .... |
| $7\frac{1}{4}$% due | 92 | .... | .... | .... | 2.27 | .... | .... |
| 5/2016 | 94 | .... | 2.27 | .... | .... | .... | .... |
| | 96 | .... | 2.02 | .... | .... | .... | .... |
| | 98 | .... | 1.24 | .... | .... | .... | .... |
| | 100 | .... | 1.00 | .... | .... | .... | .... |

Total call vol. 442. Call open int. 16,985.
Total put vol. 380. Put open int. 19,801.

3 p.m. prices of underlying issues supplied by Merrill Lynch: T-Bonds—$11\frac{3}{4}$% $131\frac{2}{32}$; $10\frac{5}{8}$% $122\frac{28}{32}$; $9\frac{7}{8}$% $116\frac{18}{32}$; $9\frac{1}{4}$% $114\frac{10}{32}$; $7\frac{1}{4}$% $94\frac{26}{32}$. T-Notes—$9\frac{5}{8}$% $105\frac{18}{32}$; $9\frac{1}{8}$% $103\frac{30}{32}$; $8\frac{1}{8}$% $100\frac{22}{32}$; $7\frac{1}{2}$% $98\frac{9}{32}$.

### Chicago Board of Trade

**Treasury bills (IMM)-$1 million; pts. of 100%**

| Strike price | Calls—Settle | | | Puts—Settle | | |
|---|---|---|---|---|---|---|
| | Sept-c | Dec-c | Mar-c | Sept-p | Dec-p | Mar-p |
| 93.25 | 0.64 | .... | .... | .... | .... | .... |
| 93.50 | 0.45 | .... | .... | 0.16 | 0.32 | .... |
| 93.75 | 0.30 | .... | .... | 0.25 | .... | .... |
| 94.00 | 0.18 | 0.29 | .... | 0.38 | .... | .... |
| 94.25 | 0.10 | 0.20 | .... | 0.55 | .... | .... |
| 94.50 | 0.05 | 0.14 | .... | 0.75 | .... | .... |

Est. vol. 176. Tues. vol. 38 calls, 1 puts.
Open interest Tues.; 7,347 calls, 1,404 puts.

**T-bonds (CBT) $100,000; points and 64ths of 100%**

| Strike price | Calls—Last | | | Puts—Last | | |
|---|---|---|---|---|---|---|
| | Sept-c | Dec-c | Mar-c | Sept-p | Dec-p | Mar-p |
| 88 | 6-28 | 6-40 | 0-00 | 1-35 | 2-49 | 3-49 |
| 90 | 5-06 | 5-27 | 0-00 | 2-18 | 3-38 | 4-45 |
| 92 | 3-57 | 4-26 | 0-00 | 3-04 | 4-28 | 5-43 |
| 94 | 2-59 | 3-37 | 4-06 | 4-03 | 5-33 | 6-51 |
| 96 | 2-10 | 2-52 | 3-25 | 5-14 | 6-45 | 8-00 |
| 98 | 1-39 | 2-14 | 0-00 | 6-34 | 8-02 | 0-00 |

Est. vol. 70,000, Tues. vol. 25,661 calls, 30,747 puts.
Open interest Tuesday; 170,880 calls, 160,935 puts.

**T-notes (CBT) $100,000; points and 64ths of 100%**

| Strike price | Calls—Last | | | Puts—Last | | |
|---|---|---|---|---|---|---|
| | Sept-c | Dec-c | Mar-c | Sept-p | Dec-p | Mar-p |
| 94 | 4-32 | 0-00 | .... | 0-63 | 1-46 | .... |
| 96 | 3-10 | 3-14 | .... | 1-43 | 2-35 | .... |
| 98 | 2-07 | 2-20 | .... | 2-36 | 3-37 | .... |
| 100 | 1-18 | 1-40 | .... | 3-48 | 4-50 | .... |
| 102 | 0-50 | 1-06 | .... | 5-09 | .... | .... |
| 104 | 0-28 | 0-46 | .... | 6-49 | .... | .... |

Est. vol. 3,700, Tues vol. 1,161 calls, 2,719 puts.
Open interest Tuesday; 37,838 calls, 18,997 puts.

Source: *The Wall Street Journal.*

Although this book deals primarily with traded option markets, it is worth mentioning that there is a vast array of over-the-counter interest rate option products, such as caps and collars, as well as a range of fixed interest instruments with option characteristics such as convertibles and warrants. The principles developed later for analysing traded interest rate options will also be of direct relevance to these instruments.

### e. Commodity options

The final type of traded option that needs to be discussed is the traditional option on physical commodities. After a somewhat chequered history, option trading has now resumed in the United States on both metals and agricultural products. Commodity option trading also occurs in London (on a non-traded basis, however), and in precious metals on a wide range of exchanges worldwide including Canadian exchanges and Amsterdam. The options are again divided into options on futures or options on cash. Commodity options are not dealt with in detail here since they are similar to the other options previously described. However, a description of two typical options may be helpful.

#### (i) CBT soybean futures option

This is an option to buy or sell one CBT 5000 bushel soybean futures contract. Premium is defined in dollars and cents per bushel.

#### (ii) European Options Exchange silver cash option

This is an option to buy or sell 250 troy ounces of silver. Premium is defined in dollars and cents per oz. At exercise, 250 ozs of physical silver are delivered.

# 3. Margining procedures for options

The marking to market procedure for futures contracts has already been described: it is the daily payment of gains and losses on a futures contract to avoid credit risk. These daily payments – called variation margin – are paid into a clearing house, which acts as a guarantor of performance to the two parties to a futures contract. The clearing process has two major functions.

1. Clearing ensures that traders on the exchange, although carrying out their transactions with other members, actually make and receive obligations with the clearing house. This has the advantage of largely eliminating credit risk, which limits the usefulness of forwards and non-exchange traded options. Traders do not have to concern themselves with the credit risk of the other traders with whom they deal as the risk is carried by the clearing house.
2. Clearing also makes trading easier as it allows transactions to be "closed out" by opposite transactions. For example, if you have sold an option, then the obligation can be voided by buying an option identical in exercise price and expiration date. This makes for considerable simplicity in administration; it becomes unnecessary to run two equal and opposite positions until expiry or exercise.
3. The clearing house safeguards its exposure by requiring members to deposit cash or collateral ('margin') to cover the risk of movement in rates. All open positions are revalued daily, and the level of initial margin must be maintained.

A similar system of clearing exists for option contracts. However, it is important to distinguish between the standard type of option traded on virtually all exchanges, where the buyer of an option has to pay the full premium at purchase, and the futures style margining system pioneered by the London International Financial Futures Exchange, where both the buyer and seller of options are margined.

## a. Premium paid options

Since the option buyer cannot by definition lose more than the option premium, if he pays the full premium in advance, no further payment can ever be required. Thus, no margins of any kind are ever required.

By contrast, the seller of the option who receives the premium in exchange for assuming a contractual obligation has to margin the short position to ensure contract performance. However, margining requirements for options can be extremely complex and vary substantially from exchange to exchange. There may also be different margin requirements for straight open or spread positions, and different rules for what offsets can be applied. Although examples of some different option margin requirements are given below, the option trader should check with the individual exchange on individual margin requirements.

---

**Option margin requirements are complex and may alter through time. It is essential for the trader to know individual exchange and individual position margin requirements before trading.**

---

For premium paid options, three margining systems need to be discussed: the Options Clearing Corporation rules for individual stock options, the London Stock Exchange currency option requirements, and the Chicago Board of Trade Treasury bond futures options. These are only illustrations. Other exchanges and other contracts may be totally different. These margin requirements also strictly apply only for relationships between the clearing member and the clearing house. Margin requirements between customers and members are subject to negotiation and may frequently be higher than those stated here.

### (i) Options on stocks (OCC)

An uncovered writer of a stock call option must deposit 15% of the stock price plus the call premium less the amount by which the stock is below the strike price. In all cases, the minimum requirement is 5% of the stock price plus the call premium. The call premium received can be set against the margin requirement. This initial margin requirement is marked to market every day in exactly the same way as a futures contract. The table below illustrates the procedure.

| *150 IBM call (100 shares)* | | | | | |
|---|---|---|---|---|---|
| Stock price | 150 | 155 | 148 | 145 | 140 |
| 15% of stock price | 2,250 | 2,325 | 2,220 | 2,175 | 2,100 |
| Call premium | 350 | 625 | 200 | 50 | 12.50 |
| Degree of out-of-money | 0 | 0 | −200 | −500 | −1,000 |
| Total margin | 2,600 | 2,950 | 2,220 | 1,725 | 1,112.50 |

It is not generally necessary to put this margin requirement up in cash; acceptable collateral such as Treasury bills and other equities are acceptable. The trader should check with his brokerage house as to which are acceptable.

A covered call writer by contrast needs to post no more margin than that required to carry the stock position in the first place, and will be credited with the option premium. So if we again take IBM at 150.

$$\text{Market value of stock} = \$15,000$$
$$\text{Regulation margin requirement on stock } (50\%) = \$7,500$$
$$\text{Less call premium} = -\$350$$
$$\text{Net initial margin} = \$7,150.00$$

Stock option spreads will also have their individual margin requirements.

### (ii) London Stock Exchange currency options

For short option positions, the London Stock Exchange charges 10% of the face value of the contract plus or minus the in- or out-of-the-money element.

**Example**

*Day 1*
Written 1 March sterling 115 call
Spot rate = $1.20
Closing premium = 6.8¢
$$\text{Margin required} = (\pounds12,500 \times \$1.20 \times 0.10) + [\$12,500 \times (\$1.20 - \$1.15)]$$
$$= \$2,125.00$$
*Day 2*: Sterling exchange rate closes at $1.25.
$$\text{Margin required} = (\pounds12,500 \times \$1.25 \times 0.10) + [\pounds12,500 \times (\$1.25 - \$1.15)]$$
$$= \$2,812.50$$
$$\text{Initial margin} = \$2,125.00$$
$$\text{Variation margin required} = \$687.50$$

Once again special spread margins operate. In addition there are special margin requirements for market-makers. Market-makers are required to deposit 130% of the daily closing premium value on all net open positions, i.e. after deducting 70% of the value of purchased positions and offsetting the values of calls against puts.

**Example**

Written 1 March sterling 115 call.    Closing premium 3¢
Purchased 1 June sterling 120 call.    Closing premium 2¢
$$\text{Margin required} = [\pounds12,500 \times \tfrac{130}{100} \times \$0.03] - [\pounds12,500 \times \tfrac{70}{100} \times \$0.02]$$
$$= \$312.50$$

### (iii) Treasury bond futures options (CBT)

The naked writer of an option must post the following margin.

$$\text{Initial margin} = \text{Option premium} + \text{Current T-bond futures margin}$$
$$- \text{ Half the amount (if any) the option is out-of-the-money}$$

With a minimum of $1,000.

**Example**

Sell September 94-00. Call at 2-35 when future is trading at 92-00.
$$\text{Receive option premium} = 163/64\text{th}(2\text{-}35) \times \$15.625$$
$$= \$2,546.88$$
$$\text{Initial margin} = \$2,546.88 + \$3,000 - (94 - 92) \times \frac{32 \times \$31.25}{2}$$
$$= \$4.546.88$$

Below are two examples of spread margins for these options.

1. *Bear call*: long call with a high exercise price
         short call with a low exercise price
   Receive net credit. Margin = difference in exercise prices.

**Example**

Buy September 94 call at 2–35
Sell September 92 call at 3–28

$$\text{Receive net credit} = 57/64\text{th (3-28 minus 2-35)} \times \$15.625$$
$$= \$890.625$$

$$\text{Initial margin} = 128/64\text{th (94-00 minus 92-00)} \times \$15.625$$
$$= \$2,000.00$$

2. *Naked straddle*: sell a call and sell a put.
   Receive both premiums. Margin = Sum of two premiums plus current T-bond futures margin.

**Example**

Sell 92-00 September call at 3-28
Sell 92–00 September put at 3–30

$$\text{Receive both premiums} = 442/64\text{th (3-28 + 3-30)} = \$6,906.25$$

$$\text{Initial margin} = \$6,906.25 + \$3,000 \text{ (futures margin)}$$
$$= \$9,906.25$$

These few examples of typical margin requirements give a flavour of the type of payments that need to be made. They also give an idea of the differences between exchanges and contracts that give rise to extremely complex margining systems.

## b. LIFFE margining system

The LIFFE margining system, which is likely in due course to be adopted in some form on the majority of other exchanges, is a much simpler and more coherent margining system. The discussion below uses the LIFFE Eurodollar futures contract option as an illustration.

For both futures and options positions, LIFFE operates a system of initial margins and variation margins. For the Eurodollar futures contract, the margining system works exactly like all futures contracts. The initial margin currently required on a long or short Eurodollar futures position is $1,000 per contract.[7] Since such initial margins are calculated on net positions, a straddle – long one futures contract and short another futures contract – generally requires a zero initial margin.

Futures profits and losses are calculated at the end of each business day ('marking to market') and the resultant payments (from those whose positions have incurred losses and to those whose positions have made profits) necessary to maintain the required level of initial margin are called variation margin.

**Example**

*Day 1*: Eurodollar futures settlement price = 89.20
    Long margin account $1,000
    Short margin account $1,000
*Day 2*: Eurodollar futures settlement price = 89.50
    Long margin account credited with $750 ($25 × 30 basis points profit)
    Short required to pay $750 into account to return level to $1,000

Margining for LIFFE Eurodollar options contracts is based on the same principles. The initial margin for an options position will be determined relative to the estimated risk of that position as determined by a risk factor, identified daily by the exchange for all trading options. This is known as a delta-based[8] margining system. The appropriate initial margin for an option is the Eurodollar futures margin of $1,000 × risk factor. For short options positions, an additional prudential risk margin is also required.

---

[7] This margin is subject to change. Traders should check with the exchange for current margins.
[8] The concept of delta is dealt with in Chapter 3.

There are two important features of this margining system which make it unique to LIFFE.

1. Both short and long options positions are marked to market, i.e. are subject to futures-style margining.
2. There is full automatic offset of initial margins for options and futures/options combinations which involve risk offsets.

In contrast to the initial margin on a futures position which remains constant at $1,000 until delivery, the initial margin on an options position can vary as the risk factor of the position varies, but will never exceed a full futures margin.

**Example**

September 15 December 90.00 call = 0.75   Risk factor = 0.67

Buyer's initial margin: $1,000 × 0.67 = $670

Seller's initial margin: $1,000 × 0.67 = $670
Illustrative prudential add-on          = $100
                                          ———
                                          $770

October 15   December 90.00 call = 1.07   Risk factor = 0.86
Buyer's variation margin (1.07 − 0.75) = 0.32
32 basis points at $25 per basis point = $800
Buyer's additional initial margin requirement = ($1,000 × 0.86) − $670 = $190
Buyer's net cash flow = +$610 (i.e. $800 − $190)
Seller's net cash flow = −$800 − $190 = −$990

The risk factor approach can be extended to portfolios of futures and options contracts. The risk factor for a portfolio of futures and options positions is the absolute value of the sum of the risk factors of the individual positions. The risk factor is:

| *Positive* | *Negative* |
|---|---|
| Long call | Short call |
| Short put | Long put |
| Long futures (+1) | Short futures (−1) |

Additional short options margins are always positive.

**Example**

September 15 December 90.00 call =  0.75   Risk factor =   0.67
             December 90.00 put  =  0.25   Risk factor = −0.33
             December futures     = 90.50   Risk factor =   1.00

| *Position* | *Risk factor* |
|---|---|
| Short 2 December futures | −2.00 |
| Long 4 December 90.00 calls | +2.68 |
| Short 2 December 90.00 puts | +0.66 |
| Total risk factor | 1.34 |

Initial margin requirement = 1.34 × $1,000 = $1,340

In this case no additional margin is required for the short puts since they are part of a synthetic long futures position with two of the long calls.

October 15 December 90.00 call =  1.56  Risk factor =   0.90
           December 90.00 put  =  0.06  Risk factor = −0.10
           December futures     = 91.50  Risk factor =   1.00

| *Position* | *Risk factor* |
|---|---|
| Short 2 December futures | −2.00 |
| Long 4 December 90.00 calls | +3.60 |
| Short 2 December 90.00 puts | +0.20 |
| Total risk factor | 1.80 |

Required additional initial margin = (1.80 × $1,000) − $1,340 = $460

The additional initial margin is more than compensated for by positive variation margin.

Loss on December futures = − $5,000 ($25 × 2 × (90.50 − 91.50) × 100)
Gain on December 90.00 calls = $8,100 ($25 × 4 × (1.56 − 0.75) × 100)
Gain on December 90.00 puts = $950   ($25 × 2 × (0.25 − 0.06) × 100)

Total profit = $4,050

Buyer's net cash flow = $4,050 − $460 − $3,590

The LIFFE margining system is extremely cash efficient, and enables large complex futures/options position to be established at minimum cost.

# 4. Delivery procedures

As with margin systems, delivery procedures vary as widely as options exchanges and options contracts. Nonetheless some examination of the delivery procedures for options contracts is called for. The delivery procedure with options on futures is simpler. The procedures for Eurodollar futures options on the Chicago Mercantile Exchange and the London International Financial Futures Exchange are given below, involving respectively premium paid and margined options.

## a. CME Eurodollar options

The CME option can be exercised on any trading day. The trading hours for the Eurodollar option are 7.30 am to 2.00 pm, but the option can be exercised up to 5.00 pm, i.e. the option can be exercised when the actual trading floor is closed. This is quite usual with all kinds of options. It provides an opportunity for an option buyer to take advantage, after the exchange has closed, of a sharp movement in interest rates whose effect on price may be eliminated before the opening of trading the following day. If the option is exercised after the exchange is closed, the seller who is called upon to accept exercise will not generally know of this until some time the following morning, which may increase his level of risk considerably.

Exercise results in a long futures position for a call buyer, and a short futures position for a put buyer. The futures position is effective on the trading day immediately following exercise, and is marked to market on the settlement that day.

### Example
A holder of the September 90.00 Eurodollar call observes on June 10 Eurodollar prices trading at 91.25 and decides to exercise the option. The option premium is exactly 1.25 at settlement on June 10.
On June 11 the buyer acquires a long Eurodollar futures position at 90.00.

$$\text{June 11 settlement price} = 91.12$$

$$\text{Buyer's margin account} = (91.12 - 90.00) \times 100 \times \$25$$
$$= \$2,800.00$$

Assume required initial margin on Eurodollar future = $2,000.00
Buyer can withdraw $800.00

$$\text{Seller's margin account} = \text{Required margin for short position June 10}$$
$$= \$2,800.00$$

Unless the buyer of the option simultaneously sells a Eurodollar future at 91.25 when exercising the option within exchange trading hours, there is no guarantee of the specific profit to the option, since the Eurodollar price could easily change substantially over night. However, the position could be effectively closed by selling a Eurodollar contract on the Singapore exchange.

Early exercise of Eurodollar options is not very frequent because the option premium normally lies above the exercise value of the option: it has time value.[9] Consider the example below.

15 October     Settlement prices
            December 90.00 call =   1.07
            December futures     = 91.00

Buyer notifies clearing house before 5.00 pm and is assigned December futures at 91.00 at opening of trading on October 16.
At opening he sells a Eurodollar future at 91.02

$$\text{Result exercise value } 91.02 - 90.00 = 1.02$$
$$\text{less option price} = 1.07$$
$$\text{An effective loss of 5 bp (basis point)} \times \$25 = \$125.$$

The buyer should have sold his option in the market at the close of the previous day. It is worth noting that any CME Eurodollar option that is in-the-money at expiration will automatically be exercised on behalf of the buyer. However, this automatic exercise does not apply to all options and in particular not to cash options.

---

[9] See Chapter 3 for a fuller discussion of this point.

## b. LIFFE Eurodollar options

The delivery procedure with LIFFE futures options is more complex, because the buyer has not paid nor the seller received the premium originally, which therefore has to be paid over at exercise.

The following cash flows occur on exercise of a Eurodollar call option whether prematurely (before 5.00 pm on any day before the last trading day) or automatically (at the end of the last trading day):

| *Buyer* | *Seller* |
|---|---|
| Pays full futures initial margin | Pays full futures initial margin |
| plus | minus |
| Option settlement price (premium) | Option settlement price (premium) |
| minus | plus |
| Difference between futures settlement price and options exercise price | Difference between futures settlement price and options exercise price |
| minus | minus |
| Existing option initial margin | Existing option initial margin |

**Example**

Exercise of one call option prior to expiration, resulting in the creation of a futures position.

Exercise price = 93.00
Futures settlement price = 95.00
Option settlement price = 2.05

| *Buyer* | *Seller* |
|---|---|
| $1,000.00 | $1,000.00 |
| plus | minus |
| $5,125.00 (premium) | $5,125.00 (premium) |
| minus | plus |
| $5,000.00 (95.00 − 93.00) | $5,000.00 (95.00 − 93.00) |
| minus | minus |
| $650.00 (existing initial margin) | $750.00 (existing initial margin) |
| equals | equals |
| $475.00 | $125.00 |

In this case of premature exercise, the buyer of the option has lost $125.00 as compared with the option premium he would have received by selling the option in the market. The net effect is exactly the same as with the CME option, although the cash flows at delivery are different.[10]

Some delivery procedures for cash options are given below; there are, however, pronounced differences between different exchanges and contracts.

## c. CBOE stock options

A CBOE stock option may be exercised at any time. To exercise an option, the holder of the option directs his broker to give exercise instructions to the Options Clearing Corporation. Brokers will normally have specific cut-off times for accepting exercise instructions on a particular day which may vary from one firm to another. Once an exercise instruction is given to the OCC, it cannot be revoked (except in the case of an exercise instruction filed in error if notice of the error is given to the OCC on the same day by the OCC clearing member that filed the instruction).

On the business day following receipt of an exercise instruction, the OCC randomly assigns the exercise to a clearing member account that reflects the writing of an option or options identical to the exercised option. The brokerage firm to which the exercise is assigned must then allocate the assignment to a customer maintaining a position as an option writer, either on a random selection basis or on a first-in, first-out basis. An option writer may not be notified that an exercise

---

[10] This description applies only to the exchange of the option for the futures position (the option delivery procedure). Delivery procedures for exchanging futures for the underlying cash instrument can be complex, especially in the case of bond futures and agricultural commodity futures. The reader should refer to individual exchanges for details.

has been assigned to him until one or more days following the date of the initial assignment to the clearing member by the Options Clearing Corporation.

The OCC also imposes rules concerning dividend payments when an option is exercised. If exercise instructions are received by the OCC before the ex-dividend date, the dividend belongs to the assigned writer of a put or the holder of a call. A problem could arise with this system for the assigned writer of a call: he may not find out about the assignment until after the ex-dividend date. Then he would be required to deliver the stock plus the dividend distribution even though the stock can only be purchased in the market on an ex-dividend basis.

The regular settlement day for stock options is the fifth business day after exercise, and settlement is carried out through the usual stock clearing corporations. However, the OCC has the authority to postpone settlement when it considers it to be necessary in the public interest. In certain circumstances when the writer of a call is unable to obtain the underlying stock – for instance if trading in the stock were suspended – the OCC may apply special settlement procedures. This could result in delayed settlement and perhaps cash settlement. In normal circumstances, however, on the fifth business day after exercise, the usual settlement procedure will involve the assigned writer of, say, a call delivering 100 shares of stock and receiving the exercise value in dollars.

### d. LIFFE cash currency options

Because the LIFFE currency option is a premium margined option, the same cash flows occur at settlement as with the Eurodollar futures contract.

**Example**

Exercise one call option prior to expiration.

Exercise price        = $1.20
Spot exchange rate     = $1.25
Option settlement price = 5.30¢

| *Buyer* | *Seller* |
|---|---|
| Pays $1,000.00 | Pays $1,000.00 |
| plus | minus |
| $1,325.00 ($0.053 × £25,000) | $1,325.00 ($0.053 × £25,000) |
| minus | plus |
| $1,250.00 (($1.25 − $1.20) × £25,000) | $1,250.00 |
| minus | minus |
| $800 (existing initial margin) | $800 |
| equals | equals |
| $275.00 | $125.00 |

The physical exchange of one currency for another will take place at an exchange rate of $1.20. In this case, the call buyer will hand over $30,000 and receive £25,000 sterling. The exchange of currencies may take place through the existing futures system requiring dollar payment two days before the settlement day, or by the delivery versus payment (DVP) system requiring payment on settlement day subject to pre-payment advice. The clearing house pays interest on cleared US dollar funds during the delivery cycle.

This section on delivery procedures does not give a complete description of procedures for all exchanges and all options. In essence, the fundamentals of delivery are simple. If an option is exercised, either a futures contract is bought and sold at a specific price, or a physical asset is bought and sold at a specific price. The major difference is that in the first case, full payment for the asset is not required at delivery, but in the latter case of a cash option full payment is required. The trader of cash options should be aware of this, and check carefully the assignment procedures of the clearing house, and the precise settlement timetable.

# Chapter 3
# The pricing of options

## 1. Introduction

One of the most important questions related to all types of options is how they should be priced in equilibrium with the price and characteristics of the underlying asset. Like any other item, an option will be priced according to the supply of and demand for the option in the market. However, because the value of an option at expiration is directly linked to the underlying asset price, it is likely that an option will be priced in equilibrium as a function of the underlying asset price. So, let us consider the simple pricing of an option.

The price of an option, or premium, can be viewed as consisting of two components: *intrinsic value* and *time value*.

### a. Intrinsic value

Intrinsic value is the profit that the holder of an option (an American option) can realize by exercising the option immediately. A call option has intrinsic value if the exercise price of the option is less than the current price of the underlying asset. A put option has intrinsic value if the exercise price of the option is greater than the current price of the underlying asset. Exhibit 3.1 illustrates the intrinsic value of a call option.

**Exhibit 3.1: Intrinsic value line**

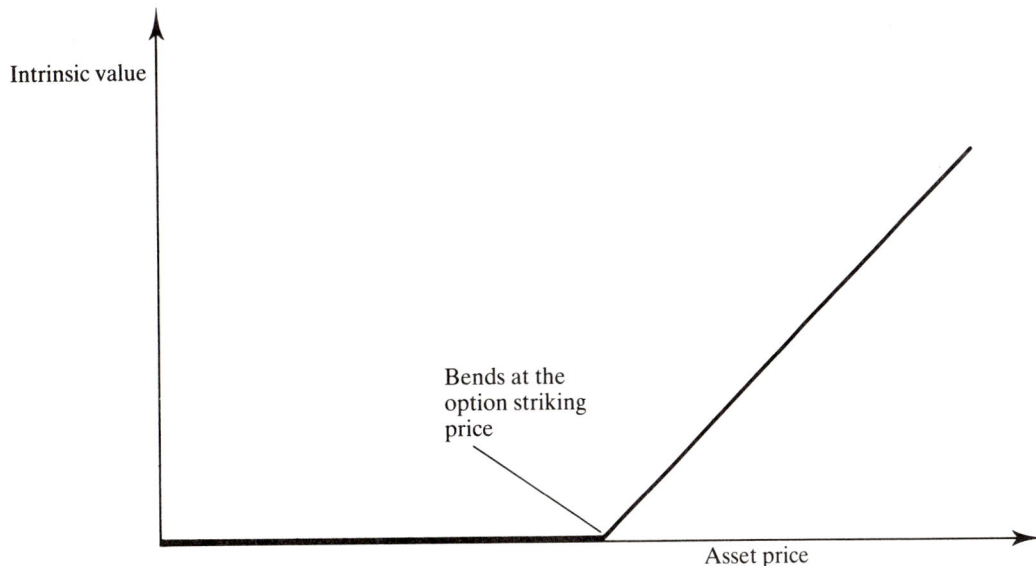

Source: LIFFE.

**Example**

An IBM call stock option with an exercise price of $125. The current IBM stock price is $128 and the intrinsic value of the IBM option is $3.

31

## b. Time value

In many cases, however, the market price of the option will be higher than its intrinsic value – the difference is known as time value. The time value of the option can be considered as the value of a continuing speculation on a favourable movement in the underlying asset price.

### Example

An IBM stock option with an exercise price of $125 is selling for $5. The current IBM stock price is $128, so the option has an intrinsic value of $3 and a time value of $2.

Exhibit 3.2 shows the typical time value of an option as the underlying asset price varies for put options and call options.

The detailed question of how time value is determined will be discussed later, but if it is thought of as the value of a bet on the future movement in the underlying asset price, the value of the bet will be related to the probability that the final asset price will exceed the exercise price of the option for out-of-the-money options, and the probability that the asset price will exceed the exercise price by more than the current margin for in-the-money options. This definition applies to call options; for put options the reverse would be the case. When considering this betting value, it is clear that the probability of the asset price exceeding the exercise price at expiration will get

## Exhibit 3.2: Time value

### a. Long call

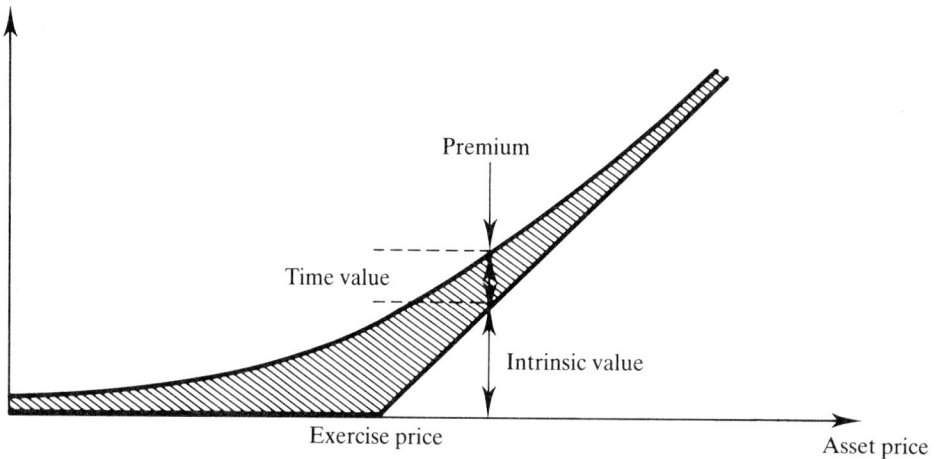

### b. Long put

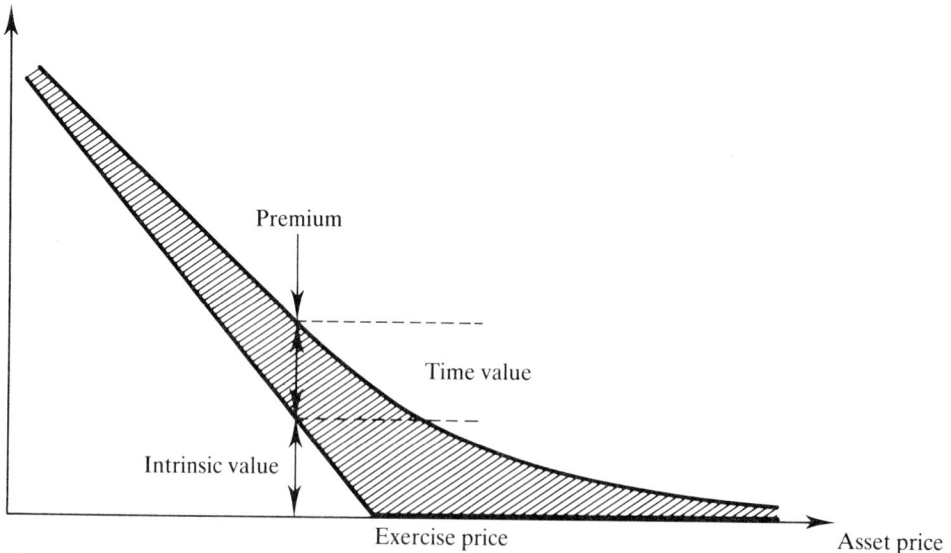

Source: LIFFE.

**Exhibit 3.3: Time value premium decay**

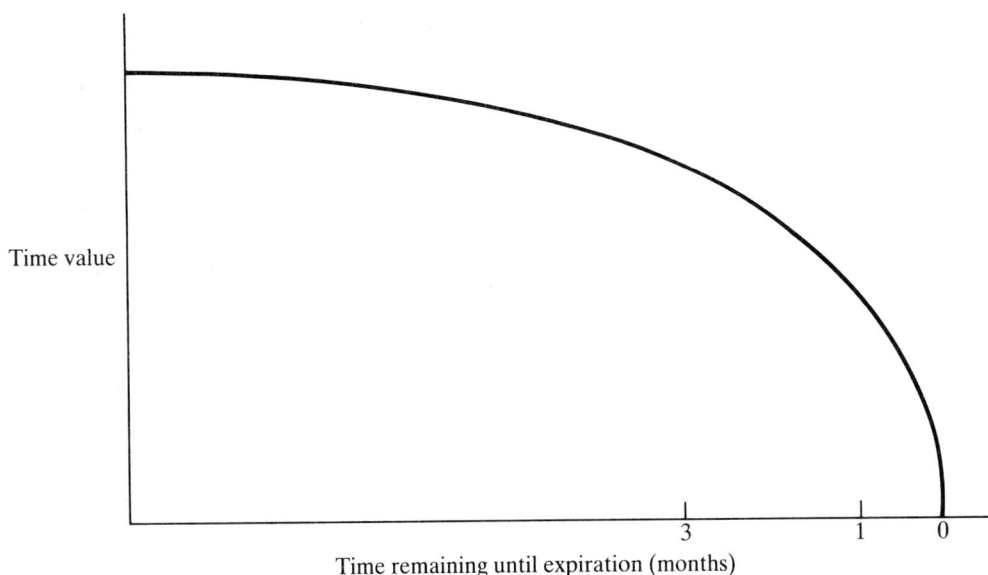

Source: LIFFE.

lower as the option gets further out-of-the-money, and hence the option's time value will get lower. Similarly, as the asset price exceeds the exercise price by greater margins, the probability of a further price advance as opposed to a retreat gets less, and the time value of the option steadily diminishes. By the same argument, the time value of the option will be at a maximum when the option is just at-the-money. This is precisely the pattern of option values shown in Exhibit 3.2.

This time value, or betting value, of an option depends crucially on how long the option has to run before expiration. A bet that the underlying asset price will rise, say, 10% from current levels is not going to have much value if the time period within which the bet will be settled is only a couple of days, but might have considerable value if the time period were two or three months. Hence the time value of the option would be expected to decline to zero at expiration. Exhibit 3.3 shows the typical decay pattern for the time value of an option.

The next step is to look more closely at how the time value of an option is determined.

## 2. Determining a fair option premium

How would a trader set about deciding what price to pay for an option? When a trader purchases the option, in essence he is buying the probability weighted average of all possible intrinsic values of the option at expiration. Since the exercise price of the option is known with certainty, the only unknown element is the probability distribution of the asset price at the expiration of the option. The price of the option will be systematically related to the shape and parameters of this distribution, save that it is known that the value of the option cannot go below zero because the trader cannot be forced to exercise the option. The easiest way to look at this is with cumulative probability distributions (see Exhibit 3.4). This is a simpler concept that it seems.

Exhibit 3.4 shows the probability that a given stock price will not be exceeded by the expiration date of a particular option. In the case shown, there is a 25% chance that the final stock price will not exceed $120, a 50% chance that the final stock price will not exceed $125, and a 75% chance that the final stock price will not exceed $130 and so on. The expected value of the stock price at expiry in this case is $125, because there is an equal probability that the final stock price will exceed $125 or will be less than $125.

Consider, however the equivalent cumulative probability distribution for an IBM stock option with an exercise price of $120 (see Exhibit 3.5).

The trader who buys an IBM option with an exercise price of $120 creates a different cumulative probability distribution to the trader who purchases the stock itself: the part of the stock price distribution below $120 is removed because, as already mentioned, the trader cannot be forced to exercise the option. This shifts the expected value of the option to the right: the new distribution has its 50:50 division at an IBM stock price of $127.50. Hence, ignoring any

**Exhibit 3.4: Cumulative probability distribution for IBM stock price**

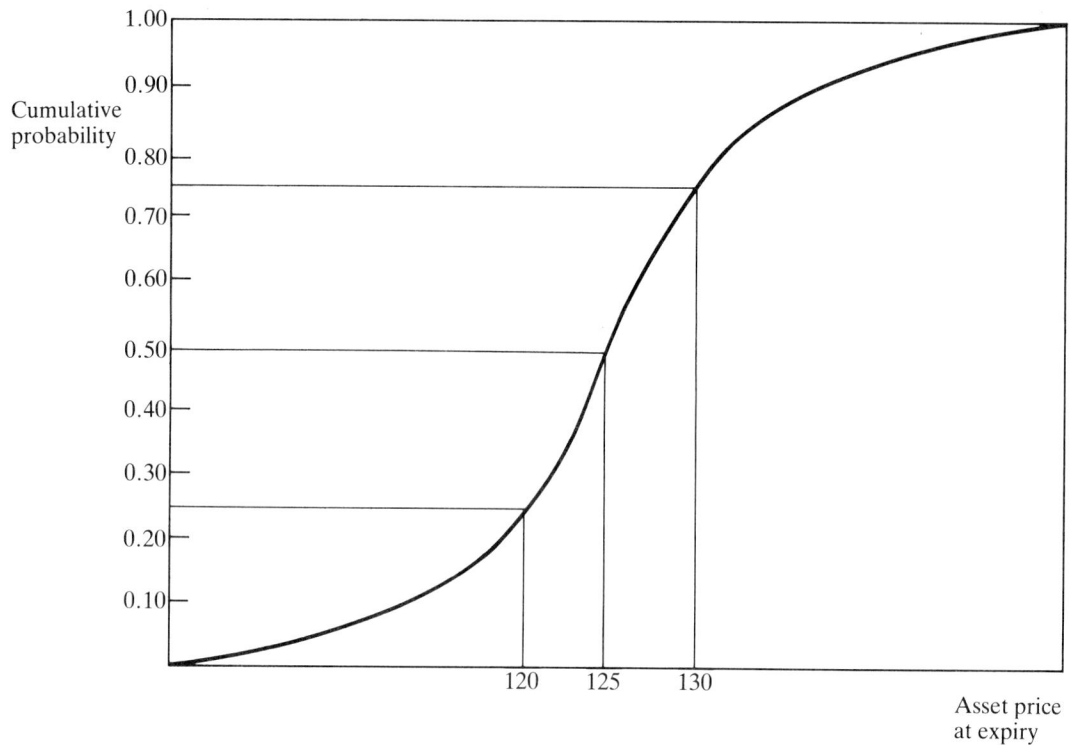

**Exhibit 3.5: Cumulative probability distribution for IBM stock option**

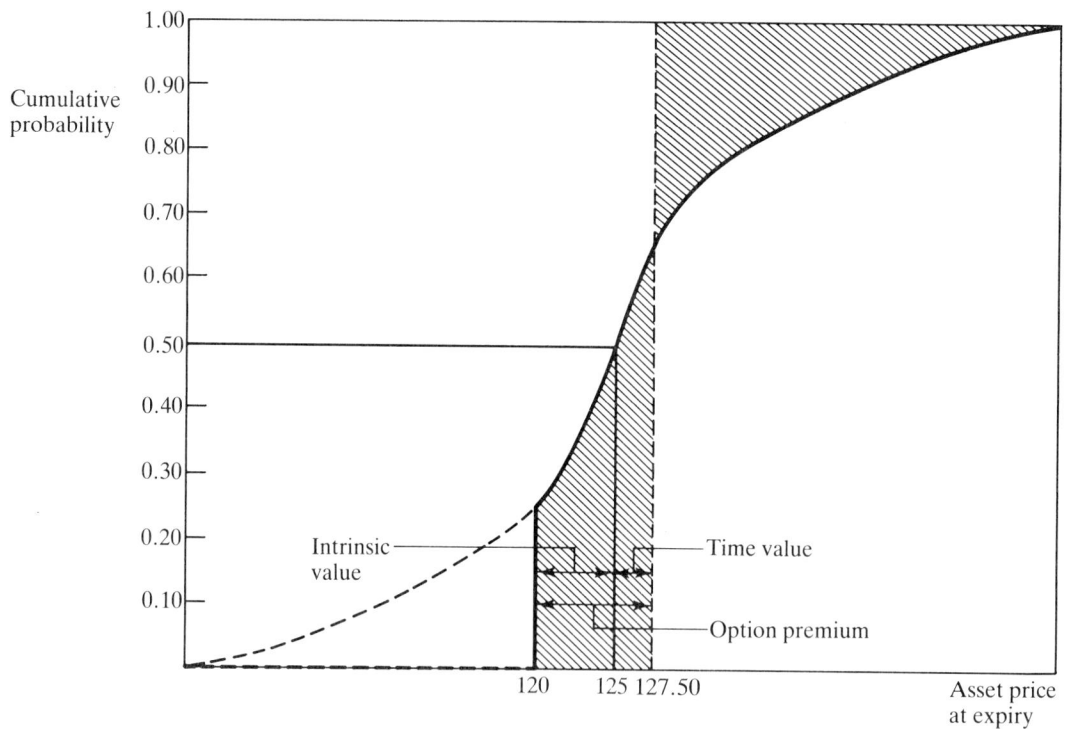

discounting of expected values back to the date of purchase of the option, the expected value of the option at expiration is $7.50, of which $5 is accounted for by intrinsic value and $2.50 by time value. In other words, the option buyer is willing to pay $2.50 to lose the part of the distribution below the exercise price of $120. The level of time value is a function of the shape of the probability distribution of the underlying asset price at expiration.

The role of option valuation is to determine the nature of this function. If this can be achieved, the fair time value can be determined and hence the fair price of the option. The process of valuation will be similar regardless of the type of option being evaluated, whether it be an option on a stock, a cash currency, or a futures contract.

Before discussing precise valuation models for options, however, it is worth thinking about the likely inputs into the kind of function just discussed.

### a. Underlying asset price

The higher the asset price for a call option, the higher the intrinsic value if the call is in-the-money and hence the higher the premium. If the call is out-of-the-money, then the higher the asset price the greater the probability that it will be possible to exercise the call at a profit and hence the higher the time value, or premium, of the option. The reverse will apply with put options.

### b. Exercise price

For an in-the-money call the lower the exercise price, the higher the intrinsic value. For an out-of-the-money call the lower the exercise price the greater the probability of profitable exercise and hence the higher the time value.

### c. Time to expiration

The longer an option has to run, the greater the probability that it will be possible to exercise the option profitably, hence the greater the time value of the option.

### d. Interest rates

The role of interest rates in the determination of option premiums is complex and varies from one type of option to another. A call option can be thought of as the right to buy the underlying asset at the discounted value of the future spot price: the greater the degree of discount the more valuable is the right, and the higher the interest rate the greater the degree of discount. So, other things being equal, option prices should rise with short-term interest rates.

### e. Volatility

Volatility is the degree to which underlying asset prices are expected to move as time passes. The greater the expected movement in the underlying asset price, the greater the probability that the option can be exercised at a profit and hence the more valuable the option. This can be seen by considering a one-year option to buy IBM stock at an exercise price of $150 when the current stock price is $130. If a purchaser were told that the price of IBM stock moves on average up or down by about 5% per year, then he would only be willing to pay very little for the option. If by contrast he were told the IBM stock price moves 40% per year, that option to buy IBM at $150 would be considerably more interesting and valuable.

These five elements are likely to appear in any model for valuing options.

## 3. Boundary conditions for options

Before trying to arrive at a precise option valuation model, it will be useful to examine what bounds can be placed on the values of options from arbitrage arguments. To avoid confusion, this section will deal with options on stock. Arbitrage conditions specific to other types of options will be discussed in later chapters. However, many of the conditions discussed below are common to non-stock options and the principles underlying arbitrage conditions are fundamentally the same.

Consider first a simple option – an American call option on a non-dividend paying stock. The option premium is written as

$$C(S, X, T)$$

where $C$ = option premium
$S$ = underlying stock price
$X$ = exercise price of the option
$T$ = time to expiration of the option

**Condition A**

The value of a call option is greater than or equal to zero.

$$C(S, X, T) \geqslant 0$$

At expiration, the owner of an option can either exercise it or let it expire. It will be exercised if $S > X$ and will then be worth its intrinsic value $S - X$. If $S \leqslant X$, the option will not be exercised and will have a value of zero. Before expiration its intrinsic value will be zero or $S - X$ if $S > X$ and it will have some positive time value.

### Condition B
The value of an American call option will always be at least as high as its intrinsic value.

$$C(S, X, T) \geqslant S - X$$

If the option is exercised when $S > X$, this involves the option holder buying the underlying stock for $X$ which he can immediately sell for $S$, reaping a profit of $S - X$. The option cannot be worth less than this immediately available profit. Before expiration the option will be worth generally more than $S - X$ if $S > X$ because of its time value. At expiration the option will be worth the maximum of $S - X$ or $O$.

### Condition C
A call option with a lower exercise price will be worth at least as much as, and generally more than, a similar option with a higher exercise price.

$$C(S, X_1, T) \geqslant C(S, X_2, T) \quad \text{if} \quad X_2 > X_1$$

This is obvious from condition B. Since the option is always worth at least as much as its intrinsic value $S - X_1$ and $S - X_1 > S - X_2$, then condition $C$ must hold.

### Condition D
A call option with a longer time to expiration will be worth at least as much as, and generally more than, a similar option with a shorter time to expiration.

$$C(S, X, T_1) \geqslant C(S_1, X, T_2) \quad \text{if} \quad T_1 > T_2$$

Consider the $C(S, X, T_2)$ option at expiration. Its value is the maximum of $S - X$ and zero; and the non-expiring option has a value by condition B greater than or equal to $S - X$. So condition D holds.

### Condition E
A call option cannot be worth more than the underlying stock.

$$C(S, X, T) \geqslant S$$

The stock is at least equivalent to a perpetual call option with a zero exercise price. If this is true then

$$S \geqslant C(S, O, \infty) \geqslant C(S, X, T) \quad \text{where} \quad X > O \quad \text{and} \quad T < \infty$$

## Exhibit 3.6: Bounds on option values

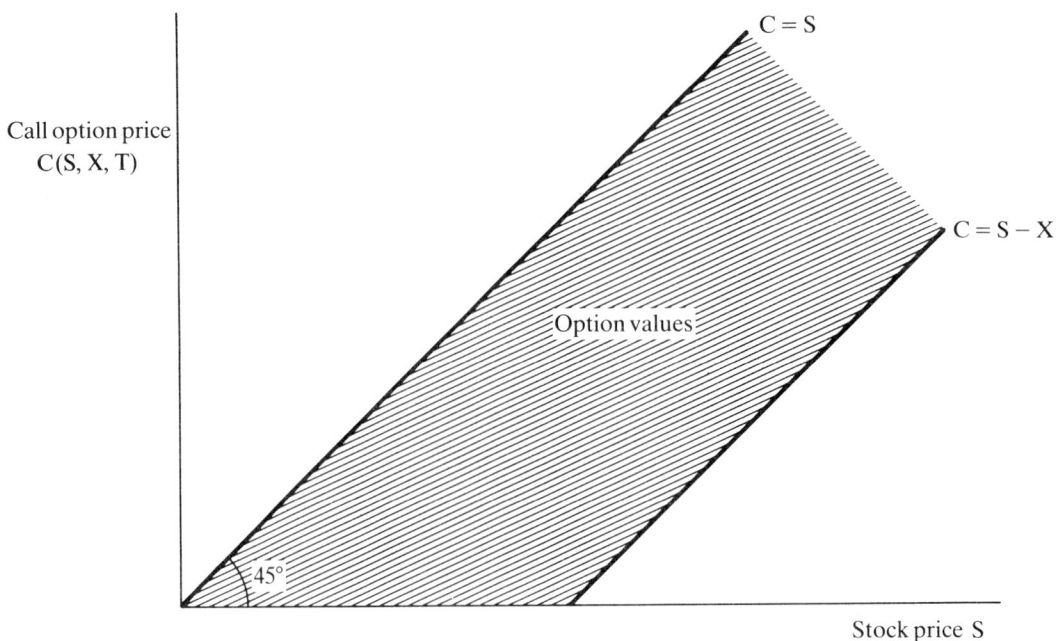

These five simple conditions, derived from first principles, give the first set of bounds on the call option value shown in Exhibit 3.6. These bounds are still very wide. To narrow them down further requires the application of what in finance theory is called *stochastic dominance*. This is a simple concept. Consider two portfolios A and B. Suppose in all states of the world, the return to portfolio A is at least equal to B and in at least one state of the world is strictly greater than B. In equilibrium, we would know that the price of A would have to be greater than the price of B. This type of argument can be used to get further restrictions on the price of options.

**Condition F**

The value of a call option will always be at least as much as the stock price minus the discounted value of the exercise price.

$$C(S, X, T) \geqslant S - Xe^{-rT}$$

where $r$ = riskless rate of interest.

Consider a discount bill which will pay an amount $X$ at the expiration of the option. Then its current price assuming continuous discounting would be $Xe^{-rT}$. Now consider two portfolios: the first A consists of a call option $C(S, X, T)$ and the discount bill priced at $Xe^{-rT}$; the second B consists of the stock at price $S$. The respective prices and returns to these portfolios are shown below.

| Portfolio | Price | Stock price at expiration $S^* < X$ | $X \leqslant S^*$ |
|---|---|---|---|
| A | $C(S, X, T) + Xe^{-rT}$ | $0 + X$ | $(S^* - X) + X$ |
| B | $S$ | $S^*$ | $S^*$ |
| Relationship of terminal values | | $V_A^* > V_B^*$ | $V_A^* = V_B^*$ |

To avoid dominance, the price of portfolio A must be greater than the price of portfolio B. Hence

$$C(S, X, T) + Xe^{-rT} > S$$
$$C(S, X, T) > S - Xe^{-rT}$$

This relationship has several interesting implications. First, it indicates that an American call option on a non-dividend paying stock will never be exercised: the call is worth more than $S - Xe^{-rT}$, but if exercised the investor would only receive $S - X$, which is less than $S - Xe^{-rT}$ for any positive interest rate. So it is always better to sell a call option to somebody else rather than exercise it. Secondly, a relationship of this kind opens up arbitrage possibilities.

**Example**

A call option with an exercise price of $35 and a time to expiration of three months is selling for $5.50. The price of the stock is $40 and the riskless rate of interest is 10%. Is an arbitrage profit available?
We know from condition F that the following condition should hold

$$C(40, 35, 3) > 40 - 35e^{-(0.10)(0.25)}$$

Now in fact, $40 - 35e^{-(0.10)(0.25)}$ is actually equal to $5.86. Hence the call option priced at $5.50 is undervalued. The investor decides to carry out the following transactions:

| | | |
|---|---|---|
| Buy 1 call option | Cash outflow | $5.50 |
| Sell short 1 share of stock | Cash inflow | $40.00 |
| Buy $34.14 of discount bonds: face value $35 | Cash outflow | $34.14 |

$$\text{Net cash inflow} = \$0.36$$

At the expiration of the option, consider four alternatives: a stock price of $30, $35, $40 or $45.

*Alternative 1: $S^* = \$30$*
Option expires worthless, receive $35 from discount bond, buy back stock at $30.

$$\text{Net cash inflow} = \$5.00$$
$$\text{Total profit} = \$5.36$$

*Alternative 2: $S^* = \$35$*
Option expires worthless, receive $35 from discount bond, buy back stock at $35.

$$\text{Net cash inflow} = \$0.00$$
$$\text{Total profit} = \$0.36$$

## Exhibit 3.7: Additional bounds on option values

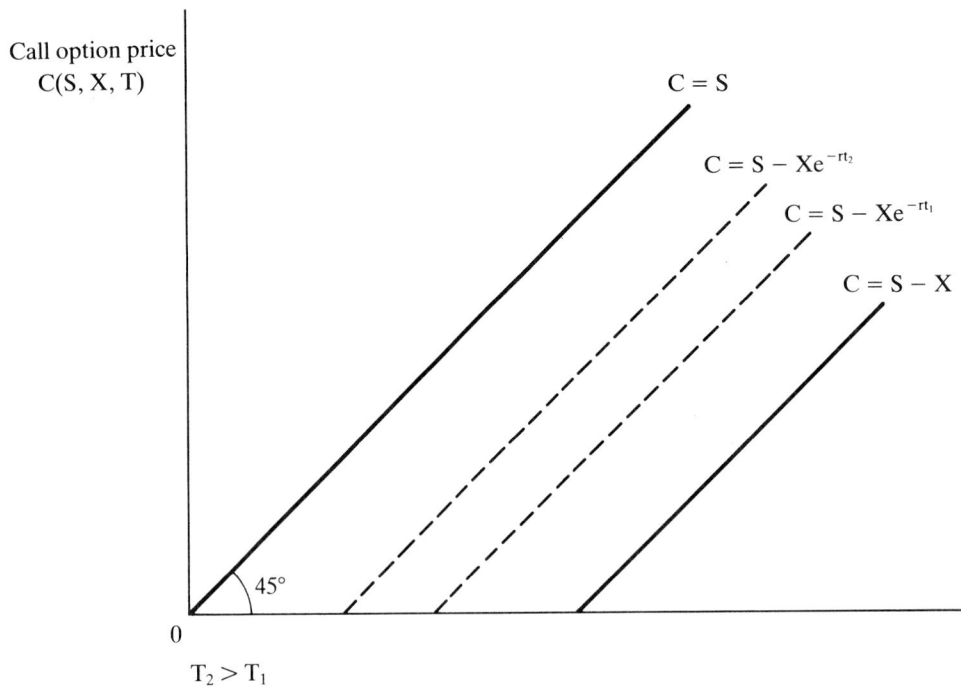

*Alternative 3*: $S^* = 40$
Option is exercised, buy stock at \$35, receive \$35 from discount bond.

$$\text{Net cash inflow} = \$0.00$$
$$\text{Total profit} = \$0.36$$

*Alternative 4*: $S^* = 45$
Option is exercised, buy stock at \$35, receive \$35 from discount bond.

$$\text{Net cash inflow} = \$0.00$$
$$\text{Total profit} = \$0.36$$

Hence there is a true arbitrage profit: whatever the eventual price of the stock, the investor will receive a riskless \$0.36 per option purchased, and if the stock price falls below \$35 he will make an even larger profit. For investors able to sell short stock readily, such a strategy could yield appreciable profits.

Condition F imposes tighter bounds on the value of the call option, as shown in Exhibit 3.7. The lower bound for the value of the option now depends upon the time to expiration: the longer the maturity, the smaller the amount $Xe^{-rT}$ and hence the higher the value of the option – exactly as predicted by condition D. The higher the value of the interest rate $r$, the smaller will be $Xe^{-rT}$ and the higher the value of the option, as mentioned earlier in the chapter. Thus a further condition can be written.

## Condition G
The value of a call option is an increasing function of the riskless rate of interest.

This approach to the value of an option can also yield further insights into the role of volatility in option pricing.[1] Condition F implies that purchasing a call option is more or less equivalent to buying the underlying stock with borrowed funds. At expiration, if the option is exercised, a purchaser owns the stock and pays off the loan of $X$ previously borrowed. However, this is a slightly unusual loan, since if the price of the stock is below the exercise price, the option holder can default on the loan by not exercising the option without penalty. The difference between the intrinsic price or value of the option $S - Xe^{-rT}$ and the actual premium $C(S, X, T)$ is effectively an insurance or risk premium, which prices how much the ability to default on the loan is worth.

---

[1] This insurance approach to options is derived from a paper by D. Galai.

38

Since the greater the volatility of the underlying stock price, the more likely it will be in the option buyer's interest to default on the loan, then the higher will be the insurance or risk premium, and the greater the value of the option. In symbols this can be expressed

$$C(S, X, T) = \begin{matrix} \text{Stock} \\ \text{price} \end{matrix} - \begin{matrix} \text{Discounted value of a} \\ \text{loan of the exercise} \\ \text{price maturing at } T \end{matrix} + \begin{matrix} \text{Insurance premium} \\ \text{to allow a no-penalty} \\ \text{default if } S \leqslant X \end{matrix}$$

Since the insurance premium fair price is a positive function of asset price volatility, then there is a further valuation condition.

**Condition H**

The value of a call option is an increasing function of the stock price volatility.

The conditions above outline all the basic characteristics of option values that can be proved from first principles by dominance. However, dominance arguments can be used to construct many other arbitrage conditions for stock options and others, which will be developed in subsequent chapters.

# 4. Option valuation models

The fair price of an option depends upon the probability distribution of the asset price at the expiration date of the option. Under certain assumptions the type of probability distribution can be characterized by its expected value and the standard deviation of the distribution. The type of probability distribution conventionally used is the log-normal distribution.[2] Based on this distribution, the most famous option valuation model, and the one most frequently used by option traders, is the one derived by Black and Scholes and simply called the *Black-Scholes model*. This section examines the original form of the model suitable for stock options. Other variants of the model suitable for different types of options will be discussed in later, specific chapters.

## a. The Black-Scholes model

The basic Black-Scholes model can be written

$$C(S, X, T) = S . N(d_1) - Xe^{-rT}N(d_2)$$

$$\text{where } d_1 = \frac{\ln (S/X) + (r + \sigma^2/2)T}{\sigma\sqrt{T}}$$

$$
\begin{aligned}
d_2 &= d_1 - \sigma\sqrt{T} \\
C &= \text{call option premium} \\
S &= \text{current asset price} \\
X &= \text{exercise price} \\
T &= \text{time to expiration} \\
\sigma^2 &= \text{instantaneous variance of the asset price (volatility)} \\
\ln &= \text{natural logarithm} \\
N(.) &= \text{cumulative normal distribution function} \\
r &= \text{riskless rate of interest.}
\end{aligned}
$$

Although the Black-Scholes option valuation formula looks complicated, it is easy to use in practice. The only variable in the formula which is not directly observable is the volatility of the underlying asset price, which can be estimated from historical or other observable data.[3] Before discussing its structure in more detail, however, it will be useful to use it to value a specific option.

**Example**

The stock price is currently $60 and the annual standard deviation of the stock price is 25%. The riskless rate of interest over six months is 10%. What is the fair price of a six-month option with an exercise price of $55?

---

[2] No attempt is made in this book to examine the precise derivation of the option valuation models discussed. The aim is to show how the trader can make use of the models. For a full discussion of the models, the reader is referred to J. C. Cox and M. Rubinstein, *Option Markets*, Prentice-Hall (1985), and for a simpler account to R. M. Bookstaber, *Option Pricing and Strategies in Investing*, Addison-Wesley (1981).

[3] The question of how to determine the level of volatility of asset prices will be discussed in detail later in this chapter.

First $d_1$ and $d_2$ are calculated.

$$d_1 = \frac{\ln(60/55) + [0.10 + (0.25)^2/2]0.5}{0.25\sqrt{0.5}}$$

$$= \frac{[0.0870 + 0.065625]}{0.17678} = 0.8634$$

$$d_2 = 0.8634 - 0.17678 = 0.6866$$

The next step is to determine the value of the cumulative normal distribution corresponding to $d_1 = 0.8634$ and $d_2 = 0.6866$, i.e. what is the probability that a final outcome will be 0.8634 standard deviations above the mean or less, and will be 0.6866 standard deviations above the mean or less. Examining the normal distribution table (see Appendix 3)

$$N(0.8634) = 0.8060 \qquad N(0.6866) = 0.7538$$

So the fair value of the call option can be determined as

$$\begin{aligned}C(S, X, T) &= C(60, 55, 6mo) \\ &= 60(0.8060) - 55e^{-(0.10)(0.5)}(0.7538) \\ &= \$8.92\end{aligned}$$

For the set of data given above, the fair value of the call option with an exercise price of $55 is just below $9. The intrinsic value of the call option is $5 and the time value is $3.92.

Although it is beyond the scope of a book of this kind to discuss the theoretical derivation of the Black-Scholes formula, it is easy to give an intuitive idea of what lies behind the formula. Consider a portfolio consisting of long call options and short the underlying stock. If an investor chooses the proportions of stock and options carefully, a riskless portfolio could be constructed, i.e. a portfolio where for small changes in the stock price, any profits or losses on the long option position will be exactly compensated for by the profits or losses to the short stock position. Since such a portfolio is essentially riskless, the investor should expect to earn on the portfolio the riskless rate of interest. This construction of a hedged portfolio for options and stock which must earn the riskless rate of interest is at the heart of the Black-Scholes option valuation model. If the rate of return is known and the price of the stock is known, it should be possible to express the price of the option as a function of these variables. The solution to that problem is the Black-Scholes formula. The option formula also simultaneously provides the hedge ratio for determining the riskless portfolio for small changes in the stock price.

$$\text{Hedge ratio} = N(d_1) = N\left[\frac{\ln(S/X) + (r + \sigma^2/2)T}{\sigma\sqrt{T}}\right]$$

In the case of the option analysed above, the value of $N(d_1) = 0.8060$, i.e. an approximately riskless portfolio would consist of long 100 options and short 81 shares of stock.

### Example
An investor buys 100 55 call options at a premium of $8.92 and sells 81 shares of stock at $60. The stock price falls to $59.50. What is the change in the value of the portfolio if no other changes take place?
The first thing to do is to derive the new fair option value.

$$d_1 = \frac{\ln(59.50/55) + [0.10 + (0.25)^2/2)]0.5}{0.25\sqrt{0.5}}$$

$$= \frac{0.07864 + 0.065625}{0.1768} = 0.81598$$

$$d_2 = 0.81598 - 0.1768 = 0.63918$$

Again using the cumulative normal distribution table

$$N(0.81598) = 0.7927 \qquad N(0.63918) = 0.7386$$

So the new fair value of the option is

$$(59.50)(0.7927) - 55e^{-(0.10)(0.5)}(0.7386) = \$8.52$$

Now examining the change in the value of the portfolio

$$\begin{aligned}\text{Drop in value of call options} &= 100 \times (\$8.92 - \$8.52) \\ &= \$40.00 \\ \text{Profit from short stock position} &= 81 \times \$0.50 \\ &= \$40.50\end{aligned}$$

Weighting the number of shares by the hedge ratio means that for a small change in the stock price, the option losses were almost exactly matched by the profits on the stock. The result would have been even closer if the hedge ratio had not been rounded up from 0.8060 to 0.81.

However, the *hedge portfolio* is riskless only for small changes in the stock price because the hedge ratio changes as the variables in the option valuation formula change. For instance, as the stock price fell from $59.50, the hedge ratio $N(d_1)$ went from 0.8060 to 0.7929. Suppose the stock price had suddenly jumped from the original $60 to $65. The new fair option value calculated from the Black-Scholes formula would be $13.19.

$$\text{Profit on 100 55 calls} = 100 \times (\$13.19 - \$8.92)$$
$$= \$427.00$$
$$\text{Loss on short 81 shares} = 81 \times (\$65 - 60)$$
$$= \$405.00$$
$$\text{Net profit} = \$18.00$$

In this case, the investor benefited from the jump in share prices. However, if the portfolio had been reversed – short 100 55 calls and long 81 shares of stock – there would have been a net loss of $18.00. As we shall see in Chapter 4 when discussing trading strategies based on option valuation models, it is important to rebalance hedge portfolios as hedge ratios alter.

---

**The Black-Scholes hedge ratio gives an approximately riskless portfolio only for small changes in the underlying asset price.**

---

## b. Option delta

The hedge ratio from the Black-Scholes model is usually called the *delta* of the option. The delta is the expected change in the option premium for a one-unit change in the price of the underlying asset. The delta of an option is a very important concept.

### (i) Delta margining

The delta of an option is the prime determinant of the risk factors used by many exchanges in determining the margin funds that are to be deposited by the seller of an option. For example, take a Eurodollar futures option with a delta of 0.5. Since it is expected to change in price by half as much as the futures price changes, it is half as risky as the future. So if the initial margin on a futures contract is $1,000, the margin for the seller of the option should be only $500.[4]

### (ii) Balanced options hedges

The delta of options is also used to construct balanced options hedges. For example suppose an investor had purchased 100 undervalued March $125 IBM calls with a delta of 0.65 and wished to sell IBM $135 calls to produce a position broadly neutral with respect to price. The IBM $135 calls have a delta of 0.30.

Since the $125 calls are expected to move by 65 cents for each $1 movement in IBM and the $135 calls are expected to move by only 30 cents, an appropriate hedge portfolio would be

$$\text{Long 100 } \$125 \text{ calls}$$
$$\text{Short } 100 \times \frac{0.65}{0.30} \quad \text{or} \quad 217 \text{ } \$135 \text{ calls}$$

### (iii) Measuring short-term profit potential of options positions

In Chapter 2, profit and loss profiles for options at expiration were displayed. However, few options traders intend to hold positions to expiration. The delta of an options position indicates how the value of the position will alter if the underlying asset price varies in the short term.

$$\text{Long 2 March } \$125 \text{ IBM calls} \quad \text{Delta} = 0.65 \times 2 = 1.30$$
$$\text{Short 2 March } \$135 \text{ IBM calls} \quad \text{Delta} = -(0.30 \times 2) = -0.60$$
$$\text{Net delta} = 0.70$$

Hence the options position would be expected to show a rise in value of 70 cents if the underlying price of IBM rose $1. This is a bullish options trade.

---

[4] This concept is discussed in more detail in the section on margining (see Chapter 2).

The fair option premium and the option delta will change as the inputs into the option valuation formula vary. The formula also gives the trader the ability to see exactly how premiums and deltas change as inputs change. In Exhibit 3.8, the impact of varying exercise prices, time to expiration, interest rates and asset price volatility is demonstrated using the simple Black-Scholes formula.

## Exhibit 3.8: Call option values

### a. Impact of maturity
Volatility = 15%   Interest rate = 10%   Current stock price = $100

| | Option premium (deltas in brackets) | | |
| Exercise price | 30-day | 90-day | 180-day |
| --- | --- | --- | --- |
| 94.00 | 6.87 (0.94) | 8.73 (0.86) | 11.24 (0.82) |
| 96.00 | 5.06 (0.87) | 7.11 (0.80) | 9.70 (0.78) |
| 98.00 | 3.46 (0.75) | 5.63 (0.72) | 8.26 (0.72) |
| 100.00 | 2.16 (0.58) | 4.33 (0.63) | 6.94 (0.66) |
| 102.00 | 1.22 (0.40) | 3.23 (0.53) | 5.75 (0.60) |
| 104.00 | 0.61 (0.24) | 2.34 (0.43) | 4.70 (0.53) |

### b. Impact of interest rate
Volatility = 10%   Maturity = 90 days   Current stock price = $100

| | Option premium (delta in brackets) | | |
| Exercise price | R = 5% | R = 10% | R = 15% |
| --- | --- | --- | --- |
| 94.00 | 7.31 (0.92) | 8.37 (0.94) | 9.44 (0.94) |
| 96.00 | 5.54 (0.85) | 6.56 (0.89) | 7.59 (0.91) |
| 98.00 | 3.97 (0.74) | 4.88 (0.80) | 5.85 (0.85) |
| 100.0 | 2.66 (0.60) | 3.43 (0.68) | 4.27 (0.75) |
| 102.00 | 1.65 (0.45) | 2.24 (0.54) | 2.93 (0.62) |
| 104.00 | 0.95 (0.30) | 1.36 (0.39) | 1.88 (0.47) |

### c. Impact of volatility
Interest rate = 10%   Maturity = 90 days   Current stock price = $100

| | Option premium (deltas in brackets) | | |
| | | Volatility | |
| Exercise price | 10% | 15% | 20% |
| --- | --- | --- | --- |
| 94 | 8.37 (0.94) | 8.73 (0.86) | 9.32 (0.80) |
| 96 | 6.56 (0.89) | 7.11 (0.80) | 7.83 (0.74) |
| 98 | 4.88 (0.80) | 5.63 (0.72) | 6.48 (0.67) |
| 100 | 3.43 (0.68) | 4.33 (0.63) | 5.28 (0.60) |
| 102 | 2.24 (0.54) | 3.23 (0.53) | 4.23 (0.53) |
| 104 | 1.36 (0.39) | 2.34 (0.43) | 3.33 (0.45) |

The responsiveness of option premiums to changes in the model inputs corresponds to the desired structure discussed earlier. Call option prices decline as the exercise price increases, and rise as time to expiration increases. An increase in the riskless rate of interest from 5% to 10% to 15% also, as predicted, causes the fair price of the option to increase steadily. Similarly, increasing volatility increases the fair price of the option. The impact of volatility is particularly important because, whereas interest rates in general do not double or treble in the short-term, asset price volatilities can change abruptly by large amounts.

The value of the at-the-money option with exercise price equal to $100 goes up by $1.85 or 54% as the implied volatility moves from 10% per annum to 20%; the out-of-the-money option at $104 increases in price by $1.97 or 145%.

This responsiveness of option premiums to asset price volatility is of immediate interest to the trader. Without options, the trader could only take a view on where asset prices were going by buying or selling the underlying asset. With options, he can also speculate on how volatile asset prices are going to be without necessarily having a view on the underlying price.

The impact of changes in the model inputs upon the option deltas is also worth examining. As already indicated, the option delta will rise with the degree the option is in-the-money: if an option is well out-of-the-money, a change in the underlying asset price will not substantially increase the probability that the option can be exercised profitably and hence the option value will not change very much; if an option is very in-the-money, most of its value will be intrinsic value rather than time value, and the intrinsic value of the option will simply move one-to-one with the underlying asset, i.e. the delta will be close to one.

The impact of time to expiration on delta also depends on whether the option is in- or out-of-the-money. If the option is in-the-money, then the amount of value constituted by intrinsic value relative to time value will diminish as the time to expiration increases, and hence the less the option will behave like the stock and the lower the option delta. By contrast the delta of the option tends to increase with time for out-of-the-money options. This can be seen in Exhibit 3.8. An in-the-money $94 exercise price option with a maturity of 30 days has a delta of 0.94 which falls to 0.82 for a 180-day option. By contrast an out-of-the-money $104 exercise price option with a maturity of 30 days has a delta of 0.24 which rises to 0.53 for a 180-day option. This has implications for the rebalancing of delta neutral option positions as the time to expiration decreases.

The impact of an increase in interest rates on the option deltas is to push them up modestly. This is intuitive because the definition of delta in the simple Black-Scholes formula contains a positive interest rate term.[5] The impact of volatility is similar to that of time to maturity. A rise in volatility tends to push down the delta of in-the-money options and push up the deltas of out-of-the-money options. Thus the Black-Scholes option valuation model possesses properties in line with arguments on how option prices ought to respond to the input variables.

This discussion of how option prices respond to the input variables suggests that the simple delta of the option may not be sufficient to characterize fully the responsiveness of option premiums to underlying variables for the purposes of trading and hedging. Several other measures of responsiveness also derived from the option valuation model are often used.

### c. Option gamma

The delta of an option increases as the option goes more in-the-money and decreases as the option goes further out-of-the-money, i.e. the delta of a call option is a positive function of the level of the stock price. The *gamma* of a option is simply a measure of the expected change in the delta of the option for a small change in the underlying stock price. Technically it is the second derivative of the option premium with respect to the stock price.

**Example**

Volatility = 15%   Interest rate = 10%
Time to expiration = 90 days   Exercise price = $100.00

Under these conditions a call option is priced at $4.33 if the underlying stock price is $100. The option delta is 0.63 and the option gamma is 0.05.

This implies that if the underlying stock price falls to $99 or rises to $101, the option delta will fall by 0.05 to 0.58 or rise by 0.05 to 0.68.

Hence the average delta over a specific stock price range will be delta $\pm \frac{1}{2}$ (gamma).

When designing neutral hedging or trading strategies, the gamma of the options will need to be taken into account.

---

[5] This effect only holds for the Black-Scholes stock option model being discussed; it will not apply to options on futures instruments.

**Example**

Volatility = 15%   Interest rate = 10%
Time to expiration = 90 days   Exercise price = $100.00
Current spot price = $100.00
Call option delta =   0.63  Call option gamma = 0.05
Put option delta = −0.37  Put option gamma = 0.05

Suppose the trader decides to buy puts and calls in a delta neutral manner.

$$\text{Ratio of puts to calls} = \frac{0.63}{0.37} = 1.7$$

Buy 10 $100 calls   Position delta =   6.30
Buy 17 $100 puts   Position delta = −6.29
Net delta =   0.01

But now consider the gamma of this position.

10 $100 calls   Position gamma = 0.50
17 $100 puts   Position gamma = 0.85
Net gamma = 1.35

If the current stock price rose by $1, we would expect the delta of the overall position to rise from 0.01 to 1.36.

Stock price up $1   Delta of call       0.68
Delta of put        0.32
Call position delta = 6.80
Put position delta  = 5.44
Net delta  = 1.36

What this means is that a position can be delta neutral initially, but if it has a relatively high gamma, it can rapidly become a bullish or bearish price trade.

## d. Option theta

Exhibit 3.8 illustrated how the time to expiration plays a considerable role in determining the fair option price. The *theta* of an option measures the expected change in the fair option premium as the time to expiration decreases.

**Example**

Volatility = 15%   Interest rate = 10%
Time to expiration = 90 days   Exercise price = $100.00
Call option price = $4.33   Option theta = 0.02

This implies that a reduction in time to expiration to 89 days, other things being equal, will reduce the option premium from $4.33 to $4.31 (4.33 − 0.02).

The time value of an option falls much more swiftly in the last few days of an options life than earlier, i.e. the theta of the option will increase rapidly as the time to expiration reduces. In general, it would pay a trader to put on a delta neutral position that would benefit as the time to expiration decreased.

## e. Option epsilon*

The *epsilon* of an option measures the responsiveness of the option premium to changes in the underlying volatility of the asset price.

**Example**

Volatility = 15%   Interest rate = 10%
Time to expiration = 90 days   Exercise price = $100
Call option price = $4.33   Option epsilon = 0.19

This implies that an increase in the underlying volatility from 15% to 16% would be expected to increase the option premium by 0.19 (from 4.33 to 4.52).

In practice the response of an option to underlying inputs will be complex because it is likely that the stock price, the time to expiration and the underlying volatility will also be changing

---

\* No standard nomenclature has been agreed for the response of option premiums to volatility: it is sometimes referred to as eta, vega, omega or kappa, as well as epsilon.

# Exhibit 3.9: Option model elasticities versus stock price

**a. Option delta**

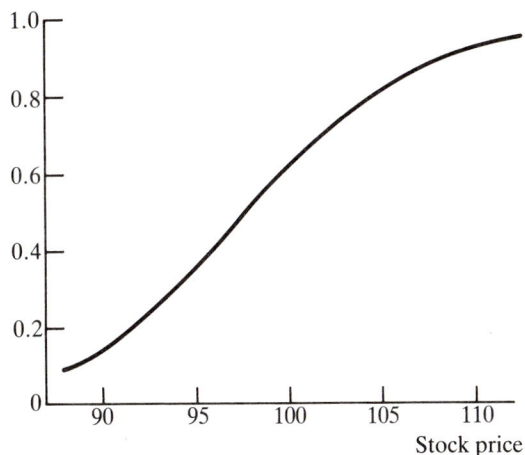

**b. Option gamma**

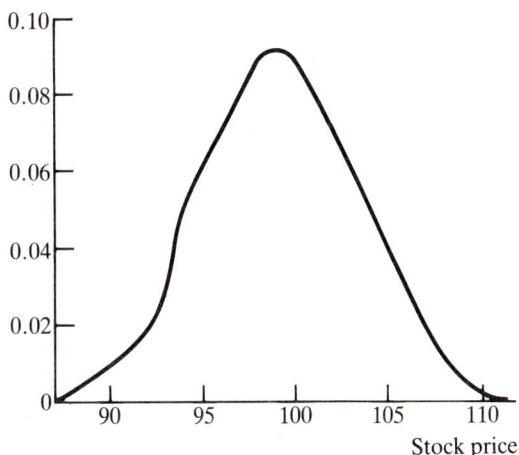

**c. Option epsilon**

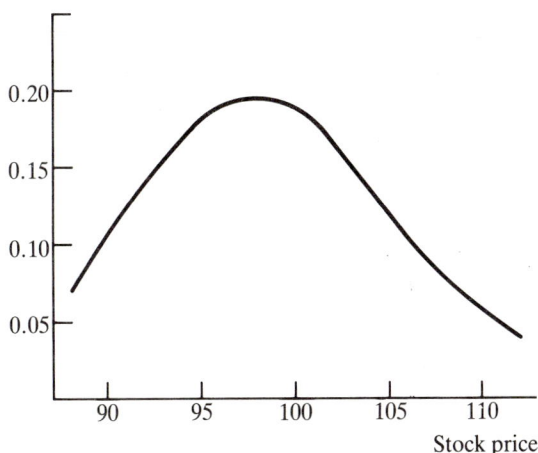

simultaneously. Moreover the delta, gamma, theta and epsilon of the option will all vary as the underlying inputs into the option valuation model change.

The graphs in Exhibit 3.9 show the responsiveness of the three parameters – delta, gamma and epsilon – to movements in the underlying stock price. The slope of the delta function (which is gamma) increases and then decreases. The maximum slope, as revealed by the gamma function, is when the call option is slightly out-of-the-money. The maximum responsiveness of the option premium to volatility is also when the option is slightly out-of-the-money, although the maximum epsilon level extends over a somewhat wider range.

It is worth considering the implications of these different parameters. Below is a table of option parameters.

*Call options*

Maturity = 90 days

| Exercise price | Premium | Delta | Gamma | Epsilon | Theta |
|---|---|---|---|---|---|
| 96 | 5.59 | 0.72 | 0.04 | 0.16 | 0.01 |
| 98 | 4.92 | 0.67 | 0.05 | 0.17 | 0.01 |
| 100 | 4.33 | 0.63 | 0.05 | 0.19 | 0.02 |
| 102 | 3.72 | 0.58 | 0.05 | 0.19 | 0.02 |
| 104 | 3.20 | 0.53 | 0.05 | 0.19 | 0.02 |

**Example**

Suppose the trader decided to wager on volatility rising while not wishing to take a view on price. He would like to be:

delta neutral – gamma positive – theta negative – epsilon positive

Suppose he sold 100 exercise price options and bought 104 exercise price options in the ratio 0.53 to 0.63 or 0.84.

|  |  | Delta | Gamma | Epsilon | Theta |
|---|---|---|---|---|---|
| 84 | 100 options short | −52.9 | −4.2 | −15.96 | 1.68 |
| 100 | 104 options long | 53.0 | 5.0 | 19.00 | −2.00 |
|  | Net | 0.1 | 0.8 | 3.04 | −0.32 |

$$\text{Total investment} = (100 \times \$3.20) - (84 \times \$4.33)$$
$$= -\$43.72$$

1. The investor draws $43.72 out of the transaction.
2. If the volatility moves 1% from the current level of 15%, the investor will obtain the expected profit of $3.04.
3. For each day that passes, the position is expected to gain $0.32.
4. If the price rises $1, the investor expects to earn profit of delta $+ \frac{1}{2}$ gamma $= \$0.50$. If the price falls $1, the new delta will be $-0.7$. Hence the average delta of $-0.3$ implies an expected profit of $0.10.

Hence if all the parameters are accurate, the position is favourable to the trader. An investor must analyse a trading position in terms of these parameters to check its suitability before commencing an options transaction. Any good valuation programme should print out these parameters for any combination of options.

# 5. Estimation of volatility

The importance of the asset price volatility as a prime determinent of fair and actual option premiums was stressed earlier in this chapter. The volatility estimate is also the only non-directly observable variable in simple Black-Scholes type option valuation models. The volatility of asset prices is usually measured as the standard deviation of daily, weekly or even monthly log price relatives annualized.

$$\text{Standard deviation} = \frac{\sum_{t=1}^{N} (X_t - \bar{X})^2}{N - 1}$$

where $N$ = number of observations
$X_t = \log(Y_t/Y_{t-1})$
$Y_t$ = observation in period $t$
$\bar{X}$ = arithmetic mean of the $X_t$.

To find the volatility, the standard deviation is multiplied by the square root of the period.

$$\text{Weekly data} \quad \text{Annual volatility} = \frac{\text{Weekly standard deviation}}{} \times \sqrt{52}$$

$$\text{Daily data}[6] \quad \text{Annual volatility} = \frac{\text{Daily standard deviation}}{} \times \sqrt{365}$$

**Example**: *IBM stock price volatility*

| Day | Stock price | Price relative ($Y_t/Y_{t-1}$) | Log price relative |
|---|---|---|---|
| 1 | 125 |  |  |
| 2 | $125\frac{3}{8}$ | 1.00300 | 0.00300 |
| 3 | $125\frac{7}{8}$ | 1.00399 | 0.00398 |
| 4 | $125\frac{1}{2}$ | 0.99702 | −0.00298 |
| 5 | $126\frac{1}{8}$ | 1.00498 | 0.00497 |
| 6 | $125\frac{7}{8}$ | 0.99802 | −0.00198 |

---

[6] Some would argue that the calculation of annual volatility from daily data should use a weighting of $\sqrt{250}$ or so, because only working days should be used.

$$\text{Mean log price relative} = \frac{0.00300 + 0.00398 - 0.00298 + 0.00497 - 0.00198}{5}$$

$$= 0.001398$$

$$\text{Daily standard deviation} = \sqrt{\frac{\begin{array}{l}(0.00300 - 0.001398)^2 + (0.00398 - 0.001398)^2 \\ + (-0.00298 - 0.001398)^2 + (0.00497 - 0.001398)^2 \\ + (-0.00198 - 0.001398)^2\end{array}}{5 - 1}}$$

$$= \sqrt{0.0000131} = 0.003625$$

$$\text{Annual volatility} = 0.003625\sqrt{365}$$
$$= 0.069 \quad \text{or} \quad 6.9\%$$

In the simple example shown above, the volatility estimate was obtained by calculating the simple historical standard deviation of log price relatives over the previous five days. Many different methods can be used to estimate volatility; in fact the best method of volatility estimation is one of the most discussed topics in option pricing. What is required is the best predictor of volatility over the life of the option; in a sense historical volatility is irrelevant except that it may have predictive ability for subsequent volatility. It will be useful to discuss some of the different approaches.

### a. Analysis of historical asset prices

In essence using historical data is simply an application of the simple standard deviation method outlined above. If the volatility of the underlying asset price is assumed to be constant, a simple historical volatility estimate will be appropriate, and the greater the number of observations, the closer the sample standard deviation will be to the actual standard deviation. If, however, volatility varies through time, the simple volatility estimation procedure outlined above will not be appropriate.

One alternative is to use only more recent data, and apply some weighting procedure to give greater importance to more recent observations. Such procedures can produce very different results depending on the weighting system adopted. Consider for instance the set of weekly closing prices for the UK pound in the period December 1984–May 1985.

*Weekly closing prices (UK pound)*

| Date | Exchange rate | Date | Exchange rate |
| --- | --- | --- | --- |
| 27/12/84 | 1.1610 | 13/3/85 | 1.0860 |
| 2/1/85 | 1.1480 | 20/3/85 | 1.1505 |
| 9/1/85 | 1.1410 | 27/3/85 | 1.2400 |
| 16/1/85 | 1.1170 | 3/4/85 | 1.2120 |
| 23/1/85 | 1.1105 | 10/4/85 | 1.2145 |
| 30/1/85 | 1.1135 | 17/4/85 | 1.2780 |
| 6/2/85 | 1.0872 | 24/4/85 | 1.2250 |
| 13/2/85 | 1.0873 | 1/5/85 | 1.2240 |
| 20/2/85 | 1.0870 | 8/5/85 | 1.2195 |
| 6/3/85 | 1.0680 | | |

Suppose we look at several different percentage weightings, where each price is given a certain percentage of the previous price as a weight. For instance, with 90% weighting, we would give the most recent rate a weight of 100, the previous one a weight of 90, the next previous one a weight of 81(90 × 0.90) and so on. The table below shows annual exchange rate volatilities using different percentage weights.

*Annual volatilities for different percentage weights*

| Percentage weight | Volatility (%) |
| --- | --- |
| 100 | 21.50 |
| 90 | 24.55 |
| 80 | 26.54 |
| 70 | 28.05 |
| 60 | 31.94 |

There are two points to be made. First, even using these simple weighting systems, the choice of weights can have a major impact on the estimated volatility. Secondly, bearing in mind the major impact of estimated volatility on fair option premiums, the statistical method used to calculate volatility plays a crucial role in the validity of any set of model option prices. There are also many different means of weighting historical data to produce forecasts such as exponential smoothing, ARIMA analysis, etc.

---

**The first task of an option analyst is to determine the best method of using historical price changes to predict future volatilities.**

---

The analyst needs to determine what is the best period of observations to use, the best weighting system, and whether to use weekly, daily or even transactions data. He also needs to explore whether information other than the simple series of closing prices might be used in volatility prediction. Parkinson[7] has suggested that better estimates of future volatility can be obtained by using the high and low prices obtained during the trading day rather than closing prices. His volatility estimator is

$$\text{Standard deviation} = \frac{0.627}{N} \sum_{i=1}^{N} \ln (H_i/L_i)$$

where $N$ = number of observations
$H_i$ = high price observed on a specific day
$L_i$ = low price observed on a specific day

Garman and Klass[8] have improved this technique, and options traders should experiment with it to see if improved volatility estimates result. Finally, other variables may be introduced into a forecasting system for volatility, e.g. the volume of trading in a stock, the behaviour of the market, or economic variables.

## b. Calculating volatilities implied by market option premiums

A different though complementary approach is to solve the option valuation model in reverse, i.e. plug in the market prices of options and determine the implied asset price volatilities that are consistent with them. This method probably gives the most reliable estimate of the current market view of volatility. The example below illustrates the procedure for a set of Eurodollar options trading on the London International Financial Futures Exchange.

*Option premiums + Implied volatilities*

Futures price = 90.30

| Exercise price | September call | | December call | |
| --- | --- | --- | --- | --- |
| | *Market price* | *Implied volatility (%)* | *Market price* | *Implied volatility (%)* |
| 89.50 | 1.00 | 2.80 | 1.20 | 2.80 |
| 90.00 | 0.60 | 2.40 | 0.90 | 2.90 |
| 90.50 | 0.40 | 2.74 | 0.60 | 2.72 |
| 91.00 | 0.25 | 2.80 | 0.40 | 2.65 |

Different market prices even for the same delivery date indicate different implied volatilities. This could arise because of imperfections in the data, and different probabilities of premature exercise according to whether the option is in- or out-of-the-money. The usual way of handling this problem is to combine the different volatility estimates to produce a single *composite volatility estimate*. The individual trader has to determine which weighting system for a set of implicit

---

[7] M. Parkinson, "The random walk problem: extreme value method for estimating the variance of the rate of return", *Journal of Business*, 1980, 53, 61–65.

[8] M. Garman and M. Klass, "On the estimation of security price volatilities from historical data", *Journal of Business*, 1980, 53, 67–78.

volatilities produces the best predictor of future volatility (and numerous articles have been written on this topic).[9]

Finally the trader will decide whether historical time series of these implied volatilities can provide additional information for forecasting purposes. A weighted combination of the best volatility forecast drawn from historical prices and the best volatility forecast drawn from current and past implied volatilities may also do better at forecasting future volatility than either alone.

The calculation of a composite implied volatility is an important tool in option valuation trading (see Chapter 4). For instance, using the implied volatilities for Eurodollar options shown on p. 48, the table below illustrates the weights used by a typical implied volatility estimation procedure.

| | September call | | | December call | | |
|---|---|---|---|---|---|---|
| Exercise price | Market price | Implicit volatility | Assigned weight (%) | Market price | Implicit volatility | Assigned weight (%) |
| 89.50 | 1.00 | 2.80 | 6 | 1.20 | 2.80 | 15 |
| 90.00 | 0.60 | 2.40 | 9 | 0.90 | 2.90 | 19 |
| 90.50 | 0.40 | 2.74 | 9 | 0.60 | 2.72 | 19 |
| 91.00 | 0.25 | 2.80 | 7 | 0.40 | 2.65 | 15 |

The weighting procedure shown[10] follows the common procedure of assigning more weight to options close to the money and with longer maturities. Most weighting systems in commercial computer packages weight individual call implied volatilities according to the sensitivity of the call option premium to volatility. Some traders may not want to use September and December option prices simultaneously to calculate a composite implied volatility since options with different expiration dates do not necessarily have the same volatility. For instance, if the option prices shown were for July, the market might expect interest rate volatility to be relatively high between July and September, but to slacken off again in the autumn months.

Given the weights shown, the composite volatility estimate is 2.74%. Now the trader can estimate fair prices given the composite estimate.

## Option premiums
Volatility = 2.74%

| | September | | | December | | |
|---|---|---|---|---|---|---|
| Exercise price | Market price | Fair price | Difference (%) | Market price | Fair price | Difference (%) |
| 89.50 | 1.00 | 0.99 | +1 | 1.20 | 1.17 | +3 |
| 90.00 | 0.60 | 0.65 | −9 | 0.90 | 0.86 | +5 |
| 90.50 | 0.40 | 0.40 | +1 | 0.60 | 0.60 | 0 |
| 91.00 | 0.25 | 0.22 | +12 | 0.40 | 0.40 | −1 |

It is possible to judge by how much each market price may be overvalued or undervalued relative to the others. However, the trader has to be certain that the market prices are ones at which he can actually trade. The natural tendency when calculating implicit volatilities is to use mid-point prices. While this may be appropriate for obtaining relative valuations, the trader will probably have to operate on the wrong side of the *bid-ask* spread and pay appropriate commissions.

For instance, suppose the bid-ask spread for the undervalued September 90 call was 0.59–0.61 and for the overvalued September 91 call was 0.24–0.26. Further suppose the trade was to buy the 90 call and sell the 91 call in a ratio of 1:2. Trading at the market prices shown will yield an expected profit, if prices moved back into line quickly, of five points from the 90 call

[9] There is a good discussion of this topic in Cox and Rubinstein (1985) *op. cit.* Two particularly useful articles are S. Beckers, "Standard deviations implied in option prices as predictors of future stock price variability", *Journal of Banking and Finance*, 1981, 5, 363–82, and H. Latané and R. Rendleman, "Standard deviations of stock price ratios implied in option prices", *Journal of Finance*, 1976, 31, 369–81.

[10] The various option calculations and estimates shown in this book were carried out on the options software package of Investor Intelligence Systems Corporation unless otherwise stated.

and six points from the two 91 calls. Now consider trading on the wrong side of the bid-ask spread.

Profit

|          |            |             |   |
|----------|------------|-------------|---|
| 90 Call  | Buy at 61  | Sell at 64  | 3 |
| 91 Call  | Sell at 24 | Buy at 23   | 1 |

The profit is reduced from an expected 11 points to an expected four points – a very substantial reduction. Commissions would reduce the expected profit even more.

Nevertheless, as we shall discuss further in Chapter 4 on options trading, the estimation of implied volatilities is a crucial input into option valuation trading.

---

**The options trader must analyse and use historical asset prices and current and historical implied volatilities to produce the best composite predictor of asset price volatility over the life of the options in question.**

---

## 6. Extensions of the options pricing model

As mentioned earlier, the simple Black-Scholes model originally designed for stocks technically only applies to European options. It was possible to use it to value American options, as long as the stock did not pay dividends, because of our proof of condition F in section 3 of this chapter. In practice, stocks pay dividends and for this and other reasons the value of American options will differ from their theoretical European values. Before discussing the problems of early exercise, however, the valuation of put options should be examined, assuming that a European pricing model is appropriate.

### a. Valuation of European put options

For European options it is possible to show the following proposition: *put-call parity*. The price of a put option is equal to the value of a European call option with the same exercise price and time to expiration, a riskless investment of the discounted value of the exercise price, and a short position in the stock.

Using the terminology developed earlier

$$P(S, X, T) = C(S, X, T) + Xe^{-rt} - S$$

Consider the following two portfolios and their returns.

|          | Return at expiration | |
|----------|:---:|:---:|
| *Portfolio* | $S^* < X$ | $S^* \geqslant X$ |
| A. $P(S, X, T)$ | $X - S^*$ | $0$ |
| B. $C(S, X, T) + Xe^{-rt} - S$ | $X - S^*$ | $(S^* - X) + X - S^*$ |
| *Result* | $VA = VB$ | $VA = VB$ |

By stochastic dominance, therefore, our result is proven.

For European options, an arbitrage possibility will exist if this condition is not fulfilled.

### Example

A three-month call option with an exercise price of $45 is selling for $8.00. A three-month put option with an exercise price also of $45 is selling for $1.00. The rate of interest is 10% and the stock price is $50. Is there an arbitrage opportunity?

It is known that the following should hold

$$C(S, X, T) = 50 + 1 - 45e^{-(0.10)(0.25)} = \$7.11$$

Since the call is actually priced at $8, it is clearly overvalued. The investor decides to carry out the following set of transactions.

|                                 |              |            |
|---------------------------------|--------------|------------|
| Write a 45 call                 | Cash inflow  | = $8.00    |
| Buy the stock at $50            | Cash outflow | = $50.00   |
| Buy a 45 put                    | Cash outflow | = $1.00    |
| Borrow discounted value of $45  | Cash inflow  | = $43.89   |
|                                 | Total net inflow | = $0.89 |

At the expiration of the options, consider three alternatives: a final stock price of $40, $45 and $50.

> *Alternative 1*: $S^* = \$40$
> 45 put is exercised, deliver stock, receive $45.
> Repay discount loan with $45. Net cash flow is zero.
> Total profit = $0.89

> *Alternative 2*: $S^* = \$45$
> Both options expire worthless.
> Sell stock at $45 and repay discount loan. Net cash flow is zero.
> Total profit = $0.89

> *Alternative 3*: $S^* = \$50$
> 45 call is exercised, deliver stock, receive $45.
> Repay discount loan with $45. Net cash flow is zero.
> Total profit = $0.89

Hence whatever happens to the price of the underlying asset, the arbitrage profit of 89 cents per option is assured. The put-call parity relationship can be combined with the call conditions discussed earlier to deduce a number of similar conditions for the put option. The American put will generally have a higher price than the European put because of the value of early exercise. Hence the circumstances above, where the put was undervalued relative to the call, would still represent an arbitrage opportunity.

For the sake of completeness the tables below show put and call prices under the simple Black-Scholes assumptions for the stock price illustrated earlier.

## Option values: Impact of maturity

Volatility = 15%   Interest rate = 10%   Current stock price = $100

| Exercise price | Call option premiums (deltas in brackets) | | |
|---|---|---|---|
| | *30-day* | *90-day* | *180-day* |
| 94.00 | 6.87(0.94) | 8.73(0.86) | 11.24(0.82) |
| 96.00 | 5.06(0.87) | 8.73(0.80) | 9.70(0.78) |
| 98.00 | 3.46(0.75) | 5.63(0.72) | 8.26(0.72) |
| 100.00 | 2.16(0.58) | 4.33(0.63) | 6.94(0.66) |
| 102.00 | 1.22(0.40) | 3.23(0.53) | 5.75(0.60) |
| 104.00 | 0.61(0.24) | 2.34(0.43) | 4.70(0.53) |

| Exercise price | Put option premiums (deltas in brackets) | | |
|---|---|---|---|
| | *30-day* | *90-day* | *180-day* |
| 94.00 | 0.09(−0.05) | 0.44(−0.11) | 0.77(−0.13) |
| 96.00 | 0.27(−0.12) | 0.76(−0.18) | 1.12(−0.18) |
| 98.00 | 0.65(−0.25) | 1.24(−0.26) | 1.59(−0.23) |
| 100.00 | 1.34(−0.41) | 1.89(−0.35) | 2.18(−0.29) |
| 102.00 | 2.38(−0.59) | 2.75(−0.45) | 2.90(−0.35) |
| 104.00 | 3.75(−0.75) | 3.80(−0.55) | 3.85(−0.42) |

The first important point is that the arbitrage condition discussed above for European put options is consistent with put option premiums being priced at below their intrinsic value. For instance, take the 104 90-day put. The price of $3.80 is fully consistent with our arbitrage condition.

$$P(S, X, T) = C(S, X, T) + Xe^{-rt} - S$$
$$= 2.34 + (104)e^{-(0.10)(90/360)} - 100$$
$$= \$3.77$$

The difference of $0.03 is due to a rounding error in the option valuation programme. This could not be the case for an American put option, because it would pay an investor to buy the option for $3.80, buy the stock for $100 and immediately exercise the option to sell the stock at $104, netting an immediate and riskless profit of $0.20 per option

## b. Valuation of American put options

This point brings up the entire question of how the simple Black-Scholes model needs to be adjusted for the early exercise characteristics of American options. Even ignoring the American put option, the problem also applies to American call options on dividend paying stocks. Consider a stock which goes ex-dividend and pays a certain dividend D at the expiration date of the option. Then look at two portfolios: A consisting of a call option and an investment to yield $(X + D)$ at the expiration date of the option, and B consisting of a share of stock.

| Portfolio | Current value | Final value | |
|---|---|---|---|
| | | $S^* < X$ | $S^* \geqslant X$ |
| A | $C(S, X, T) + (X + D)e^{-rt}$ | $X + D$ | $S^* - X + X + D$ |
| B | $S$ | $S^*$ | $S^*$ |
| Relative terminal values | | $VA > VB$ | $VA > VB$ |

Hence to avoid dominance, it is clear that

$$C(S, X, T) + (X + D)e^{-rt} > S$$
$$C(S, X, T) > S - (X + D)e^{-rt}$$

It is not clear that $S - (X + D)e^{-rt}$ will always be greater than $S - X$. For instance, consider a three-month option with an exercise price \$40 and a riskless interest rate of 10%. If the expected dividend is \$2, then $(40 + 2)e^{-(0.10)(0.25)}$ is equal to \$40.96. In these circumstances, it may be optimal to exercise the option prematurely rather than sell it, and the problem of option valuation then becomes more complex.

To illustrate that an American put is likely to be exercised early does not even require the stock to pay dividends. If the put is exercised only at maturity, its terminal value is $C(S, X, T) - S + Xe^{-rt}$. If it is exercised early, the investor will obtain $X - S$ which can be invested at the riskless rate of interest and will therefore have a terminal value of $(X - S)e^{rt}$. The question is: can we conceive of conditions under which

$$(X - S)e^{rt} > C(S, X, T) - S + Xe^{-rt}$$
$$\text{or} \quad C(S, X, T) < X(e^{rt} - e^{-rt}) + S(1 - e^{-rt})$$

The call option price can certainly fulfil this condition for a low enough stock price, and in those circumstances the American put will be exercised prematurely. The existence of dividends may reduce the probability of early exercise at certain times, but will not necessarily eliminate it. This means that calls on dividend-paying stocks and American puts generally will need some adjustment of the simple Black-Scholes formula for valuation purposes.

It is beyond the scope of this book to go into the mathematical complexities of adjusting the Black-Scholes option valuation model for the question of early exercise. However, it is worth discussing some of the approaches.[11] Any option valuation model must impose the constraint that the option value should equal the intrinsic value of the option. Thus with European puts on a non-dividend paying stock, where model prices can fall below intrinsic value, the price curve must be adjusted (see Exhibit 3.10).

This is not entirely satisfactory because the value of the put at-the-money will take into account a certain probability of the in-the-money put being worth its intrinsic value rather than its European value according to the Black-Scholes model. The true price, therefore, may be something like the dotted line shown in Exhibit 3.10. Finding the true shape of the realistic put price is, however, not easy. The binominal option pricing model pioneered by Sharpe[12] and discussed extensively in the Cox and Rubinstein book (*op. cit.*) provides a valuation formula for the American put and the American call on dividend paying stocks. Alternatively numerical approximation methods can be used to determine fair put and call values. Curve fitting techniques can then be used to determine the best price line between the intrinsic value of in-the-money options and the fair value of out-of-the-money European options that corresponds most

---

[11] Cox and Rubinstein, *Options Markets*, discusses many of the problems associated with early exercise. Important papers such as M. Brennan and E. Schwartz, "The valuation of American put options", *Journal of Finance*, 1977, 32, 449–62, and M. Parkinson, "Options pricing: the American put", *Journal of Business*, 1977, 50, 21–36, discuss the question of numerical solutions to the valuation of options where early exercise can be optimal.

[12] The first idea behind the binominal model was presented in W. Sharpe, *Investments*, Prentice-Hall, 3rd edition (1986).

**Exhibit 3.10: American put valuation**

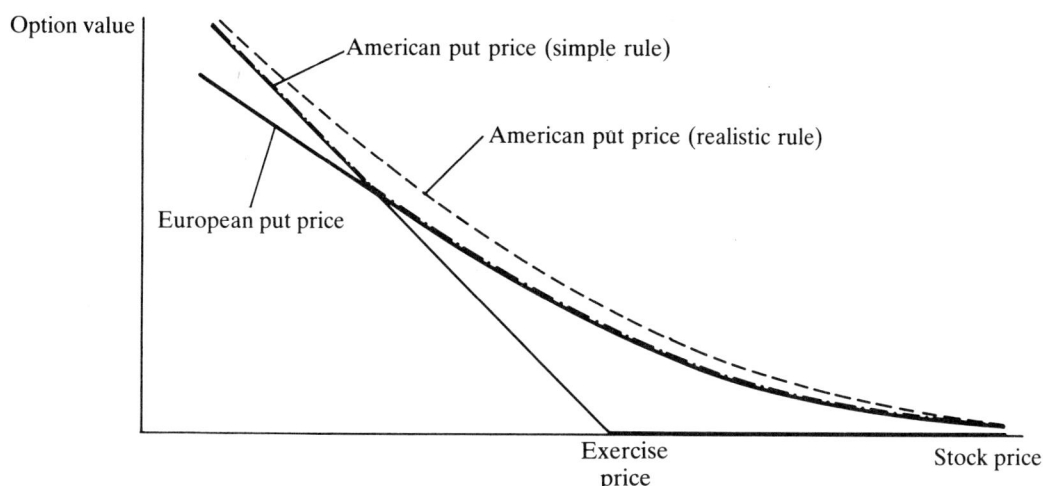

closely with the fair prices from the numerical solution.[13] The table below gives some idea of the differences that arise by using these different methods to value the American put.

*Put option values*

Volatility = 15%   Maturity = 90 days   Interest rate = 10%   Stock price = $100

| Exercise price | European | Simple American | Curve-fitted American |
|---|---|---|---|
| 94 | 0.44 | 0.44 | 1.46 |
| 96 | 0.76 | 0.76 | 2.04 |
| 98 | 1.24 | 1.24 | 2.75 |
| 100 | 1.89 | 1.89 | 3.61 |
| 102 | 2.75 | 2.75 | 4.63 |
| 104 | 3.80 | 4.00 | 5.78 |
| 106 | 5.05 | 6.00 | 7.07 |
| 108 | 6.47 | 8.00 | 8.49 |
| 110 | 8.04 | 10.00 | 10.01 |

### c. Modifications of the Black-Scholes model

The other two important major extensions of the Black-Scholes model are modifications designed to cope with different underlying assets: options on dividend paying stocks, currencies, and futures contracts; and changes needed if the underlying process by which the asset price moves is different. The modifications to cater for different underlying instruments will be discussed in each specific chapter on particular types of options; but the different price generation processes need to be analysed here.

The basic Black-Scholes assumption is that stock prices follow a continuous random walk through time. Various other processes have been suggested.

### (i) Absolute diffusion

This model assumes that stock prices do not vary continuously but discretely according to a binomial process. This is the Sharpe model mentioned earlier.

### (ii) Compound option models

For leveraged companies, the stock of the company can be regarded as an option on the value of the company. Since the call option is an option on the stock which is itself an option, the call option is a compound option. In this model, the variance or volatility of the stock price will not be constant through time and the Black-Scholes model will need to be adjusted accordingly.

---

[13] The Investor Intelligence Systems Corporation option evaluation system, from which most of the examples in this book are drawn, uses the latter approach.

## (iii) Displaced diffusion

If a firm holds a proportion of its value in risky assets and a proportion in riskless assets, the variance of the stock price will again no longer be constant as the market value of the risky assets changes. The Black-Scholes model will need to be adjusted accordingly.

## (iv) Jump processes

The conventional Black-Scholes model assumes that underlying asset prices follow a smooth path. Another possibility is that every so often the stock price jumps discretely and unpredictably – say, the impact of Brazilian frosts on coffee futures prices. Depending upon whether, in between jumps, the price path is predictable or follows a random walk, further modifications to the Black-Scholes model will be needed.

Exhibit 3.11, originally presented by Rubinstein,[14] gives an idea of how much difference these various assumptions make to the simple Black-Scholes model values. The table is for a stock with a current price of 50 when the rate of interest is 7%. The table shows the extent to which the volatility estimate in the basic Black-Scholes model needs to be adjusted to create the same option value as that determined by the alternative model. The values are normalized so that the at-the-money option with a time to expiration of 120 days is priced identically under all the assumptions.

### Exhibit 3.11: Comparative implied volatilities

$S = 50 \quad r = 1.07 \quad \sigma = 0.3$

| Exercise price | Time to expiration (in days) | | | | | | | | | | | | | | |
|---|---|---|---|---|---|---|---|---|---|---|---|---|---|---|---|
| | 10 | 40 | 120 | 200 | 270 | 10 | 40 | 120 | 200 | 270 | 10 | 40 | 120 | 200 | 270 |
| | Displaced diffusion ($\alpha = 0.5$) | | | | | Black-Scholes | | | | | Displaced diffusion ($\alpha = 1.5$) | | | | |
| 40 | 0.99 | 0.89 | 0.87 | 0.86 | 0.85 | 1.00 | 1.00 | 1.00 | 1.00 | 1.00 | 1.01 | 1.04 | 1.04 | 1.04 | 1.05 |
| 45 | 0.96 | 0.96 | 0.94 | 0.93 | 0.92 | 1.00 | 1.00 | 1.00 | 1.00 | 1.00 | 1.02 | 1.02 | 1.02 | 1.02 | 1.03 |
| 50 | 1.02 | 1.01 | 1.00 | 0.99 | 0.98 | 1.00 | 1.00 | 1.00 | 1.00 | 1.00 | 1.00 | 1.00 | 1.00 | 1.00 | 1.01 |
| 55 | 1.06 | 1.06 | 1.05 | 1.04 | 1.03 | 1.00 | 1.00 | 1.00 | 1.00 | 1.00 | 0.98 | 0.98 | 0.99 | 0.99 | 0.99 |
| 60 | 1.13 | 1.10 | 1.09 | 1.08 | 1.07 | 1.00 | 1.00 | 1.00 | 1.00 | 1.00 | 0.97 | 0.97 | 0.97 | 0.97 | 0.98 |

| Exercise price | Pure | jump | ($\sigma = 0.3$, | $\lambda = 1$) | | Compound option $\left(T = 3, \dfrac{B}{S} = 0.8\right)$ | | | | |
|---|---|---|---|---|---|---|---|---|---|---|
| 40 | 0.98 | 0.58 | 0.41 | 0.35 | 0.32 | 1.02 | 1.05 | 1.05 | 1.06 | 1.06 |
| 45 | 0.55 | 0.34 | 0.24 | 0.75 | 0.92 | 1.02 | 1.02 | 1.03 | 1.03 | 1.03 |
| 50 | 0.38 | 0.71 | 1.00 | 1.06 | 1.05 | 1.00 | 1.00 | 1.00 | 1.00 | 1.00 |
| 55 | 1.71 | 1.37 | 1.22 | 1.11 | 1.01 | 0.98 | 0.98 | 0.98 | 0.98 | 0.99 |
| 60 | * | 1.64 | 1.22 | 1.08 | 1.11 | 0.96 | 0.96 | 0.96 | 0.97 | 0.97 |

| Exercise price | Diffusion-jump ($\lambda = 1$, $\gamma = 0.8$) | | | | | Absolute diffusion | | | | |
|---|---|---|---|---|---|---|---|---|---|---|
| 40 | * | 1.61 | 1.31 | 1.25 | 1.23 | 1.07 | 1.12 | 1.12 | 1.12 | 1.12 |
| 45 | 1.48 | 1.14 | 1.11 | 1.13 | 1.15 | 1.05 | 1.05 | 1.05 | 1.06 | 1.06 |
| 50 | 0.72 | 0.86 | 1.00 | 1.07 | 1.10 | 1.00 | 1.00 | 1.00 | 1.00 | 1.00 |
| 55 | 1.35 | 1.04 | 1.04 | 1.08 | 1.10 | 0.95 | 0.95 | 0.95 | 0.96 | 0.96 |
| 60 | * | 1.40 | 1.16 | 1.13 | 1.14 | 0.92 | 0.91 | 0.91 | 0.91 | 0.91 |

* Extremely high.

There are several conclusions. First, the simple Black-Scholes model is relatively robust compared with several of the alternative models, particularly the displaced diffusion and the compound option models. The binomial process indicates that the Black-Scholes model will tend to overprice out-of-the-money options and underprice in-the-money options. Thus for a 120-day option with an exercise price of 40, the Black-Scholes volatility input would need to be increased by 12% to produce a premium equal to the binomial model premium. For a 120-day option with an exercise price of 60, the Black-Scholes volatility input would need to be reduced by 9%. These modifications are not dramatic.

The existence of jumps causes a greater problem. Major modifications need to be made to the Black-Scholes model to cater for the possibility of occasional random jumps. The trader must decide whether such modifications are appropriate for specific assets. Nonetheless, the simple model adjusted for dividends and for early exercise is capable of playing a major role in options trading and hedging strategies.

---

[14] M. Rubinstein, "A survey of option pricing models" in M. Brenner (ed), *Option Pricing*, Lexington Heath (1983).

54

# 7. Summary

This chapter has explored the basics of the pricing of options contracts. Although the discussion concentrated largely on stock options, because all the original work on options pricing was carried out in this context, the arguments apply equally well to other options. The basic options pricing model is the Black-Scholes model, which expresses the price of a call option as a function of the underlying asset price, the exercise price, the time to expiration, the interest rate and the volatility of the underlying asset price. The Black-Scholes model values fitted in with conditions placed on options premiums from dominance arguments.

Although the Black-Scholes model needs to be modified to take into account the possibility of premature exercise of American options, the payment of dividends and different underlying processes for the stock price, it remains the fundamental method for the valuing of options for trading and hedging purposes, and will be used extensively in the remainder of this book. The options trader need not, however, become too involved in the theory of option pricing models: they are simply tools to be used by the trader and hedger. The aim is to determine the best model and the best method for calculating volatilities to yield the maximum return to options trading activities and the best hedging performance.

---

**The option user's role is to:**

- **Identify the option pricing model which best fits the nature of the underlying asset and gives satisfactory trading and hedging results.**
- **Determine the best method of predicting asset price volatility given historical data and current and past option market premiums.**
- **Use the model outputs – fair prices, deltas, gammas, epsilons and thetas – to design trades which best suit his or her price and/or volatility forecasts, or to design efficient hedges.**

---

Even if the trader or hedger is very dubious about theoretical option pricing models, the assessment of the short-term performance of an option portfolio in response to changes in asset prices and volatilities requires some pricing model. A suspicious trader may use two or three different pricing models to compare under- and over-valued options.

# Chapter 4
# Trading with options

## 1. Introduction

There are many different types of options described in this book, but the majority of option trading strategies are applicable to all options. Apart from the types of arbitrage trades described in Chapter 3, options trading divides naturally into three basic types.

*Open position trading*: The trader uses options contracts to speculate on expectations of future asset price movements or asset price volatility that differ from those embedded in the current set of market prices.

*Valuation trading*: The trader buys and sells options that appear underpriced or overpriced according to a specific option valuation model. He has no particular expectations concerning the future evolution of asset prices.

*Asset-option combination trading*: The trader combines positions in the underlying asset with options positions to create more optimal risk-return characteristics.

There are three specific features of options contracts that are favourable to the professional trader. First, the fact that options can be abandoned without any other penalty other than the loss of the original premium enables the trader to limit the risk of the options position to any desired level. Second, the degree of leverage with options, particularly out-of-the-money options, can be extremely high. Finally, the large number of options combinations that can be constructed enables the trader to tailor return profiles more closely to his individual expectations than is possible with the underlying asset.

## 2. Position trading

In position trading, the general characteristic is that the current set of options prices are consistent with market expectations of future asset prices, but the trader has a different set of expectations than the market. A comparison of options positions and asset positions suggests:

|  | Asset position | Option position |
|---|---|---|
| View | Price to fall or rise relative to market expectation. | (a) Price to rise or fall relative to market expectation.<br>(b) Price volatility to be greater or less than market expectation. |
| Risk | Potentially unlimited. | Can be limited in any desired manner. |

Elementary options positions can be characterized by their profit profiles at expiration. Exhibit 4.1 illustrates the difference between a long position in GEC stock at 200p and the purchase of an at-the-money 200 call option for a premium of 20p. The option holder makes 20p less profit than a long stock position if the price rises, but has a maximum loss of 20p if the price falls. Moreover, there is a difference between the option closing value on the day of purchase and the option profit profile at expiration. If the GEC stock price were to move immediately to, say 210p, the option position could be liquidated for a substantial profit, even though the intrinsic value of the option was still 10p less than the premium. This suggests an important feature of options trading.

**Exhibit 4.1: Comparison of options and assets: profit-loss profile**

GEC 200 call option   Premium = 20p     GEC stock price = 200

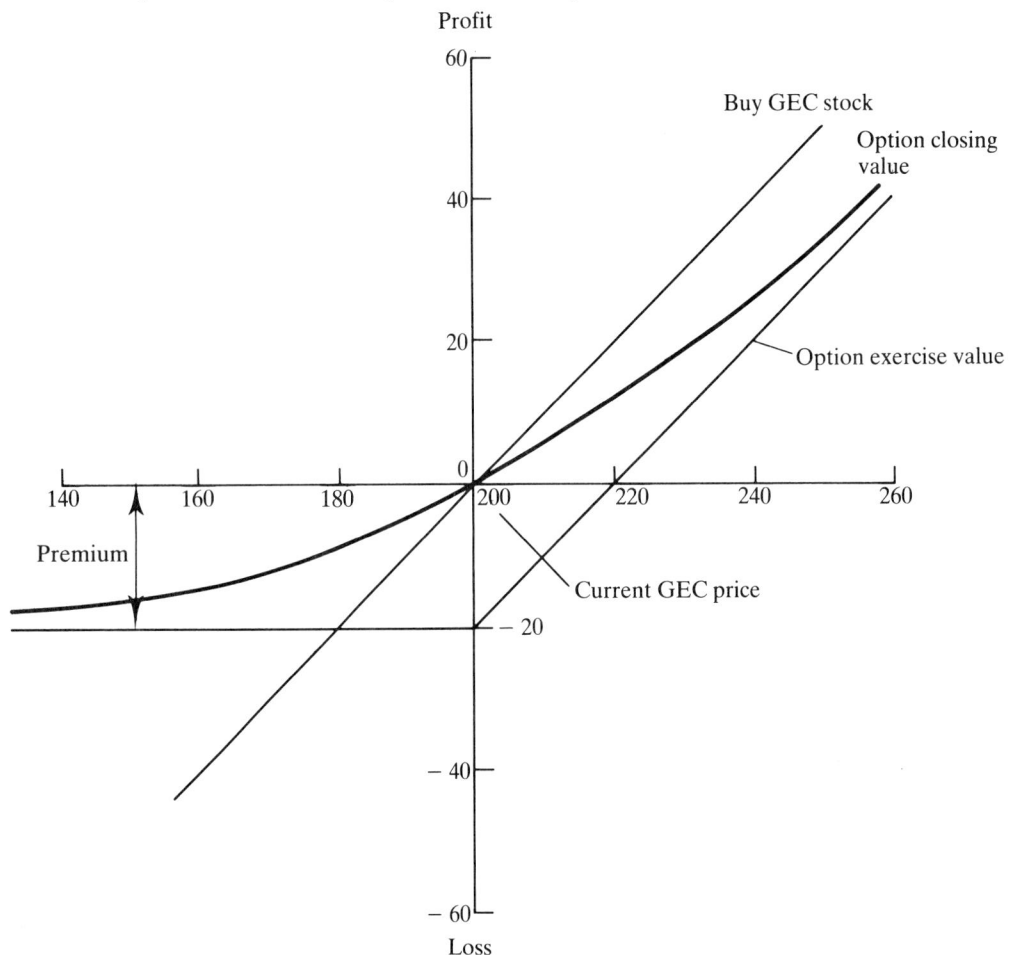

The options position profit for asset price movements before expiration is as important as the profit at expiration.

Exhibit 4.2 illustrates the dollar profit profile for a General Motors 45 put option purchased at a premium of $2.50 on 23 June 1982 for price movements occurring immediately, in two months, in four months, in five months and at expiration. The short-run profit from a downward stock price movement below $45 is high even if the option never gets in-the-money.

The other method of characterizing an option position is to look at a *risk profile* of the position rather than a profit and loss profile. A typical risk profile for the long position in GEC stock at 200p and the long 200 call at 20p are shown in Exhibit 4.3.

The trader's forecast is for a market price for GEC at the expiration of the option of 220p. Hence the expected profit on an investment in the stock is 20p, with the downward risk illustrated by the cumulative probability of a price below 200p given the trader's forecast. This cumulative probability is 19%. In the case of the option, because the trader's expected price is 220p, the expected gain from the option purchase is zero since the price increase is exactly matched by the option premium. However, if the option premium were only 15p, there would be an expected gain of 5p. In each case the individual trader has to decide which combination of expected gain and relative proportions of risk and opportunity best suit his characteristics. The option profit-loss profiles and risk profiles are the essential elements in option trading decisions.

To illustrate the basic option strategies, the following set of option premiums will be adopted. Although a set of Philadelphia currency option premiums is used, the trading strategies carry over directly to all types of options.

**Exhibit 4.2: Put option**

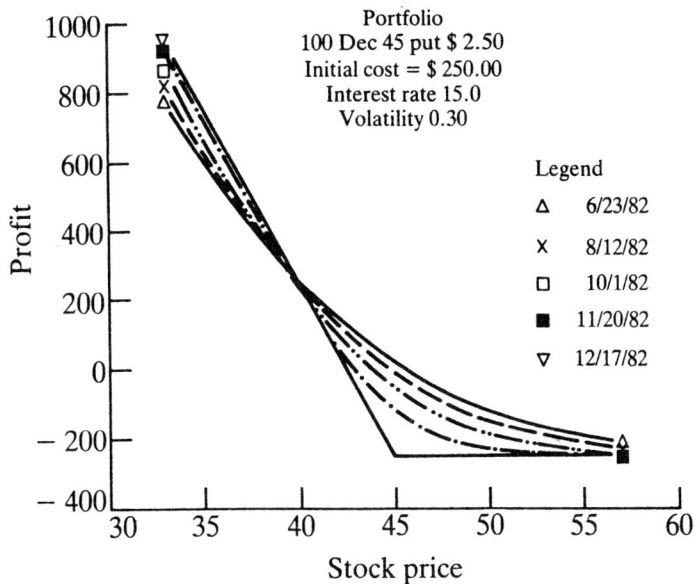

Portfolio
100 Dec 45 put $ 2.50
Initial cost = $ 250.00
Interest rate 15.0
Volatility 0.30

Legend
△  6/23/82
✕  8/12/82
□  10/1/82
■  11/20/82
▽  12/17/82

**Exhibit 4.3: Risk profile**

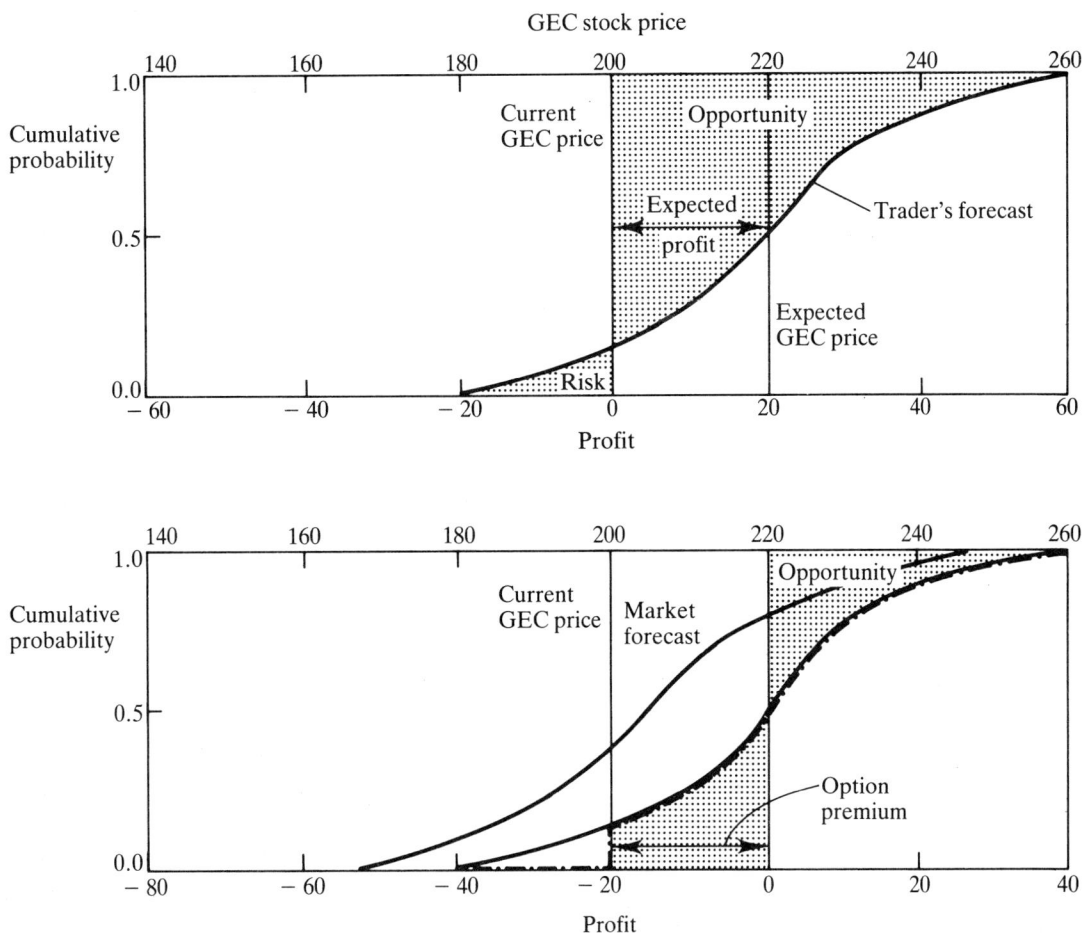

59

*Currency option premiums: March 12*

Sterling spot rate = $1.2485  June forward rate = $1.2455  September forward rate = $1.2425

| Strike price | Calls | | Puts | |
|---|---|---|---|---|
| | June | September | June | September |
| 115 | 9.85 | 9.99 | 0.29 | 1.22 |
| 120 | 5.63 | 6.63 | 1.16 | 2.61 |
| 125 | 2.70 | 4.06 | 3.13 | 4.79 |
| 130 | 1.04 | 2.29 | 6.36 | 7.77 |
| 135 | 0.31 | 1.18 | 10.53 | 11.41 |

Suppose a simple example is considered first: the purchase of an out-of-the-money call for speculation.

1. The current sterling rate is $1.2485 but is expected to rise sharply. The trader decides to buy a deep out-of-the-money June 135 call at a premium of 0.31 cents.

$$\text{Cost of option} = \$38.75 \ (\pounds12,500 \times \$0.0031)$$

2. If the rate rises to $1.3700 (+9.7%), the intrinsic value of the June 135 call will rise to 2 cents plus any time value, which represents a minimum rise of 545%.
3. If the sterling rate remains below $1.2485, the maximum loss will be $38.75.

*Buy an out-of-the-money call*

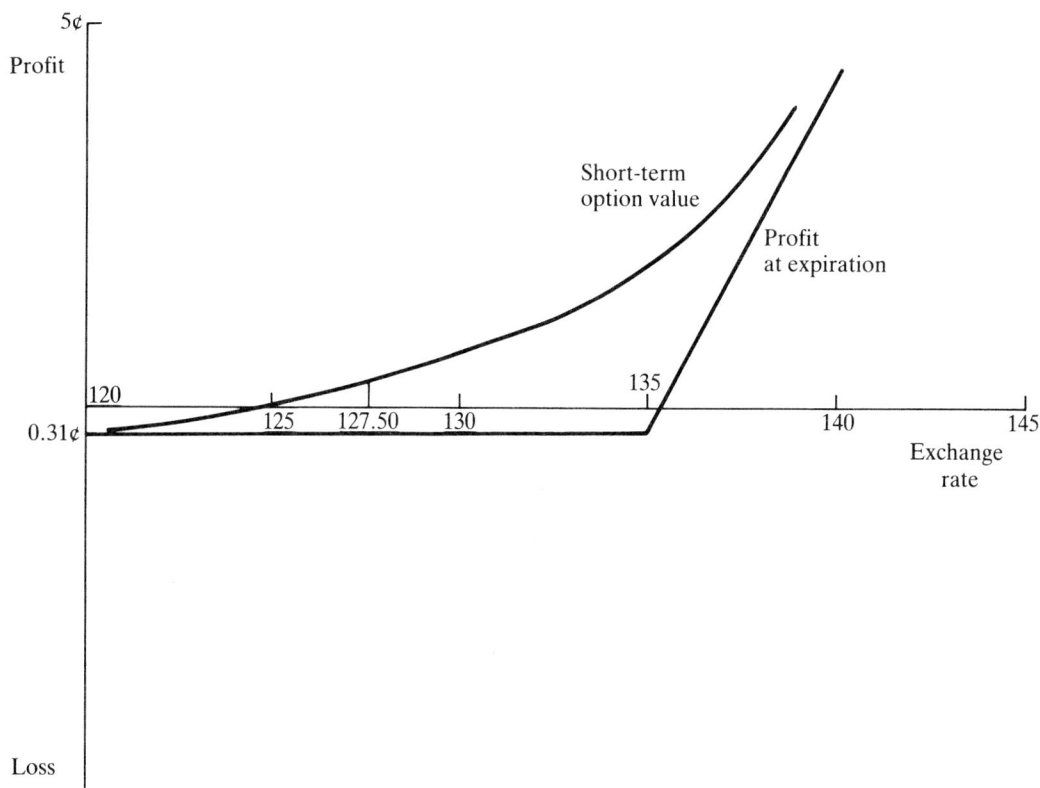

A movement to $1.2750 in the short-term would double the option premium of 0.31 ¢

## a. Bullish price expectational trades

The first basic set of option trades, of which the one just described is an example, are the *bullish price expectational trades*. These are trades designed to cater for when the trader accepts the market consensus on future asset price volatility, but believes prices are going to rise more rapidly than is anticipated by the market. The point about accepting the market consensus on volatility is important. Volatility is one of the major elements in option valuation. If volatility falls rapidly in the short-term, the option premium could decline even if the underlying asset price rises quite sharply.

Different trades can be categorized by their degree of conservatism relative to a position in the underlying asset. The major trades are described below.

### (i) The long-call (conservative)

The first strategy to be examined is the long call.

*Profit-loss matrix*

| Exchange rate at expiry | Forward purchase | Long June calls | | |
| --- | --- | --- | --- | --- |
| | | 120 call | 125 call | 130 call |
| 115 | −$1,193.75 | −$703.75 | −$337.50 | −$130.00 |
| 120 | −$568.75 | −$703.75 | −$337.50 | −$130.00 |
| 125 | +$56.25 | −$78.75 | −$337.50 | −$130.00 |
| 130 | +$681.25 | +$546.25 | +$287.50 | −$130.00 |
| 135 | +$1,306.25 | +$1,171.25 | +$912.50 | +$495.00 |

The in-the-money call behaves like a long futures position: however, the maximum loss is constrained to $703.75 for which the price paid is a profit $135 less for rises in the asset price, and a slightly larger loss for small drops in the asset price. The out-of-the money call will lose least in dollar terms if the asset price falls, but will gain least if the asset price rises. The at-the-money call will be the worst performer if the exchange rate remains around current levels, because time value decay will play a large role, and will show middle-range gains and losses for larger price falls or rises. Exhibit 4.4 illustrates the comparison between the different strategies.

The choice of the most suitable trade will depend upon the individual investor. An investor who believes the exchange rate will rise only moderately is unlikely to buy the out-of-the-money 130 call. On the other hand an investor who is expecting a major shift in the exchange rate may regard this option as very favourable in terms of expected percentage return.

This set of profits and losses only applies at expiration. If the exchange rate moves up a couple of cents in the following few days, the price of the 130 option (with a delta of 0.20) is likely to rise by around 0.40 cents, representing a percentage increase of around 40% despite the fact that the option would still be well out-of-the-money. The time-frame of the trader's exchange rate forecast is as important as the forecast itself.

### (ii) The short put (speculative)

A more speculative bullish price expectational trade would be to sell the put options. The profit-loss profiles for alternative short put strategies are shown in Exhibit 4.5. Such strategies are more

## Exhibit 4.4: The long call (conservative)

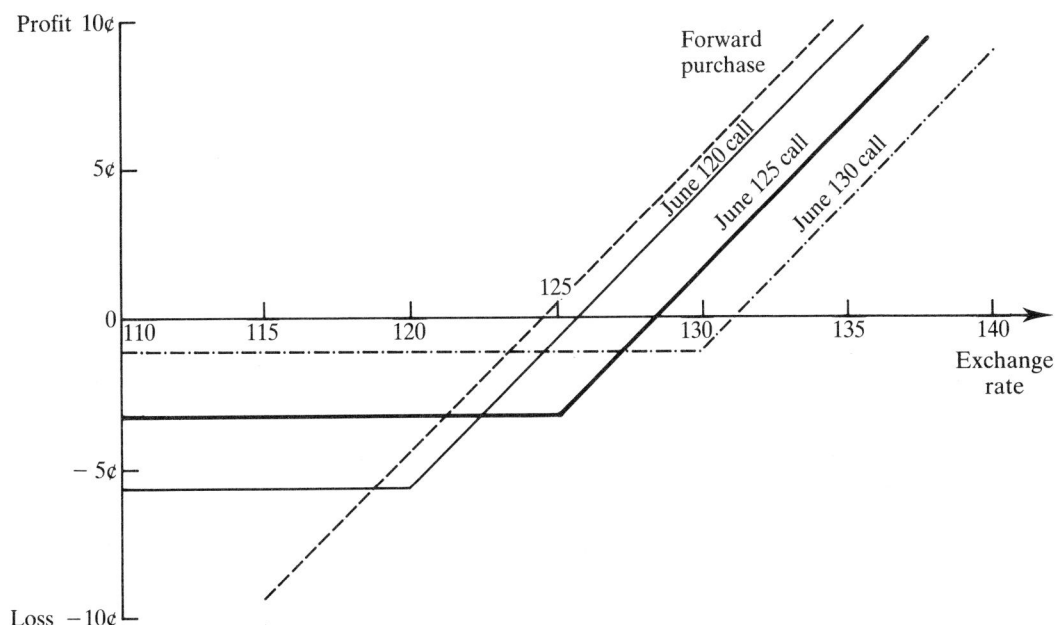

**Exhibit 4.5: The short put (speculative)**

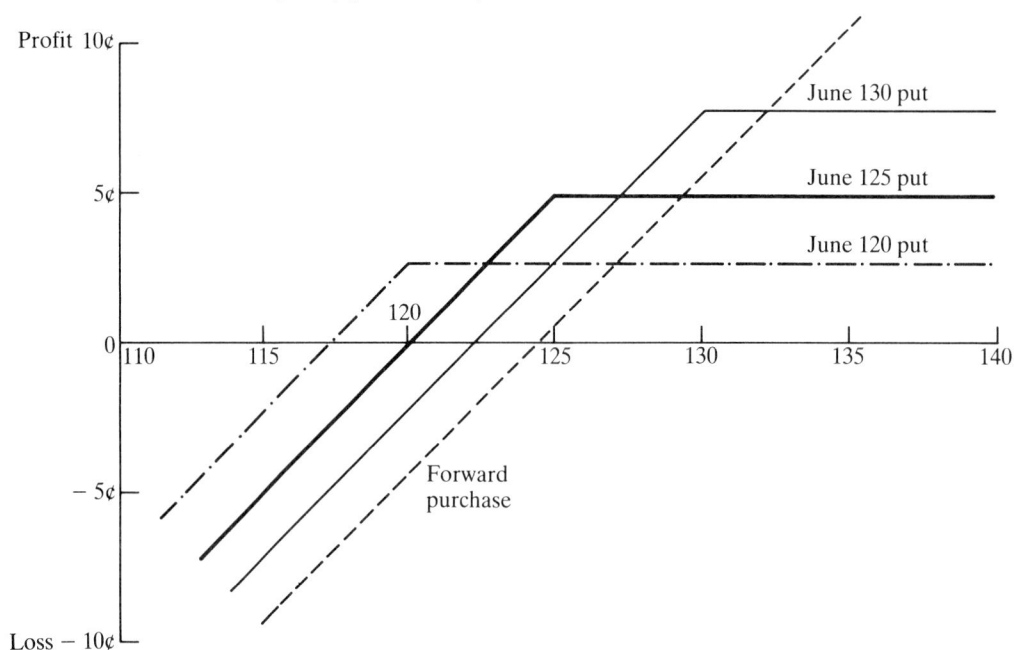

speculative than long call positions since the maximum profit is limited and the losses potentially unlimited, although less than the equivalent forward purchase by the amount of premium income received. The positions show broadly the same characteristics as the long call positions. The sale of an in-the-money put behaves very similarly to a long forward position established, but at a lower price than the current forward rate and with a maximum profit. The at-the-money put makes the maximum profit of any of the strategies if the exchange rate remains around current levels, and mid-range profits and losses if the exchange rate moves more violently. The table below compares the two at-the-money strategies with the forward position and each other.

*Profit-loss matrix*

| Exchange rate at expiration | Forward position | Long 125 call | Short 125 put |
|---|---|---|---|
| 115 | −$1,193.75 | −$337.50 | −$858.75 |
| 120 | −$568.75 | −$337.50 | −$233.75 |
| 125 | +$56.25 | −$337.50 | +$391.25 |
| 130 | +$681.25 | +$287.50 | +$391.25 |
| 135 | +$1,306.25 | +$912.50 | +$391.25 |

The short put position performs better than the long call position for modest movements in the underlying exchange rate and worse for large movements in the exchange rate.

### (iii) The vertical spread purchased (very conservative)

This common option spread involves buying a put or call option with a low exercise price and simultaneously selling a put or call option with a higher exercise price. Such a spread has the effect of limiting the loss if the underlying asset price falls, but also limiting the potential gain if the asset price rises. Any given set of option prices gives rise to a very large number of possible bullish vertical spreads – there are 40 such spreads with the currency options displayed. A small selection of vertical spreads is illustrated below.

|  |  |  |
|---|---|---|
| *Strategy A:* | Buy June 120 call | 5.63¢ |
|  | Sell June 125 call | 2.70¢ |
| *Strategy B:* | Buy June 120 call | 5.63¢ |
|  | Sell June 130 call | 1.04¢ |
| *Strategy C:* | Buy June 125 put | 3.13¢ |
|  | Sell June 130 put | 6.36¢ |

62

## Exhibit 4.6: Vertical spreads

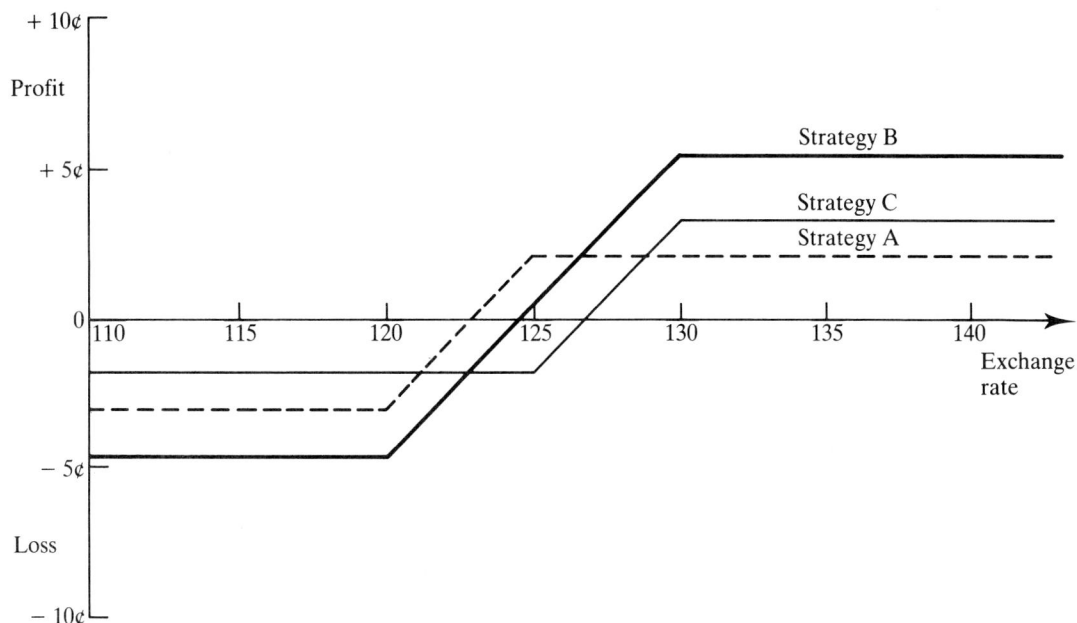

It is useful to compare the profit and loss profile for the long call and put position at 125 with the call 125–130 vertical spread and the put 125–130 vertical spread.

*Profit-loss matrix*

| Exchange rate at expiration | Short 125 put | Long 125 call | Long 125 call Short 130 call | Long 125 put Short 130 put |
|---|---|---|---|---|
| 115 | − $858.75 | − $337.50 | − $207.50 | − $221.25 |
| 120 | − $233.75 | − $337.50 | − $207.50 | − $221.25 |
| 125 | + $391.25 | − $337.50 | − $207.50 | − $221.25 |
| 130 | + $391.25 | + $287.50 | + $417.50 | + $403.75 |
| 135 | + $391.25 | + $912.50 | + $417.50 | + $403.75 |

Two points are immediately apparent. First, the put 125–130 vertical spread gives a uniformly worse profit profile over the entire range of asset prices than the call 125–130 vertical spread. This is not necessarily a sign of an arbitrage opportunity. To obtain the call spread the investor has to pay out the $207.50 at the commencement of the option trade and will be involved in borrowing costs. By contrast the buyer of the put spread will receive a net cash flow of $403.75 at the time of setting up the trade which can be invested to earn additional interest. The second feature is that both vertical spreads outperform the short put strategy throughout the exchange rate range, save for virtually no change in rates, and hence may be preferred by traders who anticipate a modest rise in the exchange rate.

## b. Bearish volatility expectational trades

So far the discussion has dealt with option trades based on expectations of where prices are going, but accepting the current market assumed level of volatility. The other major group of position trades involves the trader in taking a view on market volatility different from that contained in the current set of market prices. The market forecast of volatility over the life of the option is one of the prime determinants of option prices. If, therefore, the trader believes the market forecast of volatility is incorrect, he can put in place trades which will make profits if his forecast is realized. Such trades will have to be designed to insulate the trader from underlying price movements distinct from those induced by changes in volatility.

The major aim of the *bearish volatility expectational trades* (i.e. the trader expects lower price volatility than the market) is to benefit if prices move less than expected. Thus the trader will desire a profit profile that shows gains at or around the current level of the asset price, and losses if the price moves dramatically away from current levels. The trades available vary from conservative to speculative positions.

### (i) The straddle sold (speculative)

The short straddle involves the simultaneous sale of a call option and a put option with the same exercise price and the same maturity. In most circumstances, the straddle trade will be carried out at-the-money. The profit-loss profile for the straddle trade is shown in Exhibit 4.7. This trade is a pure volatility trade – the trader does not have a view on prices. If, for example, a trader believes volatility is going to fall, and at the same time he expects prices to fall, he will be better off selling two call options rather than a call option and a put option.

### (ii) The strangle sold (middle risk)

The short strangle follows the same trading principle as the straddle, but extends the range over which profits will accrue to the trader by selling a put option with a low exercise price and a call option with a higher exercise price, both options having the same maturity. As Exhibit 4.7 illustrates, the strangle trade loses significantly less than the straddle for price movements away from the 125 price.

### (iii) The butterfly spread purchased (conservative)

The butterfly spread purchased is one of the most famous option spreads designed not only to earn profits for the trader if the price remains around current levels, but also to limit the losses if price moves rapidly away from current levels (see Exhibit 4.7). The simple butterfly spread purchased consists of buying a call with a low exercise price, selling two middle exercise price calls and buying a call option with a high exercise price, all options having the same maturity. The profit profile of butterfly spreads often looks attractive to the options trader, but this spread involves four separate option contracts, which could involve high transactions costs, thereby outweighing the potential gains.

## Exhibit 4.7: Comparing the profit profiles: strangle, straddle and butterfly

| Strangle: | Sell June 120 put | 1.16¢ | Straddle: | Sell June 125 call | 2.70¢ |
|---|---|---|---|---|---|
| | Sell June 130 call | 1.04¢ | | Sell June 125 put | 3.13¢ |

| | Butterfly: | Buy June 120 call | 5.63¢ |
|---|---|---|---|
| | | Sell 2 June 125 call | 2.70¢ |
| | | Buy June 130 call | 1.04¢ |

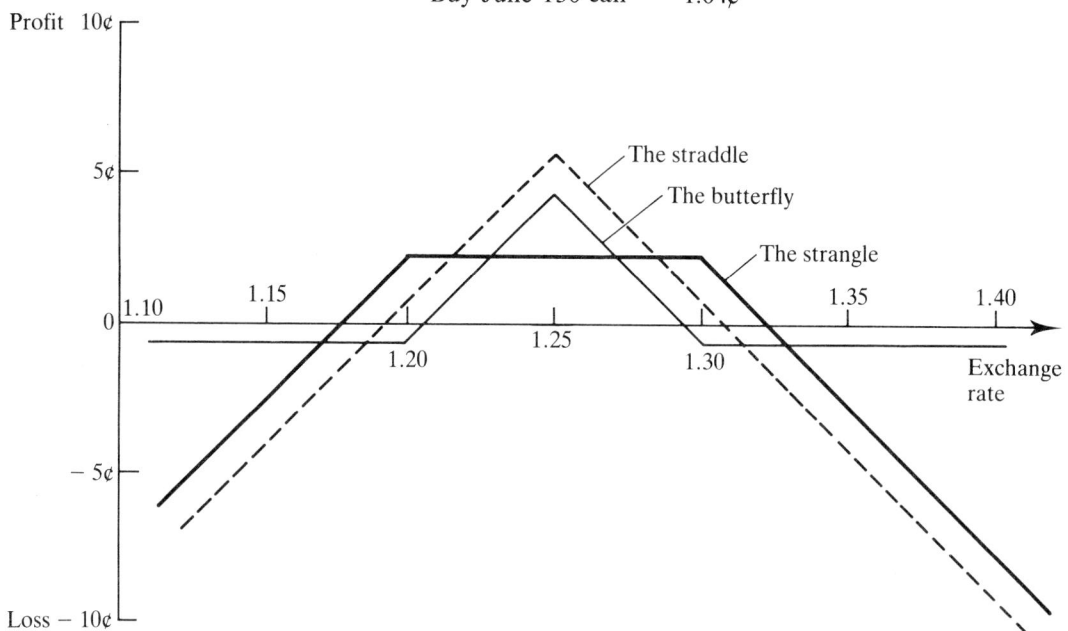

If the trader takes the opposite view, i.e. that price volatility over the life of the option will be greater than currently expected by the market, then he will do the trades in the opposite direction:

*Buy* the *Straddle* (middle risk) –
*Buy* the *Strangle* (conservative) –
*Sell* the *Butterfly* spread (speculative).

## c. Characterizing options positions

Although the major options strategies have been described, the trader may construct even more complex strategies, e.g. what would a position of short 2 120 puts, long 3 125 calls and long 2 130 puts achieve? To generalize the principles of options trading, it is sensible to develop a system for characterizing any options position – an option algebra, to use a grandiose title.

### (i) Option algebra

The task of the trader is to design a profit profile with risk-return characteristics that best fit:

1. the trader's forecast of asset prices and/or asset price volatility;
2. the trader's degree of risk aversion.

The building blocks of these strategies are:

1. forward, futures or cash asset positions;
2. long or short calls with various exercise prices and maturities;
3. long or short puts with various prices and maturities; and
4. delta neutral or ratio strategies.

There are several important features of a profit profile to be noted when devising a method of characterizing options positions. Looking at the profit profile on a graph with the X-axis and the Y-axis denominated in the same units and scale:

1. *Exercise prices* will always create *kinks* in a *profit profile.*
2. *Put* positions are *flat* above the *exercise price*, and *positive (short)* sloped or *negative (long)* sloped *below* the *exercise price.*
3. *Call* positions are *flat* below the *exercise price*, and *positive (long)* sloped or *negative (short)* sloped *above* the *exercise price.*
4. The degree of the *positive* or *negative* slope will depend on the *number* of *positions held.* The slope will always be 45° for a single option.
5. A flat slope is given a value of 0, a positive slope for a single option will be +1, a single option negative slope will be represented as −1.

The simple building blocks of the option trades can be represented in the format shown in Exhibit 4.8.

## Exhibit 4.8: Option building blocks

**a. Asset long (current price S)**

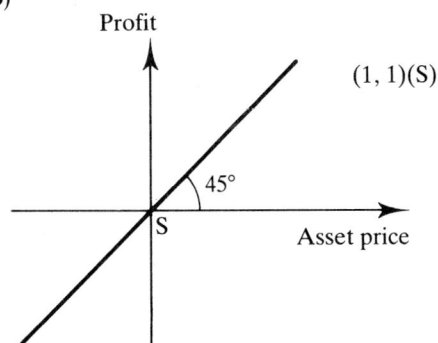

**b. Asset short (current price S)**

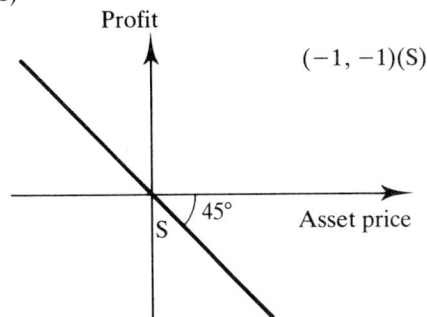

**c. Long call (exercise price E)**

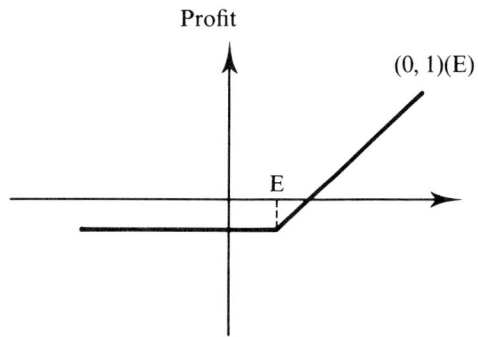

Profit

(0, 1)(E)

E

**d. Short call (exercise price E)**

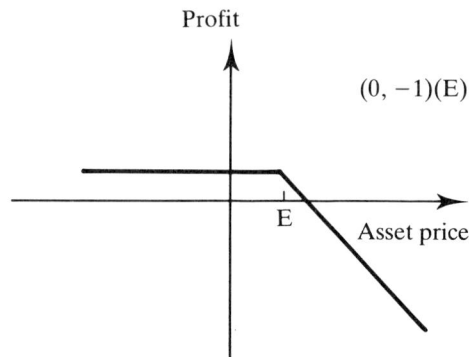

Profit

(0, −1)(E)

E

Asset price

**e. Long put (exercise price E)**

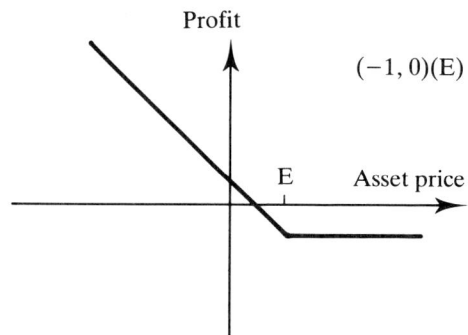

Profit

(−1, 0)(E)

E

Asset price

**f. Short put (exercise price E)**

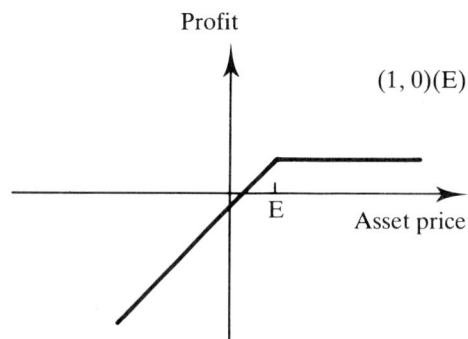

Profit

(1, 0)(E)

E

Asset price

These building block symbols can be combined to produce any options position.

Long (E) call = (0, 1)(E)
+
Short (E) (put) = (1, 0)(E)
=
Long asset = (1, 1)(E)

Thus the combination of a long call with exercise price E and a short put with exercise price E establishes an equivalent asset position established at a price of E (see Exhibit 4.9a).

**Exhibit 4.9a: Long call – short put combination**

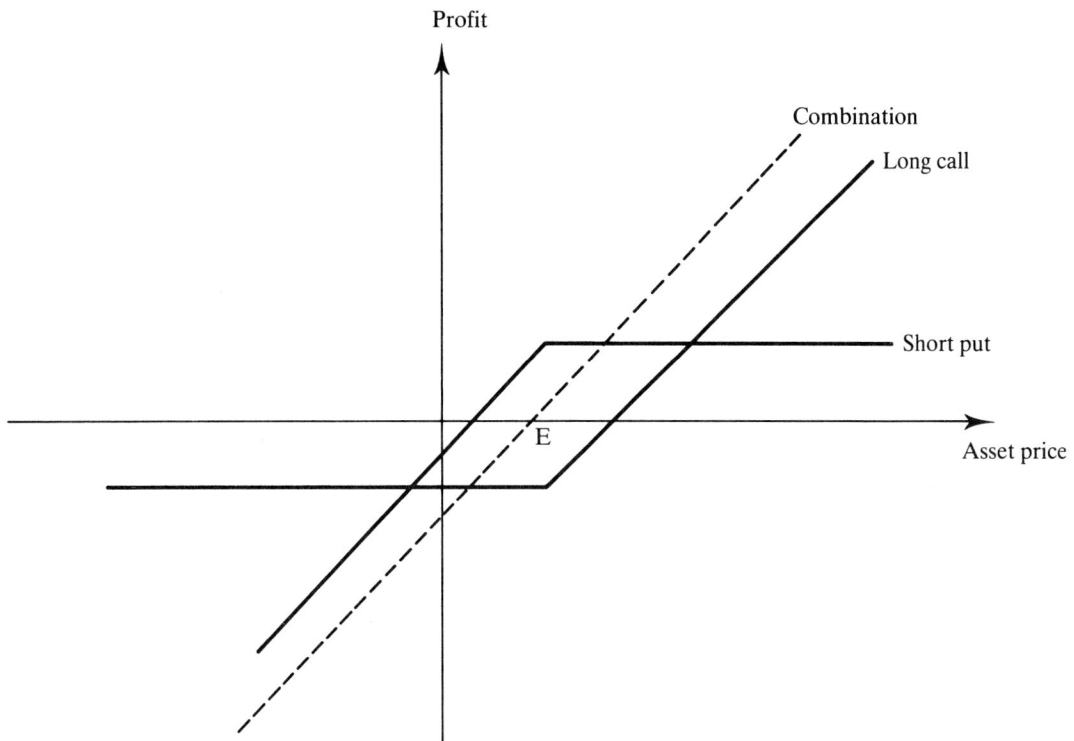

*(ii) Constructing options profiles*

A more complex options profit-loss profile can be constructed from the options described above.

**Exhibit 4.9b: A complex options combination**

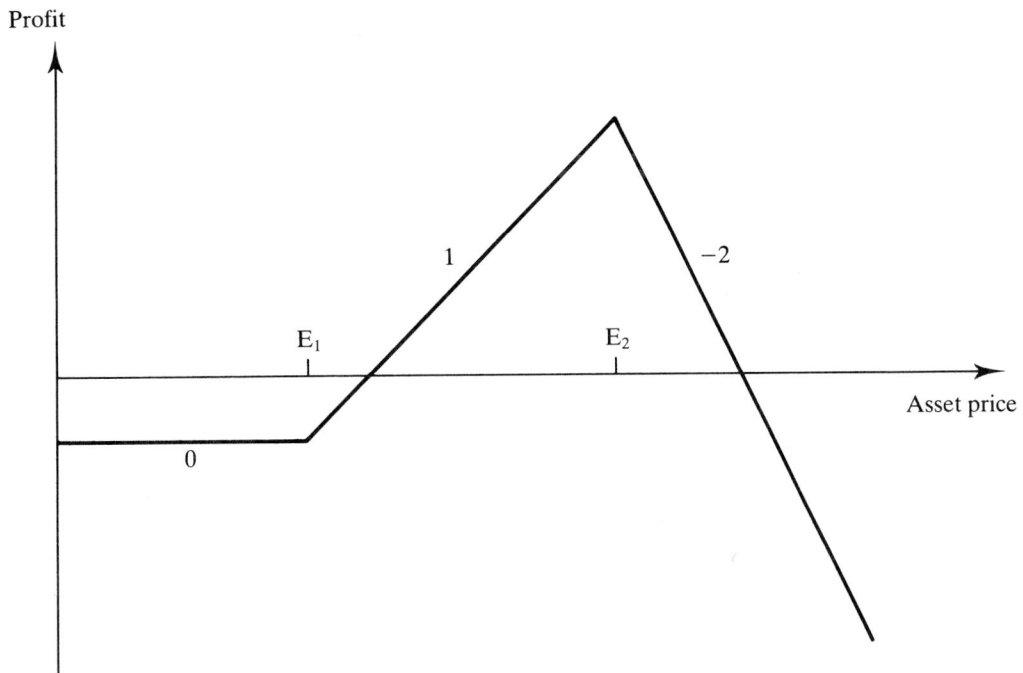

This can be expressed as:

$$(0, 1, -2)(E_1, E_2)$$

The construction is not unique. The profit profile can be constructed in different ways using different options. Below are two simple solutions.

1. *Desired position*   $(0, 1, -2)(E_1, E_2)$

   Long 1 $E_1$ call   $(0, 1, 1)(E_1, E_2)$
   +   +
   Short 3 $E_2$ calls   $(0, 0, -3)(E_1, E_2)$
   =   =
   *Desired position*   $(0, 1, -2)(E_1, E_2)$

2. *Desired position*   $(0, 1, -2)(E_1, E_2)$

   Short 2 $E_2$ calls   $(0, 0, -2)(E_1, E_2)$
   +   +
   Short 1 $E_2$ put   $(1, 1, 0)(E_1, E_2)$
   +   +
   Long 1 $E_1$ put   $(-1, 0, 0)(E_1, E_2)$
   =   =
   *Desired position*   $(0, 1, -2)(E_1, E_2)$

The same position can be constructed in many different and more complex ways.

The following two examples illustrate the desired profiles for the set of currency option premiums discussed earlier.

### Example 1

The trader believes the asset price volatility will be less than the market expectation, and decides to buy a position which has its maximum profit around the current level. However, he is cautious about the trade and decides to limit the losses for price changes above or below the current exchange rate. In other words, he would like a profit profile that looks like the one in Exhibit 4.9c.

### Exhibit 4.9c: A butterfly spread

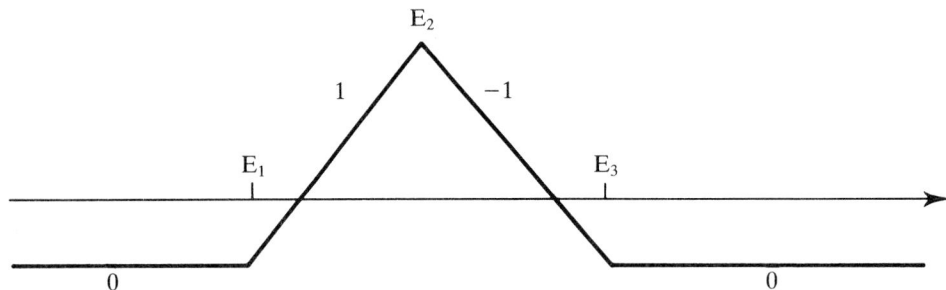

In symbolic notation this could be written

$$(0, 1, -1, 0)(E_1, E_2, E_3)$$

This is simply a description of the butterfly spread discussed earlier.

   *Desired position*   $(0, 1, -1, 0)(E_1, E_2, E_3)$
   Long 1 $E_1$ call   $(0, 1, 1, 1)(E_1, E_2, E_3)$
   +   +
   Short 2 $E_2$ calls   $(0, 0, -2, -2)(E_1, E_2, E_3)$
   =   =
   Interim position   $(0, 1, -1, -1)(E_1, E_2, E_3)$

This looks like the position the trader wanted with the exception of the unwanted negative slope above $E_3$. This can be eliminated by buying a $E_3$ call.

   Interim position   $(0, 1, -1, -1)(E_1, E_2, E_3)$
   +   +
   Long 1 $E_2$ call   $(0, 0, 0, 1)(E_1, E_2, E_3)$
   =   =
   *Desired position*   $(0, 1, -1, 0)(E_1, E_2, E_3)$

The desired position has now been achieved. Using the 120, 125 and 130 calls, this is the

$$120 - 125 - 130 \text{ butterfly}$$

**Example 2**

Suppose an investor believes the exchange rate will be $1.2000 or $1.3000 at the end of June. He will want a position that has maximum profits at $1.2000 or $1.3000 and losses elsewhere, as shown in Exhibit 4.9d.

In symbolic notation:

| | |
|---|---|
| *Desired position* | $(1, -1, 1, -1)(120, 125, 130)$ |
| Sell 1 120 put | $(1, 0, 0, 0)(120, 125, 130)$ |
| + | + |
| Sell 1 130 call | $(0, 0, 0, -1)(120, 125, 130)$ |
| = | = |
| Interim position | $(1, 0, 0, -1)(120, 125, 130)$ |
| + | + |
| Buy 1 125 put | $(-1, -1, 0, 0)(120, 125, 130)$ |
| + | + |
| Buy 1 125 call | $(0, 0, 1, 1)(120, 125, 130)$ |
| = | = |
| Interim position | $(0, -1, 1, 0)(120, 125, 130)$ |
| + | + |
| Sell 1 120 put | $(1, 0, 0, 0)(120, 125, 130)$ |
| + | + |
| Sell 1 130 call | $(0, 0, 0, -1)(120, 125, 130)$ |
| = | = |
| *Desired position* | $(1, -1, 1, -1)(120, 125, 130)$ |

Option position:  Short 2 120 puts
Short 2 130 calls
Long 1 125 put
Long 1 125 call

## Exhibit 4.9d: A twin-peaked option combination

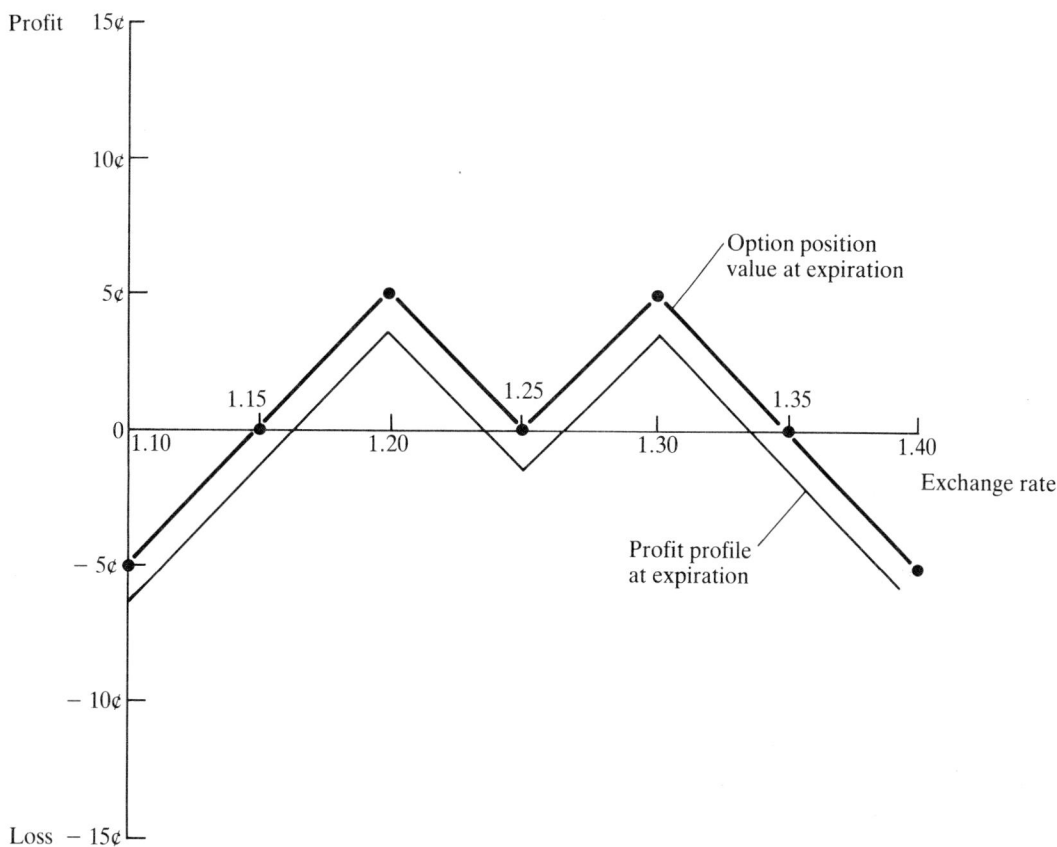

69

There is another possible way of creating the same position:

$$\textit{Desired position} \quad (1, -1, 1, -1)(120, 125, 130)$$

Sell 1 120 put     $(1, 0, 0, 0)(120, 125, 130)$

$+$          $+$

Sell 1 120 call     $(0, -1, -1, -1)(120, 125, 130)$

$=$          $=$

Interim position     $(1, -1, -1, -1)(120, 125, 130)$

$+$          $+$

Buy 2 125 calls     $(0, 0, 2, 2)(120, 125, 130)$

$+$          $+$

Sell 2 130 calls     $(0, 0, 0, -2)(120, 125, 130)$

$=$          $=$

$\textit{Desired position} \quad (1, -1, 1, -1)(120, 125, 130)$

Options position:     Short 1 120 put
                     Short 1 120 call
                     Long 2 125 calls
                     Short 2 130 calls

These symbolic notations therefore allow the trader to determine an options position which exactly matches the desired risk-return profile appropriate for the trader's set of expectations.

---

**Trading points**

1. **The variety of options combinations allows the trader to construct positions with profit profiles closely tailored to the trader's expectations.**
2. **Any specific profit profile can be achieved in a number of different ways. The trader should examine which is the lowest cost method.**
3. **Each combination has its own profit profile. The risk-return for any trade needs to be carefully assessed taking into account transactions costs and margin requirements.**

---

### (iii) Calendar spreads

Before leaving straight option trading, horizontal or calendar spreads should be discussed. So far the option spreads analysed have involved combinations of different exercise price options, whether puts or calls. Combinations of options with different maturities can also be constructed. These fall into two basic types.

*Horizontal spreads*: The purchase or sale of a short maturity option and the sale or purchase of a long maturity option both at the same exercise price.

*Diagonal spreads*: The purchase or sale of a short maturity option at one exercise price and the sale or purchase of a long maturity option at a different exercise price.

In each case the aim is to benefit from the differential effect of time decay on short and long maturity options. Once again the set of currency option premiums described earlier is adopted. Exhibit 4.10 shows June profits for a vertical bull spread, a June-September horizontal spread at an exercise price of 125, and a June-September diagonal spread at exercise prices of 120 and 125. The simple horizontal spread is a classic volatility trade, with a profit-loss profile like a straddle position, though with limited losses. The diagonal spread resembles a vertical bull spread save that profits are generally lower, though it makes profits over a wider range and loses money significantly less rapidly than a vertical spread for small to medium exchange rate declines. These spreads provide a further range of possibilities for the professional spread trader.

An options trader should also be aware of how important it is to have a position that is responsive to only the variable which the trader is forecasting. A trade concerned only with a bullish price forecast should be neutral in terms of volatility. A trade concerned only with a

**Exhibit 4.10: Spread profits in June**

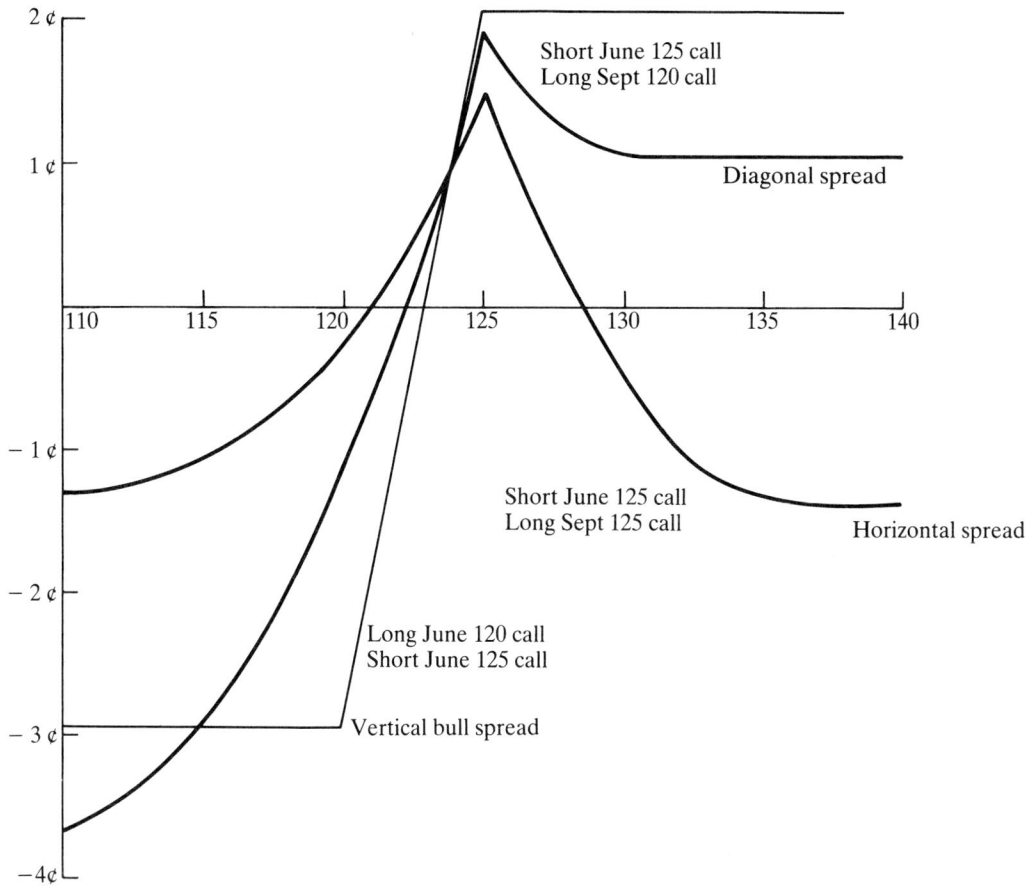

bullish volatility forecast should be neutral in terms of the underlying asset price level. This can be analysed further by considering again the set of currency option premia we have been working with, but now showing the deltas, gammas, epsilons and thetas of the different options (see the table below). All calculations are based on an implied volatility initially of 12%.

*June options*

Spot rate = $1.2485   Forward rate = $1.2455

| Exercise price | Premium | Delta* | Gamma* | Epsilon* | Theta* | Exercise price | Premium | Delta* | Gamma* | Epsilon* | Theta* |
|---|---|---|---|---|---|---|---|---|---|---|---|
| 115 | 9.85 | 0.93 | 0.02 | 0.09 | 0.01 | 115 | 0.29 | −0.09 | 0.02 | 0.21 | 0.01 |
| 120 | 5.63 | 0.74 | 0.04 | 0.21 | 0.01 | 120 | 1.16 | −0.26 | 0.04 | 0.21 | 0.01 |
| 125 | 2.70 | 0.49 | 0.05 | 0.25 | 0.02 | 125 | 3.13 | −0.51 | 0.05 | 0.25 | 0.02 |
| 130 | 1.04 | 0.25 | 0.04 | 0.20 | 0.01 | 130 | 6.36 | −0.75 | 0.04 | 0.20 | 0.01 |
| 135 | 0.31 | 0.10 | 0.02 | 0.11 | 0.01 | 135 | 10.53 | −0.90 | 0.02 | 0.11 | 0.01 |

\* Delta – slope of option price movement over asset price movement.
 Gamma – rate of change of slope.
 Epsilon – sensitivity to volatility changes.
 Theta – sensitivity to time.

### (iv) *Volatility trades*

The volatility trader is forecasting volatility to rise. He considers two alternatives: buying a 125 straddle: or buying a 120–125 strangle.

125 straddle   Buy one 125 call   Delta =   0.49
          Buy one 125 put   Delta = −0.51
               Net delta = −0.02

Although this trade is almost delta neutral, a small upwards movement in the underlying asset price is expected to cause a modest loss to the position. However, the gamma of the position is interesting. The 125 call and the 125 put both have a gamma of 0.05. This implies that a 1 cent upward movement in the forward rate will increase the delta of the 125 call option to 0.54 and decrease the delta of the put option to 0.46. The net delta of the position will then be +0.08 and the position will no longer be even approximately price neutral.

---

**Volatility option trades need to be rebalanced regularly to maintain their neutrality with respect to price.**

---

120–125 strangle    Buy one 120 put    Delta = −0.26
               Buy one 125 call    Delta =    0.49
                          Net delta =    0.23

This trade is not even remotely price neutral: the amount of each option will need to be ratioed to get delta neutrality.

$$\text{Ratio of 120 puts to 125 calls} = \frac{0.49}{0.26} = 1.88$$

Buy 19 120 puts    Delta = −4.94
Sell 10 125 calls    Delta =    4.90
              Net delta = −0.04

The position will need rebalancing if the underlying asset price changes significantly.

### (v) Price trades

Ensuring volatility neutrality with price trades is more difficult, since any simple option position will be responsive to both volatility changes and price changes. The only alternatives are a simple position in the cash, futures or forward markets, or a price trade which involves a combination of options which can be tailored to produce approximate volatility neutrality. The major trades of this type are the *vertical spreads* discussed earlier (see p. 62).

(see p. 62)

Bullish vertical spread    Buy June 120 call    Epsilon =    0.21
                     Sell June 125 call    Epsilon = −0.25
                            Net epsilon = −0.04

Although the trade does not have a profit-loss profile particularly sensitive to volatility, nonetheless if volatility rises, the position will show losses even if the underlying price does not alter. This can be handled by ratioing the vertical spread.

$$\text{June 120 call} - \text{June 125 call ratio} = \frac{0.25}{0.21} = 1.19$$

Buy 119 June 120 calls    Epsilon =    24.99
Sell 100 June 125 calls    Epsilon =    25.00
                   Net epsilon = −0.01

In practice in this case the trader is not likely to be concerned about such a minor lack of volatility. The important point is that the only price trades that can be approximately volatility neutral are spread trades.

---

**If a trader wishes to trade price forecasts while remaining volatility neutral, he will use vertical option spreads.**

---

### (vi) Option theta

This chapter has been looking at the reaction of option premiums to underlying asset price changes and volatility. The final effect the trader must consider is that of *theta*, the sensitivity of the option premium to the passage of time.

To appreciate the impact of time decay and the period within which price changes occur on the profitability of option trades, the graphs in Exhibit 4.11 examine the profit behaviour of a representative set of stock option trades – with General Motors as the underlying stock – for

# Exhibit 4.11: General Motors option profit profiles

### Stock price $46\frac{3}{4}$

| Strike price | Calls September | Calls December | Puts September | Puts December |
|---|---|---|---|---|
| 40 | $7\frac{1}{2}$ | $8\frac{1}{4}$ | $\frac{1}{2}$ | $1\frac{1}{8}$ |
| 45 | $3\frac{3}{4}$ | 5 | $1\frac{5}{8}$ | $2\frac{1}{2}$ |
| 50 | $1\frac{1}{8}$ | $2\frac{5}{16}$ | $4\frac{1}{2}$ | $5\frac{3}{8}$ |

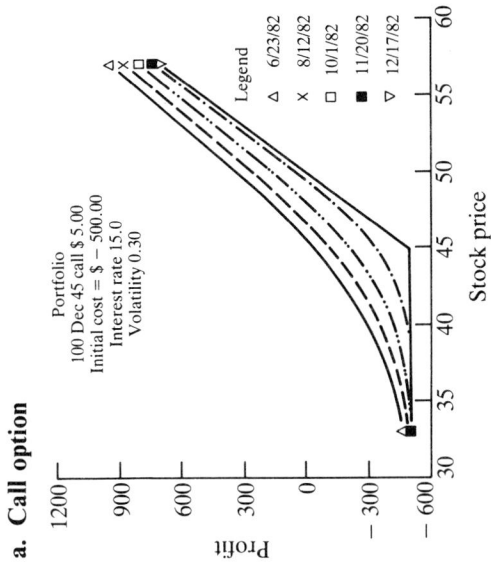

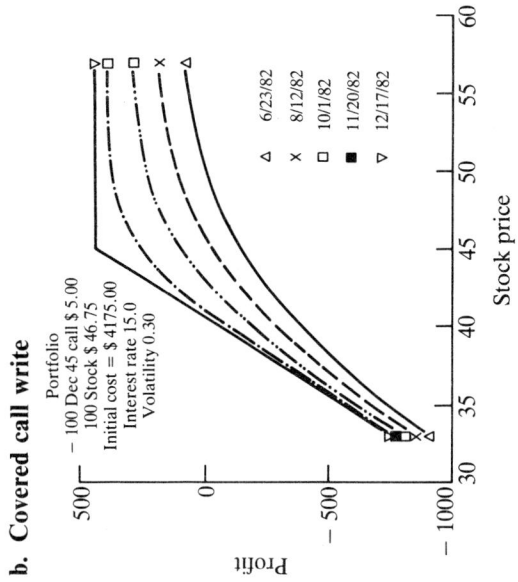

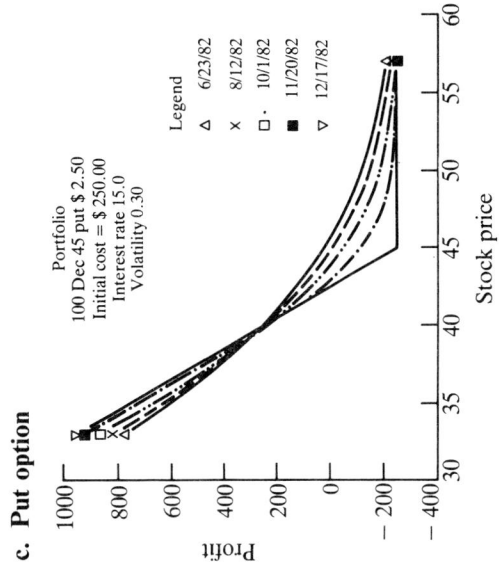

a. Call option

b. Covered call write

c. Put option

73

# Exhibit 4.11: General Motors option profit profiles (*cont.*)

## d. Straddle

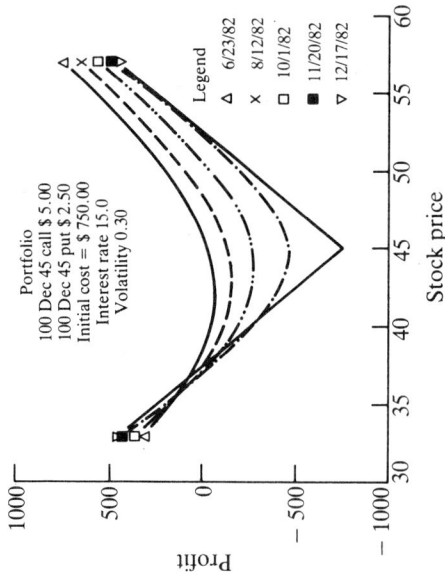

Portfolio
100 Dec 45 call $ 5.00
100 Dec 45 put $ 2.50
Initial cost = $ 750.00
Interest rate 15.0
Volatility 0.30

Legend
△ 6/23/82
✕ 8/12/82
□ 10/1/82
■ 11/20/82
▽ 12/17/82

Profit

Stock price

## e. Unbalanced short straddles

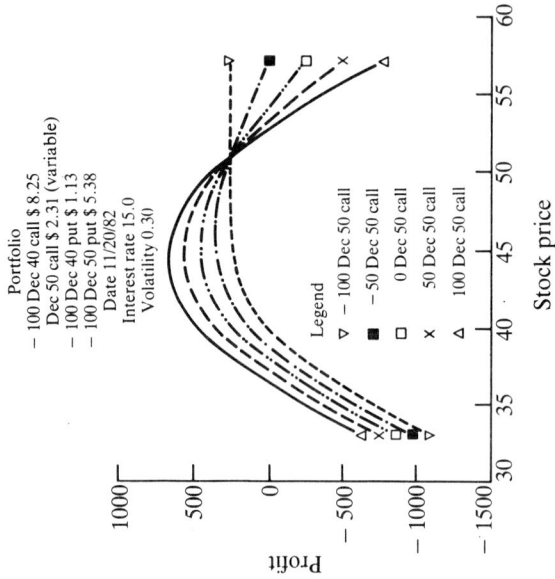

Portfolio
100 Dec 40 call $ 8.25
Dec 50 call $ 2.31 (variable)
− 100 Dec 40 put $ 1.13
− 100 Dec 50 put $ 5.38
Date 11/20/82
Interest rate 15.0
Volatility 0.30

Legend
▽ − 100 Dec 50 call
■ − 50 Dec 50 call
□ 0 Dec 50 call
✕ 50 Dec 50 call
△ 100 Dec 50 call

Profit

Stock price

## f. Short strangles

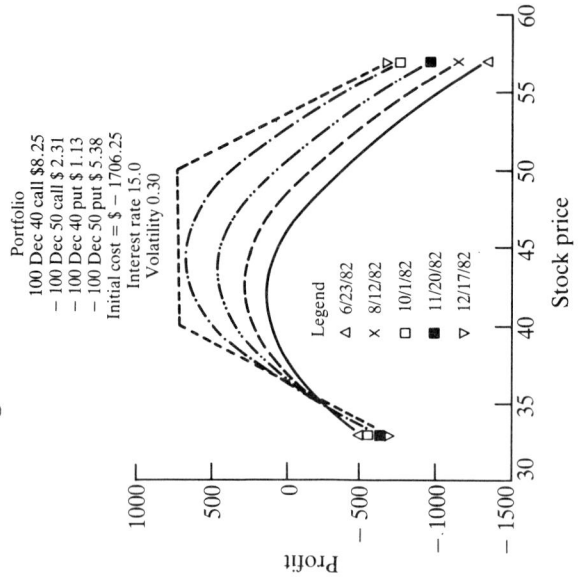

Portfolio
100 Dec 40 call $8.25
− 100 Dec 50 call $ 2.31
− 100 Dec 40 put $ 1.13
− 100 Dec 50 put $ 5.38
Initial cost = $ − 1706.25
Interest rate 15.0
Volatility 0.30

Legend
△ 6/23/82
✕ 8/12/82
□ 10/1/82
■ 11/20/82
▽ 12/17/82

Profit

Stock price

## g. Butterfly spread

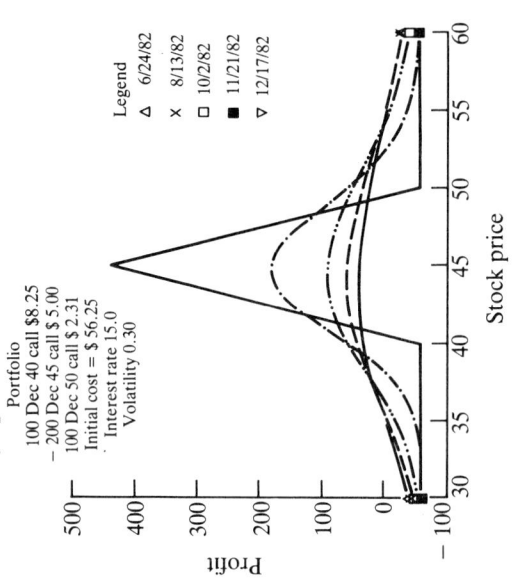

Portfolio
100 Dec 40 call $8.25
− 200 Dec 45 call $ 5.00
100 Dec 50 call $ 2.31
Initial cost = $ 56.25
Interest rate 15.0
Volatility 0.30

Legend
△ 6/24/82
✕ 8/13/82
□ 10/2/82
■ 11/21/82
▽ 12/17/82

Profit

Stock price

74

# Exhibit 4.11: General Motors option profit profiles (cont.)

## h. Unbalanced butterfly spread

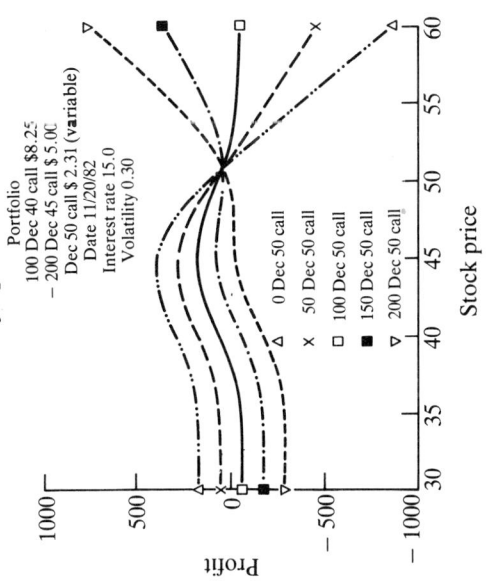

Portfolio
100 Dec 40 call $8.25
− 200 Dec 45 call $ 5.00
Dec 50 call $ 2.31 (variable)
Date 11/20/82
Interest rate 15.0
Volatility 0.30

△   0 Dec 50 call
×   50 Dec 50 call
□   100 Dec 50 call
■   150 Dec 50 call
▽   200 Dec 50 call

## i. Unbalanced butterfly spread

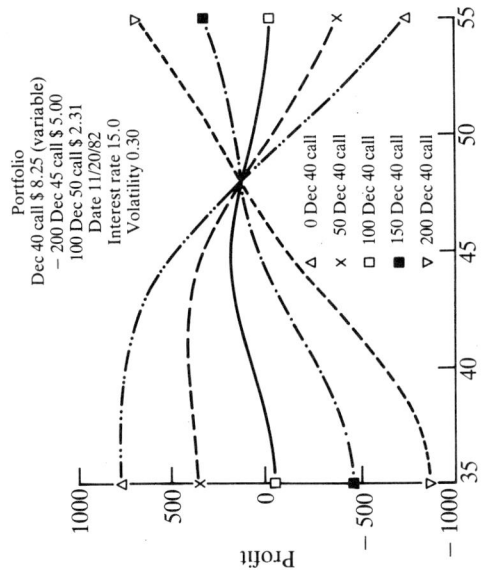

Portfolio
Dec 40 call $ 8.25 (variable)
− 200 Dec 45 call $ 5.00
100 Dec 50 call $ 2.31
Date 11/20/82
Interest rate 15.0
Volatility 0.30

△   0 Dec 40 call
×   50 Dec 40 call
□   100 Dec 40 call
■   150 Dec 40 call
▽   200 Dec 40 call

## j. Flattened butterfly

Portfolio
100 Dec 40 call $8.25
Dec 45 call $ 5.00 (variable)
100 Dec 50 call $ 2.31
Date 1 /20/82
Interest rate 15.0
Volatility 0.30

Legend
△  − 300 Dec 45 call
×  − 250 Dec 45 call
□  − 200 Dec 45 call
■  − 150 Dec 45 call
▽  − 100 Dec 45 call

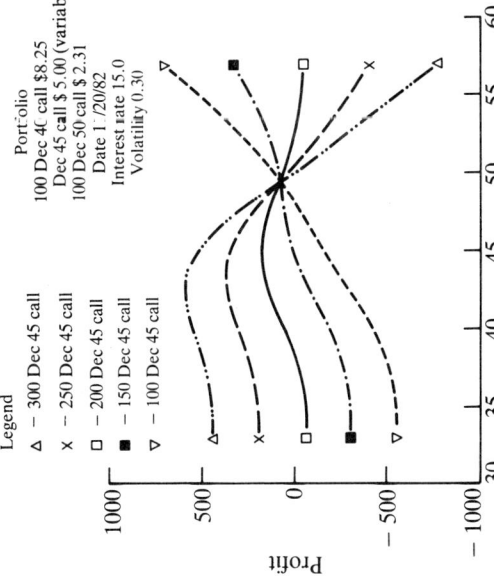

## k. Bullish price spread

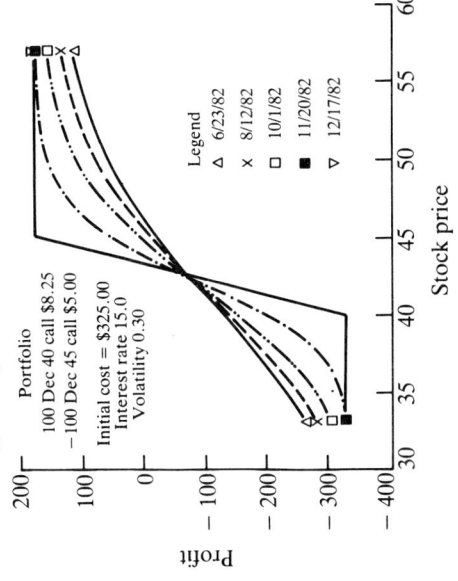

Portfolio
100 Dec 40 call $8.25
−100 Dec 45 call $5.00
Initial cost = $325.00
Interest rate 15.0
Volatility 0.30

Legend
△   6/23/82
×   8/12/82
□   10/1/82
■   11/20/82
▽   12/17/82

75

**Exhibit 4.11: General Motors option profit profiles** (*cont.*)

## m. Time spread

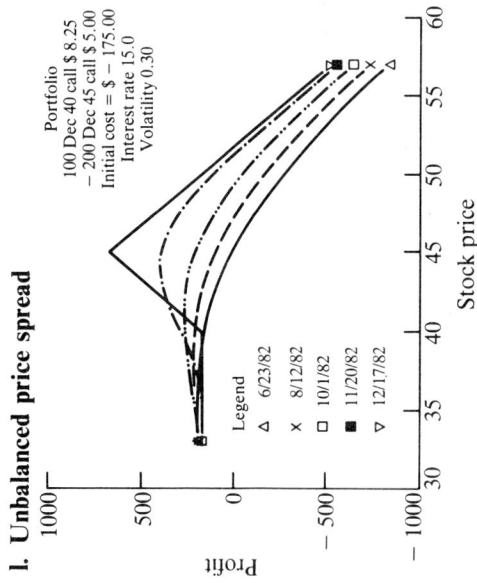

Portfolio
− 100 Sept 45 call $ 3.75
100 Dec 45 call $ 5.00
Initial cost = $ 125.00
Interest rate 15.0
Volatility 0.30

Legend
△  6/23/82
×  7/15/82
□  8/6/82
■  8/28/82
▽  9/17/82

## o. Short option portfolio

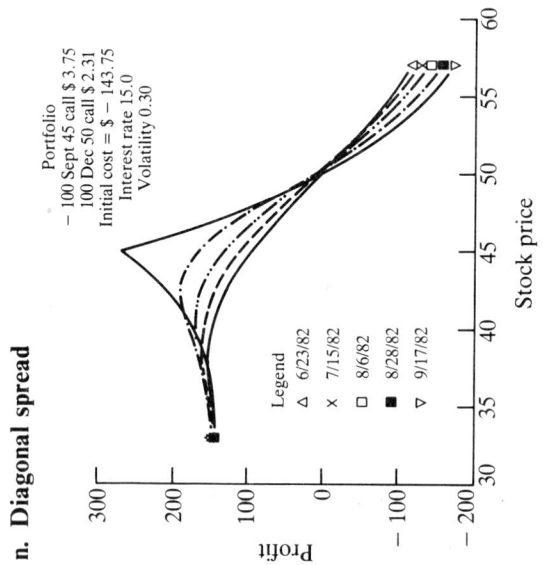

Portfolio
−100 Dec 40 call $8.25
−100 Dec 40 put $1.13
−100 Dec 50 put $5.38
Initial cost = $ −1475.00
Interest rate 15.0
Volatility 0.30

Legend
△  6/23/82
×  8/12/82
□  10/1/82
■  11/20/82
▽  12/17/82

## l. Unbalanced price spread

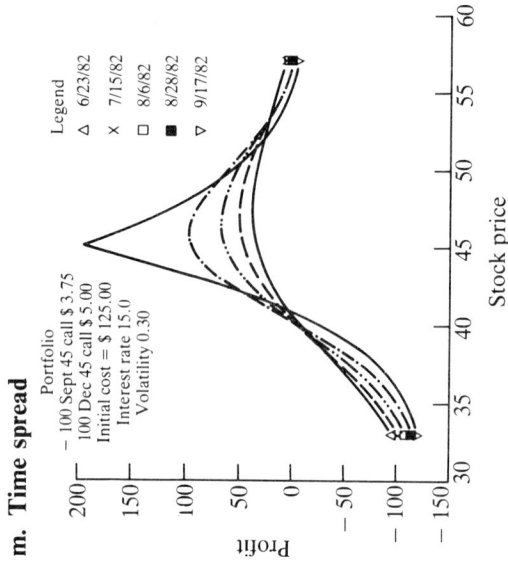

Portfolio
100 Dec 40 call $ 8.25
− 200 Dec 45 call $ 5.00
Initial cost = $ − 175.00
Interest rate 15.0
Volatility 0.30

Legend
△  6/23/82
×  8/12/82
□  10/1/82
■  11/20/82
▽  12/17/82

## n. Diagonal spread

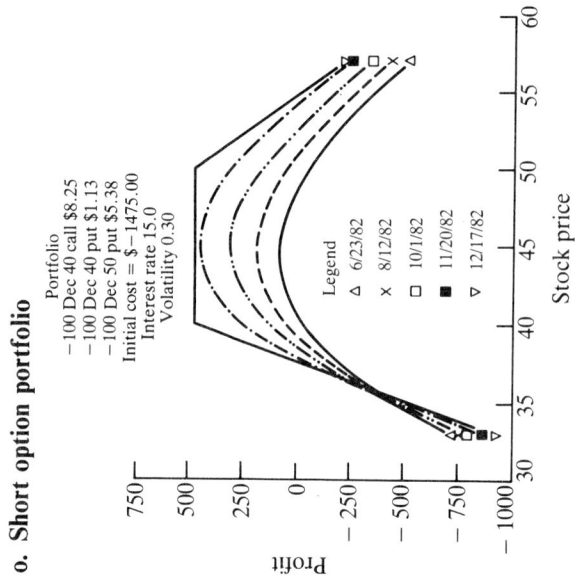

Portfolio
− 100 Sept 45 call $ 3.75
100 Dec 50 call $ 2.31
Initial cost = $ − 143.75
Interest rate 15.0
Volatility 0.30

Legend
△  6/23/82
×  7/15/82
□  8/6/82
■  8/28/82
▽  9/17/82

different time horizons up to expiration. Many of the trades show substantially different profit profiles before maturity compared with the profit at expiration. A trader should be aware of the impact of time to expiration on the potential profitability of his position.[1] Moreover, the profit profiles would look different again if the volatility of the option were allowed to alter in the short-term. This can be illustrated by considering buying a Eurodollar straddle at 90.50 with 70 days to expiration and volatility 2.25% and examining the position five days later if the price has remained static but volatility has changed.

Day 0   Volatility = 2.25%  Eurodollar futures price = 90.25
         June 90.50 call price = 0.25
         June 90.50 put price = 0.50
         Buy the June 90.50 straddle

Alternative 1  Volatility = 2.50%  Eurodollar futures price = 90.25
         June 90.50 call price = 0.27
         June 90.50 put price = 0.52
       Net profit = 4bp × \$25 = \$100.00

Alternative 2  Volatility = 2.00%  Eurodollar futures price = 90.25
         June 90.50 call price = 0.20
         June 90.50 put price = 0.45
       Net loss = 10bp × \$25 = \$250.00

The trader must remember that the interim profit to an option trading position is a complex function of time, movements in asset prices and shifts in volatility. The option trader should therefore carefully assess whether the particular trade that he is putting on is suitable for his forecasts of both price and volatility, and will not be too sensitive to the reduction in the maturity of the option over time. Exhibit 4.12 summarizes the behaviour of common options trades as underlying variables change, and should prove a useful summary for the options trader.

## Exhibit 4.12: Characteristics of option strategies

| Strategy | Price bias | Volatility bias | Profit potential | Loss potential | Time decay |
|---|---|---|---|---|---|
| Long call | Bullish | Bullish | Unlimited | Limited | Hurts |
| Short call | Bearish | Bearish | Limited | Unlimited | Helps |
| Long put | Bearish | Bullish | Unlimited | Limited | Hurts |
| Short put | Bullish | Bearish | Limited | Unlimited | Helps |
| Bull price spread | Bullish | Neutral | Limited | Limited | Mixed |
| Bear price spread | Bearish | Neutral | Limited | Limited | Mixed |
| Long butterfly | Neutral | Bearish | Limited | Limited | Helps |
| Short butterfly | Neutral | Bullish | Limited | Limited | Hurts |
| Long condor | Neutral | Bearish | Limited | Limited | Helps |
| Short condor | Neutral | Bullish | Limited | Limited | Hurts |
| Long straddle | Neutral | Bullish | Unlimited | Limited | Hurts |
| Short straddle | Neutral | Bearish | Limited | Unlimited | Helps |
| Long strangle | Neutral | Bullish | Unlimited | Limited | Hurts |
| Short strangle | Neutral | Bearish | Limited | Unlimited | Helps |
| Call ratio spread | Neutral to bullish | Bearish | Limited | Unlimited | Helps |
| Call ratio backspread | Neutral to bullish | Bullish | Unlimited price up Limited price down | Limited | Mixed |
| Put ratio backspread | Neutral to bearish | Bullish | Unlimited price down Limited price up | Limited | Mixed |

Source: Table courtesy of Chronometrics Inc and the Chicago Mercantile Exchange.

---

[1] I am grateful to my colleague at New York University, Professor Steve Figlewski, for providing me with these General Motors option profit profiles.

Exhibit 4.13 presents suggestions for the options positions which will show the maximum profit for any combination of price and volatility expectation relative to the original capital employed. The influence of time decay and the degree of risk aversion of the trader are ignored here, though they can easily be taken into account by reviewing the previous table. As always in these matters, the suggested trades should have a health warning attached – all trades are carried out at the trader's own risk. It should also be remembered that these are short-term trades; very different strategies would be adopted if it was intended to hold positions through to expiration on a regular basis.

## Exhibit 4.13: Possible option trading strategies

(Maximum return as percentage of capital employed)

| Price level forecast \ Price volatility forecast | Volatility to rise | Volatility to remain stable | Volatility to fall | Volatility outlook unknown |
|---|---|---|---|---|
| Price to rise sharply | *Buy* short maturity out-of-the-money *calls* | *Buy* short maturity out-of-the-money *calls* | *Sell* short maturity out-of-the-money *puts* | *Buy* epsilon neutral *vertical spreads* with both legs out-of-the-money |
| Price to rise modestly | *Buy* short maturity out-of-the-money *calls* | *Buy* short maturity out-of-the-money *calls* | *Sell* short maturity out-of-the-money *puts* | *Buy* epsilon neutral *vertical spreads* with the near leg at-the-money |
| Price to remain stable | *Buy* short maturity out-of-the-money *puts* or *calls* | *Sell* short maturity at-the-money *puts* or *calls* | *Sell* short maturity out-of-the-money *puts* or *calls* | Do not trade |
| Price to decline modestly | *Buy* short maturity out-of-the-money *puts* | *Buy* short maturity out-of-the-money *puts* | *Sell* short maturity out-of-the-money *calls* | *Sell* epsilon neutral *vertical spreads* with the far leg at-the-money |
| Price to decline sharply | *Buy* short maturity out-of-the-money *puts* | *Buy* short maturity out-of-the-money *puts* | *Sell* short maturity out-of-the-money *calls* | *Sell* epsilon neutral *vertical spreads* with the far leg at-the-money |
| Price outlook unknown | *Buy* delta neutral short maturity *straddles* or *strangles* at-the-money | Do not trade | *Sell* delta neutral short maturity *straddles* or *strangles* at-the-money | Do not trade |

## 3. Valuation trading

This popular type of trading, which might be termed pseudo-arbitrage, is based on the use of the option valuation models discussed earlier. The aim is to profit from evidence of misvaluation of options indicated by the model, while insulating the overall position from movements in the underlying asset price. There are two basic approaches.

### a. Absolute volatility estimation

Here the trader will establish his best prediction of the volatility of the underlying asset price over the maturity of the options being examined.[2] By plugging this volatility estimate into an option valuation, mispriced options can be identified. The trader will then:

1. buy options where model prices are greater than market prices;
2. sell options where model prices are less than market prices.

To avoid exposure to underlying asset price movements, the options position needs to be hedged either with an asset position, cash or futures, or an opposite options position. However, hedging with cash or futures leaves the hedger more exposed to the risk that the response of the options position will not be matched exactly to that of the hedging position as asset prices and volatilities change. Other things being equal, it is generally better to hedge options positions with other

[2] The question of volatility estimation has been discussed previously in Chapter 3.

options positions when valuation trading. When constructing the hedge portfolio, which will naturally involve the use of the option deltas to design the hedge, the trader will also need to decide whether to adopt deltas consistent with his volatility predictions or those consistent with the implied volatilities embedded in the existing set of market prices. In hedging options with options, it is also useful to keep the responsiveness of the long and short position deltas to the underlying asset price and its volatility as nearly equal as possible. These hedge portfolios will need to be regularly rebalanced to keep the position almost riskless through time.

## b. Relative volatility estimation

Rather than attempting to trade on the basis of absolute volatility estimates, which suffer from all the problems of volatility estimation discussed earlier, most valuation trading prefers to rely on the estimation of implied volatility from option market prices. The procedure can be outlined very simply:

1. Use the option valuation model to estimate the implied volatility for each option.
2. Combine the implied volatilities to produce the best composite volatility measure.
3. Estimate fair prices for the options of a specific maturity using the composite volatility estimate.
4. Compare fair prices and actual market prices to identify relatively undervalued and overvalued options.
5. Construct hedged portfolios by buying undervalued and selling overvalued options in proportions which are as much as possible neutral in terms of delta, gamma, epsilon and theta.
6. Monitor movement in option prices and the relationship of fair prices and market prices, rebalancing when necessary to preserve the riskless character of the hedge portfolio.
7. Liquidate position and take profits when fair prices and market prices are deemed to have moved back sufficiently closely in line.

A detailed case study of a valuation trade is now analysed,[3] explaining fully the basics of valuation trading.

## c. Valuation trade case study

The trader observes the following set of LIFFE June Eurodollar *call* option prices; the options have 70 days to go to expiration.

| June futures price = 90.25 | Strike price | Premium |
|---|---|---|
| | 89.00 | 1.30 |
| | 89.50 | 0.88 |
| | 90.00 | 0.46 |
| | 90.50 | 0.27 |
| | 91.00 | 0.11 |
| | 91.50 | 0.03 |

*Step 1*

The trader estimates the implied volatilities.

| Strike price | Premium | Implied volatility | Composite weighting |
|---|---|---|---|
| 89.00 | 1.30 | 2.52% | 5 |
| 89.50 | 0.88 | 2.51% | 14 |
| 90.00 | 0.46 | 2.02% | 40 |
| 90.50 | 0.27 | 2.40% | 24 |
| 91.00 | 0.11 | 2.32% | 13 |
| 91.50 | 0.03 | 2.18% | 4 |
| Composite | | 2.25% | 100 |

It is clear that certain options, particularly the 89.00 and the 89.50, look relatively overvalued, and the 90.00 looks relatively undervalued.

---

[3] The particular valuation trade analysed here uses LIFFE Eurodollar futures options. However, the trading principles will be identical for all types of options.

## Step 2

Determine fair prices and deltas for the options assuming the volatility of 2.25%.

| Strike price | Premium | Fair price | Percentage difference | Delta |
|---|---|---|---|---|
| 89.00 | 1.30 | 1.28 | 1 | 0.92 |
| 89.50 | 0.88 | 0.85 | 3 | 0.80 |
| 90.00 | 0.46 | 0.50 | −8 | 0.61 |
| 90.50 | 0.27 | 0.25 | +9 | 0.39 |
| 91.00 | 0.11 | 0.10 | +8 | 0.20 |
| 91.50 | 0.03 | 0.03 | −14 | 0.08 |

The obvious options trades will involve buying the 90.00 call and selling either or both of the 90.50 and the 91.00 calls. Although the 89.00 and 89.50 calls both have higher implied volatilities, the percentage misvaluation is much smaller because they are relatively deep in-the-money.

Before making a final decision on the trade, however, the trader decides to examine the sensitivity of the option premiums and option deltas to changes in asset prices and volatilities. These sensitivities are all calculated relative to the fair prices of the options.

| Strike price | Premium | Delta | Gamma | Volatility | Time |
|---|---|---|---|---|---|
| 89.00 | 1.28 | 0.92 | 0.16 | 0.06 | 0.00 |
| 89.50 | 0.85 | 0.80 | 0.31 | 0.11 | 0.00 |
| 90.00 | 0.50 | 0.61 | 0.43 | 0.15 | 0.00 |
| 90.50 | 0.25 | 0.39 | 0.43 | 0.15 | 0.00 |
| 91.00 | 0.10 | 0.20 | 0.32 | 0.11 | 0.00 |
| 91.50 | 0.03 | 0.08 | 0.17 | 0.06 | 0.00 |

Because the 90.00 call and the 90.50 call are equidistant in exercise price from the futures price of 90.25, the gamma, volatility and time sensitivity of the two options are almost exactly equal. It thus makes sense to buy the 90.00 calls and sell the 90.50 calls. The proportionality for a hedged portfolio is given by the ratio of the two deltas.

$$\text{Number of 90.50 calls to match 1 90.00 call} = \frac{0.61}{0.39} = 1.56$$

Trader buys 100 90.00 calls
sells 156 90.50 calls

## Step 3

It is difficult to determine a definitive expected profit figure for this trade, because the actual profit will depend upon when the misvaluation corrects itself, if it does, and what volatility and the asset price have done in the meantime.

However, the simplest estimate of expected profit is obtained by assuming that the option prices return immediately to their fair values.

$$\text{Expected profit from June 90.00 calls} = 100 \times \$25 \times [100 \times (0.50 - 0.46)]$$
$$= \$10,000.00$$
$$\text{Expected profit from June 90.50 calls} = 156 \times \$25 \times [100 \times (0.27 - 0.25)]$$
$$= \$7,800.00$$
$$\text{Total expected profit} = \$17,800.00$$

The next step to illustrate the attributes of valuation trading is to assume that the option prices go back into line with the fair values under a range of conditions after a certain amount of time. The table below gives the fair prices for a period of five days in the future (i.e. the options now expire in 65 days) and various Eurodollar futures prices and volatilities.

Several points emerge from this table. First, although in most cases when options prices moved in line with fair prices, the position showed a profit, the profit in all cases was significantly different to the profit that would have been achieved if the change to fair prices had occurred

| Volatility | Futures price | 90 call premium | Profit | 90.50 call premium | Profit | Total profit |
|---|---|---|---|---|---|---|
| 2.00 | 89.50 | 0.12 | (85,000) | 0.03 | 93,600 | 8,600 |
| 2.00 | 90.25 | 0.45 | (2,500) | 0.20 | 27,300 | 24,800 |
| 2.00 | 91.00 | 1.03 | 142,500 | 0.62 | (136,500) | 6,000 |
| 2.25 | 89.50 | 0.15 | (77,500) | 0.05 | 85,800 | 8,300 |
| 2.25 | 90.25 | 0.48 | 5,000 | 0.23 | 15,600 | 20,600 |
| 2.25 | 91.00 | 1.05 | 147,500 | 0.65 | (148,200) | (700) |
| 2.50 | 89.50 | 0.18 | (70,000) | 0.07 | 78,000 | 8,000 |
| 2.50 | 90.25 | 0.52 | 15,000 | 0.27 | 0 | 15,000 |
| 2.50 | 91.00 | 1.07 | 152,000 | 0.69 | (163,800) | (11,300) |

immediately without any change in the underlying asset price and the volatility of that asset price.

The difference of $2,800 in profit from the expected level when the volatility remained at 2.25% and the futures price at 90.25 can be largely explained by a rounding error, since options prices are constrained to move in basis point jumps. Nonetheless changes in asset prices and volatility substantially change the profitability of the position. Even though matching the gamma and volatility sensitivity helps to protect against the hedged portfolio becoming risky, this still only helps if the movements in price and volatility are not too extreme. For movements upwards in price and volatility as shown above, rebalancing is required to protect the expected profitability of the hedge portfolio.

To examine the impact of rebalancing, it is assumed that in the worst case result, when the volatility increased to 2.50% and the futures price to 91.00, the movements occurred on a steady basis, appropriate rebalancing was carried out on a daily basis, and that the degree of over and undervaluation was eliminated steadily day by day.[4]

**Day 0**  Buy 100 June 90.00 calls
Sell 156 June 90.50 calls

**Day 1**  Futures price = 90.40   Volatility = 2.30%
June 90 call        Delta = 0.67   Price = 0.56
June 90.50 call   Delta = 0.46   Price = 0.34
Hedge ratio = 0.67/0.46 = 1.46
Sell 10 June 90.50 calls
Realized $loss = 10 \times \$25 \times 100 \times (0.34 - 0.27)$
    $= \$1,750.00$

*Position*   Long 100   Call 90.00
    Short 146   Call 90.50

**Day 2**  Futures price = 90.55   Volatility = 2.35%
June 90 call        Delta = 0.73   Price = 0.71
June 90.50 call   Delta = 0.52   Price = 0.39
Hedge ratio = 0.73/0.52 = 1.40
Sell 6 June 90.50 calls
Realized $loss = 6 \times \$25 \times 100 \times (0.39 - 0.27)$
    $= \$1,800.00$

*Position*   Long 100   Call 90.00
    Short 140   Call 90.50

**Day 3**  Futures price = 90.70   Volatility = 2.40%
June 90 call        Delta = 0.77   Price = 0.82
June 90.50 call   Delta = 0.59   Price = 0.48
Hedge ratio = 0.77/0.59 = 1.31

---

[4] This is only one of an almost infinite number of ways the changes in price and volatility, and the return to fair prices, could occur over the period. However, it should still serve to give the trader an idea of how the rebalancing of the portfolio can eliminate substantially the risks discussed.

Sell 9 June 90.50 calls
Realized *loss* = 9 × \$25 × 100 × (0.48 − 0.27)
$$= \$4,725.00$$

*Position* Long 100  Call 90.00
    Short 131  Call 90.50

**Day 4** Futures price = 90.85  Volatility = 2.45%
June 90 call    Delta = 0.82  Price = 0.95
June 90.50 call   Delta = 0.65  Price = 0.58
Hedge ratio = 0.82/0.65 = 1.26
Sell 5 June 90.50 calls
Realized *loss* = 5 × \$25 × 100 × (0.58 − 0.27)
$$= \$6,625.00$$

*Position*  Long 100  90.00 calls
    Short 126  90.50 calls

**Day 5** Futures price = 91.00  Volatility = 2.50%
June 90 call    Delta = 0.85  Price = 1.07
June 90.50 call   Delta = 0.70  Price = 0.69
All remaining positions liquidated
June 90.00 call profit = 100 × \$25 × [100 × (1.07 − 0.46)]
$$= \$152,500$$
June 90.50 call loss   = 126 × \$25 × [100 × (0.69 − 0.27)]
$$= \$132,300$$
Total net profit = \$5,300.00

Even with daily rebalancing, the profitability of the return to fair prices is substantially reduced compared with the case of no change in Eurodollar futures prices and their volatility. This is because even on a daily basis the shifts in price and volatility were large enough to mean that the number of losing 90.50 calls was persistently higher than required for a riskless hedge. Nonetheless, daily rebalancing was certainly sufficient to protect the misvaluation trade against loss. The result would have been slightly different if instead of realizing losses on the 90.50 calls to rebalance, it had been decided to purchase further 90.00 calls. In that case the net profit would have only been \$3,400.00.

The valuation trader needs to watch carefully the progress of his position. Frequent and careful rebalancing of the options positions may be necessary. No matter how closely the sensitivity of delta and the option premium to factors such as the asset price and volatility are matched, significant changes in those variables can easily eliminate the expected profits to valuation trades if rebalancing is not carried out frequently enough. This means an important lesson for the valuation trader.

---

**The expected profit to a valuation trade needs to be large enough to cover the transactions costs involved in frequent rebalancing and still show a sufficient return to capital employed.**

---

The position also works the other way. In the case of the Eurodollar option valuation trade discussed, downward movements in prices and/or volatility produced windfall gains by reducing the price of the 90.50 call more than proportionately to the fall in the price of the 90.00 call.

---

**The need for rebalancing is asymmetric. If the price and/or volatility moves in favour of the valuation trade, not rebalancing will increase trading profits.**

---

The valuation trader also needs to be aware of two other major points. First, there is no guarantee that expected profits from the elimination of misvalued options will be achieved before the expiration date of the options. If the option hedge has to be maintained for a long period, the transactions costs associated with frequent rebalancing could substantially reduce or even eliminate expected profits. The pattern of decay of time value may also play a more important role if the hedge portfolio has to be maintained for a long period. Second, the correct identification of undervalued or overvalued options, whether in absolute or relative terms, depends crucially on the validity of the pricing model used and on the accuracy of volatility estimates.

---

**A trader needs a good valuation model to make good valuation trades.**

---

## 4. Combined asset-options positions

This chapter has concentrated on positions involving solely options, either singly or in combinations. An additional set of strategies combines options positions with underlying asset positions to achieve another and different set of risk-return profiles. Asset-options positions fall broadly into three categories:

1. buying options to protect underlying asset positions;
2. writing options against underlying asset positions, and
3. pyramiding asset positions with additional options positions.

### a. Options for protection

The purchase of options for protection can be best understood by the use of an example. Consider an investor who has established a £1,000,000 cash sterling position at $1.15, when the current sterling-dollar rate is $1.22. The trader obviously has a substantial profit, but is still bullish on the sterling exchange rate. However, he is also of the opinion that he would like to lock in some of his profits in the event of an unexpected and rapid decline in the exchange rate. One solution is to buy in-the-money put options. Imagine the sterling $1.25 put is trading at a premium of 5.0 cents.

$$\text{Number of puts:} \frac{£1,000,000}{£25,000} = 40 \text{ contracts}[5]$$
$$\text{Cost of protection} = 40 \times £25,000 \times \$0.05 = \$50,000$$
$$\text{Guaranteed FX position profit} = £1,000,000 \times (\$1.25 - \$1.15)$$
$$= \$100,000$$
$$\text{Minimum net guaranteed profit} = \$50,000$$

This compares with a current realizable profit to the FX position if liquidated of $70,000 (£1,000,000 × ($1.22 − $1.15). Hence the maximum opportunity loss if the exchange rate – which is effectively the insurance premium – falls, is $20,000, and will be less if the puts still have time value when sold. The trader's position is that, if the currency rate does fall sharply, the sterling puts can be exercised at $1.25 or sold at a profit in the market, while additional profits over $50,000 will be earned if the exchange rate rises above $1.25. The combined position profit and loss profile at expiration is shown in Exhibit 4.14. What has happened is the effective purchase of a 125 call at a negative price of −5 cents. In practice the trader will want to compare this position in terms of commissions and transactions costs to simply liquidating the FX position at a profit of $70,000 and buying the $1.25 out-of-the-money call.

Alternative strategies for buying protection for profitable underlying asset positions could involve buying at-the-money puts or out-of-the-money puts. In each case the effect is to set up a synthetic call options position either at-the-money or in-the-money. In each case, the trader will have to determine whether this is cheaper than simply liquidating the position and using some of the proceeds to buy the call direct. Whether the trader is happier dealing in in-the-money puts, at-the-money puts or out-of-the-money puts will depend upon his degree of risk aversion and how

---

[5] LIFFE and CME contract sizes have been used in this example. If Philadelphia or London Stock Exchange options had been used, the number of contracts would be 80.

**Exhibit 4.14: Cash-put position**

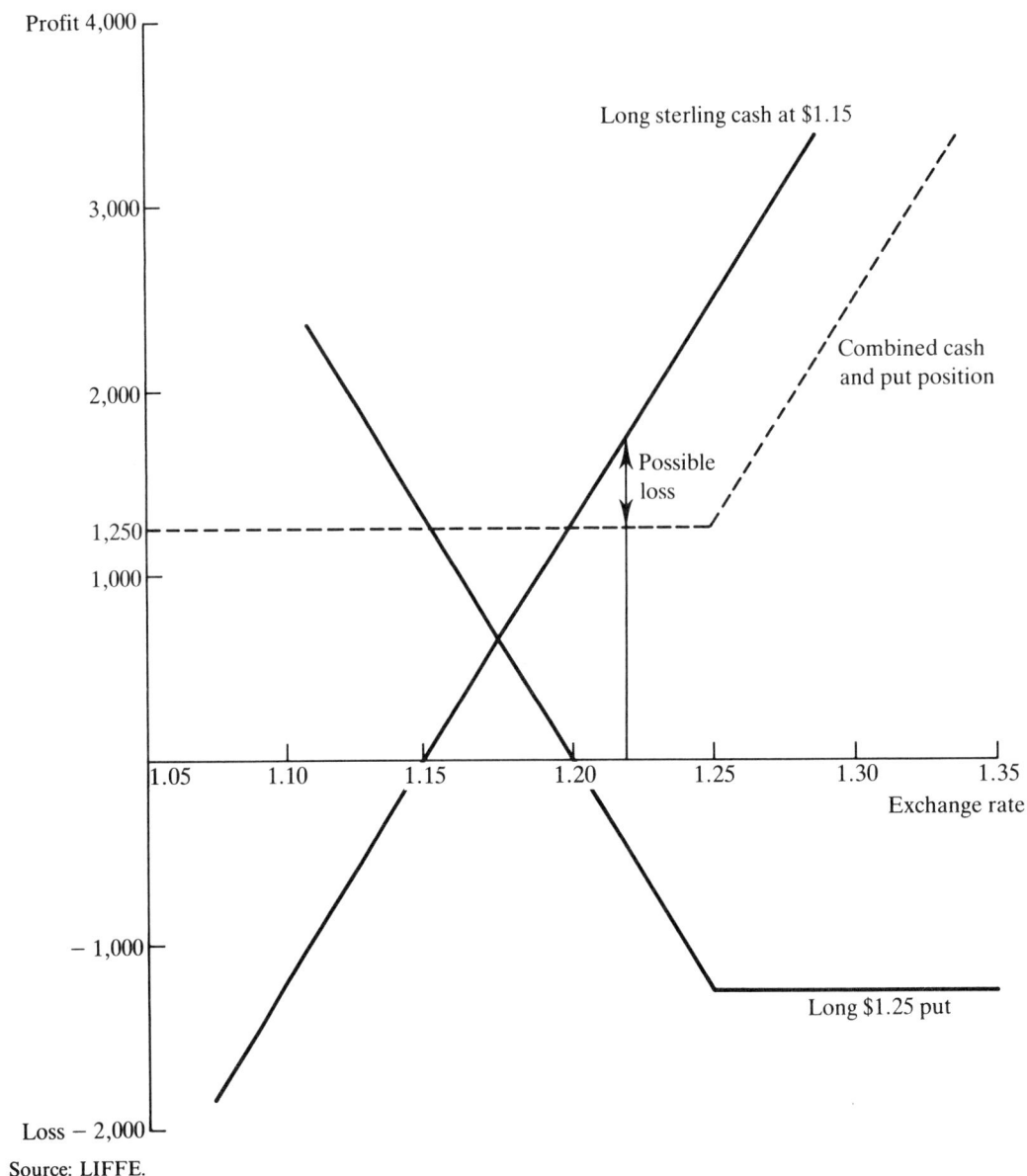

Source: LIFFE.

bullish he is in his asset price forecasts. For instance consider the profit and loss profiles for the above position, or buying a 115 put at 0.10 cents or a 120 put at 2.25 cents.

*Profit-loss matrix*

| Exchange rate | Underlying asset | Plus 115 put 10 × 40 × 2.5 | Plus 120 put 225 × 40 × 2.5 | Plus 125 put 500 × 40 × 2.5 |
|---|---|---|---|---|
| 1.10 | − $50,000 | − $1,000 | + $27,500 | + $50,000 |
| 1.15 | 0 | $1,000 | + $27,500 | + $50,000 |
| 1.20 | + $50,000 | $49,000 | + $27,500 | + $50,000 |
| 1.25 | + $100,000 | + $99,000 | + $77,500 | + $50,000 |
| 1.30 | + $150,000 | + $149,000 | + $127,500 | + $100,000 |

If the trader is confident about rising exchange rates, but wants to avoid losses in the case of a totally unexpected decline, buying an out-of-the-money put may be acceptable insurance. The precise choice always belongs in the realm of personal preference.

Similar protection trades can be achieved by buying call options when holding a profitable short asset position.

1. **Buy puts to protect long and profitable asset positions. Buy calls to protect short and profitable asset positions.**
2. **Always compare the cost of such strategies with simply liquidating the asset position and replacing with a simple option position.**

## b. Covered option writing

Just as the discussion of simple option position trading analysed the relative profits and losses to alternative strategies of buying calls and selling puts and vice versa, so an alternative to buying puts to protect a profitable underlying asset position would be to write calls against it. Exhibit 4.15 below shows the result of simultaneously holding an established sterling position at $1.15 with a current sterling exchange rate of $1.22 and writing a $1.25 call at a premium of 2.10 cents.

Since buying puts for protection creates artificial long calls, and selling calls for protection establishes artificial short puts, the question of which is the better depends on exactly the same arguments as were discussed under an open position trading. In the case shown above, between an exchange rate of $1.18 and $1.27, the artificial short put position created by the covered 125 call write gives higher profits than the FX position protected by a 125 put purchase. Beyond that exchange rate change, the opposite is the case. Thus the final decision will be a function of the trader's exchange rate forecast and the level of transactions costs of the various alternatives:

1. liquidate the position and do nothing;
2. liquidate the position and buy calls;
3. liquidate the position and sell puts;

## Exhibit 4.15: A covered call write

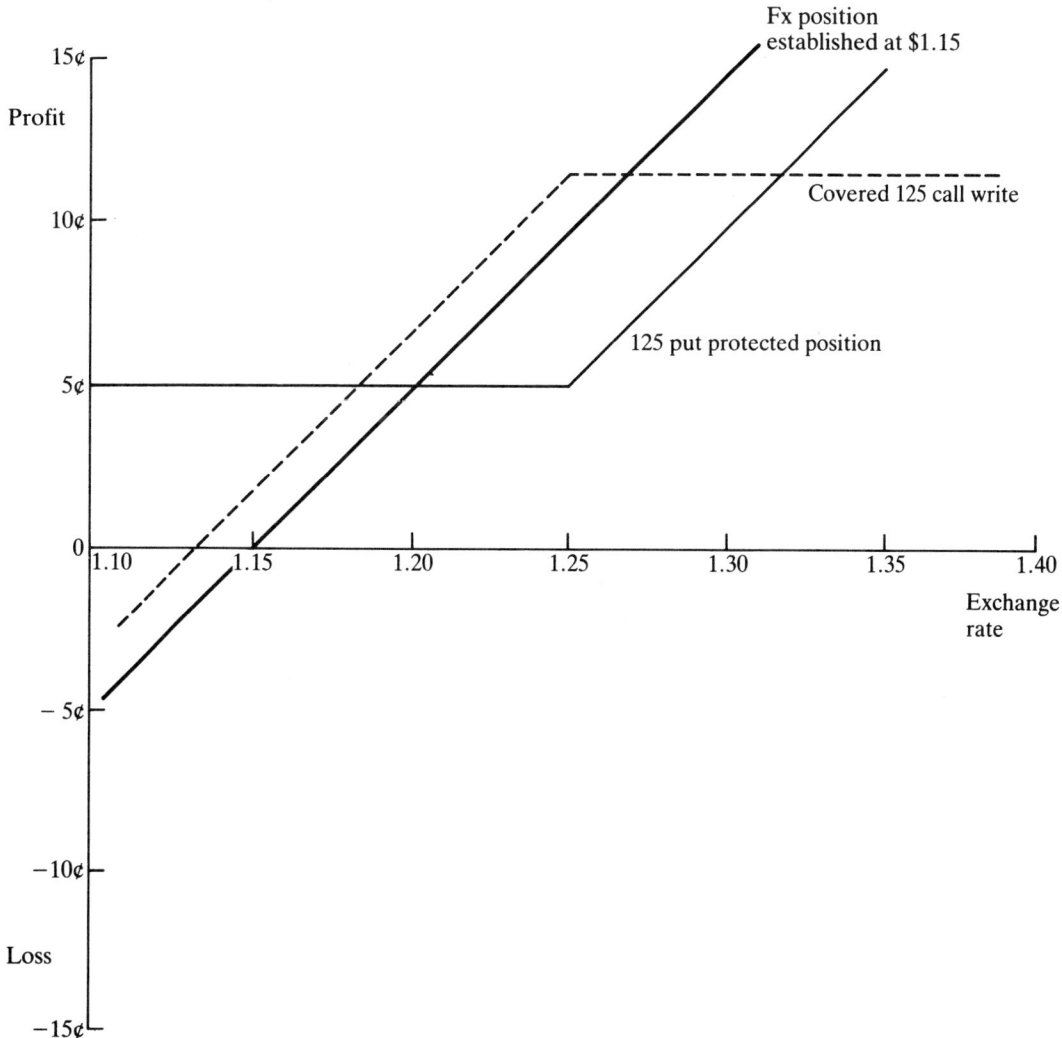

4. buy puts and add to the position;
5. write calls against the position.

Similar arguments apply for the writing of put options against short positions.

### c. Pyramiding asset and options positions

So far the combined trades discussed have involved the use of options to reduce the risk of underlying asset positions. Options can also be used in addition to underlying asset positions to produce a profit profile somewhere between that of a straight options position and a straight asset position. Such positions are sometimes termed Texas hedges (although not, presumably, within earshot of serious Texan options traders).

Exhibit 4.16 shows a typical Texas hedge using the LIFFE Eurodollar option. The profit profile shows that the Texas hedge gives up some of the profit appreciation of the futures position to eliminate a significant proportion of the downside risk. By mixing options and futures in different proportions, any position between a straight future and a straight call option can be obtained. Take a position in three Eurodollar futures contracts and use the symbolic notation discussed earlier; the profit profiles for the different possible positions can then be analysed:

| | | |
|---|---|---|
| 3 long ED futures | Price E | (3, 3) (E) |
| 2 long futures + 1 E call | | (2, 3) (E) |
| 1 long future + 2 E calls | | (1, 3) (E) |
| 3 E calls | | (0, 3) (E) |

### Exhibit 4.16: Bullish Texas option hedge (long ED futures + long call)

Buy June ED future at 88.70 and June ED 88.50 call at 0.34

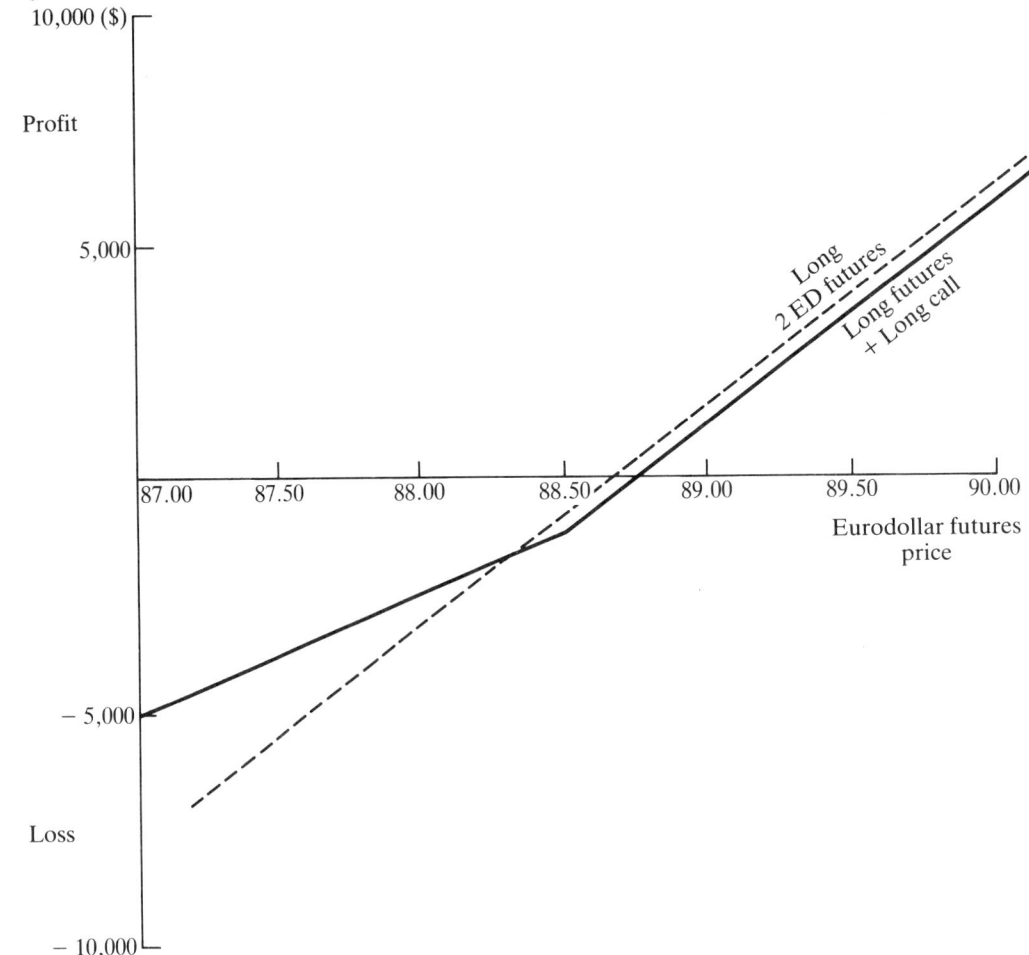

Source: LIFFE.

In addition, pyramiding could be used to add call options to a profitable futures position. Consider the profit profile in Exhibit 4.16 if the futures position had been purchased at 88.00 and, say, an ED 88.50 call purchased at 0.34.

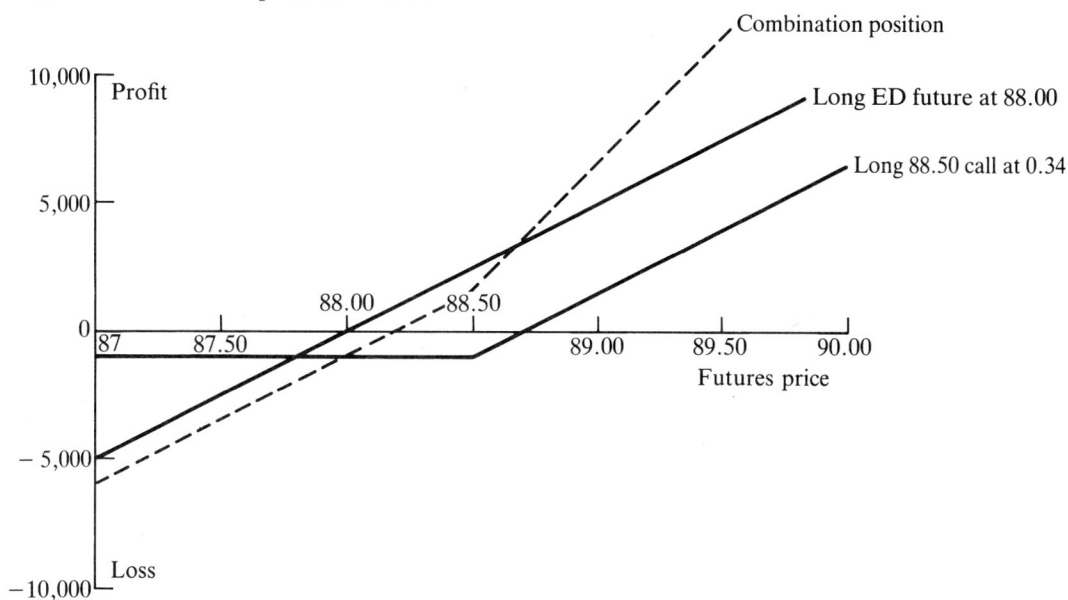

By using some of the variation margin to the futures position to buy call options, a significant return benefit could be obtained for further rises in Eurodollar futures prices at a small cost in lower profits if the exchange rate falls.

### d. Conversions and boxes

The principle of combining options and asset positions can also be used to set up arbitrage or almost arbitrage trades. In option algebra, a *long call + short put* is equivalent to a *long asset*.

Long call (0, 1) (E)
+
Short put (1, 0) (E)
=
Long asset (1, 1) (E)

This is not quite the underlying asset because the actual asset price will be different to the exercise price of the two options. If, for example, the underlying asset price is greater than the exercise price, the trader would expect the cost of the call option to exceed the premium income from the put – the difference representing the payment for establishing the asset position at below the fair market price.

To establish a flat or arbitrage position, the artificial asset could be sold against the actual long asset.

Sell call = (0, −1) (E)
Buy call = (−1, 0) (E)
Buy asset = (1, 1) (E)
Net position = (0, 0) (E)

This type of arbitrage is known as a *conversion*. It would be carried out if the net cost of the option position differed from the net advantage or disadvantage of purchasing the asset away from the market price.

### Example

```
June ED futures price = 92.00
June ED call 91.00    =  1.20
June ED put 91.00     =  0.16
```

|  | Cash Inflow | Outflow |
|---|---|---|
| Buy put | — | 0.16 |
| Sell call | 1.20 | — |
| Buy future | — | — |
| Net credit | 1.04 | |

**June** (at expiration)

| | | | *ED futures price* | | |
| --- | --- | --- | --- | --- |
| | | *90.00* | *91.00* | *92.00* | *93.00* |
| | Put | +1.00 | 0 | 0 | 0 |
| | Call | 0 | 0 | −1.00 | −2.00 |
| | Future | −2.00 | −1.00 | 0 | +1.00 |
| | Net | −1.00 | −1.00 | −1.00 | −1.00 |

No matter what happens to the futures price at the expiration of the option, there is a net credit to the arbitrageur of four basis points. The profit would in fact be slightly higher because of the opportunity to invest the net credit of 1.04 for the period to June to earn interest.

Thus this appears to be an absolutely certain arbitrage. The only conceivable problem is that of potential early exercise because the Eurodollar option on the CME is an American option. This danger is not as severe with the Eurodollar futures option as it is with stock options, currency options and others. Nevertheless it still exists, and hence the arbitrageur will be interested in finding misvalued options that create potential conversions where the written option position is well out-of-the-money so as to decrease the probability of early exercise during the life of the conversion. For instance, with an underlying asset price of 92.00, it would be better to do a conversion involving the 93.00 puts and calls than the example using the 91.00 options.

The trader will also be hoping that the option misvaluation will correct itself before expiration, when the position can be unwound and the arbitrage profit taken.

### Example: Seven days later

*Alternative 1*

ED futures price = 91.40
June 91.00 call  = 0.75
June 91.00 put  = 0.35

$$\text{Net cash flow on liquidation} = (91.40 - 92.00) + 0.35 - 0.75$$
$$= -1.00$$
$$\text{Net profit} = 1.04 - 1.00 = 0.04$$

*Alternative 2*

ED futures price = 92.50
June 91.00 call  = 1.60
June 91.00 put  = 0.10

$$\text{Net cash flow on liquidation} = (92.50 - 92.00) + 0.10 - 1.60$$
$$= -1.00$$
$$\text{Net profit} = 1.04 - 1.00 = 0.04$$

The *reversal* arbitrage is the exact opposite of the conversion. It involves selling a put option, buying a call option and selling the underlying asset.

$$\text{Sell put} \quad = (1, 0) \text{ (E)}$$
$$\text{Buy call} \quad = (0, 1) \text{ (E)}$$
$$\text{Sell asset} \quad = (-1, -1) \text{ (E)}$$
$$\text{Net position} = (0, 0) \text{ (E)}$$

### Example

ED futures price = 92.00
June 92.50 put  = 0.95
June 92.50 call  = 0.39

$$\text{Net cash flow} = 0.95 - 0.39 = 0.56$$

| | *Futures price* | | | | |
| --- | --- | --- | --- | --- | --- |
| *At expiration* | *90.00* | *91.00* | *92.00* | *93.00* | *94.00* |
| Put | −2.50 | −1.50 | −0.50 | 0 | 0 |
| Call | 0 | 0 | 0 | +0.50 | +1.50 |
| Asset | +2.00 | +1.00 | 0 | −1.00 | −2.00 |
| Net | −0.50 | −0.50 | −0.50 | −0.50 | −0.50 |

$$\text{Net profit} = 0.06 \ (\$150)$$

A *box* arbitrage is similar to the conversion and reversal arbitrages, but avoids the use of the underlying asset by buying and selling two artificial assets established at different effective prices.

*Debit box*   Buy low exercise price call
Sell high exercise price call
Sell low exercise price put
Buy high exercise price put

$$(0, 1, 1) \, (E_1, E_2)$$
$$+$$
$$(0, 0, -1) \, E_1, E_2)$$
$$+$$
$$(1, 0, 0) \, (E_1, E_2)$$
$$+$$
$$(-1, -1, 0) \, (E_1, E_2)$$
$$=$$
$$(0, 0, 0) \, (E_1, E_2)$$

This is a perfectly flat position, where the net cash outflow is hoped to be less than the difference in the two option strike prices.

$$\text{Profit} = (\text{Difference in exercise prices}) - \text{Net debit}$$

**Example**

ED futures price = 92.00
June 91.50 call  = 0.75
June 92.50 call  = 0.20
June 91.50 put  = 0.17
June 92.50 put  = 0.57

$$\text{Net debit} = (0.20 - 0.75) + (0.17 - 0.57)$$
$$= -0.95$$
$$\text{Box profit} = (92.50 - 91.50) - 0.95 = 0.05$$

| At expiration | *Futures price* | | | | |
|---|---|---|---|---|---|
|  | *91.00* | *91.50* | *92.00* | *92.50* | *93.00* |
| 91.50 call | 0 | 0 | 0.50 | 1.00 | 1.50 |
| 92.50 call | 0 | 0 | 0 | 0 | -0.50 |
| 91.50 put | -0.50 | 0 | 0 | 0 | 0 |
| 92.50 put | 1.50 | 1.00 | 0.50 | 0 | 0 |
| Net | 1.00 | 1.00 | 1.00 | 1.00 | 1.00 |

So the profit is earned for all possible futures prices at expiration.

The opposite box arbitrage trade is called a *credit box*.

*Credit box*   Sell low exercise price call
Buy high exercise price call
Buy low exercise price put
Sell high exercise price put

$$(0, -1, -1) \, (E_1, E_2)$$
$$+$$
$$(0, 0, 1) \, (E_1, E_2)$$
$$+$$
$$(-1, 0, 0) \, (E_1, E_2)$$
$$+$$
$$(1, 1, 0) \, (E_1, E_2)$$
$$=$$
$$(0, 0, 0) \, (E_1, E_2)$$

Here the arbitrageur hopes that the net cash inflow will be more than the difference between the exercise prices

$$\text{Profit} = \text{Net credit} - (\text{Difference in exercise prices})$$

In the case of the debit box, the position will have to be financed whereas with the credit box, funds will be available for investment. Because the trader is buying mostly in-the-money calls and puts and selling out-of-the money or less in-the-money options, the dangers posed by early exercise are reduced. The trader also has to remember that the arbitrage profits from such trades have to be large enough to cover commissions and bid-ask spreads. For instance, a more realistic assessment of the conversion discussed earlier might see the following price spreads and commissions.

### Example
ED futures price = 92.00–92.01
June 91.00 call   =   1.19–1.21
June 91.00 put   =   0.15–0.17

Futures commission in and out   $20.00
Options commission in and out   $10.00

| | Cash | |
| --- | --- | --- |
| | *Inflow* | *Outflow* |
| Buy put | — | 0.17 |
| Sell call | 1.19 | — |
| Buy future | — | — |

Net credit = 1.02
Equivalent to 102 ticks × $25 = $2,550.00
Less commissions = $40.00

Invest at 10% for three months

Terminal value = $2,510.00 × 1.025
= $2,572.75
Net payout at expiration = 100 ticks × $25
= $2,500.00
Net profit = $72.75

Of which interest component = $62.75

Virtually all the notional (before interest income) arbitrage profit of four ticks or $100 has disappeared because of the bid-ask spreads and commissions. This effect will be even worse with arbitrage trades involving net debits. By contrast market-makers operating on the right side of the bid-ask and not paying commissions may well find significant numbers of worthwhile conversions, reversals and box trades.

# Chapter 5
# Hedging with options

## 1. Introduction

Unlike the trading strategies discussed extensively in the previous chapter, many of the details of hedging with option contracts are peculiar to specific contracts. Nevertheless, there are certain principles of options hedging which can be usefully discussed in a general way. The hedger's objective is always to reduce risk by temporarily offsetting a current or expected position in the cash market with a matching but opposite position in the futures, forward or options markets.

Consider a currency position: if the cash position in a currency is likely to be adversely affected by higher exchange rates than those currently anticipated, the hedger could *buy* currency *call* options and the profits on the calls – if anticipated exchange rates rise – will provide compensation for losses on the cash position. A similar result could be achieved by *selling put* options: if exchange rates rise, the put options will expire worthless or at least reduced in value and the hedger will regain all or some of the original premium to compensate for the impact of the exchange rate rise on the cash position. If lower exchange rates are the worry, the hedger could *buy put* options or *sell call* options. This hedging principle applies with options written on any underlying assets.

---

**Cash position**

**Rising asset prices adverse: buy calls or sell puts.**
**Falling asset prices adverse: buy puts or sell calls.**

---

In contrast to hedging in the forward or futures market,[1] which attempts to lock in a specific asset price or value for the hedger, an options hedge is more like the purchase of an insurance contract. For the price of an option (the insurance premium), the buyer is protected (insured) against an adverse movement in the underlying asset price, while preserving some of the benefits of a favourable movement in the price.

Different options provide different types of insurance. Consider the following set of currency option premiums.

**Example**

| *December calls* | | |
|---|---|---|
| *Exercise price* | *Premium* | *December forward rate = $1.1950* |
| $1.15 | 5.65¢ | |
| $1.20 | 2.70¢ | |
| $1.25 | 1.03¢ | |

By selling dollars forward for December delivery, the exchange rate of $1.1950 can be locked in exactly.

*Buy $1.25 call*

By paying a premium of 1.03 cents, the hedger is insured against the exchange rate in December going above $1.25, i.e. an excess on the policy of 5.50 cents. The hedger will achieve a better result than the forward hedge if the exchange rate falls below $1.1847 ($1.1950 − $0.0103).

---

[1] For a full description of hedging with futures contracts, see M. D. Fitzgerald, *Financial Futures*, Euromoney Publications (1983).

*Buy $1.20 call*

By paying a premium of 2.70 cents, the investor is insured against the exchange rate rising above $1.20, i.e. an excess of 0.50 cents, and will do better than the forward hedge if the rate falls below $1.1680.

*Buy $1.15 call*

By paying a premium of 5.65 cents, the investor is insured against rates being above $1.15, i.e. 4.50 cents better than the forward hedge, and will do better than the forward hedge if the rate falls below $1.1385.

|  | Best guaranteed rate | Breakeven rate |
| --- | --- | --- |
| Forward | $1.1950 | $1.1950 |
| $1.25 call | $1.2603 | $1.1847 |
| $1.20 call | $1.2270 | $1.1680 |
| $1.15 call | $1.2065 | $1.1385 |

This simple example illustrates the major features of options hedging. Hedging with different options allows the hedger a choice of alternative hedging costs and alternative guaranteed asset prices (exchange rates in this case). To continue the insurance analogy: the hedger can decide which level of risk to accept and which insurance premium to pay.

But the best guaranteed exchange rate achievable with an options hedge is always worse than can be guaranteed with a forward or futures hedge. However, with an options hedge, there is always a breakeven level at which the rate achieved will be more favourable than the rate achieved with the forward or futures hedge.

## 2. Designing hedges with options

The question of which type of hedge is suitable for which type of exposure is the most crucial decision for the hedger. There are two basic inputs into the type of exposure. First, whether the level of exposure is *known with certainty* to the hedger or is totally or partially *unknown*.

A typical case would be a fixed commitment to import machine tools at a specific future date, where the importer knows he must buy a fixed amount of foreign currency for a specific date – this is a certain known exposure. The other would be a contract for tender situation where a contractor is bidding for a contract in a foreign currency, but has no idea whether he will get the contract – he faces an uncertain foreign exchange exposure.

The second input is whether the level of exposure is *symmetrical* or *asymmetrical*. A symmetrical exposure is one where the unhedged position is equally exposed to a rise or fall in the underlying asset price, i.e. the hedger benefits if the asset price moves one way and is hurt if the asset price moves the other way. An asymmetrical exposure is one where the hedger will be hurt if the asset price moves one way and will not benefit or will benefit in a restricted manner if the asset price moves the other way.

An example would be a financial institution which has issued an interest rate cap guarantee to a customer. The customer benefits and the financial institution is hurt if interest rates fall; but the financial institution does not benefit totally if interest rates rise because there is a cap on the interest rate the customer will have to pay.

The choice of type of hedge to use also depends on the objective of the hedger. Is the aim of the hedger to minimize asset price risk on a specific transaction, or to smooth out the pattern of returns through time, thereby reducing return variance? Or does the hedger wish to achieve a minimum return with certainty while maintaining the possibility of gaining extra returns? Or is the aim to alter the risk structure of a given asset-liabilities mix to a more desired level? Hedgers can vary – from the importer with fixed exchange rate transactions exposure to portfolio managers who want to reduce the volatility of an asset portfolio where the exposure is uncertain and no specific time frame is involved.

Options represent an appropriate hedge vehicle when:

| *Exposure is* | *The hedger's objective is to* |
| --- | --- |
| Uncertain | Smooth out returns |
| and/or | and/or |
| Asymmetrical | Guarantee a minimum return |

If an options hedge is chosen, the hedger has a further decision to make: should the options hedge be a *fixed hedge* or a *ratio hedge*. We examined examples of fixed hedges when exploring the insurance properties of options. The aim with a fixed hedge is to limit the maximum possible loss on a hedged position, or to guarantee a minimum return. Generally, with a fixed hedge, the full amount of the underlying exposure is hedged with options and the options are closed out either by sale or exercise when the underlying exposure is eliminated. There is no question of rebalancing during the life of a fixed option hedge, although as with any other kind of hedge, changes in the hedger's view about likely asset prices or a reassessment of the nature of the underlying exposure may lead to lifting all or part of a hedge before its original intended life is complete.

By contrast a *ratio* or *delta hedge* is designed to maintain a combined cash and options position with a zero delta through time on a continuous basis. Such a hedge may need frequent rebalancing and will be more risky than a fixed hedge because the number of contracts required will be larger. Delta hedges are often used when hedging over-the-counter (OTC) options positions written by financial institutions. Ratio hedges are designed to be delta neutral. Moreover, ratio hedge performance can be affected by changes in implied volatility. More advanced ratio hedging strategies will not only try to achieve delta neutrality, but also try to keep constant the sensitivities of the two sides of the hedged position to changes in delta (or gamma), as well as trying to achieve volatility (epsilon) and time (theta) neutrality.

Even when the exposure is traditional two-way certain, and the hedger wishes to lock in a specific return and/or minimize risk, an options hedge is not necessarily the less advantageous hedge. Often it will depend upon how much hedging is carried out. For instance, if options are priced fairly, a large portfolio of options purchased on a continuous basis should provide exactly the same (or a slightly better) overall hedge result as a classic forward hedge.

Whereas for a single hedge, a currency option would be viewed as expensive compared with a forward hedge, over time many of the option hedges will make windfall profits compared with the forward hedge. Overall for continuous hedging, the two types of hedge appear to achieve very similar results.

---

### Option hedging points

1. **If you hedge a lot, you will probably find options hedges achieve much the same result as other hedges.**
2. **For asymmetrical and/or uncertain exposures, option hedges are particularly suitable.**
3. **For guaranteeing a minimum return, option hedges are suitable.**
4. **Think of option hedges as insurance transactions.**

---

## a. Hedging strategies

We shall examine some alternative hedging strategies. Interest rate hedges using the LIFFE Eurodollar futures option will be used. Although individual options will have different methods for determining the precise number of options contracts for a suitable hedge, the principles outlined here apply to all options hedges.[2]

Consider a treasurer who is intending to borrow $10 million on 15 December 1986 which is the delivery day for the December futures contract.

Exhibit 5.1 illustrates the interest rate exposure. The current futures price for December delivery is 90.00, which indicates an equivalent London interbank offer rate of 10% because the LIFFE Eurodollar futures price is defined as 100 – Libor. The futures price is taken to represent the market consensus on the interest rate that will prevail in December, or more precisely it is priced off the forward-forward rate for December. Hence if the December rate is higher than the current December rate of 10% when December comes around, the hedger will lose money because of higher borrowing costs; if rates are lower, the hedger will benefit.

The hedger always measures his exposure relative to the forward-forward rate prevailing for December at the current date. If we examine Exhibit 5.1 – remembering that if interest rates rise futures prices fall – we see that the solid black line through a futures price of 90.00 represents the

---

[2] I am grateful to the London International Financial Futures Exchange and Dr. Jacques Pezier of Investment Intelligence Systems Corporation for the provision of the hedge diagrams used below.

## Exhibit 5.1: Borrowing exposure

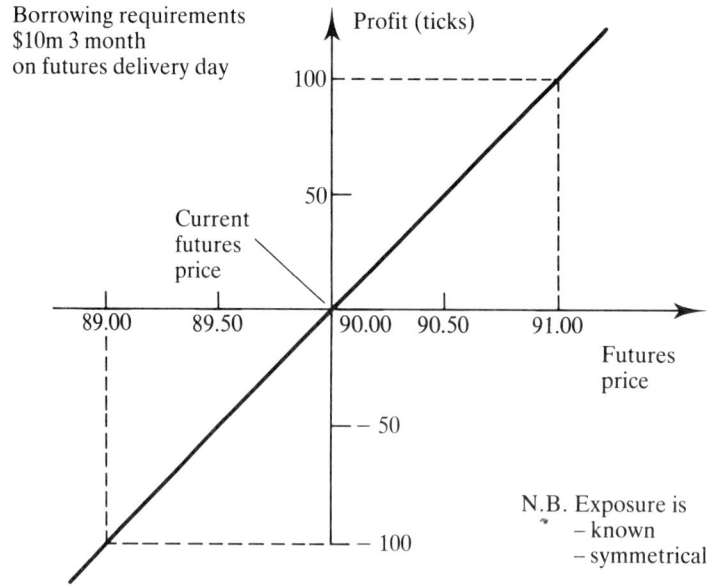

Borrowing requirements
$10m 3 month
on futures delivery day

Profit (ticks)

Current
futures
price

Futures
price

N.B. Exposure is
– known
– symmetrical

Source: LIFFE.

treasurer's exposure. If the Libor rate rises to 11%, the futures price falls to 89.00 equivalent, and the hedger has to pay 100 basis points more in interest on $10 million or $25,000 in cash.

### (i) The futures hedge

What are the alternatives open to the hedger? First, he could hedge the exposure with futures. Since he loses money if interest rates rise, he will want to put on a futures position that makes money if rates rise, i.e. he will sell futures. Since the hedger plans to borrow $10 million, he sells 10 Eurodollar futures contracts at a price of 90.00 (Eurodollar contracts are denominated in $1,000,000 units). The net hedged position is shown in Exhibit 5.2.

By selling futures contracts at 90.00, the hedger compensates exactly for losses on his cash market exposure. The net hedged position shown by the broad black line displays zero profits and

## Exhibit 5.2: Perfect fixed hedge with futures

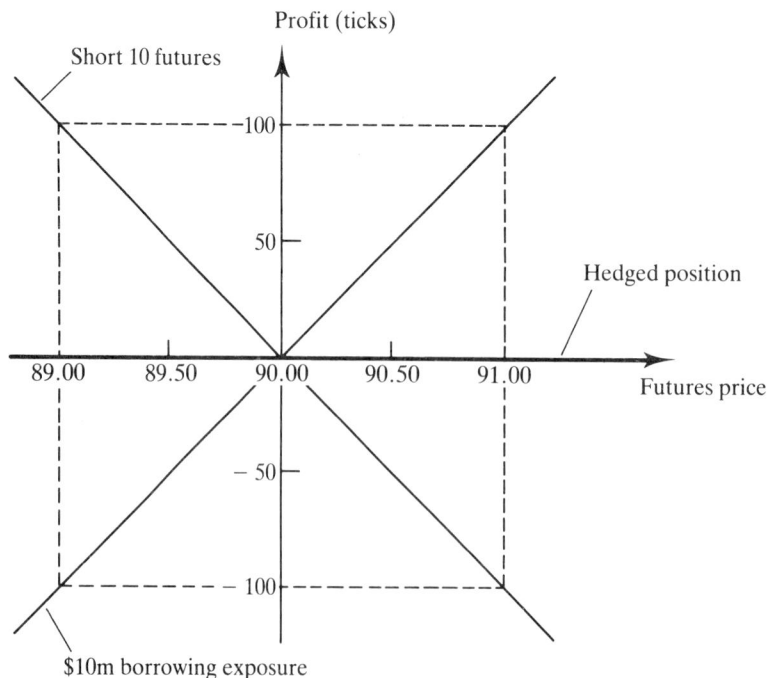

Profit (ticks)

Short 10 futures

Hedged position

Futures price

$10m borrowing exposure

Source: LIFFE.

## Exhibit 5.3: Partial fixed hedge with futures

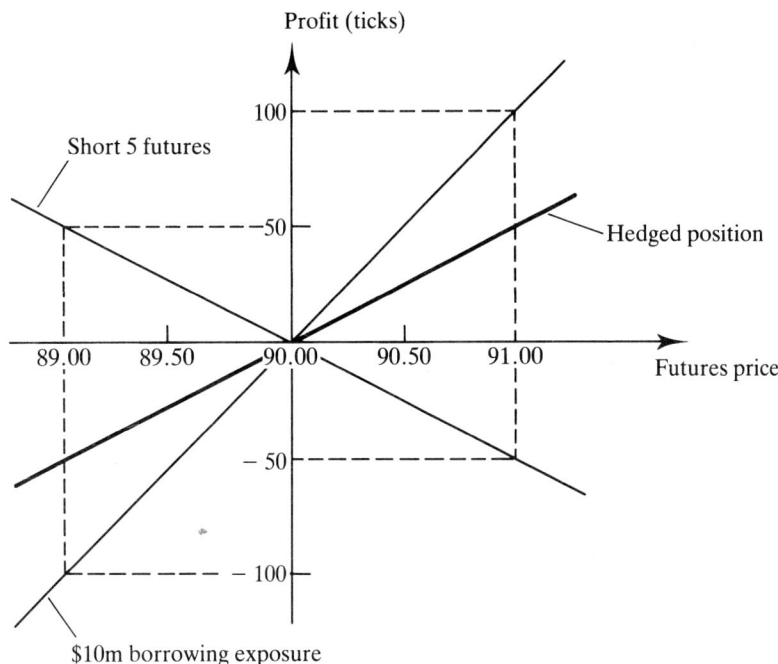

Source: LIFFE.

losses no matter what happens to the underlying December Libor rate and futures prices. Whatever happens the treasurer will be able to borrow the required $10 million at 10% (plus any commercial margin).

There is no necessity for the hedger to put on futures contracts to the full face value of the exposure. By choosing the number of contracts, the hedger can alter the slope of the hedged position in any way he likes. Exhibit 5.3 illustrates the hedge position where five rather than 10 futures contracts are sold. Such a position might be favoured by a hedger who was convinced rates were going to fall, but thought the risk of maintaining a full open exposure of $10 million was too high.

### (ii) The fixed option hedge

An alternative hedge would be to buy put options which will also gain in value if Eurodollar futures prices fall (Eurodollar interest rates rise). A fixed hedge with Eurodollar put options is shown in Exhibit 5.4. The hedger purchases 10 Eurodollar December put options with an exercise price of 90.00 for a premium of 0.75. The value of the hedged position at expiry is then obtained by adding the profit or loss on the put position to the profit or loss on the underlying cash exposure. The dotted line indicates the final hedged position. At an unchanged futures price of 90.00, the cash position shows a zero profit and loss while the hedger has lost the put premium. As the price rises above 90.00 (i.e., interest rates fall below 10%), the put is worthless but the hedger gradually profits from paying less interest on his borrowings. Eventually when futures price rise to 90.75 (interest rates fall to 9.25%), the hedger begins to achieve net borrowing costs lower than would be achieved with the full futures hedge. At futures prices below 90.00, losses on the cash position are matched by gains on the put position, and the net loss stays steady at the level of the put premium of 75 basis points.

A similar fixed hedge could be achieved by selling calls, and that hedge is also shown in Exhibit 5.4. The hedge achieved by selling call options gives a better result than the put hedge over quite a wide range. The call hedge is better than the put hedge in terms of profit and loss between a futures price of 88.50 (Libor of 11.50%) and a futures price of 91.50 (Libor of 8.50%). The call hedge outperforms the futures hedge for futures prices of 89.25 (Libor of 10.75%) and above, and underperforms for larger interest rate rises. The put hedge outperforms the futures hedge for futures prices of 90.75 (Libor of 9.25%) and above. However, the maximum loss on the hedged position with the short call hedge is still unlimited, while that with the long put is limited to the put premium.

95

## Exhibit 5.4: Fixed hedge with put option

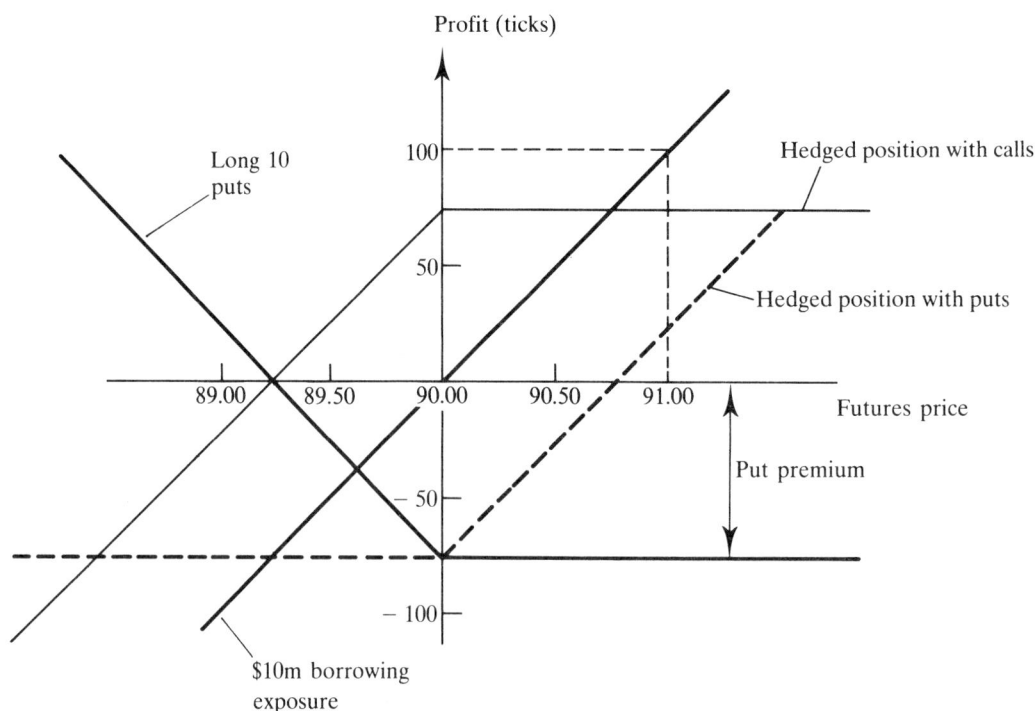

Source: LIFFE.

### (iii)  The ratio option hedge

The next step is to examine the equivalent ratio hedge of this particular exposure. In the case above, the delta of the option is estimated to be 0.67, indicating that a price neutral, or delta neutral, hedge involving buying the 90.00 put option would involve matching 15 put options against the $10 million of cash exposure. The profit and loss profiles for this ratio hedge are shown in Exhibit 5.5.

The aim of a delta hedge is to make the hedged position riskless for small changes in the underlying asset price, i.e. profits or losses to the cash position should be more or less exactly compensated for by profits or losses on the options position. We also know that such a hedge will never be perfect, because the delta changes whenever the underlying asset price changes. The heavy dotted line in Exhibit 5.5 shows the short-term behaviour of the ratio hedged position. As suggested the profit-loss profile is horizontal for the area immediately around the current futures price of 90.00, and then curves up on both sides showing a net profit to the hedge position.

This looks attractive to the hedger. It arises because of the changing delta. Suppose the delta of 0.67 gives an almost perfect hedge around 90.00. The price falls to 89.50. Because this is a put option, its delta will increase as it goes in-the-money. If the delta increases, it means that fewer than 15 put options are required to effectively hedge the $10 million cash position, i.e. the hedger is over-hedged. Since, however, it is the put option position that is making money, while the cash position is losing, the hedged position earns windfall profits as shown in the exhibit.

The same happens if the futures price rises to 90.50. Now the delta of the put option falls as the put option goes out of the money. Hence more than 15 put options would be required to match the $10 million cash exposure, and the position is under-hedged. However, now it is the cash position that is making money, and the put option position that is losing, so once again the hedged position earns a windfall profit again, as shown in Exhibit 5.5.

What this means is that as long as the delta used is an accurate assessment of the option's likely price movement in relation to changes in the asset price, then in the short-term the hedged position will show zero profits for small movements in the underlying asset price, and windfall profits if the asset price moves significantly either up or down. However, this ignores the question of volatility risk and time risk even in the short-term. Since the hedged position is long put options and long cash, then a decline in implied volatility will reduce the value of the put options without necessarily impacting upon the cash position. That would result in a short-term loss to the hedged position even with no asset price movement.

96

**Exhibit 5.5: Ratio hedge with put options**

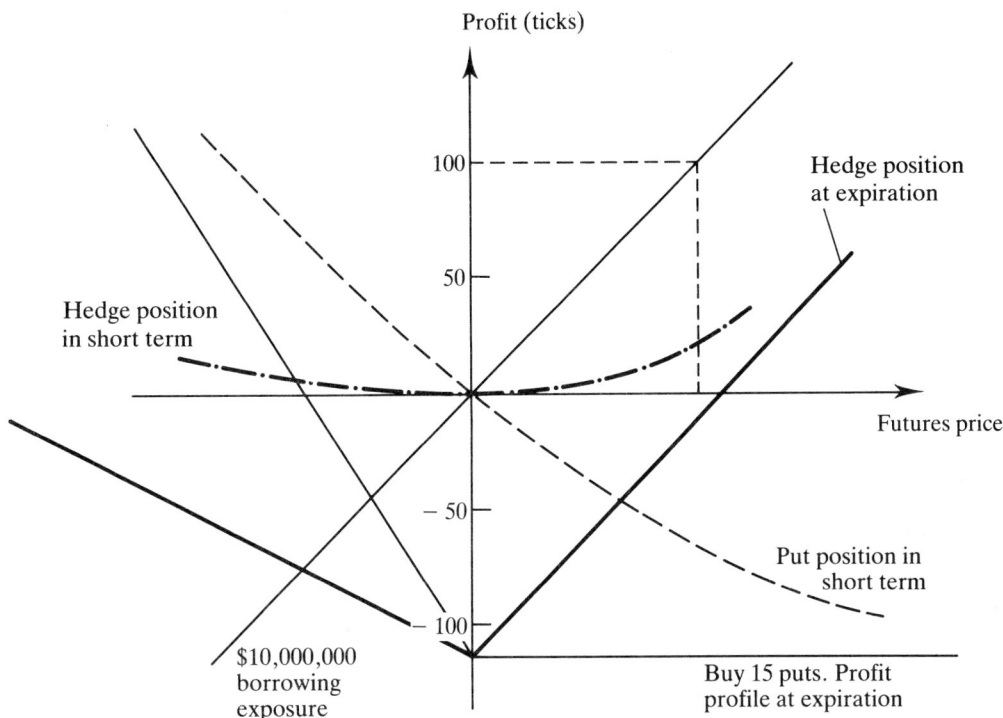

Source: LIFFE.

This is one of the dangers when trying to maintain a permanently hedged position of options on the one hand, and cash or futures on the other. It applies particularly in reverse: hedging an over-the-counter (OTC) option position written with a cash or futures position always exposes the hedger to volatility risk.

---

**A hedge of a cash or futures position with options or vice-versa always exposes the hedger to volatility risk in the short-term.**

---

The point about time or theta risk is easily seen in Exhibit 5.5. Although the delta hedge of 15 put option contracts is neutral to price changes in the short-term, the impact of time on the time value of the put options will produce losses to the hedge over its life. Assuming no further rebalancing were carried out over the period of the hedge, the final profit-loss profile is shown by the heavy black line in Exhibit 5.5. If the futures price expires at 90.00, the put options expire worthless, and per $1 million cash position the loss is $112\frac{1}{2}$ basis points (i.e. one and a half times the put option premium). This is technically an unfair assessment since it assumes an unlikely scenario – the ratio hedge is put on and left alone over its life. Nevertheless, it emphasizes the point that since a delta hedge will invariably demand more contracts than a fixed hedge, the maximum possible loss with a delta hedge will be greater than a fixed hedge, though it cannot be assessed exactly once the likelihood of rebalancing is introduced.

When an option hedge is basically a substitute for a forward or futures hedge it is appropriate to use a fixed hedge; when an option hedge is designed to continuously hedge a position, a delta hedge will be appropriate.

---

1. **Where an option is used to hedge a specific transaction at a specific date, the option hedge should be for the full face value of the exposure.**
2. **Where the hedge is of another option position, or where it is designed to continuously hedge a cash position rather than at a specific date, a delta or ratio hedge will be used.**

---

### (iv) Gamma and volatility neutral hedges

It is worth discussing how it might be possible to reduce the need for rebalancing as delta changes with the underlying asset price, and reduce the impact of changes in volatility on hedge performance. The table below shows the output from a typical option valuation programme.[3]

**Calls**

| Price | Premium | Delta | Gamma | Volatility | Days |
|-------|---------|-------|-------|------------|------|
| 135.00 | 15.00 | 1.00 | 0.00 | 0.00 | 0.01 |
| 140.00 | 10.54 | 0.84 | 0.02 | 0.18 | 0.01 |
| 145.00 | 6.87 | 0.67 | 0.03 | 0.27 | 0.02 |
| 150.00 | 4.11 | 0.49 | 0.04 | 0.30 | 0.02 |
| 155.00 | 2.24 | 0.32 | 0.03 | 0.27 | 0.02 |
| 160.00 | 1.10 | 0.19 | 0.02 | 0.20 | 0.02 |
| 165.00 | 0.49 | 0.10 | 0.02 | 0.13 | 0.01 |

**Puts**

| Price | Premium | Delta | Gamma | Volatility | Days |
|-------|---------|-------|-------|------------|------|
| 135.00 | 0.43 | −0.08 | 0.01 | 0.11 | 0.01 |
| 140.00 | 1.15 | −0.18 | 0.02 | 0.20 | 0.02 |
| 145.00 | 2.55 | −0.33 | 0.03 | 0.27 | 0.02 |
| 150.00 | 4.80 | −0.51 | 0.04 | 0.30 | 0.02 |
| 155.00 | 7.92 | −0.68 | 0.03 | 0.27 | 0.02 |
| 160.00 | 11.78 | −0.81 | 0.02 | 0.20 | 0.02 |
| 165.00 | 16.17 | −0.90 | 0.02 | 0.13 | 0.01 |

This shows the sensitivities for various exercise prices for a 90-day LIFFE sterling currency option. Suppose it was necessary to hedge a short sterling position of £1,000,000. The current sterling rate is $1.50. To maintain a delta neutral position, one could envisage using the at-the-money 150 calls with a delta of 0.49.

$$\text{Number of contracts} = \frac{£1,000,000}{£25,000} \times \frac{1}{0.49} = 81.6 \text{ or } 82 \text{ contracts}$$

But the gamma of the call is 0.04, i.e. if the exchange rate moves to $1.51, the delta of the option will move from 0.49 to 0.53 and the hedge will be unbalanced. Consider what happens to this position if everything else remains unchanged, but the exchange rate moves to $1.55 one day later.

$$\text{Fair price of \$1.50 call} = 6.97 \quad \text{Delta} = 0.66$$
$$\text{Cash position loss} = £1,000,000 \, (\$1.55 - \$1.50)$$
$$= \$50,000$$
$$\text{Options position gain} = 82 \times (\$0.0697 - \$0.0411) \times £25,000$$
$$= \$58,630$$

Thus a net gain of $8,630 is realized – good for the hedger but an indication that delta neutrality is not sufficient to maintain a neutral hedge for significant price movements. Now consider creating the delta neutral hedge using a spread of options.

$$\text{Buy 145 call} \quad \text{Delta} = \ \ 0.67$$
$$\text{Sell 155 call} \quad \text{Delta} = -0.32$$
$$\text{Net delta} = \ \ 0.35$$
$$\text{Net gamma} = \ \ 0.03 - 0.03 = 0.00$$
$$\text{Number of option spreads for full hedge} = \frac{£1,000,000}{£25,000} \times \frac{1}{0.35}$$
$$= 114 \text{ spreads purchased}$$
$$\text{Fair price of 145 call} = 10.61$$
$$\text{Fair price of 155 call} = 4.23 \quad \text{FX rate} = \$1.55$$
$$\text{Cash position loss} = \$50,000$$
$$\text{Options position gain} = 114 \, (\$0.1061 - \$0.0687) \, £25,000$$
$$- 114 \, (\$0.0423 - \$0.0224) \, £25,000$$
$$= \$49,875.00$$

---

[3] This table is from the Investor Intelligence Systems Corporation option valuation program.

The cash position loss is closer to the option position gain – the gamma neutral hedge was a more effective hedge. The gamma neutral hedge is also more effective at protecting against volatility changes, since on examining the sensitivity to volatility, the 145 call appears as sensitive as the 155 call.

Consider the exchange rate movement to $1.55, but this time let volatility move to 10% which will harm the long option position.

$$\text{Fair price of 145 call} = 10.00$$
$$\text{Fair price of 150 call} = 5.70$$
$$\text{Fair price of 155 call} = 2.71$$
$$\text{Cash position loss} = \$50,000$$
$$\text{150 call option position} = 82 \, (\$0.0570 - \$0.041) \, £25,000$$
$$= \$32,800$$
$$\text{Net loss} = \$17,200$$

The hedge proves ineffective in the face of a significant change in implied volatility.

$$\text{145} - \text{155 option spread position} = 114 \, (\$0.1000 - \$0.0687) \, £25,000$$
$$- 114 \, (\$0.0271 - \$0.0224) \, £25,000$$
$$= \$75,810$$
$$\text{Net gain} = \$25,810$$

Although the hedger would be satisfied with the net gain, this is not an effective hedge if volatility changes. Why is this? Look at the volatility sensitivity of the two options at 10% volatility and the FX rate at $1.55.

$$\text{145 call volatility sensitivity} = 0.00$$
$$\text{155 call volatility sensitivity} = 0.30$$

The reason is that at $1.55 the 145 call has no time value (it is priced at $0.10) and hence is not sensitive to small changes in volatility. The 155 call premium is entirely time value and hence its sensitivity to volatility is extremely high. Since the position is long the 145 call and short the 155 call, this has favoured the hedger. Consider, therefore, a volatility change to 20%.

$$\text{Fair price of 145 call} = 11.68$$
$$\text{Fair price of 155 call} = 5.75$$
$$\text{145} - \text{155 option spread position} = 114 \, (\$0.1168 - \$0.0687) \, £25,000$$
$$- 114 \, (\$0.0575 - \$0.0224) \, £25,000$$
$$= \$37,050$$

This is a better hedge but still results in a net loss of $12,950. Hence although the hedge is delta neutral and gamma neutral, the option spread hedge remains exposed to the risk of volatility change. However, the exposure is generally asymmetric – the benefits to the hedge of a fall in volatility from 15% to 10% considerably outweigh the costs of a rise in volatility from 15% to 20%. The effect would be reversed if the exchange rate had fallen significantly rather than rising as in our example. Nonetheless, the option spread hedge will be a better hedge against underlying asset price changes (this is more important when the option hedge involves short options positions), and will provide better volatility protection than a simple option hedge.

The hedge will be more volatility neutral if there are smaller changes in volatility. Suppose we look at a rise to 16% and a fall to 14%.

*14% volatility*

$$\text{Fair price of 145 call} = 10.44$$
$$\text{Fair price of 155 call} = 3.93$$

*16% volatility*

$$\text{Fair price of 145 call} = 10.79$$
$$\text{Fair price of 155 call} = 4.53$$

*14% volatility*

$$\text{Option position gain} = 114 \, (\$0.1044 - \$0.0687) \, £25,000$$
$$- 114 \, (\$0.0393 - \$0.0224) \, £25,000$$
$$= \$53,580$$

*16% volatility*

$$\text{Option position gain} = 114\ (\$0.1079 - \$0.0687)\ £25,000$$
$$- 114\ (\$0.0453 - \$0.0224)\ £25,000$$
$$= \$46,455$$

A 1% rise in volatility still involves a loss of around \$3,500.00. Even so, if a simple hedge with the 150 option had been used, and volatility fell to 14%, performance would be worse.

$$\text{Fair price of 150 call} = 6.69$$
$$\text{Option gain} = 82\ (\$0.0669 - \$0.0411) \times £25,000$$
$$= \$52,890.00$$

The impact of the volatility change has been to reduce the net hedge benefit from \$8,630 to \$2,890. This change of \$5,740 is significantly greater than the change from a net loss of \$125.00 to a net loss of \$3,545.00 for the option spread (for a volatility shift from 15% to 16%).

---

1. **Delta neutral, gamma neutral options hedges can be created by using options spreads.**
2. **Hedges with options spreads provide better protection against volatility changes than simple hedges.**

---

## b. Hedging OTC positions

One of the primary hedging uses of traded options is to hedge over-the-counter (OTC) positions written by banks and other financial institutions. Over-the-counter options are designed to suit the needs of individual clients, and can therefore have contract sizes, exercise prices and expiration dates which do not correspond to the limited range of values that characterize the traded options market. The aim is to determine a traded option position which will best mimic the over-the-counter option position through time. However, the question of how to hedge an over-the-counter option position depends crucially on whether the financial institution in some sense guarantees to buy the option back before expiration at a fair price or whether the buyer of the option simply has the right to exercise it.

Consider a bank which evaluates a specific currency option with an exercise price of \$1.30 which is at-the-money and comes up with a fair price of, say, 5 cents. Because it is a customized OTC option, the bank is able to demand a premium of 5.5 cents, giving an expected commercial margin over the fair price of 0.5 cents. If the bank promises to buy the option back at a fair price on a continuous basis, then it will try to construct an opposite hedge position which exactly matches in profit the fair price of the option, originally 5 cents, as it moves upward. If, on the other hand, all the option buyer can do is exercise the option, then to protect the commercial margin of 0.5 cents, since this is originally an at-the-money option, the bank only needs to hedge movements in the intrinsic value of the option, currently zero, above 5 cents. This means that hedging strategies would be totally different.

---

1. **If the seller of an OTC option promises to buy it back before expiration at a fair price, he should design an equivalent but opposite option position which will match movements in the fair price of the OTC option continuously in the period before expiration.**
2. **If the buyer of an OTC option only has the right to exercise it, then the seller only needs to hedge upward movements in the intrinsic value of the option that exceed the original fair price.**

---

What are the problems that face the writer of a customized OTC option wishing to hedge the position in the traded options market? A minor problem is a *size mismatch*: since the size of the traded option is fixed, hedging broken amounts exactly is not possible. In the case of Eurodollar options (used so far in this chapter) a maximum size mismatch of \$500,000 can occur. With other types of options it will generally be smaller, because the average contract size is smaller. However, the hedger can do nothing about this problem.

### (i) Price mismatches

An *exercise price mismatch* can be handled by using a mixture of options on either side of the OTC exercise price to produce a combination which behaves similarly to the option in the middle. Exhibit 5.6 shows an example of this. A $10 million 90.20 exercise price call has been written and has been hedged by the purchase of 90.00 calls and 90.50 calls. To produce a weighted average exercise price of 90.20, the hedge will involve buying six 90.00 calls and four 90.50 calls.

$$0.6 \ (90.00) + 0.4 \ (90.50) = 90.20$$

However, the profit-loss profile of this hedge shown in Exhibit 5.6 does not show a perfect hedge. The hedged position makes money if the price remains around 90.20 and loses money for significant movements in the underlying asset price. This arises because the price of the over-the-counter option is not simply the linear combination of the option premiums on either side.

### Exhibit 5.6: Exercise price mismatch

Exposure   Short $10 m   90.20 call

Cover   Long 6   90.00 calls
        Long 4   90.50 calls

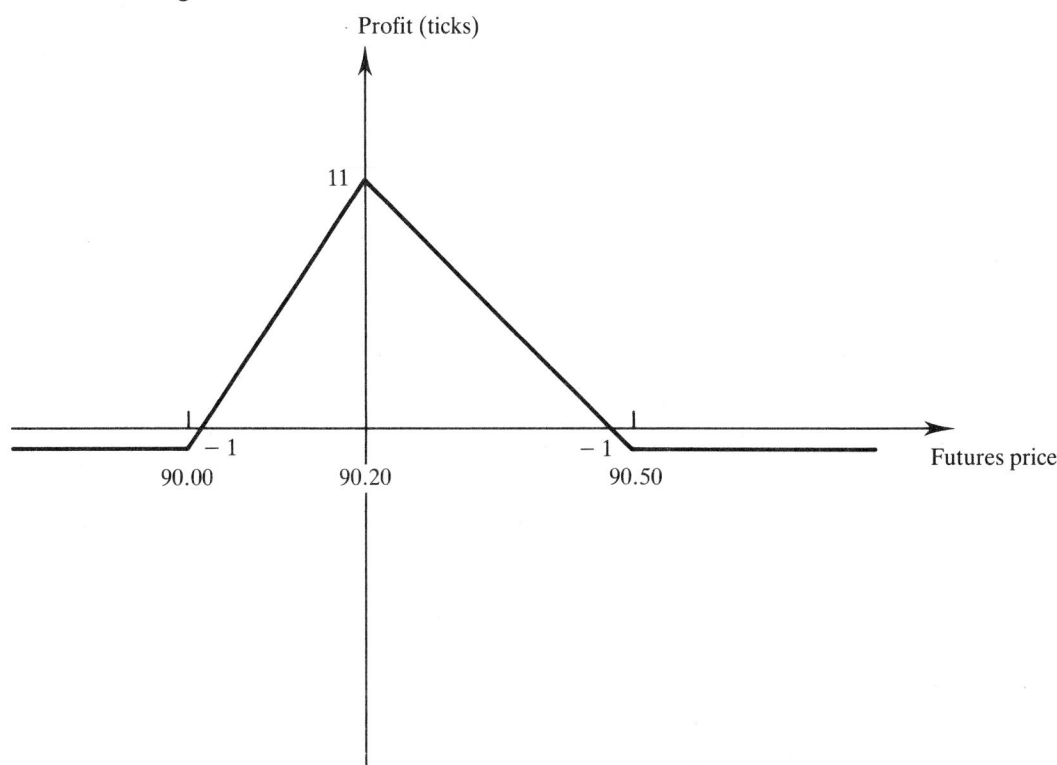

For instance, assuming an implied price volatility of 2.0%, the table below shows the fair prices for LIFFE Eurodollar call options.[4] All options are assumed to be 90 days in length. The futures price is 90.00.

| Exercise price | Premium |
| --- | --- |
| 89.00 | 1.06 |
| 89.50 | 0.66 |
| 90.00 | 0.36 |
| 90.50 | 0.16 |
| 91.00 | 0.06 |

Using the same volatility, the fair price of a 90.20 option is 0.27. But the effective cost of his hedge is

$$(0.6)(0.36) + (0.4)(0.16) = 0.28$$

The profits and losses at expiry indicate the type of pattern shown in Exhibit 5.6.

_____

[4] The model used to produce these fair values is described in Chapter 8.

*Final futures price = 90.00 or below*

All options expire worthless.

$$\text{Net loss} = 0.27 - 0.28 = -0.01 \text{ or one basis point}$$

*Final futures price = 90.20*

90.20 and 90.50 options expire worthless. Intrinsic value of 90.00 option (0.6) (0.20) or 0.12.

$$\text{Net profit} = 0.12 - 0.28 + 0.27 = 0.11$$

*Final futures price = 90.50*

90.50 expires worthless. Intrinsic value of 90.00 option is (0.6) (0.50) or 0.30. Intrinsic value of 90.20 option is also 0.30. Net loss again equals 0.01 or one basis point.

$$\text{Net loss} = 0.30 - 0.28 + 0.27 - 0.30 = -0.01$$

*Final futures price = 91.00*

Intrinsic value of 90.00 option is (0.6) (1.00) or 0.60. Intrinsic value of 90.20 option is 0.80. Intrinsic value of 90.50 option is 0.20. Net loss again equals 0.01 or one basis point.

$$\text{New low} = -0.28 + 0.27 + 0.60 + 0.20 - 0.80 = -0.01$$

From the point of view of the OTC writer, the aim is to charge the buyer a commercial margin over the cost of the hedge portfolio, which is 0.28, and hope that the price will remain around 90.20, in which case an additional windfall profit will accrue. In trading parlance, what has happened is that the hedge position is exactly the same as a delta neutral butterfly with 90.00, 90.20 and 90.50 exercise price options.

---

**The algebra developed earlier for designing trading strategies is equally useful for designing hedge strategies.**

---

The exercise price mismatch hedge discussed above is called an interpolative hedge – the exercise price to be hedged is between two exercise prices of traded options. An extrapolative hedge may need to be used for an exercise price mismatch. This could arise if a customer wants an option very out-of-the-money or very in-the-money, so that the desired exercise price lies outside the range of current traded exercise prices. For instance, supposing the OTC writer sold a $10 million 89.00 call at a fair price of 1.06 plus commercial margin and 89.50 and 90.00 were the lowest exercise prices available on LIFFE.

In our option algebra, the written OTC option has a description

$$(0, -1)(89.00)$$

Supposing it were hedged by buying 10 89.50 calls. The profile would then be

$$(0, -1, 0)(89.00, 89.50)$$

However, a closer match to the exercise price could be found by going long 89.50 calls and short 90.00 calls

$$89.00 = (2)(89.50) - (1)(90.00)$$

In our option algebra, this would give rise to a position equivalent to the reverse type of butterfly spread

$$(0, -1, 1, 0)(89.00, 89.50, 90.00)$$

Both hedging strategies are shown in Exhibit 5.7.

The purchase of the 89.50 call options turned the OTC position into the equivalent of a vertical spread sold which loses 10 basis points for all prices above 89.50. The purchase of 20 89.50 calls and the sale of 10 90.00 calls creates the effective sale of a butterfly spread which gains 10 basis points above or below 89.00 and 90.00 and loses 40 basis points at a futures price of 89.50. Which hedge position is preferable is up to the individual hedger. However, the additional margin required to guarantee against a hedge position loss will generally be less with the vertical spread

**Exhibit 5.7: Extrapolated hedges**

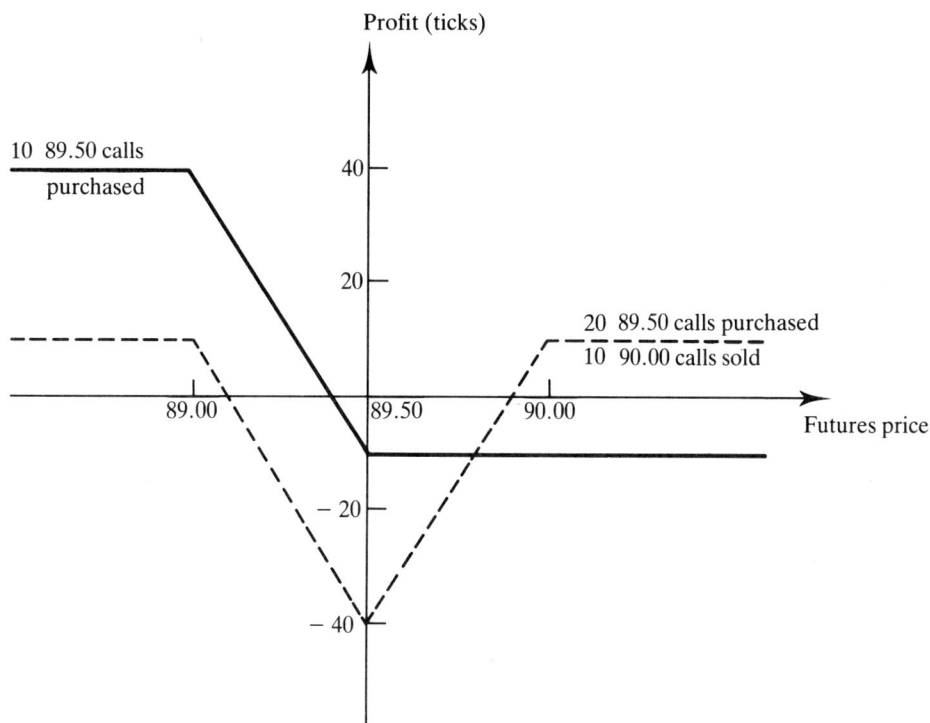

hedge than the sold butterfly hedge. In the case above, to guarantee absolutely against a hedge loss at expiration in the case of the butterfly, the hedger would have to sell the OTC option at a minimum price of 1.56. In the case of the vertical spread hedge, the price would need to be 1.16.

## (ii) Expiration mismatches

The other major type of mismatch that can occur with hedging over-the-counter options is where the expiration date of the OTC option does not correspond to that of the traded option or options being used to hedge it. If the hedger uses the traded option with an expiration date after the expiration date of the OTC option, the time value of the traded option will be greater than that of the OTC option, and this difference will be lost by the hedger if a major change in the underlying asset price occurs and both options become worthless. The simple way to handle this is by linear interpolation and extrapolation among the traded options.

**Example: Current date August 1**

A bank writes a $10 million OTC 90.00 call option expiring on November 1. The option is written on the cash three-month interest rate. Current traded option prices are:

| Delivery date | Futures price | Option premium | Option delta |
|---|---|---|---|
| September 15 | 90.00 | 0.27 | 0.50 |
| December 15 | 89.70 | 0.33 | 0.40 |
| March 16 | 89.45 | 0.36 | 0.36 |

Implied volatility = 2.10%

Using this implied volatility, and a linear interpolation to obtain a suggested November 1 futures price of 89.85, the fair price of a November 1 90.00 call is 0.31 with a delta of 0.44.

The traditional interpolative hedge would involve buying a mixture of September 90 calls and December 90 calls to duplicate the November 1 call.

Sell 10 November 1 calls at 0.31
Buy 5 September calls  at 0.27
Buy 5 December calls  at 0.33
Net inflow per $1,000,000 = 1 basis point

This interpolative hedge can only be maintained until September 15, at which point the September options and futures will expire. The interpolative hedge will then need to be replaced with a simple hedge using

103

December options or an extrapolative hedge using December and March options. Such an extrapolative hedge can be placed immediately on August 1.

Sell 10 November 1 calls at 0.31
Buy 15 December calls   at 0.33
Sell  5 March calls       at 0.36
Net outflow per $1,000,000 = 1/2 basis point

Exhibit 5.8 shows the hedge results on September 15 for the simple hedge of buying 10 December 90 calls immediately, the interpolative hedge and the extrapolative hedge. The simplest hedge is the most risky. The extrapolative hedge is actually better at producing a neutral hedge position over the range of futures prices shown. Exhibit 5.9 shows the result of the extrapolative hedge (established on August 1) at the expiration date of the OTC option for a range of equivalent futures prices on November 1. On the assumption of no change in implied volatility, and no change in the spread between different futures prices (which we have made throughout) the maximum loss on the hedge position is nine basis points per $1 million or $225. In general, if an extrapolative hedge is going to be required eventually to cover an over-the-counter option position, it may as well be put on immediately unless there is a large time-gap between the current date and the eventual date at which the extrapolative hedge will be required.

Putting on the extrapolative hedge in the ratio shown would not create a perfectly delta neutral hedge.

*Delta*

OTC 10 November 90 call short          $10 \times (-0.44) = -4.4$
Buy 15 December 90 calls              $15 \times (0.40) = 6.0$
Sell 5 March 90 calls                 $5 \times (-0.36) = -1.8$

Net delta $= -0.2$

The position would be expected to lose modestly in the short-term if interest rates fell and Eurodollar futures prices rose. Because of the $1 million size of the Eurodollar contracts, this modest degree of delta non-neutrality cannot be removed.

Another point needs to be stressed for all these hedges of broken dates with mixtures of traded options designed to effectively duplicate the underlying position. Although simple linear interpolation and extrapolation produces effective hedged positions within specific profit and loss boundaries, in all the cases shown it was assumed that volatility remained constant. If, by

## Exhibit 5.8: Hedge results: September 15

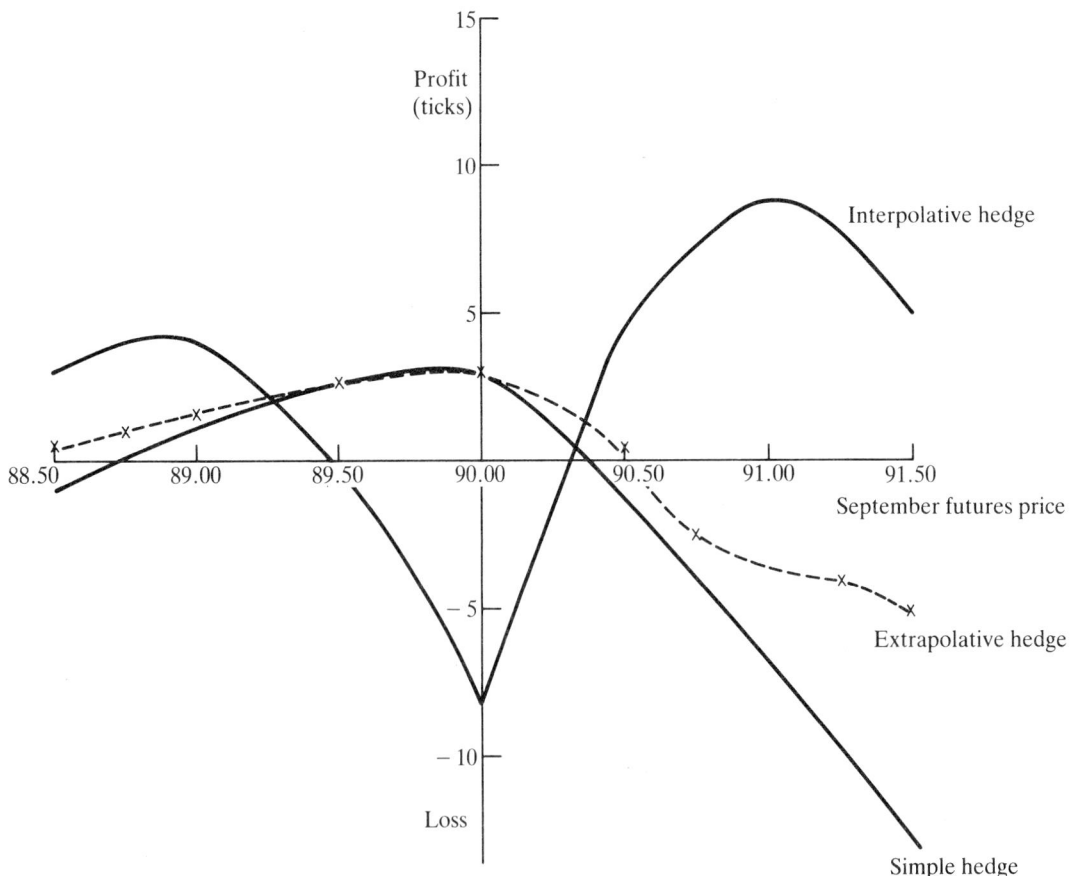

**Exhibit 5.9: Extrapolative hedge: November 1**

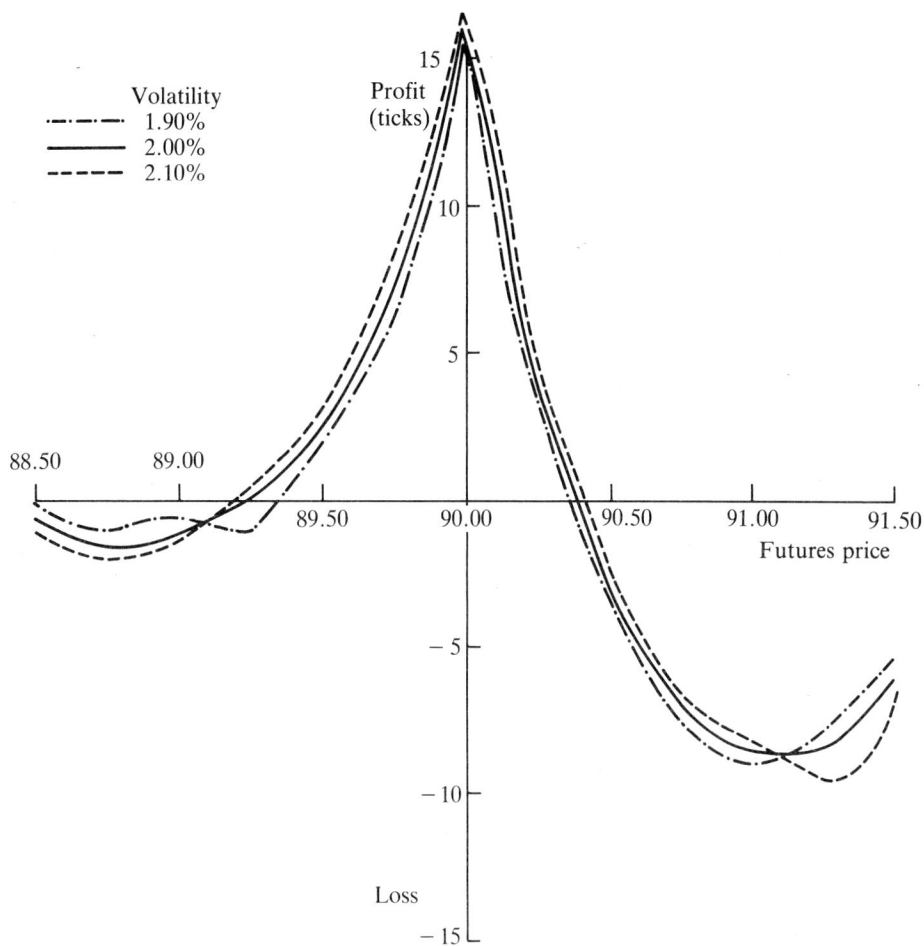

contrast, volatility were to change significantly, it could have an impact upon the boundaries within which the final hedge results will lie. Exhibit 5.9 illustrates the impact of letting the volatility move to 2.00% and up to 2.20%. This level of change of volatility has only a modest impact upon hedge profitability, with the maximum range being no more than two basis points or $50 per $1,000,000 exposure.

### c. Hedging uncertain cash flows

This chapter has discussed the differences between futures or forward hedges and option hedges, and various aspects of hedging options with options. It is now appropriate to analyse in more detail the hedging of uncertain cash flows. The approach so far has been to consider hedging with options rather than futures, so that the loss is limited if the cash flow does not actually materialize. An alternative hedging strategy is to hedge only the expected value of the uncertain cash flow rather than the full value of the cash flow. A typical case of this would be the contract to tender where firms bid for contracts denominated in foreign currencies.

To keep the hedge examples consistent, we will use the $10 million cash exposure when there is a 60% probability that the cash flow will occur and a 40% probability that it will not. Exhibit 5.10 illustrates the nature of the exposure, with the expected exposure shown by the dotted line. The first alternative is to use futures contracts to hedge the expected exposure, by selling six futures contracts at a price of 90.00. This produces a zero expected hedge position (see Exhibit 5.11), though the *ex post* hedge result will give rise to a windfall gain or loss depending on whether or not the cash flow occurs. If the cash flow occurs, $4,000,000 is left unhedged, which will result in a profit if rates fall and a loss if rates rise. If the cash flow does not occur, the hedger has an exposed short futures position of six contracts which will make money if rates rise and lose money if rates fall. Assuming, however, a lengthy sequence of such hedges, and that the hedger is able to correctly identify the probability distribution of expected cash flows, unexpected gains and losses over the hedge sequence will sum to more or less zero and the *ex post* overall hedge performance will approximate the expected hedge performance.

**Exhibit 5.10: Uncertain exposure**

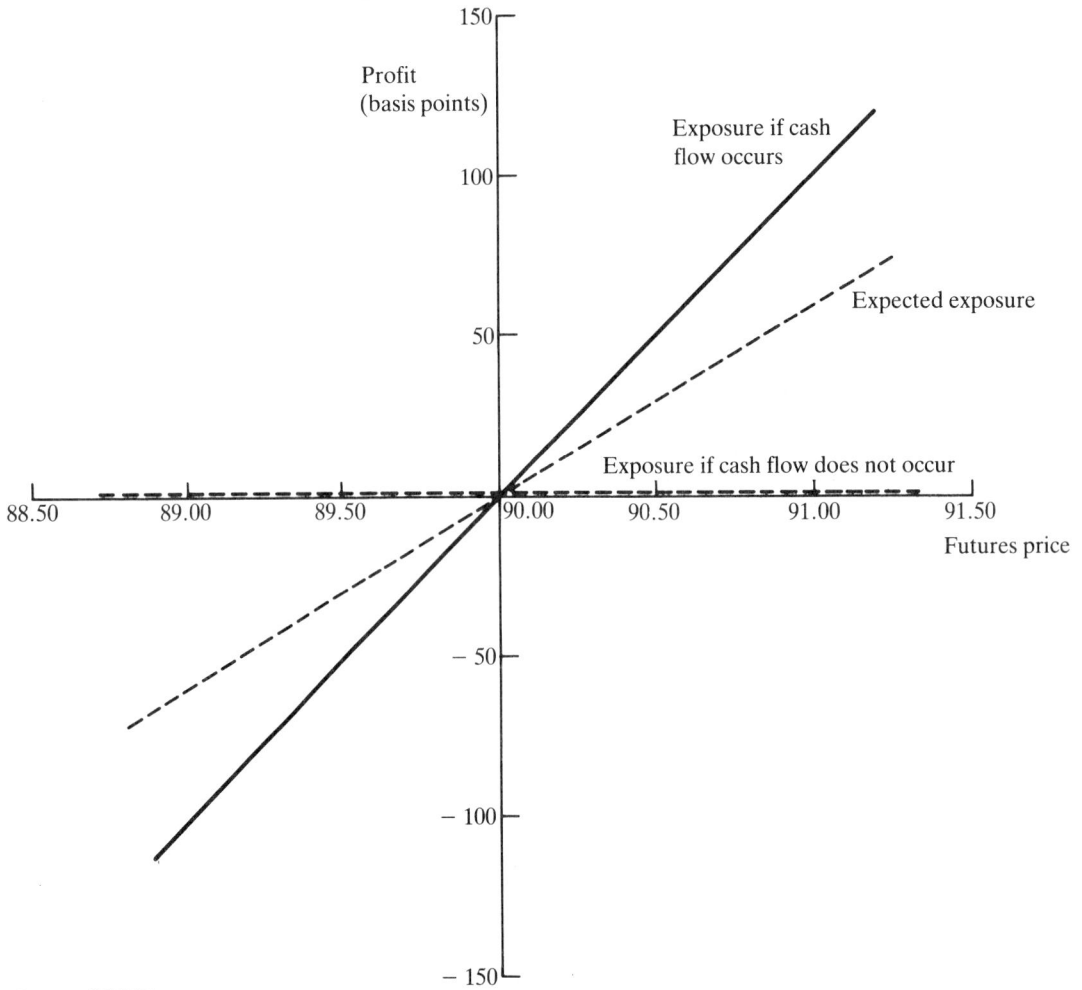

Profit (basis points)

Exposure if cash flow occurs

Expected exposure

Exposure if cash flow does not occur

Futures price

Source: LIFFE.

**Exhibit 5.11: Probability weighted hedge of uncertain exposure**

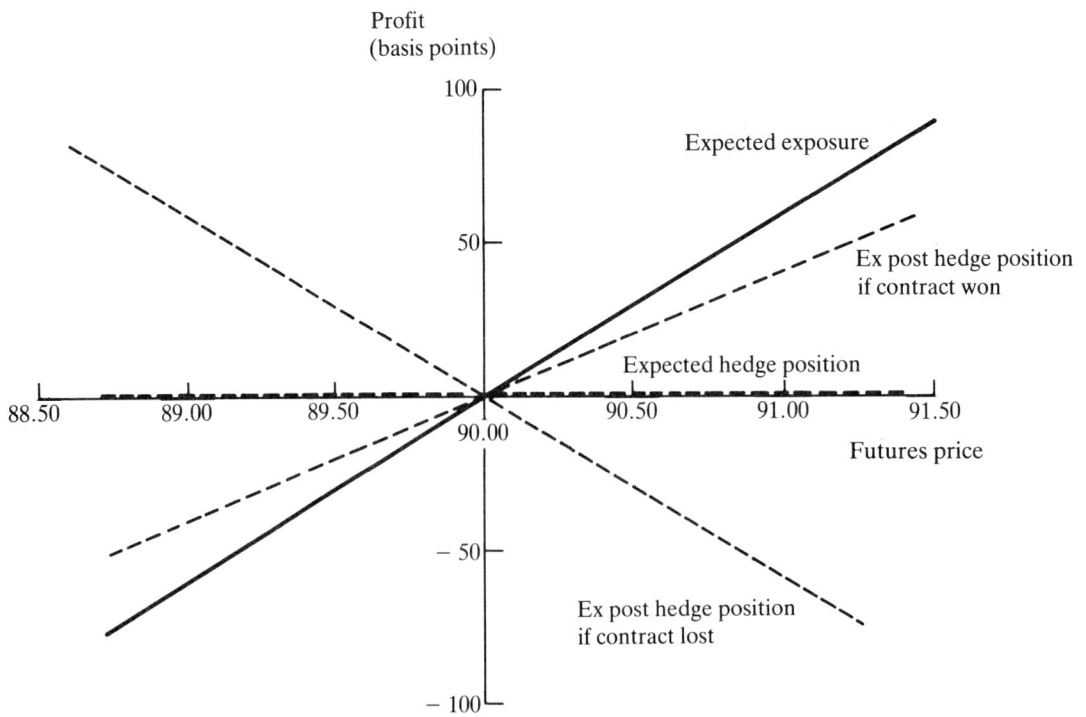

Profit (basis points)

Expected exposure

Ex post hedge position if contract won

Expected hedge position

Futures price

Ex post hedge position if contract lost

Source: LIFFE.

106

**Exhibit 5.12: Option hedge of uncertain exposure**

Profit
(basis points)

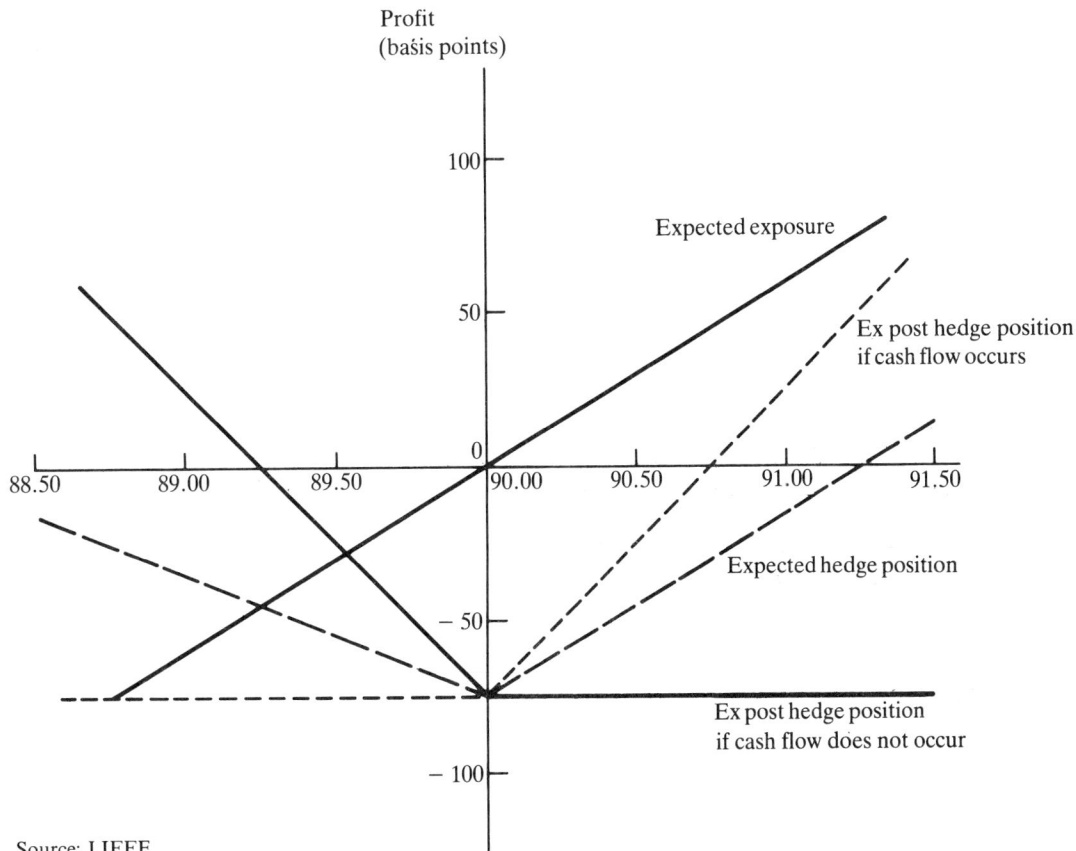

Source: LIFFE.

The alternative is to hedge this type of exposure with options. Exhibit 5.12 shows the alternative hedge positions when the uncertain cash flow is hedged by buying put options. The expected result is similar to that of a ratio hedge of a certain exposure. If the cash flow does not occur, the hedger simply has an open Eurodollar put position.

If the cash flow occurs, the hedger has a synthetic 90.00 call option position established at a price of 75 basis points (the same as the premium on the put). The expected hedge position is therefore a synthetic straddle position established for a price of 75 basis points. The maximum loss to the position is the 75 basis points, and the hedger will earn windfall profits if the Eurodollar futures price falls sharply and the cash flow does not occur, or rises sharply and the cash flow does occur. If only a few hedges are envisaged, the hedger may well prefer the profit and loss profile of the options hedge to the potentially unlimited gains and losses of the probability weighted futures hedge. In practice, the two approaches can be combined, hedging the minimum exposure which is regarded as certain with futures, and hedging the rest of the exposure with options.

---

1. For uncertain exposures in the cash market, hedging the expected exposure with futures or forwards will minimize risk and will secure the expected result *ex post* over a sufficient number of hedges. It is a risky strategy for an isolated hedge.
2. Hedging the maximum exposure with options limits losses to the premium of the options and retains some of the benefit if the asset price moves in favour of the cash position.
3. Hedging the minimum certain exposure with futures and the maximum value of the remaining exposure with options achieves a degree of risk reduction and retains some of the benefits from extreme price movements.
4. The hedger should also explore the possibility of hedging some of the expected exposure by buying options and some by selling options.
5. The point is to design an expected hedge profit and loss profile that best suits the individual hedger.

---

## d. Cylinder hedges

This chapter has largely concerned itself with 'direct' hedging, i.e. hedging underlying asset or option positions with simple option hedges, whether on a matching basis or ratioed using delta. However, as the trading strategies chapter has implied, it is possible to add option positions to underlying cash positions to achieve a variety of hedge results. The most common of these are *cylinder hedges*.

### (i) Basic cylinders

The aim here is to offset the cost of a straight option hedge by the simultaneous sale of an option position. For instance, suppose an effective long Eurodollar position is established at a price of 92.00. The option premiums are:

| March | *Exercise price* | *91.00* | *91.50* | *92.00* | *92.50* | *93.00* |
|-------|-----------------|---------|---------|---------|---------|---------|
|       | Call            | 0.98    | 0.52    | 0.19    | 0.03    | 0.00    |
|       | Put             | 0.01    | 0.05    | 0.22    | 0.56    | 1.03    |

The March Eurodollar future is priced at 91.97.

A simple hedge to cover the position would be to buy the 92.00 put option. The cost could then be reduced, albeit only slightly in this case by selling the 92.50 call. Exhibit 5.13 shows that the effective result, instead of the creation of an artificial call option, is the creation of an artificial bull spread. The logic of this can be seen, using symbolic notation from the trading chapter (Chapter 4).

| Original position | (1, 1, 1) (92.00, 92.50) |
|-------------------|--------------------------|
| Long 92.00 put    | (−1, 0, 0) (92.00, 92.50) |
| Short 92.50 call  | (0, 0, −1) (92.00, 92.50) |
| Result            | (0, 1, 0) (92.00, 92.50) |

**Exhibit 5.13: Cylinder hedges**

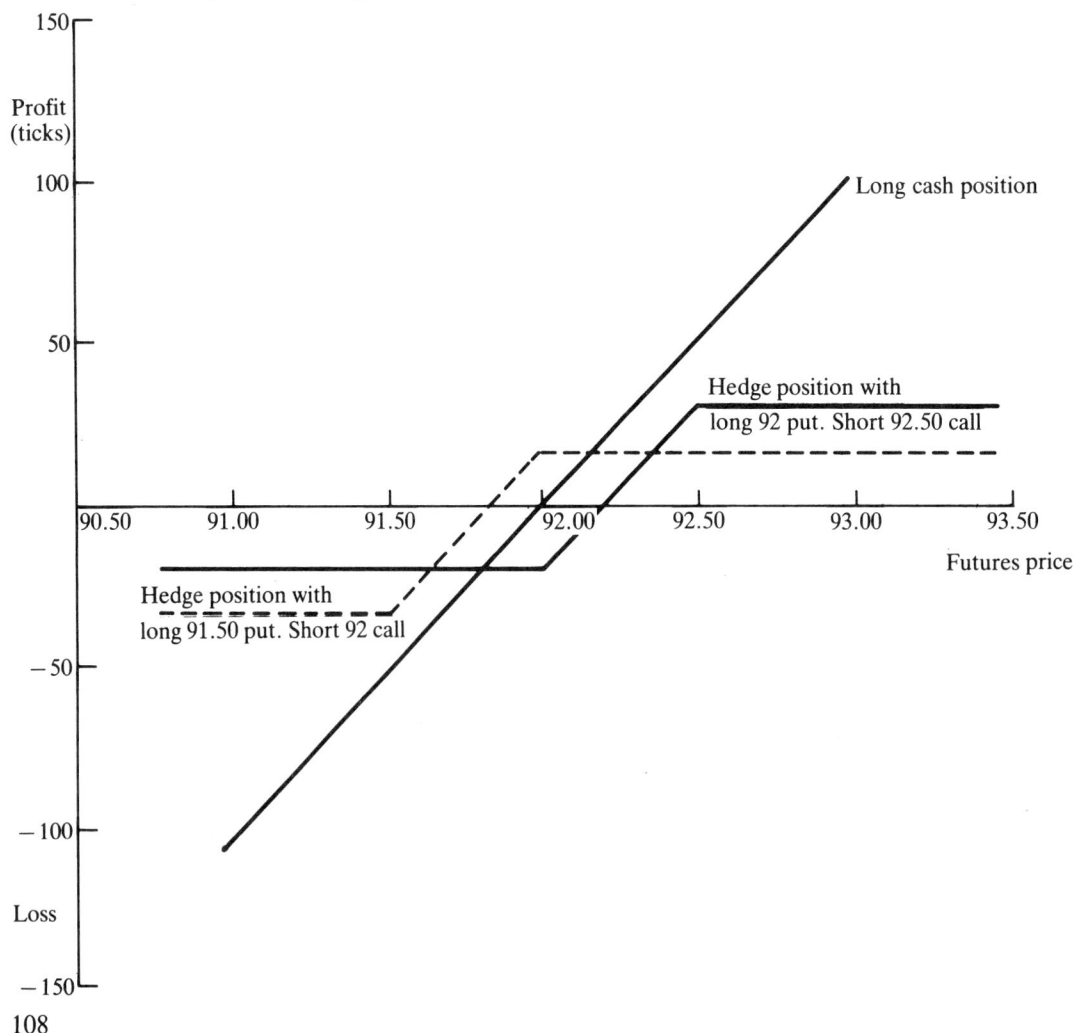

108

Many variants of this cylinder strategy could be devised, e.g. buying the 91.50 put and selling the 92.00 call. This position is also shown in Exhibit 5.13.

Artificial futures positions created from put and call options at the same exercise price can be used as a hedging substitute for actual futures positions.

| Original position | (1, 1) (92.00) | Artificial short future |
|---|---|---|
| Long 92.00 put | (−1, 0) (92.00) | (−1, −1) (92.00) |
| Short 92.00 call | (0, −1) (92.00) | |
| Result | (0, 0) (92.00) | |

The cost of the artificial future would be 0.22 minus 0.19 or three basis points. The price is consistent with the difference between the price at which the long Eurodollar position is established and the current price of the March Eurodollar three-month contract of 91.97. In this case, there is no purpose in constructing a March future from options contracts, since the net effect is to create an identical futures price to the one actually trading. However, if the hedger spots a violation of put-call parity conditions in the market, so that an artificial futures contract can be constructed at a more advantageous price than the actual futures price, this construction may be worth doing. More importantly, this ability to mix put and call options together to duplicate futures positions is useful when there is no actual future trading on the underlying asset. This is specifically the case with options written on individual stocks.

### (ii) Rotated cylinders

Another type of cylinder hedge enables the hedger to preserve the benefits of extreme favourable movements in asset prices, while paying the price of retaining the adverse impact of extreme unfavourable movements. Such a hedge might be suitable where the hedger wishes to protect

### Exhibit 5.14: Rotated cylinder hedges

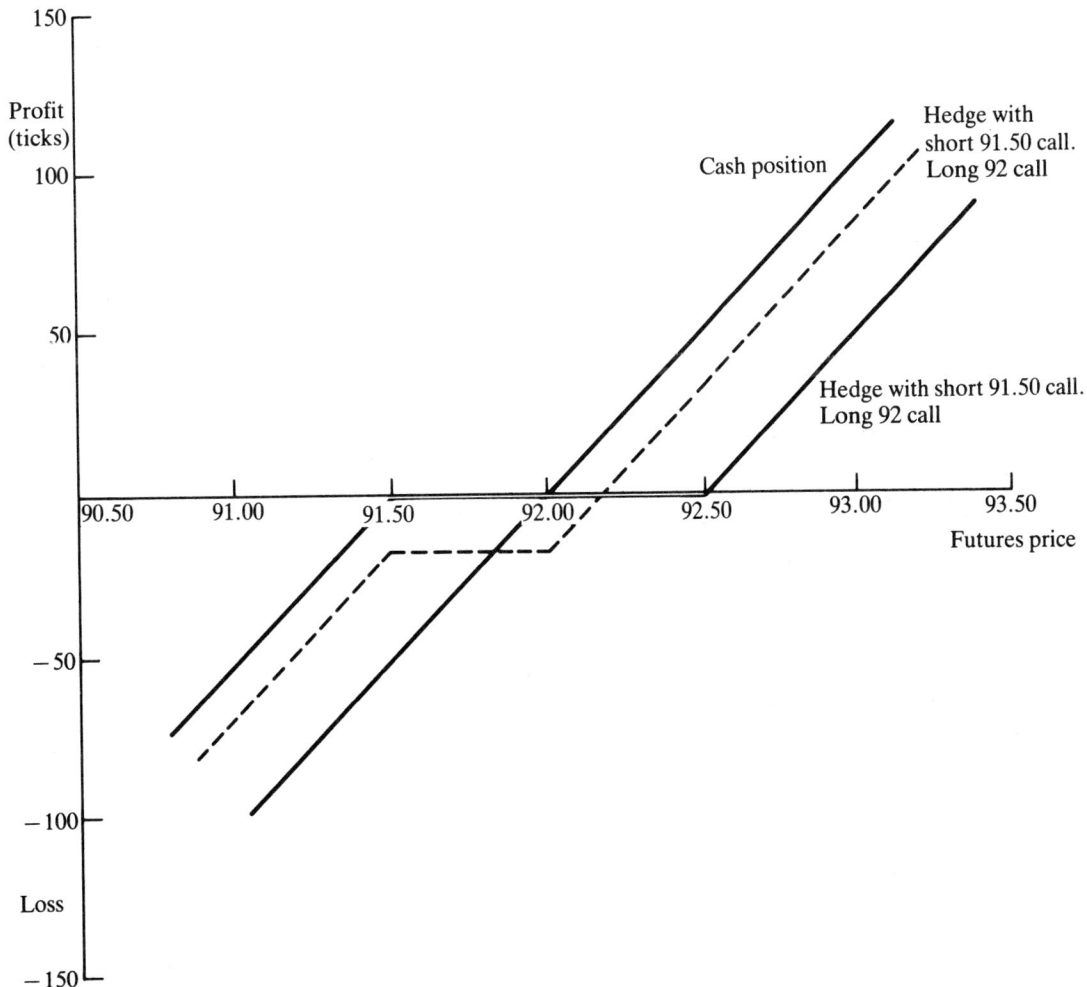

against modest adverse movements in asset prices, but is convinced that if the price moves in a big way, it will be in a favourable direction. For the long position at 92.00 discussed previously, this type of hedge could be achieved by selling a low exercise price call and buying a high exercise price call.

| | | |
|---|---|---|
| Original position | (1, 1, 1, 1) | (91.50, 92.00, 92.50) |
| Short 91.50 call | (0, −1, −1, −1) | (91.50, 92.00, 92.50) |
| Long 92.50 call | (0, 0, 0, 1) | (91.50, 92.00, 92.50) |
| Result | (1, 0, 0, 1) | (91.50, 92.00, 92.50) |

This hedge is shown in Exhibit 5.14, together with a similar hedge using the 91.50 call and the 92.00 call.

Besides simple option hedging of cash positions, combinations can be constructed to suit any particular pattern of asset price forecasts made by the hedger.

## 3. The hedging process

The essence of successful hedging with options lies not just in the kind of hedge design discussed in this chapter, but also in ensuring that it takes place within the context of an efficient hedge management. The hedge process should at the very least involve the hedger in the following steps:

1. The determination of a set of forecasts for the underlying asset prices over the likely time horizon of the hedge. This should include probability distributions of these anticipated price changes.
2. A careful analysis of past and expected volatility information to forecast volatility changes over the life of the hedge.
3. The preparation of a profit-loss matrix for different option hedging strategies for alternative movements in asset prices.

| Hedging strategies | Futures hedges | | Call option hedges | | Put option hedges | | Mixed hedges | |
|---|---|---|---|---|---|---|---|---|
| | Full | Partial | Simple | Ratio | Simple | Ratio | Simple | Ratio |
| Asset prices | Hedge results | | | | | | | |
| Mean hedge results | | | | | | | | |

4. Further analysis of the hedge profit-loss matrix by a sensitivity analysis of the implied volatility in the option prices.
5. The determination of the optimal hedge based on the hedger's set of price and volatility forecasts.

The choice of the hedge design is only the first step, however. Three further steps are:

a. hedge monitoring;
b. hedge adjustment; and
c. hedge evaluation.

### a. Hedge monitoring

Management must ensure that it has an information system capable of monitoring the complex exposures involved in options positions, which have so many expiration dates and strike prices. The following information should always be available in up-to-date form.

(i) *Cash position.* This includes not just the original estimated exposure, but any changes to it through time. The net opportunity or realized loss or gain to the underlying cash position must be identified, whether that exposure be in stocks, bonds, short-term cash positions, or currencies.

(*ii*) *Option position.* The size and profit or loss to the option position must be clearly identified. Any margin commitments on an option position need to be known, together with the imputed interest cost estimated over the life of the hedge.

(*iii*) *Basis risk.* When there is a discrepancy between the instrument being hedged and the instrument on which the option is written, e.g. the hedging of an option on a currency cash position with a Chicago Mercantile option on a currency future, relative profits and losses to the hedged position must be broken down into those due to overall asset price and basis movement.

(*iv*) *Volatility risk.* Because of the importance of rate volatility in option premium determination, implied volatilities of option prices need to be carefully monitored, and the impact on hedge profitability and efficiency determined.

(*v*) *Financing requirements.* To make sure sufficient financial resources are continuously available to maintain the hedge, margin financing requirements need to be carefully monitored.

(*vi*) *Fulfilment of forecasts.* Original forecasts for underlying asset prices and/or volatilities should be compared with realized data, for any necessary adjustments to the forecast to be made. Hedges based on historical correlation and regression information should also be regularly checked against new market data. For ratio hedges, it is important to ensure that the deltas from any option valuation model being used are good predictors of how option premiums change with asset prices. The same applies to thetas, epsilons and gammas.

## b. Hedge adjustment

The aim of a monitoring system is to provide management with the information it needs to determine whether hedges should be adjusted over the course of their life. There are various reasons for hedges having to be adjusted.

(*i*) *Alterations in exposure.* The optimal hedge size will alter if the cash market exposure changes because of unexpected cash flows. This may involve realizing losses on options contracts no longer required for a hedging function.

(*ii*) *Alterations in risk preference.* Previous hedging strategies may not be appropriate if the management of the firm is changed, or the overall goals of the firm alter.

(*iii*) *Asset price projections.* The profit-loss matrix illustrated above places price forecasts at the pivotal point in the design of options hedges. If the hedger changes his mind about the probability distribution of future asset prices, the optimal hedge may also change.

(*iv*) *Volatility changes.* From time to time options may become misvalued (see the discussion in Chapter 4). Thus, if a hedger has purchased call options with a specific exercise price, and at some point during the life of the hedge their implicit volatility appears high relative to the consensus, he might switch his hedge to calls with a different exercise price which appear cheaper, and hope to realize the misvaluation profit.

(*v*) *Increasing liquidity and finer spreads.* Options nearing expiration may be switched into more distant contracts during the life of the hedge as liquidity improves and spreads in these contracts narrow.

## c. Hedge evaluation

The most exciting part of hedging comes after the hedge is ended, i.e. discovering why the hedge did not perform in the way anticipated. Measuring hedge efficiency with options hedges is not as easy as with futures hedges. With futures it is a question of how close is the final effective asset price or interest or exchange rate to the one anticipated at the start of the hedge. Options, by contrast, behave like insurance contracts, and offer only a best guaranteed result, but could easily do better. Consequently, for a single transaction, no measure of option hedge efficiency seems acceptable. Over a series of transactions, the options hedges can be examined to see how they have performed relative to theoretical futures or forward hedges.

One final point on option hedging. People are all-important in the hedging process. The design and implementation of option hedging strategies is a complex process, which will only be successfully implemented by a first-class hedging team. Moreover, the relationships between the hedging team and senior management must be close, with exact divisions of authority made clear.

## 4. Hedging case study

### Scenario A: 15 October 1986

A treasurer of a multinational company is expecting to receive the proceeds of the sale of its chemical division on 15 December 1986, which he intends to invest for three months until it is required. Although the final value of the sale price has not yet been settled, the treasurer is confident that the minimum amount will be $50 million and has established the following probability function for the value.

| Amount | Probability | |
|--------|-------------|--|
| $50,000,000 | 0.10 | |
| $55,000,000 | 0.20 | |
| $60,000,000 | 0.30 | Mean forecast amount = $60,000,000 |
| $65,000,000 | 0.20 | |
| $70,000,000 | 0.10 | |

Interest rates have recently been extremely volatile, and the treasurer is worried that rates may have fallen below current rates by December. However, there is a distinct possibility that interest rates may rise. The following price and interest rate data is available to the treasurer.

Cash 3-month rate $8\frac{1}{2}$–$8\frac{5}{8}$

### Eurodollar futures prices

| | |
|--|--|
| December 1986 | 91.18 |
| March 1987 | 90.82 |
| June 1987 | 90.50 |

### Eurodollar options prices

| Exercise price | December Call | December Put | March Call | March Put | June Call | June Put |
|----------------|---------------|--------------|------------|-----------|-----------|----------|
| 90.00 | 1.20 | 0.02 | 0.99 | 0.17 | 0.87 | 0.37 |
| | (0.94) | (−0.06) | (0.76) | (−0.24) | (0.64) | (−0.36) |
| 90.50 | 0.75 | 0.07 | 0.65 | 0.33 | 0.59 | 0.59 |
| | (0.82) | (0.18) | (0.61) | (−0.39) | (0.50) | (−0.50) |
| 91.00 | 0.42 | 0.22 | 0.39 | 0.57 | 0.38 | 0.88 |
| | (0.60) | (−0.40) | (0.44) | (−0.56) | (0.37) | (−0.63) |
| 91.50 | 0.17 | 0.49 | 0.21 | 0.89 | 0.23 | 1.23 |
| | (0.34) | (−0.66) | (0.29) | (−0.71) | (0.25) | (−0.75) |
| 92.00 | 0.05 | 0.87 | 0.10 | 1.28 | 0.12 | 1.62 |
| | (0.14) | (−0.86) | (0.16) | (−0.84) | (0.16) | (−0.84) |
| 92.50 | 0.01 | 1.33 | 0.04 | 1.72 | 0.06 | 2.06 |
| | (0.04) | (−0.96) | (0.08) | (−0.92) | (0.09) | (−0.91) |

Figures in brackets are option deltas.

### Decision

The hedger decides to lock in a specific interest rate on the certain $50 million using the December futures contract.

Anticipated rate    100 − Futures price − 0.125 (to get a bid rate)
100 − 91.18 − 0.125 = 8.70%

Buy 50 December Eurodollar futures at 91.18

The hedger decides to hedge the mean value of the additional possible cash flows using options because it is an uncertain cash flow.[5]

$$\text{Mean additional value} = \$10,000,000$$

The treasurer has a choice of options hedges, each of which will provide a different locked-in rate and a different rate at which the options hedge will give the same result as the futures hedge.

These are some of the call option strategies.

*Buy 90.50 calls*
The treasurer locks in a minimum investment rate of 9.375% at a total cost of 0.75.

Best guaranteed rate = 8.625%        Breakeven rate = 9.45%

*Buy 91.00 calls*
The treasurer locks in a minimum investment rate of 8.875% at a total cost of 0.40.

Best guaranteed rate = 8.475%        Breakeven rate = 9.10%

*Buy 91.50 calls*
The treasurer locks in a minimum investment rate of 8.375% at a total cost of 0.17.

Best guaranteed rate = 8.205%        Breakeven rate = 8.87%

Another alternative available to the treasurer is to sell put options. As already mentioned, selling puts tends to produce better hedge results for modest changes in the asset price, but the maximum protection is limited and losses are potentially unlimited if the put moves in the wrong direction.

Four alternative strategies are examined all using the December option contracts:

|   |   | *Expenditure* |
|---|---|---|
| A. Buy 10 90.50 calls | 8.625% | $18,750 |
| B. Buy 10 91.00 calls | 8.475% | $10,000 |

|   |   | *Income* |
|---|---|---|
| C. Sell 10 91.00 puts | — | $5,000 |
| D. Sell 10 91.50 puts | — | $12,250 |

Since ratio hedges have not been used, no hedge rebalancing is anticipated and the hedge is simply evaluated at December 15. Assume to start with that the actual purchase price is indeed $60 million.

### Hedge analysis: 15 December 1986

$$\text{Cash interest rate} = 8\tfrac{8}{16} - 8\tfrac{11}{16}$$

### Eurodollar futures price

| December | March | June |
|---|---|---|
| 91.31 | 91.25 | 90.94 |

### Eurodollar options prices

|   | *December* | |
|---|---|---|
| *Exercise price* | *Calls* | *Puts* |
| 90.50 | 0.81 | 0 |
| 91.00 | 0.31 | 0 |
| 91.50 | 0.00 | 0.19 |

### Futures hedge

$$\$50,000,000 \text{ invested at } 8\tfrac{9}{16}\% \text{ for 3 months}$$
$$\text{Interest income} = \$1,070,312.5$$

$$\text{Futures profit} = 50 \times \$25 \times (91.31 - 91.18) \times 100$$
$$= \$16,250$$

---

[5] A cautious hedger might also choose to hedge the extra $10 million above the mean with out-of-the-money options.

$$\text{Effective interest rate} = \frac{\$1,070,312.50 + \$16,250}{\$50,000,000} \times \frac{12}{3}$$
$$= 8.69\%$$

The effective interest rate is almost exactly the 8.70% predicted originally; the difference is due to rounding error with the interest rates in the cash market fixed in sixteenths.

### Options hedge

$$\$10,000,000 \text{ invested at } 8\tfrac{9}{16}\%$$
$$\text{Interest income} = \$214,062.50$$

### Options hedge A

$$\text{Options profit} = 10 \times \$25 \times (0.81 - 0.75) \times 100$$
$$= \$1,500$$

$$\text{Effective interest rate} = \frac{\$214,062.50 + \$1,500}{\$10,000,000} \times \frac{12}{3}$$
$$= 8.62\%$$

### Options hedge B

$$\text{Options loss} = 10 \times \$25 \times (0.31 - 0.40) \times 100$$
$$= \$2,250$$

$$\text{Effective interest rate} = \frac{\$214,062.50 - \$2,250}{\$10,000,000}$$
$$= 8.47\%$$

### Options hedge C

$$\text{Options gain} = 10 \times \$25 \times (0.22 - 0.00) \times 100$$
$$= \$5,500$$

$$\text{Effective interest rate} = \frac{\$214,062.50 + \$5,500}{\$10,000,000}$$
$$= 8.78\%$$

### Options hedge D

$$\text{Options gain} = 10 \times \$25 \times (0.49 - 0.19)$$
$$= \$7,500$$

$$\text{Effective interest rate} = \frac{\$214,062.50 + \$7,500}{\$10,000,000}$$
$$= 8.86\%$$

Each of the four option hedges gives different effective interest rates. The call hedges give results almost exactly in line with those best guaranteed rates estimated at the beginning of the hedge, because although the Eurodollar futures price rose over the period, it was only by a modest amount, and resulted in the loss of virtually all the time value represented by the original option premiums.

Since the futures price change was modest, the put hedges also outperformed the call hedges by a considerable margin, and gave a better performance than the outright futures hedge. For the best call option hedge with the 90.50 call, and the best put hedge with the 91.50 put, Exhibit 5.15 shows the futures price range within which the put hedge will outperform the call hedge. Exhibit 5.16 shows how the hedge results alter for the call option hedge if, instead of the mean cash flow of $60 million occurring, the other possible cash flows are observed. The range of outcomes for an option hedge is difficult to predict when hedging an uncertain cash flow. However, over a large sequence of outcomes, assuming the probability distribution of the uncertain cash flows is correctly identified, the best guaranteed rates and breakeven rates determined in advance should be valid.

The case study can be extended to a more complex example, where the exposure date is not December 15 but January 30.

## Exhibit 5.15: Call hedge versus put hedge

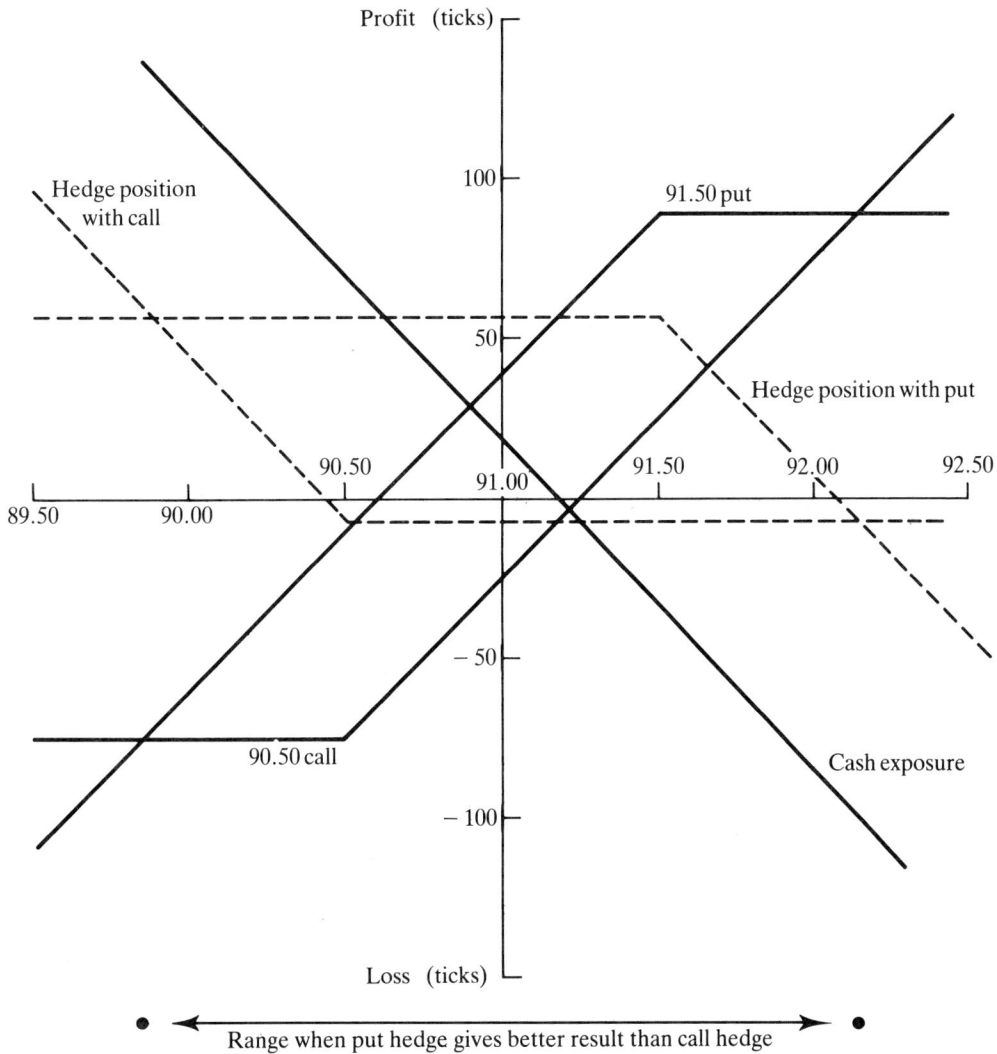

**Scenario B: 15 October 1986**
The expected cash flow is as before; the exposure date is January 30.

*Decision*

The hedger decides to lock in a specific interest rate on the certain $50 million using an interpolation hedge involving the December and March futures contracts. In December he will roll over the December contracts into March and hedge the basis risk with March-June futures straddles.

*Anticipated rate*

| | | |
|---|---|---|
| December | $100 - 91.18 - 0.125 = 8.70$ |
| March | $100 - 90.82 - 0.125 = 9.06$ |

*Interpolating for January 30*

$$(8.70)(\tfrac{1}{2}) + (9.06)(\tfrac{1}{2}) = 8.88\%\ [6]$$

Buy 25 December ED3 futures at 91.18
Buy 25 March ED3 futures at 90.82

The hedger again decides to hedge the mean additional $10 million with options. However, to

---

[6] This interpolation has been simplified slightly to 50:50, because Dec. 15–Jan. 30 actually contains 46 days and Feb. 1–Mar. 15 43 days.

## Exhibit 5.16: Call hedge for alternative cash flows

Hedge result is valid only if the additional $10,000,000 is received.

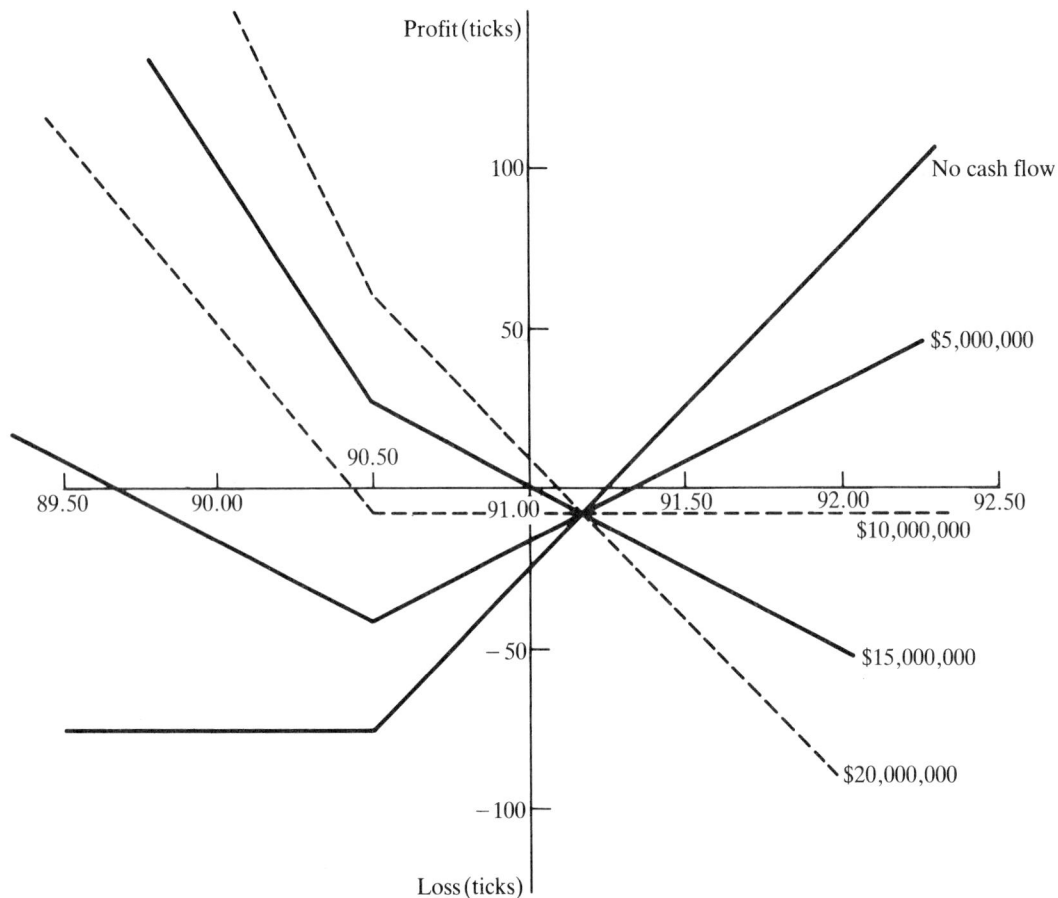

avoid transactions costs and minimize possible loss of time value, he decides to try an extrapolation hedge with the 91.00 calls.

Buy 15 March 91.00 call options at 0.39
Sell   5 June   91.00 call options at 0.38

This should behave much like a January 91.00 call. Using linear interpolation, the January 91.00 call would cost 0.40 and hence have a best guaranteed rate of 8.475%.

For the sake of illustration, only a single option hedge is used; many other hedge designs could be considered.

*Hedge analysis: January 30*

$$\text{Cash rate} = 8\tfrac{7}{8} - 9\%$$

| | |
|---|---|
| March futures price   90.80 | March 91.00 call   0.18 |
| June futures price   90.52 | June 91.00 call   0.26 |

*Futures hedge*

The futures profit has to take into account the selling of the 25 December futures on December 15 at 91.31, and the purchase of 25 additional March futures at 91.25, and the simultaneous purchase of 25 March-June straddles. That is the net position on December 15 changes from long 25 December futures and 25 March futures to long 75 March futures and short 25 June futures.

$$\text{Profit on December futures on December } 15 = 25 \times \$25 \times (91.31 - 91.18) \times 100$$
$$= \$8,125.00$$

$$\text{Loss on March futures purchases on October } 15 = 25 \times \$25 \times (90.80 - 90.82) \times 100$$
$$= -\$1,250$$

116

$$\text{Loss on March futures purchased on December 15} = 50 \times \$25 \times (90.80 - 91.25) \times 100$$
$$= -\$56,250$$

$$\text{Profit on June futures sold on December 15} = 25 \times \$25 \times (90.94 - 90.52) \times 100$$
$$= \$26,250$$

$$\text{Net futures loss} = (\$23,125)$$

Invest \$50,000,000 at $8\frac{7}{8}\%$

$$\text{Interest income} = \$1,109,375$$
$$\text{Effective interest rate} = \frac{\$1,109,375 - \$23,125}{\$50,000,000} \times \frac{12}{3}$$
$$= 8.69\%$$

In this case, although the achieved rate is higher than the cash rate on October 15, there is a significant difference between the expected rate of 8.88% and the rate achieved of 8.69%. This is because of basis risk: interpolated hedges for dates between delivery dates are more risky than hedging for delivery dates. The hedger will have to decide whether the level of basis risk is sufficiently large to change his hedge decisions.

### Options hedge

$$\text{Loss on 15 March 91.00 calls} = 15 \times \$25 \, (0.18 - 0.39) \times 100$$
$$= -\$7,875$$
$$\text{Gain on 5 June 91.00 calls} = 5 \times \$25 \times (0.38 - 0.26) \times 100$$
$$= \$1,500$$
$$\text{Net options loss} = -\$6,375$$

\$10,000,000 invested at $8\frac{7}{8}\%$

$$\text{Interest income} = \$221,875$$
$$\text{Effective interest rate} = \frac{\$221,875 - \$6,375}{\$10,000,000} \times 4$$
$$= 8.62\%$$

In this case, the options hedge has not performed much worse than the futures hedge, and has supplied an effective interest rate substantially better than the best guaranteed rate of 8.475%.

It is interesting to determine how the performance of the options hedge would be affected if the volatility implied in the options premiums were to change over time. Below are some fair options premiums on January 30 for alternative volatilities of 2.00% and 2.20%.

| *2.00%* | *2.20%* |
|---|---|
| March 91 call 0.16 | March 91 call 0.19 |
| June 91 call 0.24 | June 91 call 0.28 |

*2.00% volatility*

$$\text{Net options loss} = -\$6,875$$
$$\text{Effective interest rate} = 8.60\%$$

*2.20% volatility*

$$\text{Net options loss} = -\$6,250$$
$$\text{Effective interest rate} = 8.63\%$$

Reasonably large changes in volatility have little impact upon the result of the options hedge.

The alternative hedges illustrated above are only a small selection of those that could be implemented. However, hopefully this case study illustrates in practical terms the hedging principles outlined earlier in the chapter. It should also provide the basic information for the reader to work through other hedges and compare the results. For that reason, the tables below present a complete set of fair options premiums for the dates December 15 and January 30.

### Price information: December 15

Eurodollar futures prices December 91.31
         March  91.25
         June   90.94

*Eurodollar options prices* (volatility = 2.10%)

| Exercise price | December | | March | | June | |
|---|---|---|---|---|---|---|
| | *Call* | *Put* | *Call* | *Put* | *Call* | *Put* |
| 90.00 | 1.31 | 0 | 1.29 | 0.04 | 1.13 | 0.19 |
| 90.50 | 0.81 | 0 | 0.87 | 0.82 | 0.79 | 0.35 |
| 91.00 | 0.31 | 0 | 0.52 | 0.27 | 0.51 | 0.57 |
| 91.50 | 0 | 0.19 | 0.27 | 0.52 | 0.31 | 0.87 |
| 92.00 | 0 | 0.69 | 0.12 | 0.87 | 0.17 | 1.23 |
| 92.50 | 0 | 1.19 | 0.04 | 1.29 | 0.18 | 1.64 |

## Price information: January 30

| Eurodollar futures prices | March | 90.80 |
|---|---|---|
| | June | 90.52 |

*Eurodollar options prices* (volatility = 2.10%)

| Exercise price | March | | June | |
|---|---|---|---|---|
| | *Call* | *Put* | *Call* | *Put* |
| 90.50 | 0.44 | 0.14 | 0.47 | 0.45 |
| 91.00 | 0.18 | 0.38 | 0.26 | 0.74 |
| 91.50 | 0.05 | 0.75 | 0.13 | 1.11 |
| 92.00 | 0.01 | 1.21 | 0.06 | 1.54 |
| 92.50 | 0.00 | 1.70 | 0.02 | 2.00 |
| 93.00 | 0.00 | 2.20 | 0.01 | 2.49 |

# Chapter 6
# Stock and stock index options

## 1. Introduction

Stock option contracts were among the earliest traded options contracts. Their essence is – as described earlier in Chapter 2 – very simple. They give the holder the right to buy or sell a specific quantity of the underlying stock at a specific price.

### Example: Call option

An investor buys one IBM July 150 call on the Chicago Board Options Exchange at a premium of $5 per share. He acquires the right between now and July to acquire 100 shares of IBM at $150 per share.

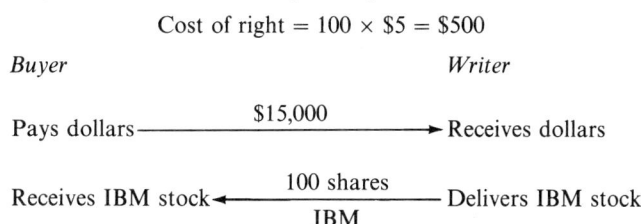

Cost of right = 100 × $5 = $500

| Buyer | | Writer |
|---|---|---|
| Pays dollars | $15,000 → | Receives dollars |
| Receives IBM stock | ← 100 shares IBM | Delivers IBM stock |

### Example: Put option

An investor buys one BP October 550 put on the London Stock Exchange at a premium of 53p per share. He acquires the right between now and October to deliver 1,000 shares of British Petroleum at a price of £5.50 per share.

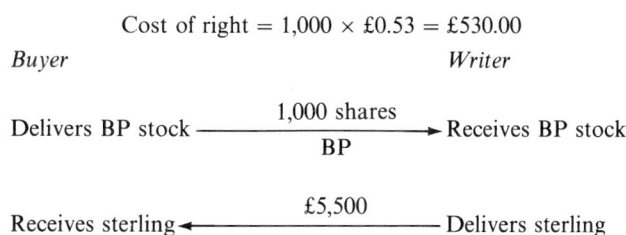

Cost of right = 1,000 × £0.53 = £530.00

| Buyer | | Writer |
|---|---|---|
| Delivers BP stock | 1,000 shares BP → | Receives BP stock |
| Receives sterling | ← £5,500 | Delivers sterling |

Individual stock options are traded on a wide variety of stock exchanges and options exchanges worldwide. All are premium paid options, where the full value of the option premium has to be paid by the option buyer in advance.

Stock index options can be options on cash or options on futures.

### Example: Call option

An investor buys one *Financial Times* Stock Exchange 100 July 1600 call option at a premium of 50. He acquires the right between now and July to buy the index at an effective level of 1600. Settlement is for cash at £10 per point.

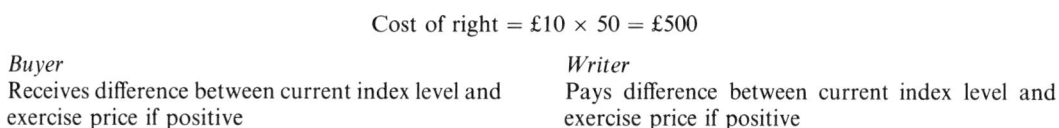

Cost of right = £10 × 50 = £500

| Buyer | Writer |
|---|---|
| Receives difference between current index level and exercise price if positive | Pays difference between current index level and exercise price if positive |

So if the index is at 1,675 and option is exercised, the writer will pay the buyer (75 × £10) or £750.

**Example: Put option**

An investor buys one S & P 500 September 245 put option on the Chicago Mercantile Exchange at a premium of 9.45. He acquires the right to set up between now and September a short position in the S & P 500 September futures contract at 245.

$$\text{Cost of right} = 9.45 \times \$500 = \$4,725.00$$

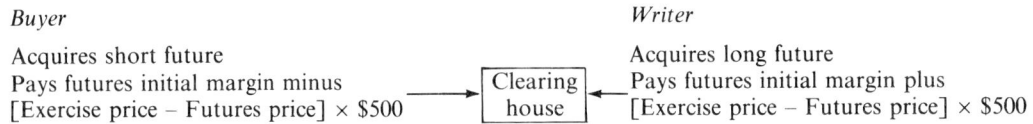

*Buyer*                                                                 *Writer*

Acquires short future                                          Acquires long future
Pays futures initial margin minus                    Pays futures initial margin plus
[Exercise price – Futures price] × $500       [Exercise price – Futures price] × $500

Clearing house

So if the futures margin is $3,000, and the index is at 240 when the option is exercised, the buyer will pay into the clearing house [$3,000 – (245 – 240)$500] or $500 and the writer will pay ($3,000 + (245 – 240)$500) or $5,500.

The final point to note about individual stock options is that they are American options which are not dividend protected, i.e. the holder of a call option will not receive dividends on the stock while he holds the option, yet he is fully exposed to the impact on the option price of any price falls that may occur when the stock goes ex-dividend. This increases the chance of early exercise, and makes the job of valuing individual stock options more difficult. The individual stock options are, however, protected against such changes as stock splits and stock dividends. This dividend effect may also play a role with stock index options, if there is a bunching of dividends on the stocks that make up the index at certain times in the year.

## 2. Pricing stock options and stock index options

Chapter 3 describes the fundamental methods for determining the fair value of an option on an individual stock and explains the principles of the Black-Scholes option valuation model.

$$C(S, X, T) = SN(d_1) - Xe^{-rt}N(d_2)$$

where   $C(S, X, T)$ = call premium

$$d_1 = \frac{\ln(S/X) + [r + \sigma^2/2]T}{\sigma\sqrt{T}}$$

$$d_2 = d_1 - \sigma\sqrt{T}$$

$S$ = current stock price

$X$ = exercise price

$r$ = riskless interest rate

$\sigma$ = volatility of stock price

$T$ = time to expiration

$N(.)$ = cumulative normal distribution.

This model will apply to both a European option and an American option as long as no dividends are paid (see Chapter 3). When dividends are paid, the possibility of premature exercise exists to obtain the dividend payment for a call option. Cox and Rubinstein (*op. cit.*) show that the following arbitrage conditions will apply for a call option.

1. A call should never be exercised at any time other than the expiration date or just before an ex-dividend date.
2. If the present value of the maximum dividends to be paid during the remaining life of the call will be at all times less than the concurrent present value of the interest that can be earned on the strike price during the remaining life of the call, the call should not be exercised before the expiration date.
3. If at any time it is optimal to exercise a call, it is never optimal to leave unexercised an otherwise identical call that has either a lower striking price or a shorter time to expiration.

As an example of a position around an ex-dividend day, assume the stock price after the dividend is paid falls to the current value minus the dividend $S - D$.

$$\text{Value of holdings} = S - D + D - X = S - X$$

This compares with non-exercise when the trader holds $C(S - D, X, T)$. Since there exists some value of $S$ for which

$$S - X > C(S - D, X, T)$$

early exercise may well be optimal. Cox and Rubinstein develop some similar arbitrage propositions for put options.

1. If throughout a period ending with time $t$ until expiration the present value of the minimum dividends to be paid during the remainder of this period will at all times be greater than the concurrent present value of the interest that can be earned on the exercise price during the remainder of the period, then the put should never be exercised before the end of the period.
2. If at any time it is optimal to exercise a put, then it is never optimal to leave unexercised an otherwise identical put that has a higher strike.

The difference with the exercise conditions for call options is that with call options it is only necessary to evaluate likelihood of early exercise at each ex-dividend point. It may, by contrast, be optimal to exercise the put at any time before the last ex-dividend date during the life of an option. In these circumstances the simple valuation procedure of the Black-Scholes model has to be altered. Several different approaches have been suggested.

## a. The Merton dividend model

The first and simplest dividend adjustment is due to Merton.[1] This applies to a European option where the underlying stock pays dividends which are assumed to be paid continuously with a constant dividend yield. The Black-Scholes model then becomes

$$C(S, X, T) = e^{-dS} N(d_1) - e^{-rX} N(d_2)$$

$$\text{where} \quad d_1 = \frac{\ln (S/X) + [r - d + \sigma^2/2]T}{\sigma \sqrt{T}}$$

$$d_2 = d_1 - \sigma \sqrt{T}$$

$C(S, X, T) = $ call premium

$S = $ current stock price

$X = $ exercise price

$T = $ time to expiration

$\sigma = $ volatility

$N(.) = $ cumulative normal distribution

$r = $ riskless interest rate

$d = $ dividend yield

## b. The Roll dividend model

An analytical solution to the problem of a dividend paying stock and an American call option on it has been suggested by Roll,[2] Geske[3] and Whaley.[4] This model can be written

$$C(S, X, T) = S[N_1(b_1) + N_2(a_1, -b_1; -\sqrt{t/T})]$$

$$- Xe^{-rT}[N_1(b_2) e^{r(T-t)} + N_2(a_2, b_2; -\sqrt{t/T})]$$

$$+ \alpha D^{-rT} N_1(b_2)$$

---

[1] R. C. Merton, "The theory of rational option pricing", *Bell Journal of Economics and Management Science*, 1973, 4, 141–83.

[2] R. Roll, "An analytic valuation formula for unprotected American options on stocks with known dividends", *Journal of Financial Economics*, Nov. 1977, 251–58.

[3] R. Geske, "A note on an analytical formula for the unprotected American call options on stocks with known dividends", *Journal of Financial Economics*, Dec. 1979, 375–80.

[4] R. W. Whaley, "On the valuation of American call options on stocks with known dividends", *Journal of Financial Economics*, June 1981, 207–11.

where   $C(S, X, T)$ = call premium

$N_1(a)$ = cumulative normal distribution

$N_2(a, b; \rho)$ = bivariate cumulative normal distribution with upper integral limits $a$ and $b$ and correlation coefficient $\rho$

$$a_1 = \frac{\ln(S/X) + (r + \sigma^2/2)T}{\sigma\sqrt{T}}$$

$$a_2 = a_1 - \sigma\sqrt{T}$$

$$b_1 = \frac{\ln(S/S_t^*) + (r + \sigma^2/2)t}{\sigma\sqrt{T}}, \qquad b_2 = b_1 - \sigma\sqrt{T}$$

$S_t^*$ = solution to $C(S_t^*, X, T - t) = S_t^* + \alpha D - X$
    where $C(.)$ is the original Black-Scholes value

$S$ = current stock price

$T$ = time to expiration

$X$ = exercise price

$r$ = riskless rate

$\sigma$ = volatility of $S$

$D$ = dividend

$t$ = time until the $XD$ date

$\alpha$ = known decline in the stock price at $XD$ as a proportion of the $D$.

This model appears to be the best analytical dividend adjustment model developed to date, although Sterk[5] suggests that it tends to alleviate rather than cure observed discrepancies between actual market prices and simple Black-Scholes model prices. It is worth experimenting with the model to see if its modifications are useful in their option hedging and trading decisions. Two important points to note are that the trader will need to forecast the dividend – although this may not be too difficult given the conservative dividend policies of most firms and the short period to expiration of most traded options. Some historical research will also be necessary to predict the value of $\alpha$ on the day after the ex-dividend day.

## c. The binomial pricing model

The other major approach to the problem of early exercise of calls with dividend paying stocks is the binomial option pricing model originally suggested by Sharpe and developed by Cox, Ross and Rubinstein.[6]

The assumption here is that there are only two possibilities for the asset price in the next period – up or down by a specific amount. Consider a simple example.

Current asset price = 200        Cost of borrowing = 8%

At each step $\pm$ 10% with equal probability

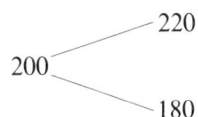

```
            220
          /
     200
          \
            180
```

The value of the call is that which avoids an arbitrage profit. The hedge ratio is 0.50,[7] that is 100 options are matched with 50 shares of stock.

[5] W. E. Sterk, "Option pricing: dividends and the in- and out-of the money bias", *Financial Management*, Winter 1983, 47–53.

[6] J. C. Cox, S. A. Ross and M. Rubinstein, "Option pricing: a simplified approach", *Journal of Financial Economics*, Sept. 1979, 7, 229–63.

[7] This concept is explained later.

|  | At expiry | | |
| --- | --- | --- | --- |
| | *Now* | *S = 180* | *S = 220* |
| Write 100 calls | $100X$ | 0 | (2,000) |
| Buy 50 shares | (10,000) | 9,000 | 11,000 |
| Borrow at 8% | $10,000 - 100X$ | $(10,000 - 100X)1.08$ | $(10,000 - 100X)(1.08)$ |
| Net profit | 0 | 0 | 0 |

There is clearly only one $X$ value which will ensure there is no net arbitrage profit.

$$9,000 - (10,000 - 100X)(1.01) = 0$$

$$X = \$16.67$$

In more general terms, the option price with one period to expiration can be written

$$C = (pC_u + (1 - p)C_d)/r$$

where $C$ = call premium

$$C_u = \text{Max}\,(0, uS - X)$$

$$C_d = \text{Max}\,(0, dS - X)$$

$$r = 1 + \text{riskless rate}$$

$$u = 1 + \%\ \text{up move}$$

$$d = 1 + \%\ \text{down move}$$

$$p = \frac{r - d}{u - d}$$

The corresponding hedge ratio used above is

$$\frac{C_u - C_d}{(u - d)S}$$

We will see how the ratio of 50 shares of stock to 100 options and the fair price of $16.67 are derived.

$$p = \frac{1.08 - 0.90}{1.10 - 0.90} = 0.90$$

$$C = [0.90(20) + (1 - 0.90)(0)]/1.08$$

$$= 18/1.08 = \$16.67$$

$$\text{Hedge ratio} = \frac{C_u - C_d}{(u - d)S} = \frac{20 - 0}{(1.10 - 0.09)(200)} = \frac{1}{2}$$

If this is extended to a two-period example:

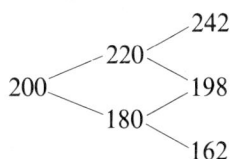

```
                          242
                  220<
          200<           198
                  180<
                          162
```

It is possible to find the fair option values in the first period via the formula and then take them back to zero.

$$C_{u1} = [0.90(42) + (1 - 0.90)0]/1.08$$

$$= \$35.00$$

$$C_{d1} = [0.90(0) + (1 - 0.90)0]/1.08$$

$$= 0$$

$$C = [0.90(35) + (1 - 0.9)0]/1.08$$

$$= \$29.17$$

It should be clear that extending this model to an indefinite number of periods will pose no computational problems. The general expression for the $n$-period binomial model can be written

$$C = \left[ \sum_{j=0}^{n} \left( \frac{n!}{j!(n - j)!} \right) p^j (1 - p)^{n-j} \max\,[0, u^j d^{n-j} S - X] \right] \Big/ r^n$$

Cox and Rubinstein (*op. cit.*) also show that this complicated expression can be written more simply as

$$C = S\Phi[a; n, p'] - Xr^{-n}\Phi[a; n, p]$$

$$p = (r - d)/(u - d) \qquad p' = (u/r)p$$

$a$ is the smallest integer (non-negative) greater than

$$\ln (X/Sd^n)/\ln (u/d)$$

If $a > n$, $c = 0$

$$\Phi[a; n, p] = \text{complementary binomial distribution function}$$

This is how the general formula works in the two-period case shown above.

$$\text{Max} (0, u^j d^{n-j}S - X)$$

$$j = 0 \qquad \text{Max} (0, -38) \qquad 0$$

$$j = 1 \qquad \text{Max} (0, -2) \qquad 0$$

$$j = 2 \qquad \text{Max} (0, 42) \qquad 42$$

$$C = \left[ \frac{(2!)}{(2!)(0!)} (0.90)^2 (1 - 0.90)^0 42 \right] \Big/ (1.08)^2$$

$$= \frac{(0.90)^2 42}{(1.08)^2} = \$29.17$$

The Black-Scholes model is in fact the limiting case of this binomial model when the number of periods is extended to continuous trading.

The next question in the binomial process is to choose the levels of the up and down parameters and the probability of an up and down movement respectively. Jarrow and Rudd[8] suggest the following parameters to make the binomial process approximate the lognormal process for the stock price which is assumed in the standard Black-Scholes model.

$$\text{Probability of up or down} = \tfrac{1}{2}$$

$$u = (r - \sigma^2/2)T/n + \sigma\sqrt{T/n}$$

$$d = (r - \sigma^2/2)T/n - \sigma\sqrt{T/n}$$

Cox and Rubinstein (*op. cit.*) also show how different parameters in the binomial model can be used to characterize the alternative processes for stock returns described towards the end of Chapter 3.

Returning to the original problem of dividends creating early exercise opportunities for the American call option, Cox and Rubinstein again provide a binomial solution to this problem.

The process starts one period before expiration. At expiration in the binomial model, the final stock price will be either

$$\begin{array}{ll} & v = 0 \text{ if final period is not an } XD \text{ date} \\ S \cdot u(1 - \delta)^v & \\ & v = 1 \text{ if final period is an } XD \text{ date} \\ \text{or} \quad S \cdot d(1 - \delta)^v & \\ & \delta = \text{dividend yield} \end{array}$$

The binomial process then looks like

$$\text{Max} [0, Su(1 - \delta)^v - X] = C_u$$
$$C$$
$$\text{Max} [0, Sd(1 - \delta)^v - X] = C_d$$

Then

$$C = \text{Max} [S - X, (p \cdot C_u + (1 - p)C_d)/r]$$

$$\text{where} \quad p = (r - d)/(u - d)$$

$$\text{Hedge ratio} = (C_u - C_d)/(u - d)S$$

[8] R. A. Jarrow and A. Rudd, *Option Pricing*, Dow Jones Irwin (1983).

The following is a simple example of this.

## Example

Asset price = 200     Exercise price 180
$u = 1.10, d = 0.90$
Riskless rate = 5%     Dividend yield = 7%
Expiration day is $XD$ day.

$$C_u = \text{Max} \, [0, (200(1.10)(1 - 0.07) - 180)]$$

$$= \text{Max} \, [0, 24.6] = 24.6$$

$$C_d = \text{Max} \, [0, (200(0.90)(1 - 0.07) - 180)]$$

$$= \text{Max} \, [0, -12.6] = 0$$

$$C = \text{Max} \left[ (200 - 180), \frac{(1.05 - 0.90)}{(1.1 - 0.90)} \, 24.6/1.05 \right]$$

$$= \text{Max} \, [20, 17.57] = 20$$

This process can be solved backwards to zero in an arbitrary number of steps, following the derivation of Cox and Rubinstein.

$n$ periods remain to expiration     $\bar{v}(n, i)$ = number of $XD$ days
during next $(n - i)$ periods

$C(n, i, j)$ = value of call $(n - i)$ periods in future
given stock price $S$ will have changed to
$u^j d^{n-i-j}(1 - \delta)^{\bar{v}(n, i)} S$ where $j = 0, 1, 2, \ldots, n - i$

$$\bar{v}(n, i) = \sum_{k=1}^{n-i} v^k$$

At expiration $i = 0$

$$C(n, 0, j) = \text{Max} \, [0, u^j d^{n-j}(1 - \delta)^{\bar{v}(n, 0)} S - X] \text{ for } j = 0, 1, \ldots, n$$

One period before expiration $i = 1$

$$C(n, 1, j) = \text{Max} \left[ u^j d^{n-1-j}(1 - \delta)^{\bar{v}(n, 1)} S - X, \frac{pC(n, 0, j + 1) + (1 - p)C(n, 0, j)}{r} \right]$$

for $j = 0, 1, \ldots, n - 1$

And for $i$ periods before expiration

$$C(n, i, j) = \text{Max} \left[ u^j d^{n-i-j}(1 - \delta)^{\bar{v}(n, i)} S - X, \frac{pC(n, i - 1, j + 1) + (1 - p)C(n, i - 1, j)}{r} \right]$$

for $j = 0, \ldots, n - i$

Finally with $n$ periods before expiration $i = n$

$$C = C(n, n, 0) = \text{Max} \left[ S - X, \frac{pC(n, n - 1, 1) + (1 - p)C(n, n - 1, 0)}{r} \right]$$

$$\text{Hedge ratio} = \frac{C(n, n - 1, 1) - C(n, n - 1, 0)}{(u - d)S}$$

We have dealt here with only a constant dividend yield $\delta = D/S$. However, this type of model can be expanded to include constant dividends or indeed more general dividend models. Jarrow and Rudd (*op. cit.*) also point out that current practice is to break down the sub-periods into around 150–200, though other authors suggest that as low as 50 iterations give good results. It will be up to the individual trader and hedger to determine his required level of accuracy.

## d. Valuing American puts

Similar binomial models can also be applied to the problem of pricing American puts. Starting with the simple case of the put option with constant dividend yield $\delta$, with one period to expiration, the usual system is

$$P_u = \text{Max}\ [0, X - u(1 - \delta)^v S]$$

$$P$$

$$P_d = \text{Max}\ [0, X - d(1 - \delta)^v S]$$

As usual

$$P = [p \cdot P_u + (1 - p)P_d]/r$$

$$p = \frac{r - d}{u - d} \qquad \text{Hedge ratio} = \frac{P_u - P_d}{(u - d)S}$$

Once again there will be some stock price at which the put should be exercised immediately. This will be the stock price at which

$$(pP_u + (1 - p)P_d)/r = X - S$$

The procedure for valuing American puts is identical to valuing call options, save for reversing the difference between stock prices and exercise prices. It is also worth pointing out several other approaches to American put pricing: the Parkinson numerical integration method,[9] the Brennan and Schwartz finite difference method[10] and the Geske and Johnson polynomial approximation.[11] The interested reader with a mathematical mind should refer to these.

### e. Some interim conclusions

So far the reader is probably lost in a maze of mathematical formulae, and it is time to give some conclusions for the use of different models for call and put options on individual stocks. There is sufficient evidence of biases in the simple Black-Scholes model to necessitate something being done about it for call options on dividend-paying stocks. The choice is between the analytical approach of Roll, Geske and Whaley and the binomial approach of Cox, Ross and Rubinstein. On balance, the use of the latter model is likely to lead to the best results and – most important – it is a simple model to programme for the computer and estimated values do not require too much processing time. Several computer models are already available which implement the Cox, Ross and Rubinstein binomial approach. For American put options, the simple Black-Scholes model is not appropriate; here the choice is probably between the binomial model and the Geske and Johnson polynomial approximation model. I would tend to rely on the binomial model in practice, but there may be interesting reported results of the Geske and Johnson model. The final important point is that although all these models look mathematically messy, they are easily programmable for the micro-computer and easily usable in practice.

### f. Option elasticities and betas

Certain other features of individual stock option behaviour require a digression on volatility aspects of the underlying securities.[12] The simplest model for the pricing of capital assets suggests that the expected return on a stock can be expressed as a function of the expected return on the so-called market portfolio – a market-value weighted portfolio of all risky assets. This is usually written

$$\hat{R}_j = R_F + (\hat{R}_m - R_F)\frac{\sigma_j \rho_{jm}}{\sigma_m}$$

where $\hat{R}_j$ = expected return on asset $j$

$R_F$ = riskless rate of interest

$\hat{R}_m$ = expected return to market portfolio

$\sigma_j, \sigma_m$ = standard deviations of expected returns for asset $j$ and the market respectively

$\rho_{jm}$ = correlation coefficient of expected returns on asset $j$ and the market

[9] M. Parkinson, "Option pricing: the American put", *Journal of Business,* Jan. 1977, 21–36.

[10] M. Brennan and E. Schwartz, "The valuation of American put options", *Journal of Finance,* May 1977, 449–62.

[11] R. Geske and H. Johnson, "The American put option valued analytically", *Journal of Finance,* 39, Dec. 1984, 1511–24.

[12] No attempt is made here to give an in-depth analysis of such topics as betas, market models, capital asset pricing models, etc. For this the reader is referred to W. F. Sharpe, *Investment,* Prentice-Hall, 3rd edition (1986).

This is often written as

$$\hat{R}_j = R_F + \beta_j(\hat{R}_m - R_F)$$

Sometimes a similar relationship is expressed as an ex post regression model of the form

$$R_{jt} = \alpha_j + \beta_j R_{mt} + \varepsilon_{jt}$$

This is known as the *market model*: it is consistent under certain circumstances with the ex ante *capital asset pricing model* if $\alpha_j = (1 - \beta_j)R_F$ since the CAPM can be rewritten

$$\bar{R}_j = R_F(1 - \beta_j) + \beta_j \hat{R}_m$$

The beta of a security measures the response of the return to an individual stock to a movement in the market portfolio. So if alpha is ignored and assets with betas of 2.0 and 0.5 respectively are considered, then the former will be expected to be twice as volatile as the market and the latter half as volatile as the market (see Exhibit 6.1).

## Exhibit 6.1: Security and market returns

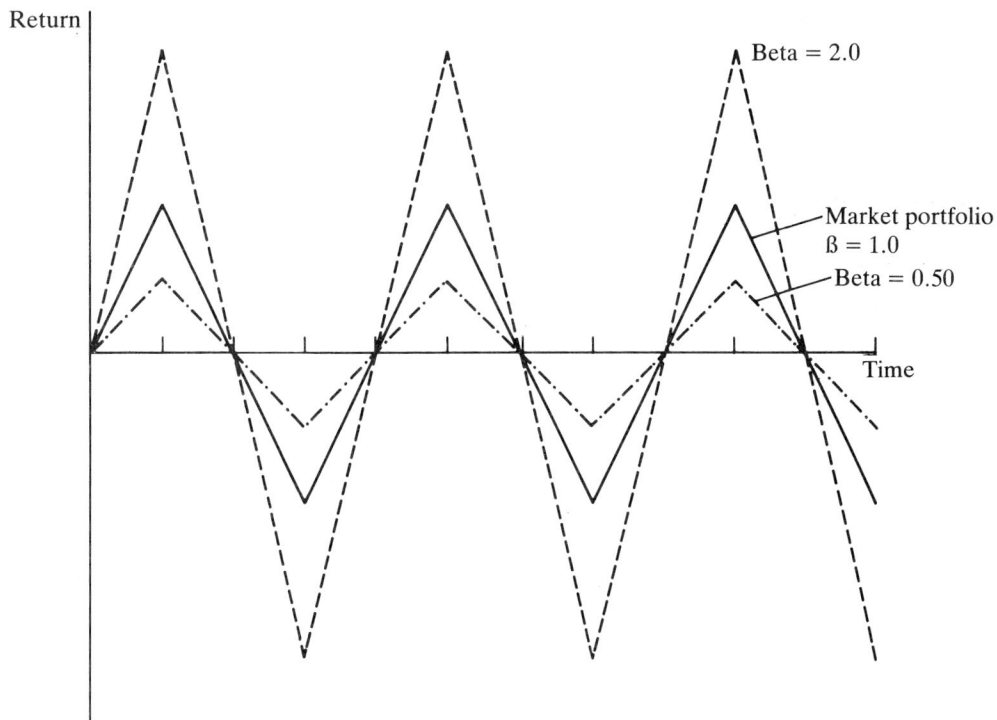

The beta of an option can now be established. The delta of an option relates changes in the premium to changes in the price of the stock.

$$dO = \Delta . dS$$

$$\Delta = \text{delta of option}$$

To express this in percentage terms, i.e. relate the percentage change in the price of the option to the percentage change in the price of the stock:

$$\frac{dO}{O} = w . \frac{dS}{S}$$

$$dO = O . w . \frac{dS}{S}$$

So that

$$\Delta = \frac{O . w}{S}$$

$$w = \frac{S . \Delta}{O} = \text{volatility of the option}$$

127

Now we also know that

$$\frac{dS}{S} = \beta_S \cdot \frac{dM}{M}$$

Therefore

$$\frac{1}{w}\frac{dO}{O} = \beta_S \frac{dM}{M}$$

Hence

$$\frac{dO}{O} = w \cdot \beta_S \frac{dM}{M}$$

So that the beta of the option $\beta_O = w \cdot \beta_S$.

This will be a very useful relationship in designing specific option trades and hedges referred to later.

### g. Stock index options

So far we have concentrated on the pricing of options on individual stocks. Now we turn to options on stock indices. Here the distinction is between options on futures and options on cash. Options on stock index futures contracts can be priced according to the Black model.

$$C(S, X, T) = e^{-rT}(F \cdot N(d_1) - X \cdot N(d_2))$$

where $\quad C(S, X, T) =$ call option premium

$$d_1 = \frac{\ln(F/X) + (\sigma^2/2)T}{\sigma\sqrt{T}}$$

$$d_2 = d_1 - \sigma\sqrt{T}$$

$F =$ current futures price

$X =$ option exercise price

$r =$ riskless rate

$T =$ time to expiration

$\sigma =$ volatility of futures price

$N(.) =$ cumulative normal distribution

The simplest model for pricing options on cash indices is the Merton proportional dividend model.[13]

$$C(S, X, T) = e^{-dS}N(d_1) - e^{-rX}N(d_2)$$

$$d_1 = \frac{\ln(S/X) + [r - d + \sigma^2/2]T}{\sigma\sqrt{T}}$$

$$d_2 = d_1 - \sigma\sqrt{T}$$

$d =$ continuous dividend yield

Black[14] has also shown that in arbitrage-free equilibrium, the futures price should bear the following relationship to the spot price.

$$F = Se^{(r-d)T}$$

What this means is that the value of the option on cash and the value of the option on the future should be identical if the futures price corresponds to that implied by the Black model, i.e.

---

[13] The rationale for this is that because the index is written on many stocks, different stocks will be paying dividends at different times and the assumption of a continuous constant dividend payout may not be unreasonable. This will not be the case if there is a bunching of dividend payments within the year, which can give rise to substantial variations in the dividend yield on the index at different times.

[14] F. Black, "The pricing of commodity contracts", *Journal of Financial Economics*, 1976, 3, 167–79.

if the future's price lies above the spot price by exactly enough to compensate for the dividend yield lying below the riskless interest rate, and vice versa if the dividend yield is above the riskless interest rate. Asay[15] further demonstrates that to avoid arbitrage, the volatility of the future's price should equal the volatility of the spot index. This has in general not been the case with options on cash indices.

Two closely related options are the cash option on the S & P 100 index on the Chicago Board Options Exchange and the futures option on the S & P 500 index traded on the Chicago Mercantile Exchange. The S & P 100 index is designed to mimic the broader-based S & P 500 index, although it is likely that it will display some non-systemic risk relative to the S & P 500 index because of the fewer number of stocks. This was confirmed in a recent paper by Asay.[16] As shown in Exhibit 6.2, the volatility of the S & P 500 index was somewhat lower than that of the CBOE S & P 100 index at around 14.0% compared with 16.3%. By contrast, the volatility of the S & P 500 futures contract was much higher at 19.2%. The exhibit also shows the prices of options and implied volatilities. Both sets of options – the S & P 500 futures options and the CBOE 100 options – seem to trade off the futures price and its volatility rather than the cash index volatility. This suggests that the futures price is frequently trading out of line with the cash index underlying it, which can give rise to arbitrage potential.

## Exhibit 6.2: Futures, spot and option implied volatility

| Date | | S & P 500 futures | | | CBOE 100 physical | |
| --- | --- | --- | --- | --- | --- | --- |
| | | Premium (discount) futures | Implied volatility off spot model | Implied volatility off futures model | Implied volatility off spot model | Implied volatility off futures model |
| Mar 18 | | | | | | |
| 150 | Call | 0.45 | 0.17 | 0.19 | 0.17 | 0.19 |
| | Put | | 0.20 | 0.19 | 0.21 | 0.19 |
| Mar. 25 | | | | | | |
| 155 | Call | 0.48 | 0.16 | 0.17 | 0.17 | 0.18 |
| | Put | | 0.18 | 0.17 | 0.21 | 0.19 |
| Mar. 31 | | | | | | |
| 155 | Call | (1.06) | 0.12 | 0.17 | 0.15 | 0.19 |
| | Put | | 0.22 | 0.18 | 0.23 | 0.19 |
| Apr. 8 | | | | | | |
| 155 | Call | (1.00) | 0.12 | 0.18 | 0.14 | 0.18 |
| | Put | | 0.20 | 0.17 | 0.23 | 0.19 |
| Apr. 15 | | | | | | |
| 160 | Call | (0.55) | 0.13 | 0.16 | 0.13 | 0.17 |
| | Put | | 0.18 | 0.15 | 0.24 | 0.21 |
| Apr. 22 | | | | | | |
| 160 | Call | (0.62) | 0.13 | 0.17 | 0.12 | 0.19 |
| | Put | | 0.19 | 0.16 | 0.29 | 0.23 |
| Apr. 29 | | | | | | |
| 165 | Call | 0.18 | 0.14 | 0.15 | 0.17 | 0.19 |
| | Put | | 0.18 | 0.16 | 0.25 | 0.24 |

Exponential weighted volatility from historic price series (ending 22 April 1983):

S & P 500 index   = 14.0%
CBOE 100 index = 16.3%
S & P 500 futures = 19.2%

Source: Chicago Mercantile Exchange.

---

[15] Michael R. Asay, "A note on the volatility of stock index futures and the pricing of options", *Journal of Futures Markets*.

[16] Michael R. Asay, "Pricing options on stock index physicals and stock index futures", *Market Perspectives*, Chicago Mercantile Exchange, May 1983.

A recent paper by Evnine and Rudd[17] offers several reasons why the pricing of cash index options differs from the theoretical models.

1. There is great difficulty in hedging the options with some sort of cash portfolio that adequately matches the index.
2. Cash settlement procedures may cause uncertainties for options' buyers and writers that could influence options pricing.
3. The dividend stream for the index is not continuous and level.
4. The distribution of returns on a cash index may not be the same as that assumed in the Black-Scholes model.

Evnine and Rudd find numerous violations of arbitrage restrictions put-call parity and the binomial pricing model for cash index options in the United States. The message is probably that it is too early to tell what is the best model for valuing index options. The simple Black model appears to work well for futures options such as the S & P 500 options on the Chicago Mercantile Exchange, but neither the Merton proportional dividend model nor the binomial model appears to work well for the cash index options.

## 3. Hedging aspects of stock and stock index options

### a. Individual stock option hedges

Hedging individual stock positions with specific stock options follows all the principles outlined in the chapter on hedging. The holder of a long position in a specific stock can offset potential negative price movements in the stock in several ways, assuming it is inconvenient for some reason to sell the stock.

*Alternative 1: Creating an artificial short stock position*

The hedger can create an artificial stock position in the stock by selling simultaneously a call option and buying a put option. The following assumptions are made:

$$\text{Stock price} = \$80 \qquad \text{Annual volatility} = 30\%$$

$$\text{Time to expiration} = 3 \text{ months} \qquad \text{Riskless interest rate} = 10\%$$

$$\text{Dividend yield on stock} = 5\%$$

*Option prices*[18]

| Exercise price | Call | Put |
| --- | --- | --- |
| 75 | 7.85 | 2.26 |
| 80 | 5.02 | 4.31 |
| 85 | 3.00 | 7.17 |

If the hedger buys an at-the-money put and sells an at-the-money call

$$\text{Net cash inflow} = \$5.02 - \$4.31 = \$0.71$$

This can be invested at 10% to yield $0.71 (1.025) = $0.728 after three months.

|  | *Position at expiry* | | |
| --- | --- | --- | --- |
|  | $S^* < 80$ | $S^* = 80$ | $S^* > 80$ |
| Stock | $S^*$ | 80 | $S^*$ |
| Call | 0 | 0 | $(S^* - 80)$ |
| Put | $80 - S^*$ | 0 | 0 |
|  | 80 | 80 | 80 |

In addition the hedger will receive $0.728 interest plus principal plus 5% dividend on the stock which amounts to 80(0.0125) or $1. Hence the net guaranteed value of the stock position at

---

[17] J. Evnine and A. Rudd, "Index options: the early evidence", *Journal of Finance*, July 1985, 743–56.
[18] These prices have been calculated using the simple Merton proportional dividend model, but assuming the possibility of early exercise.

expiration is \$81.73. This can be compared with the position if the stock were originally sold at \$80 and the entire sum invested in the money market at 10%. In that case, the net value after three months would be \$82. Hence, the hedger has locked in very closely the expected residual value of the stock investment if the stock were to reach its expected value of $80(1.025)/1.0125$ or \$80.99.

The danger with this type of hedging strategy is that the call which is sold may be exercised early. Assuming that the price does go down as the hedger expects, then the call will be most unlikely to be exercised. However, to be safe perhaps the hedger would prefer to use the 85 out-of-the-money call, i.e he buys the 85 put and sells the 85 call.

$$\text{Net cash flow} = \$7.17 - \$3.00 = \$4.17$$

This can be borrowed at 10% for a repayment of \$4.17 (1.10) or \$4.587 after three months.

|  | *Position at expiry* | | |
|---|---|---|---|
|  | $S^* < 85$ | $S^* = 85$ | $S^* > 85$ |
| Stock | $S^*$ | 85 | $S^*$ |
| Call | 0 | 0 | $(S^* - 85)$ |
| Put | $85 - S^*$ | 0 | 0 |
|  | 85 | 85 | 85 |

In addition the hedger will receive a dividend of \$1 but have to repay \$4.587. Hence the net guaranteed return will be \$81.41 – slightly less than with the at-the-money call but still a very satisfactory hedge result. In practice, the actual pattern of dividend payments would need to be taken into account in calculating the cash flows, and the hedger will wish to see if any of the options are misvalued, giving the ability to create the artificial short stock position at an advantageous price which will give a higher final return than the \$82 obtained by selling the stock and investing in the money market.

## *Alternative 2: Buying a put option*

The hedger can perform the traditional option hedge of buying a put option. Look at buying the 80 at-the-money put.

$$\text{Net cash flow} = -\$4.31$$

This can be borrowed at 10% for a final repayment of \$4.418

|  | *Position at expiry* | | |
|---|---|---|---|
|  | $S^* < 80$ | $S^* = 80$ | $S^* > 80$ |
| Stock | $S^*$ | 80 | $S^*$ |
| Put | $S^* - 80$ | 0 | 0 |
|  | 80 | 80 | $S^*$ |

$$\text{Minimum guaranteed value} = \$80 + \$1 - \$4.418 = \$76.58$$

Breakeven over straight sale    Solve $S^* + \$1 - \$4.418 = \$82$

$$S^* = \$85.42$$

## *Alternative 3: Selling a call option*

The hedger can set up a covered call write position. Try selling the at-the-money 80 call.

$$\text{Net cash inflow} = \$5.02$$

This can be invested to yield \$5.02 (1.025) = \$5.15

|  | *Position at expiry* | | |
|---|---|---|---|
|  | $S^* < 80$ | $S^* = 80$ | $S^* > 80$ |
| Stock | $S^*$ | $S^*$ | $S^*$ |
| Call | 0 | 0 | $(S^* - 80)$ |
|  | 80 | 80 | 80 |

Guaranteed value above final stock price of 80 = $80 + $1 + $5.15 = $86.15

Breakeven over straight sale   $S* + $1 + $5.15 = $82$

$$S* = \$75.85$$

In other words, the covered call write strategy outperforms the put purchase strategy for a range of stock prices from $69.70 to $89.57 – a remarkably large range.

### Alternative 4: Sell the at-the-money call, but buy an out-of-the-money put for protection

Try selling the 80 call and buying the 75 put.

$$\text{Net cash inflow} = \$5.02 - \$2.26$$

$$= \$2.76$$

This can be invested to yield $2.76 (1.025) = $2.83.

|  | | | Position at expiry | | |
|---|---|---|---|---|---|
|  | $S* < 75$ | $S* = 75$ | $75 < S* < 80$ | $S* = 80$ | $S* > 80$ |
| Stock | $S*$ | 75 | $S*$ | 80 | $S*$ |
| 80   Call | 0 | 0 | 0 | 0 | $S* - 80$ |
| 75   Put | $75 - S*$ | 0 | 0 | 0 | 0 |
|  | 75 | 75 | $S*$ | 80 | 80 |

Net minimum value = $75 + $1 + $2.83 = $78.83

Net maximum value = $80 + $1 + $2.83 = $83.83

### Alternative 5: Sell an in-the-money call, buy an out-of-the-money call

Try selling the 75 call, buying the 85 call.

$$\text{Net cash inflow} = \$7.85 - \$3.00 = \$4.85$$

This can be invested to yield $4.85 (1.0251) = $4.971.

|  | | | Position at expiry | | |
|---|---|---|---|---|---|
|  | $S* < 75$ | $S* = 75$ | $75 < S* < 85$ | $S* = 85$ | $S* > 85$ |
| Stock | $S*$ | 75 | $S*$ | 85 | $S*$ |
| 75   Call | 0 | 0 | $(S* - 75)$ | (10) | $(S* - 75)$ |
| 85   Call | 0 | 0 | 0 | 0 | $S* - 85$ |
|  | $S*$ | 75 | 75 | 75 | $S* - 10$ |

Net value below $75.   $S* + $4.971 + $1 = S* + 5.971$

Between $75–$85        $75 + $4.971 + $1 = $80.971$

Above $85              $S* + $4.971 + $1 - $10 = S* - $4.029$

All five alternatives are shown in Exhibit 6.3. It represents the usual expiration profit/loss diagram plus all the net cash flow associated with dividend payments and borrowing/investments.

The main message is that options provide a wide variety of hedging possibilities for the holders of long stock positions. The individual hedger will have to decide for himself which if any of these strategies will be suitable, and whether he wishes to hedge an entire stock position or only part of it.

All these hedge strategies can be used in reverse if the hedger has an effective short position in the stock. The typical case would be where the hedger is anticipating cash flows at a future date which he intends to use to buy specific stocks. His alternatives are to borrow the funds and buy

132

**Exhibit 6.3: Alternative stock option hedges**

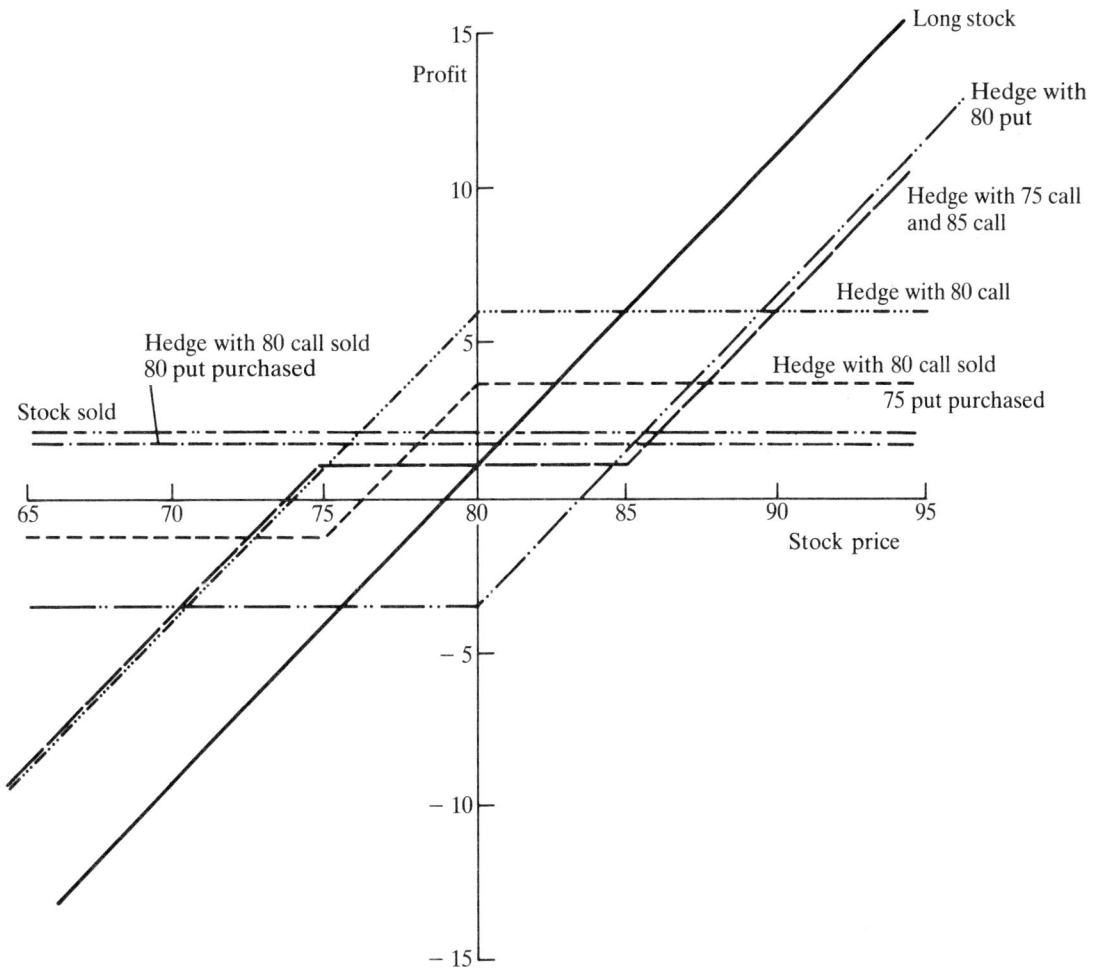

the stock immediately or use one of the hedges to fix the price at which the stock can be purchased in the future. Consider this by analysing the setting up of an artificial long position in the above stock at $80.

*Alternative 1*

Borrow $80 for 3 months    Cost = 80(1.025) = $82

Dividend offset = $1

Net cost of stock in 3 months = $81.00

*Alternative 2*

Buy 80 call    Sell 80 put

Net cash outflows = $5.02 − $4.31

= $0.71

This will be borrowed at 10% for three months.   Repayment = $0.73.
Option position guarantees cost at expiry of $80.

Net cost = $80.73

This represents a saving of $0.21 on the cost of the stock. Other hedges and their profiles can also be thus analysed.

When discussing stock option hedging we have looked only at hedges for a specific date – if, say, the would-be purchaser were uncertain about the time he was going to receive the funds, he might wish to use a ratio hedge. Ratio hedges are discussed fully in Chapter 5. We have also only looked so far at hedging individual option positions. The behaviour of large and complex portfolios of options and stocks is discussed in Chapter 9.

## b. Stock index option hedges

Hedging with stock index options requires a further discussion of stock indices and stock index futures. As already mentioned, a variety of index products are traded and it is important to distinguish between the different underlying instruments. The difference between the underlying indices can be brought out by considering the two most successful cash options contracts traded in the United States: the American Stock Exchange major market index (MMI) and the Chicago Board Options Exchange Standard and Poor's 100 index.

The major market index is a *price-weighted index* measuring the performance of 20 blue-chip stocks listed on the New York Stock Exchange. The index value is found by summing the price of the individual stocks and dividing that sum by a divisor. The divisor changes from time to time to account for stock prices and stock dividends which would otherwise result in arbitrary jumps in the index unrelated to fundamental stock price movements. The formula for the index is

$$\text{MMI} = \sum_{i=1}^{20} p^{(i)}/d$$

$p^{(i)}$ = price in dollars of an individual issue

$d$ = divisor

The MMI tends to track very closely with the famous Dow-Jones industrial average, which is itself a price-weighted index of 30 major stocks. According to the American Stock Exchange, the long-run correlation coefficient of the MMI with the Dow-Jones industrial average index is 0.97, making the MMI a very close proxy for the other index.

The structure of a value-weighted index is best introduced by considering the S & P 500 index, probably the most frequently used extended stock index in the United States. The S & P 500 is a *capitalization (or market value) weighted index* of 500 shares listed on the New York Stock Exchange. According to Standard and Poor's these 500 stocks are selected with the aim of achieving a distribution by broad industry groupings that approximates the distribution of these groupings in the New York Stock Exchange common stock population. This method of index construction means that instead of weighting the individual prices, the total market values of the corporation are used.

### Example

Consider an index consisting of four stocks.

| Stock | Price | Number of shares | Capitalization |
|---|---|---|---|
| 1 | 45 | 50,000,000 | 2,250,000,000 |
| 2 | 70 | 50,000,000 | 3,500,000,000 |
| 3 | 150 | 100,000,000 | 15,000,000,000 |
| 4 | 80 | 150,000,000 | 12,000,000,000 |
| Total | 345 | | 32,750,000,000 |

Suppose we want both indices to start at 100 on Day 1. The divisor for a price-weighted index would be 3.45.

$$\text{Price-weighted index} = \frac{345}{3.45} = 100$$

The divisor for the value weighted index would be 327,500,000

$$\text{Value-weighted index} = \frac{32,750,000,000}{327,500,000} = 100$$

Now suppose we move ahead to Day 2, and observe the following sets of stock prices.

| Stock | Price | Number of shares | Capitalization |
|---|---|---|---|
| 1 | 47.50 | 50,000,000 | 2,375,000,000 |
| 2 | 75.00 | 50,000,000 | 3,750,000,000 |
| 3 | 151.00 | 100,000,000 | 15,100,000,000 |
| 4 | 84.00 | 150,000,000 | 12,600,000,000 |
| | 357.50 | | 33,825,000,000 |

$$\text{Price-weighted index} = \frac{357.50}{3.45} = 103.62$$

$$\text{Value-weighted index} = \frac{33,825,000,000}{32,750,000,000} = 103.28$$

Note the difference between the two values on Day 2. The reason is that the percentage increase in each share was different.

| Stock | % price change |
|---|---|
| 1 | +5.56 |
| 2 | +7.14 |
| 3 | +0.67 |
| 4 | +5.0 |

Because the largest capitalization stock had the lowest percentage price change, and constituted 44.6% of the total market capitalization as opposed to only 42.2% of the total price, this tended to drag down the value of the index. The effect would have been even worse if, for instance, that stock had consisted of 200,000,000 shares priced at $75.50, up from $75 on Day 1. The values of the price indices on Days 1 and 2 would then be

$$\text{Price index Day 1} \quad \frac{45 + 70 + 75 + 80}{2.70} = 100.00$$

$$\text{Price index Day 2} \quad \frac{47.50 + 75.50 + 75.00 + 84}{2.70} = 104.44$$

The difference is thus accentuated between the price index and the value index. From the point of view of measuring portfolio performance, it would seem more appropriate to consider a large value-weighted index. However, price-weighted indices such as the Dow-Jones industrial average retain their popularity. The differences between the different indices suggest interesting option spread trades, which will be discussed later in the chapter.

The final type of stock index that is worth mentioning is the value line index on which options and futures are traded on the Kansas City Board of Trade. This is an *equally-weighted geometric index* of some 1,700 stocks representing 96% of the dollar value of all US equities. The stocks are drawn from the New York Stock Exchange, the American Stock Exchange and the over-the-counter market. How such an index would work for the four stocks discussed above is shown in the following example.

**Example**

Stock   (Day 2/Day 1)

| 1 | 47.50/45 | = 1.0556 |
| 2 | 75/70 | = 1.0714 |
| 3 | 151/150 | = 1.0067 |
| 4 | 84/80 | = 1.0500 |

$$\text{Arithmetic average} = \frac{1.0556 + 1.0714 + 1.0067 + 1.0500}{4}$$

$$= 1.04593$$

$$\text{Geometric average} = \sqrt[4]{(1.0556)(1.0714)(1.0067)(1.0500)}$$

$$= 1.04565$$

Equal weight arithmetic index   Day 2   104.59

Equal weight geometric index   Day 2   104.57

The downward bias of the geometric index compared with the arithmetic index is worth noting; and this effect will clearly grow with time. This can be seen by considering a portfolio of two stocks both priced at $50, with $1 million in each stock. Stock 1 then goes to $100 and stock 2 falls to $25.

$$\text{Portfolio value} = \$2,000,000 + \$500,000 = \$2,500,000$$

$$\text{Portfolio return} = \frac{2,500,000}{2,000,000} - 1 = 0.25 \text{ (or 25\%)}$$

$$\text{Arithmetic index } [100 \text{ (Day 1)}] = \left[ \left( \frac{\$100}{\$50} + \frac{\$25}{\$50} \right) \Big/ 2 \right] \times 100 = 125$$

$$\text{Geometric index } [100 \text{ (Day 1)}] = \sqrt{\left[ \frac{100}{50} \times \frac{25}{50} \right]} \times 100 = 100$$

Thus the geometric index has completely missed the increase of 25% in the value of the portfolio, which is captured by the arithmetic index. The value line index has two noteworthy features compared with the others.

1. The process of equal weights will mean that the price changes in small stocks have a relatively larger market impact.

135

2. For any given increase in market prices, assuming some dispersion of price changes across individual stocks, the index will be biased downwards compared with arithmetic indices.

Other stock indices will normally fall into one of these categories. Thus, for example, the New York Stock Exchange composite index is a market capitalization arithmetic index, the *Financial Times* 30 index in the UK is a price-weighted arithmetic index, the *Financial Times* Stock Exchange 100 index is a market value weighted arithmetic index, and so on. The same applies to indices traded on other stock exchanges worldwide.

The investor should also check whether the index is a so-called dividend reinvested index or not. Some indices assume the investment of dividends in the stock, thereby changing its market capitalization; others merely consider price changes. Several exchanges also trade options on sub-indices such as the oil index on the American Stock Exchange and the technology index on the Pacific Stock Exchange in the United States.

The concept of options on stock index futures has already been described, together with the relationship between stock index futures prices and stock index cash values. We now turn our attention to hedging strategies with stock index options. First, however, hedging stock portfolios with stock futures will be briefly discussed. The concept of beta was discussed earlier in the chapter. By selling stock index futures, the hedger is able to reduce or eliminate the systematic risk of his portfolio. To do this, he would first estimate the portfolio beta of his existing portfolio.

| Stock | Price | Holding | Beta | Market value |
|-------|-------|---------|------|--------------|
| 1 | $45 | 100,000 | 1.10 | 4,500,000 |
| 2 | $60 | 250,000 | 1.05 | 15,000,000 |
| 3 | $70 | 150,000 | 0.80 | 10,000,000 |
| | | | Total | 30,000,000 |

$$\text{Weighted portfolio beta} = (1.1)\frac{4.5}{30} + (1.05)\frac{15}{30} + (0.80)\frac{10.5}{30}$$

$$= 0.97$$

Suppose the September S & P 500 futures contract on the Chicago Mercantile Exchange is priced at 240.00. Then a complete hedge would involve selling a number of contracts determined by

$$\frac{\text{Dollar value of portfolio}}{\text{Dollar value of current spot index (say 238)}} \times \text{Beta of portfolio}$$

In this case

$$\frac{\$30,000,000}{238.00 \times \$500} \times 0.97 = 245 \text{ contracts}$$

The guaranteed value of the index locked in is then 240.00 or $30,309,278. The betas of individual stocks and stock portfolios must naturally be taken into account in designing optimal hedges involving stock index options. The rules to follow are:

---

**Full hedge**

$$\text{Number of contracts} = \frac{\text{Market value of portfolio}}{\text{Market value of index on which option is written}} \times \text{Portfolio beta}$$

**Ratio hedge**

$$\text{Number of contracts} = \frac{\text{Market value of portfolio}}{\text{Market value of index on which option is written}} \times \frac{\text{Portfolio beta}}{\text{Option delta}}$$

---

Below are two examples using the S & P 100 cash index options on the CBOE (data for 18 June 1986).

| Strike price | Calls | | | Puts | | |
|---|---|---|---|---|---|---|
| | June | July | August | June | July | August |
| 225 | $9\frac{5}{8}$ | $11\frac{1}{8}$ | $12\frac{7}{8}$ | $\frac{1}{16}$ | $1\frac{1}{16}$ | $2\frac{1}{4}$ |
| 230 | $4\frac{7}{8}$ | $7\frac{5}{8}$ | 9 | $\frac{3}{16}$ | $2\frac{7}{16}$ | $3\frac{1}{2}$ |
| 235 | $1\frac{3}{16}$ | $4\frac{5}{8}$ | $6\frac{1}{4}$ | $1\frac{9}{16}$ | $4\frac{1}{2}$ | $6\frac{3}{8}$ |
| 240 | $\frac{1}{16}$ | $2\frac{11}{16}$ | $4\frac{1}{8}$ | $5\frac{5}{8}$ | $7\frac{1}{2}$ | $8\frac{7}{8}$ |
| 245 | — | $1\frac{5}{16}$ | $2\frac{1}{2}$ | $12\frac{7}{8}$ | — | — |

Close index 234.46

First, consider a straightforward put hedge of the small portfolio of stocks analysed earlier: using the at-the-money 235 puts priced at $6\frac{3}{8}$. The portfolio manager decides to put on a full hedge with August options.

$$\text{Number of contracts} = \frac{\$30,000,000}{\$100 \times 234.46} \times 0.97$$

$$= 1,241 \text{ contracts}$$

$$\text{Cost of hedge for 2 months} = \$791,137.50$$

This represents a cost of approximately 2.6% of the face value of the portfolio. The hedger's view of the market will determine whether this hedge cost is acceptable to retain some of the benefits of favourable movements in stock market prices. The alternative, as before, is to construct an option hedge which will create an artificial short position in the S & P 100. This would involve buying 1,241 235 puts but selling 1,241 235 calls.

$$\text{Net cost} = 241(\$6.375 - \$6.25) \times \$100 = \$15,512.50$$

The important point about these hedges of a portfolio position with stock index options is that the portfolio manager retains the non-systematic or individual risk of the stock. In other words, this type of hedge allows him to trade the relative performance of a stock portfolio. For instance, consider the artificial short index position created with the 235 calls: the S & P 100 index falls 10%, but the value of the stock portfolio only falls 7% because the stocks have outperformed the index.

$$\text{Stock index value} = 211.01 \qquad \text{Portfolio value} = \$27,900,000$$

$$235 \text{ call premium} - 0.00 \qquad 235 \text{ put premium} = 24.00$$

$$\text{Option position profit} = [(24.00 - 6.375)100 + (6.25)(100)](1,241)$$

$$= \$2,962,887.50$$

$$\text{Net position value} = \$30,862,888$$

Thus the portfolio manager has a net profit over his original portfolio of $862,880. If, on the other hand, the original portfolio had fallen by 10% – the same percentage as the S & P 100 index – its terminal value would have been $27,000,000 and the net position value $29,962,887.50, representing a small loss of $37,113. In other words, an almost perfect hedge. If the stocks had performed worse than the market as a whole, the hedge position would show a net loss. This illustrates the difference between hedging with a portfolio of individual stock options and hedging with stock index options.

---

1. A full hedge of a stock portfolio with a portfolio of artificial short stock positions created from individual stock options will eliminate all risk, both systematic and non-systematic.
2. A full hedge of a stock portfolio with a portfolio of individual stock put options will, at a cost, eliminate all risk and preserve the benefits of upward price movements in the individual stocks.

3. A full hedge of a stock portfolio with an artificial short index position created from stock index options, or with short index futures positions, will eliminate the systematic risk of a portfolio but leave the non-systematic risk.
4. A full hedge of a stock portfolio with stock index put options will, at a cost, eliminate systematic risk, but not non-systematic risk, while preserving the benefit of upward price movements in the stock prices.

---

The portfolio manager who is considering selling call options against the portfolio as a partial hedge, should also think about the respective merits of selling individual stock calls or stock index calls. Selling calls against an underlying asset position creates a short put position, but with the stock index calls any potential losses on the artificial short put could be reduced by anticipated relative superior performance of the individual stocks over the underlying index. Programmes of writing stock index options against underlying stock portfolios have become very popular.

The choice before the portfolio manager is even wider than this because there is no necessity for him to fully hedge the portfolio with a single strategy. He might, for instance, choose to hedge a proportion of his stocks, where he anticipates average or inferior relative performance with individual stock options, while hedging the rest with stock index options.

## 4. Trading and arbitrage with stock options

The fundamental aspects of trading with options are outlined in Chapter 4. This chapter outlines some specific arbitrages and trades that can be carried out because of the special characteristics of options on stocks. Many of these trades are combination trades involving mixtures of individual stock options and stock index options.

### a. Trading relative stock strength

A purchaser buying individual put or call stock options is speculating on the overall strength or weakness of the stock price, i.e. he is taking on both the systematic and non-systematic risk of the stock. The concept of beta as a measure of systematic risk and the role of the option beta was discussed in the pricing section. Suppose a put option is purchased on the S & P 500 index in an appropriate ratio determined by the beta of IBM. This would constitute a portfolio which would have approximately zero systematic risk, but continue to bear the non-systematic risk of IBM, i.e. it would be a relative strength trade.

### Example

IBM stock price = $150.00      150 call premium $10.00
Beta = 1.10      Delta = 0.50

$$\text{S \& P 500 230 call premium} = 8$$
$$\text{Delta} = 0.50$$
$$\text{S \& P 500 index spot} = 224$$

$$\text{Beta of IBM 150 call} = \frac{\text{Stock beta} \times \text{Stock price}}{\text{Option price}} \times \text{Option delta}$$

$$= \frac{1.10 \times \$150.00 \times 0.5}{\$10.00} = 8.25$$

$$\text{Beta of S \& P 500 230 call} = \frac{224 \times 0.5}{8} = 14.00$$

To create a beta neutral position, the IBM call and the S & P 500 call will have to be purchased in a specific ratio of

$$\frac{\text{S \& P 500 call beta}}{\text{IBM call beta}} \times \frac{\text{Value of IBM call}}{\text{Value of S \& P call}} = \frac{8.25}{14.00} \times \frac{\$1,000}{\$4,000} = 0.15$$

To create the neutral position, the IBM call should be purchased and the S & P 500 calls sold in a ratio of 100 IBM to 15 S & P options. Assume the deltas remain reasonably accurate for a 1% movement in the index, and that IBM rises by more than its beta would suggest, by say 1.25%, reflecting investor interest in the computer industry.

$$\text{New IBM option price} = \$10.00 + [\$150.00 \times 0.0125 \times 0.50]$$
$$= \$10.9375$$

$$\text{New S \& P 500 option price} = 8 + [224 \times 0.01 \times 0.50]$$
$$= 9.12$$

$$\text{Net profit on position} = 100(100)(\$10.9375 - \$10.00) - 15(9.12 - 8)\$500$$
$$= \$975.00$$

By contrast if the IBM stock price had behaved exactly in line with its beta of 1.10

$$\text{IBM option price} = \$10.00 + (\$150.00 \times 0.011 \times 0.50)$$
$$= \$10.825$$

And in these circumstances, the net profit would have been

$$\text{Net profit} = 100(100)(\$10.825 - \$10.00) - 15(9.12 - 8)\$500$$
$$= -\$150$$

Thus the position shows a modest change in value, because the true hedge ratio should have been 14.7 contracts rather than 15. The other point about this position, however, is that as long as the stock does outperform, the profit is likely to be greater than that suggested because of favourable movements in delta.

Suppose the index rises but the IBM price rises more than proportionately, then the delta of the IBM option will rise more sharply than that of the index option, and the position will unbalance in favour of the IBM option which is the one making money. Similarly if the index falls but IBM does not fall proportionately, its delta will not decline as rapidly as that of the S & P option, and the position will once again be over-weighted with IBM which is showing the more favourable price developments.

The trader needs to remember that there is still a volatility exposure: he has purchased IBM volatility and sold stock market index volatility; if during the period IBM displays less volatility than the market as indicated by beta, this could affect the profitability of the trade. Nonetheless, this combination of individual stock options and index options allows the option trading of relative strength or weakness.

Another version of this strategy would involve trading sub-index options against index options. For instance, it would be possible to trade the oil and gas index on the American Stock Exchange against a widely based index such as the S & P 100 index on the CBOE. To do this, it would first be necessary to establish a beta relationship between the AMEX oil index and the S & P 100.

$$\text{Return}_t \text{ (AMEX oil)} = \alpha + \beta \text{ Return}_t \text{ (S \& P 100)} + e_t$$

Assume for the sake of convenience that this beta is 1.10.

## Example

| | | |
|---|---|---|
| AMEX oil index level = 131.62 | July 130 call $3\frac{3}{4}$ | Delta = 0.58 |
| CBOE S & P 100 index level = 234.46 | July 235 call $4\frac{5}{8}$ | Delta = 0.48 |

Suppose the trader believes the market is due to fall, but oil stocks will outperform the market. The aim is to construct a trade which will show zero profit or loss for a modest percentage fall in the S & P 100 index, and an equivalent fall in the AMEX oil option suggested by the beta.

Consider a 1% decline in the S & P 100

$$\text{New index} = 232.12 \qquad \text{Fall} = 2.34$$

Equivalent fall in AMEX oil index = 1.1%

$$\text{New index} = 130.17 \qquad \text{Fall} = 1.45$$

$$\text{Implied price change in S \& P 100 call option}^* = 2.34 \times 0.48$$
$$= 1.12$$

$$\text{New value of option} = 4\frac{5}{8} - 1.12 = 3.50$$
$$\text{Rounded to 16th} = 3\text{–}08$$
$$\text{Implied price change in AMEX oil index option} = 1.45 \times 0.58$$
$$= 0.84$$

$$\text{New value of option} = 3\frac{3}{4} - 0.84 = 2.91$$
$$\text{Rounded to 16th} = 2\text{–}15$$

Hence the ratio for an appropriate trade is

$$100 \text{ S \& P 100 options: } 100 \times \frac{3\text{–}08}{2\text{–}15} = 119$$

---

* In practice we might want to use the gamma of the option in determining its responsiveness to a 1% change in the index.

Hence sell 100 S & P 100 call options and buy 119 AMEX oil index options. This trade should show approximately zero profit and loss if the S & P 100 declines modestly and the negative return on the oil index is 1.10 times the return on the S & P 100. If by contrast the oil index performs relatively better than the S & P 100, its negative return will be less than that predicted by the beta relationship, and the trade will show a profit.

This same principle of relative performance can be used to trade any pair of index options. Popular trades might include:

### (i) Major market index versus CBOE S&P 100 index

Here the trade is of a price-weighted narrow index versus a value-weighted wide index. A trader would buy the MMI option and sell the S & P option if he expected either the 20 companies in the MMI index to relatively outperform the overall market, or the high dollar stock prices to do better than low dollar stock prices. If the trader believed the reverse, he would buy the S & P 100 options and sell the MMI options.

### (ii) Value line index versus S&P 100 index

This is a classic small firm returns versus large firm returns trade, because the value line index is equally weighted while the S & P 100 is market value weighted. Wherever possible it is better to be short calls or long puts on the Kansas City Board of Trade value line index options because of the downward bias in geometric indices mentioned earlier.

### (iii) CBOE S&P 100 index versus NYSE beta index

This is a trade for an investor who believes historical betas are not good predictors of future betas in rapidly moving markets. The New York Stock Exchange index is a market value weighted index of a group of high beta stocks. Hence a trader who believes high beta securities perform better than their historic betas would suggest in bull markets, and worse in bear markets, could if he thought the market was going to rise, buy NYSE beta index calls and sell CBOE S & P 100 index calls.

Numerous other index option spread strategies are possible. In all cases neutrality is determined as in the example above for the AMEX oil index option versus the S & P 100 index option.

## b. Arbitrage with stock options

The section on pricing has already discussed some of the fundamentals of arbitrage with stock options. Below is an example of arbitrage for an American stock option written on a dividend paying stock.

**Example: Conversion arbitrage**

A conversion consists of selling a specific exercise call, buying an identical exercise price put, and simultaneously buying the security with borrowed funds.

|  |  | At any time $t$, $S^* < X$ | $0 \leqslant t \leqslant T$ $S^* \geqslant X$ |
|---|---|---|---|
| Sell call | $C(S, X, T)$ | $0$ | $-(S^* - X)$ |
| Buy put | $-P(S, X, T)$ | $X - S^*$ | $0$ |
| Buy stock | $-S$ | $S^* + D_t$ | $S^* + D_t$ |
| Borrow | $S + P - C$ | $(C - P - S)(1 + R_t)$ | |
| Net | $0$ | $(C - P - S)(1 + R_t) + X + D_t$ | |

$D_t$ = value at $t$ of all dividends received between initiation of the conversion and time $t$
$R_t$ = interest rate between now and $t$

Since to avoid arbitrage, the net cash flow at any point must not be positive, then

$$C - P \leqslant S - \frac{X}{(1 + R_t)} - \frac{D_t}{(1 + R_t)} \leqslant S - \frac{X}{(1 + R_t)}$$

If we then consider a reversal with all the cash flows reversed, the condition for no arbitrage would be

$$C - P \geqslant S - \frac{X}{(1 + R_t)} - \frac{D_t}{(1 + R_t)} \geqslant S - \frac{D_t}{(1 + R_t)} - X$$

The final arbitrage bounds become

$$S - \frac{D_t}{(1 + R_t)} - X \leqslant C - P \leqslant S - \frac{X}{(1 + R_t)}$$

This is rather general since $t$ can vary anywhere between $O$ and $T$. But call options will only be exercised either at expiration or immediately prior to a dividend payment day.

Consider a stream of dividend payments $D_1 \ldots D_T$. If the call is exercised in period 1, then the arbitrage condition is

$$(C - P - S)(1 + R_1) + X \leqslant O$$

$$C - P - S \leqslant \frac{X}{(1 + R_1)}$$

$$C - P \leqslant S - \frac{S}{(1 + R_1)}$$

If the call is exercised in period 2, then the arbitrage condition is

$$(C - P - S)(1 + R_2) + D_1(1 + {_1}R_2) + X \leqslant O$$

$$C - P \leqslant S - \frac{X}{(1 + R_2)} - \frac{D_1}{(1 + R_2)}(1 + {_1}R_2)$$

where ${_1}R_2$ is the interest rate for funds invested or borrowed between period 1 and 2.

**Example**

| | Calls | | Puts | |
|---|---|---|---|---|
| Exercise price | 3-month | 6-month | 3-month | 6-month |
| 420 | 40 | 60 | 7 | 13 |
| 460 | 20 | 35 | 24 | 30 |
| 500 | 7 | 20 | 50 | 55 |

Current stock price = 450
3 + 6-month rates = 12%

A 16p dividend is expected in four months

*Arbitrage limits*

*3-month options*

| Exercise price | $(S - X)$ | $(C - P)$ | $(S - X)/1 + R_T$ |
|---|---|---|---|
| 420 | 30 | 33 | 42.2 |
| 460 | −10 | −4 | −2.4 |
| 500 | −50 | −43 | −35.5 |

*6-month options*

| Exercise price | $S - \dfrac{D_t}{1 + R_t} - X$ | $C - P$ | $S - \dfrac{X}{1 + R_t}$ | $S - \left[\dfrac{X + D_t(1 + {_t}R_T)}{1 + R_T}\right]$ |
|---|---|---|---|---|
| 420 | 14.6 | 47 | 46.2 | 38.38 |
| 460 | −25.4 | 5 | −7.70 | 0.64 |
| 500 | −65.4 | −43 | −30.77 | 12.91 |

There appears, therefore, to be an arbitrage profit available with the 420 six-month option.

*Original position*

| | |
|---|---|
| Sell 420 call (6-month) | +60 |
| Buy 420 put (6-month) | −13 |
| Buy stock | −450 |
| Borrow | +403 |

Assume call is not exercised

| At expiration | S = 400 | S = 500 |
|---|---|---|
| Call | 0 | −80 |
| Put | 20 | 0 |
| Stock | 400 | 500 |
| Borrowing | −403 (1.06) | −403 (1.06) |
| Dividend invested | 16 (1.02) | 16 (1.02) |
| | 9.14 | 9.14 |

Assume call is exercised

|  | 420 | 450 | 480 | 510 |
|---|---|---|---|---|
| Call | 0 | − 30 | − 60 | − 90 |
| Put (worst case) | 0 | 0 | 0 | 0 |
| Stock | 420 | 450 | 480 | 510 |
| Borrowing | − 403(1.04) | − 403(1.04) | − 403(1.04) | − 403(1.04) |
| Net | 0.88 | 0.88 | 0.88 | 0.88 |

Hence, as indicated, a pure arbitrage profit does exist whether the call is exercised early prior to the payment of the 16p dividend or whether it is not exercised prior to maturity. The only further points to note about this arbitrage are the possibilities of uncertain future interest rates and uncertain dividends. In these cases, the arbitrage conditions should be worked out using the maximum and minimum values for interest rates and dividends.

# Chapter 7
# Currency options

## 1. The basics

Traded currency options are divided into two types: options on cash, and options on futures.

A *cash currency option is* the right to buy or sell a fixed quantity of one currency in exchange for a specific quantity of another currency in a ratio determined by a specific exchange rate at or before a specific date in the future.

A *futures currency option is* the right to buy or sell a traded currency futures contract at a specific futures price at or before a specific date in the future.

A typical comparison would be between the LIFFE sterling currency option and the CME currency option.[1]

**Example**
*LIFFE*
Buy a June call option at an exercise price of $1.2500 for a premium of 3.5 cents.
This buys the right to purchase between now and June £25,000 sterling for $31,250 (£25,000 × $1.25)

$$\text{Cost of right} = £25,000 \times \$0.035 = \$875 \text{ [2]}$$

If the option is exercised, the option holder must deposit physical dollars in exchange for sterling.

*CME*
Buy a June call option at an exercise price of $1.2500 for a premium of 3 cents.
This buys the right to establish between now and June a long sterling futures position at an original price of $1.2500.

$$\text{Cost of right} = £25,000 \times \$0.03 = \$750.00$$

If the option is exercised, a long futures position will be established for the trader at $1.2500 which would be immediately marked to market.

**Exercise**
Spot rate $1.3000        Futures price = $1.2950

*LIFFE*

| Holder | Writer |
|---|---|
| £25,000 | $31,250 |

If holder sells £25,000 spot
$$\text{Profit} = \$32,500 \ (£25,000 \times \$1.3000)$$
$$-\$31,250 - \$875$$
$$= \$375.00$$

*CME*

| Holder | Writer |
|---|---|
| Long future at $1.2500 | Short future at $1.2500 |

Holder's margin account = £25,000
$$\times (\$1.2950 - \$1.2500)$$
$$= \$1,125.00$$
If holder immediately closes out futures contract at $1.2950
$$\text{Profit} = \$1,125.00 - \$750.00$$
$$= \$375.00$$

All the major currency option contracts quoted at the three largest exchanges – the Philadelphia Stock Exchange, the Chicago Mercantile Exchange and LIFFE – trade for a fixed

---

[1] Details of all currently traded currency options contracts are given in Appendix 2.
[2] Because of the LIFFE margining system, not all of the $875 would need to be paid immediately.

quantity of non-US currency, with the exchange rate represented in US$ per currency unit. The contracts can be represented in the following way:

*Cash*

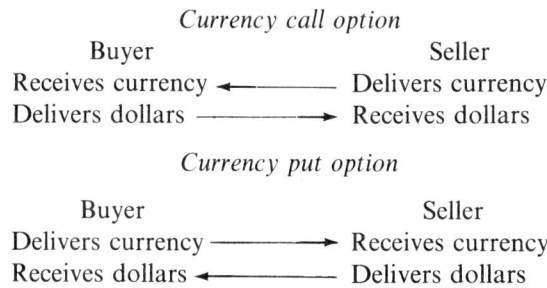

*Future*

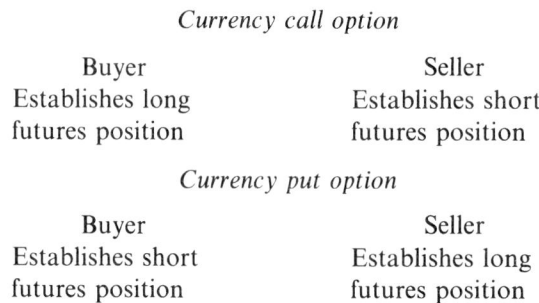

This quotation system is not universal to all currency options. Some exchanges quote foreign exchange futures and options in terms of a fixed quantity of US dollars including, for instance, the DM currency option on LIFFE.

This means that the right implied by the currency call and put options is reversed. The trader and hedger should check carefully the rights and obligations associated with a specific option before entering into a trade. For the remainder of this chapter the discussion of currency options procedures on traded markets will be confined to Philadelphia, CME and LIFFE options. After the basic characteristics of the traded currency options, the next most important elements are the exercise and margining procedures.

## a. Exercise procedures

### (i) Philadelphia

Since the full premium is paid in advance, the exercise procedure involves the exchange of one physical currency for another. The option holder notifies his clearing member of intention to exercise on any business day, and must notify his clearing member before the expiration day of the contract which is the Saturday before the third Wednesday of the delivery month (on a March, June, September, December cycle).

Purchaser    Delivers dollars through clearing member to the Option Clearing Corporation bank account in the United States.

Seller    Delivers currency to the Option Clearing Corporation bank account in the relevant country.

### (ii) LIFFE

The exercise system on LIFFE is more complex, because of the futures-style margining system for options. On notification of intention to exercise, various interim payments must be made by options buyers and sellers via their clearing members to the clearing house (ICCH).

1. Both parties must put up a full currency futures initial margin.
2. The full option settlement premium is debited to the buyer and credited to the seller.
3. Variation margin is calculated between the exercise price of the option and the spot exchange rate at exercise and is credited and debited to buyer and seller appropriately.
4. Delivery of currencies takes place at the spot rate.

**Example**

Exercise of a call option with an exercise price $1.1000 and a risk factor = 0.70. The spot exchange rate is $1.15 and the option settlement premium is 5.10 cents.

| Buyer | Seller |
|---|---|
| $1,000 (futures margin) | $1,000 (futures margin) |
| + | − |
| $1,275 (premium) | $1,275 |
| − | + |
| $1,250 (($1.15 − $1.10) × £25,000) | $1,250 |
| − | − |
| $700 (existing initial margin) | $800 (existing initial margin) |
| = | = |
| $325 | $175 |

In addition to these cash flows, the holder of the call will either have to pay dollars to the clearing house two days before the settlement day (the third Wednesday of the delivery month), or through the delivery versus payment system (DVP) requiring dollar payment on the settlement day subject to prepayment advice. Corresponding sterling payment by the option writer to the ICCH is made through the protected payment system, while payment of sterling to the option holder can be made through the protected payment system or by cheque.

The aim of this rather complex procedure is to ensure settlement of all outstanding profits and losses at the beginning of the exercise and delivery cycle, while leaving the clearing house holding a full futures deposit from each party during the cycle. That futures deposit will be returned to both parties at the conclusion of the delivery process.

### (iii) Chicago Mercantile Exchange

Option holders may exercise on any trading day by giving notice to the clearing member. Exercise results in a long futures position for a call buyer or a put seller, and a short futures position for a call seller and a put buyer. The futures position is effective on the trading day immediately following exercise, and is marked-to-market to the settlement that day.

**Example**

A June $1.3000 call option is purchased at a premium of 3.0 cents. On April 15 the call is exercised and the April 15 futures settlement price is $1.4000.

Assuming the holder does not sell the future in the market before the close of trading on April 16, when the future settles at $1.3950. The trader's margin account is credited with

$$(\$1.3950 - \$1.3000) \times £25,000 = \$2,375.00$$

The trader is free to withdraw the excess over the future initial margin.

$$\text{Profit} = \$2,375 - \$750 \ (£25,000 \times \$0.03)$$
$$= \$1,625.00[3]$$

## b. Margining

Systems of options margining were discussed in Chapter 2. It is difficult to make specific statements about margining systems because they are varied and change frequently. The main difference for currency options is between systems which require full payment of the premium by the buyer, and systems such as LIFFE which margin both long and short options positions futures-style. Methods of margining short positions vary from clearing house to clearing house, and should be checked for individual transactions.

## 2. Pricing of currency options

The basic principles of pricing options along the lines of the Black-Scholes model discussed in Chapter 3 can be applied to currency options.[4]

[3] The trader could have locked in a higher profit by selling a futures contract at $1.4000 on April 15 simultaneously with giving notice of exercise.

[4] Once again it is not proposed to discuss the detailed theory of currency option pricing here. The interested reader is referred to M. S. Garman and S. W. Kohlhagen, "Foreign currency option values", *Journal of International Money and Finance*, 1983, pp. 231–37 and J. Orlin Grabbe, "The pricing of call and put options on foreign exchange", *Journal of International Money and Finance*, 1983, 2, 239–53.

## a. Cash options: premiums paid

The value of the call option for European options on cash currency where the full premium is paid in advance can be written:

$$C(S, X, T) = e^{-r_F T}[SN(d_1) - e^{-r_d T}XN(d_2)]$$

$$\text{where} \quad d_1 = \frac{\ln(S/X) + (r_D - r_F + \sigma^2/2)T}{\sigma\sqrt{T}}$$

$$d_2 = d_1 - \sigma\sqrt{T}$$

and   $S$ = spot rate of currency to be acquired in domestic units per foreign unit

$X$ = exercise price in domestic units per foreign unit

$T$ = time to expiration

$r_F$ = foreign riskless interest rate

$r_D$ = domestic riskless interest rate

$\sigma$ = annual volatility of spot exchange rate

However, it is often convenient to rewrite this in terms of the forward exchange rate:

$$C(S, X, T) = e^{-r_D T}(FN(d_1) - XN(d_2))$$

$$\text{where} \quad d_1 = \frac{\ln(F/X) + (\sigma^2/2)T}{\sigma\sqrt{T}}$$

$$d_2 = d_1 - \sigma\sqrt{T}$$

$F$ = forward exchange rate in terms of domestic units per foreign unit

The *delta* of the option is still derived as the first derivative of the option premium from the original valuation model as

$$\Delta = e^{-r_F T}N(d_1)$$

This model is very similar to the original Black-Scholes model. The difference arises because the original model assumed stocks did not pay dividends, whereas a holding of foreign currency can clearly be invested to earn the foreign riskless interest rate.

The model can also be used to value European put options on cash currency, since a simple *put-call parity* condition exists. A long call and a short put position at the same exercise price $X$ will behave like a long forward position at a price $X$.

Let $S^*$ be the spot rate at expiry.

|  | $S^* < X$ | $S^* = X$ | $S^* > X$ |
|---|---|---|---|
| Long call | 0 | 0 | $S^* - X$ |
| Short put | $-(X - S^*)$ | 0 | 0 |
| Combination | $S^* - X$ | $S^* - X$ | $S^* - X$ |
| Long forward | $S^* - F$ | $S^* - F$ | $S^* - F$ |

Hence the combination: long call, short put, short forward is always worth $F - X$ at expiry; hence now

$$\text{Call} - \text{put} = (F - X)e^{-r_D T}$$

Exhibit 7.1 gives typical figures from the simple Garman-Kohlhagen option valuation model for cash sterling options.

146

## Exhibit 7.1: Numerical illustration of London Stock Exchange sterling options (European approximation)

Sterling spot = $1.20          Rus = 10%
Volatility = 15% per annum     Ruk = 12%

| Exercise price | 90-day | 180-day | 270-day |
|---|---|---|---|
| | | *Maturity* | |
| 110 call | 10.00 | 10.01 | 10.23 |
| put | 0.58 | 1.56 | 2.47 |
| 115 call | 6.00 | 6.78 | 7.31 |
| put | 1.69 | 3.10 | 4.20 |
| 120 call | 3.22 | 4.29 | 5.01 |
| put | 3.79 | 5.37 | 6.54 |
| 125 call | 1.48 | 2.53 | 3.28 |
| put | 6.93 | 8.37 | 9.47 |
| 130 call | 0.59 | 1.39 | 2.06 |
| put | 10.91 | 12.00 | 12.90 |
| Forward | 119.42 | 118.87 | 118.35 |

In the case of cash currency options, however, a European pricing model is unlikely to give entirely accurate results. With a European option, the boundary condition for a call option can be shown to be

$$\text{Call} > (F - X)\, e^{-r_D T}$$

However, since an American option can be exercised at any time, we know that

$$\text{Call} > S - X$$

Consequently if the spot rate is greater than the forward rate for a currency, it is likely that an American call will be priced higher than a European option. This is illustrated in Exhibit 7.2. Similar considerations apply to the American put (Exhibit 7.3).

The possibility of premature exercise can be looked at in another way. A deep in-the-money option will behave almost identically to a spot position (see Chapter 4), but in some cases the spot

## Exhibit 7.2: Comparison of the American call vs. the European call

Because the American offers more exercise opportunities, the American call value can only be greater than or equal to the European call value.

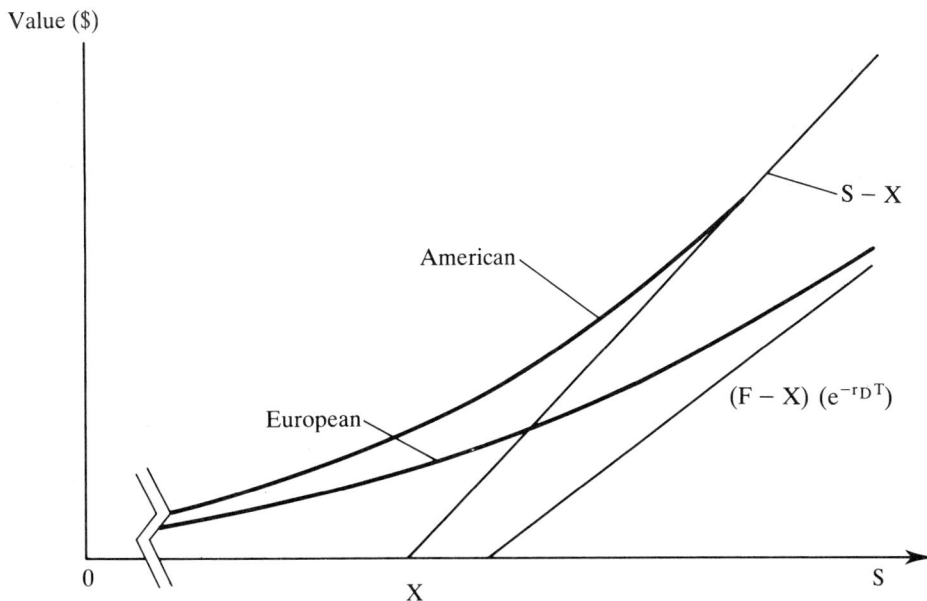

**Exhibit 7.3: Comparison of the American put vs. the European put**

Value ($)

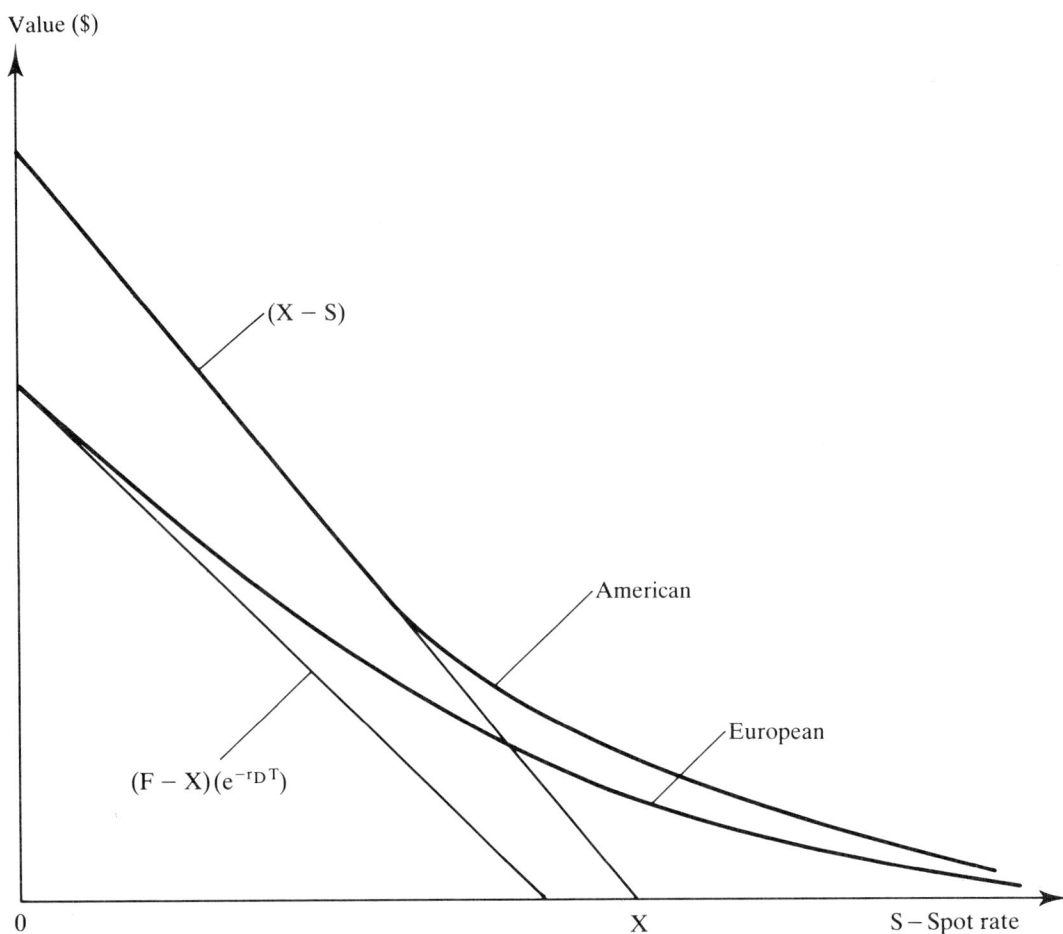

Source: The London Stock Exchange.

can be held cheaper than the option. To hold spot currency effectively costs the difference between the borrowing cost of the currency domestically and the rate at which the funds can be invested (the cost of carry). If the cost of carry is negative, and since the cost of holding the option is positive (there is no interest on the premium), it may be sensible to exercise the option prematurely. It may sometimes be worth exercising the option even if the cost of carry is positive. The reverse arguments apply to a put option.

Hence it will be necessary to adjust the simple European model to value American options. Since no analytical models for American currency options are available, numerical, binomial or curve-fitting techniques have to be used. One simple approximation often used is simply to assume

$$\text{American} = \text{Maximum (European, Intrinsic value)}$$

The table below shows some typical results for a true American model, the simple adjustment shown above, and a European model. The differences are significant but not extreme. The response of the currency option values to changes in volatility is shown in Exhibit 7.4.

*Call options*

Sterling spot = \$1.20    $R_D = 10\%$    $R_F = 12\%$    Volatility = 15%    Maturity = 90 days

| Exercise price | American | Modified European | European |
|---|---|---|---|
| 110 | 10.04 | 10.00 | 9.77 |
| 115 | 6.10 | 6.00 | 6.00 |
| 120 | 3.23 | 3.22 | 3.22 |
| 125 | 1.48 | 1.48 | 1.48 |
| 130 | 0.59 | 0.59 | 0.59 |

148

## Exhibit 7.4: Sensitivity analysis of call prices to volatility

Time values of options near the money vary about proportionally to volatility.

90-day call option

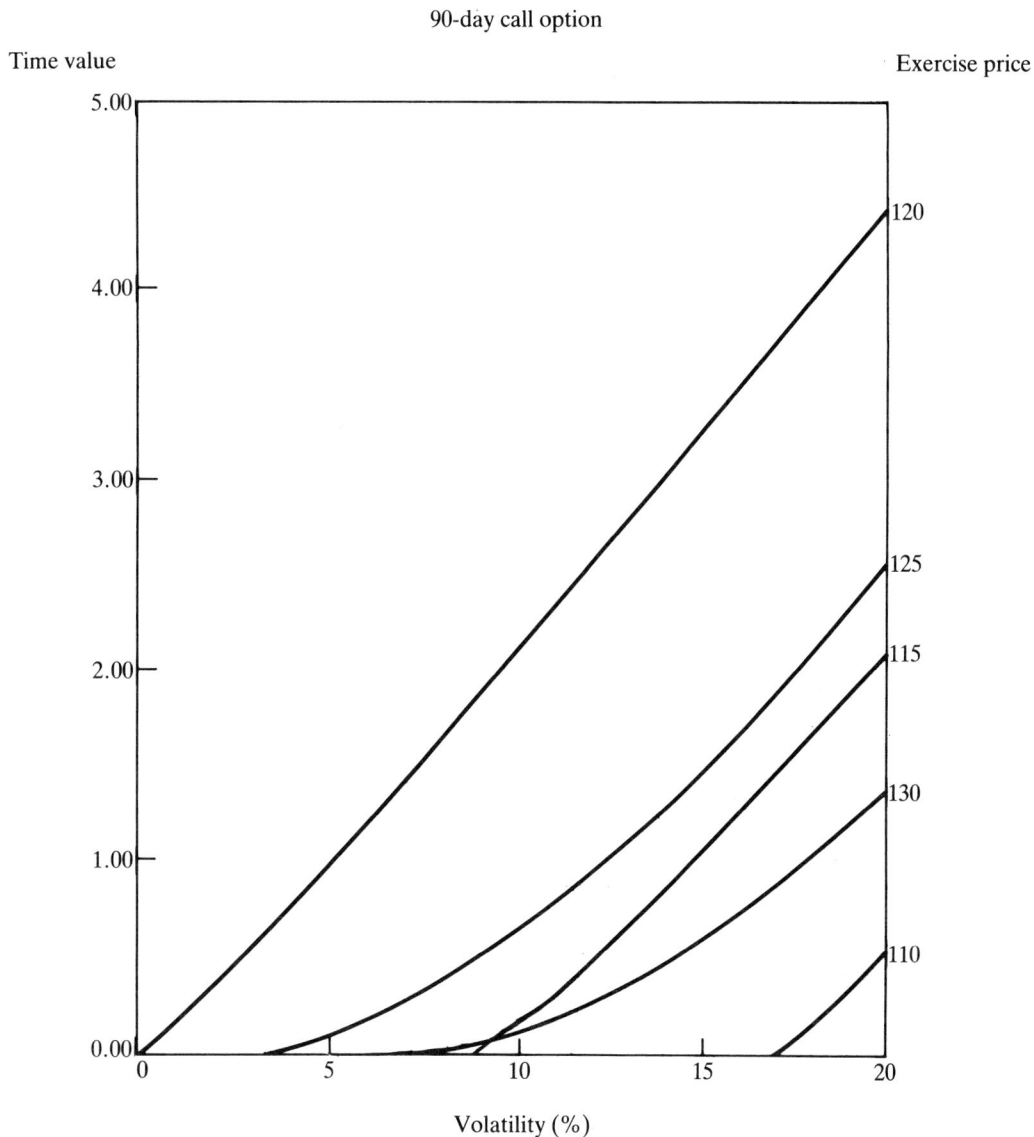

Source: The London Stock Exchange.

## b. Cash options: premiums margined

A slightly different valuation model is used when instead of the full premium of the option having to be paid in advance, the premiums are margined futures-style and it is assumed interest is paid on initial margins. Since the option seller will no longer obtain the premium on which he could earn interest, he will need to be compensated by a higher premium. In fact the premium on an equivalent LIFFE option of the same exercise price and maturity should be

$$LIFFE = Philadelphia \ (e^{r_D T})$$

giving a valuation formula

$$C(S, X, T) = FN(d_1) - XN(d_2)$$

Typical relative values are shown in the table (on p. 150), where $A$ is LIFFE margining, and $B$, full payment of premium by long.

Sterling spot = $1.20     US interest rate = 10%
Volatility     = 12.5%     UK interest rate = 12%

| Exercise price | 90-day A | 90-day B | 180-day A | 180-day B | 270-day A | 270-day B |
|---|---|---|---|---|---|---|
| 115 | 5.65 | 5.51 | 6.34 | 6.04 | 6.89 | 6.41 |
| 120 | 2.70 | 2.64 | 3.67 | 3.49 | 4.36 | 4.06 |
| 125 | 1.03 | 1.01 | 1.91 | 1.82 | 2.58 | 2.40 |
| 130 | 0.31 | 0.30 | 0.90 | 0.85 | 1.43 | 1.33 |

The interest rate factor on these options also applies to the option deltas, which will now simply be

$$\Delta = N(d_1)\left(\frac{e^{r_D T}}{e^{r_F T}}\right)$$

In practice the relationship, which yields the possibility of arbitrage strategies, is unlikely to be so simple. The main reason for early exercise with the cash option is that the funds tied up in the option do not yield a return, compared with a positive return to holding the spot in a negative carry market. Under the LIFFE margining system, there are effectively no funds tied up in the options position. Any profits earned on a deep in-the-money option have already been paid through the variation margin system and can be invested at market rates, while it is assumed that interest is payable on initial margin. Hence, the discrepancies between actual market prices for American options and theoretical European option prices may not be as large for LIFFE currency options as for Philadelphia and UK Stock Exchange options. Lack of trading liquidity for LIFFE deep in-the-money options may still make early exercise the only way of efficiently closing out an options position, but the frequency of early exercise and hence its value will be less than for options with full premium payment.

### c. Futures options: premiums paid

The option valuation formula for a premium paid option on a currency future is identical to that for an option on cash save that the *futures price* replaces the *forward price*. Assuming that arbitrage keeps the currency futures price and the forward price closely in line, the values of a European cash call should be identical with a futures call. The differences arise when the American option is considered. The boundary condition $(F - X)e^{-r_D T}$ has to be replaced with the intrinsic value of the option $(F - X)$. Although this will generally lie above the simple European option values, the value may lie below the cash American option in a negative cost of carry market. This can be seen in Exhibit 7.5.

Early exercise is still more likely with paid premium options on futures than margined options on cash. For an option on a futures contract, the interest lost on funds tied up in the option may exceed the time value of the option. Deep in-the-money options have profit profiles almost identical to the underlying futures contract, but the futures contract only required an initial

### Exhibit 7.5: Bounds on option values

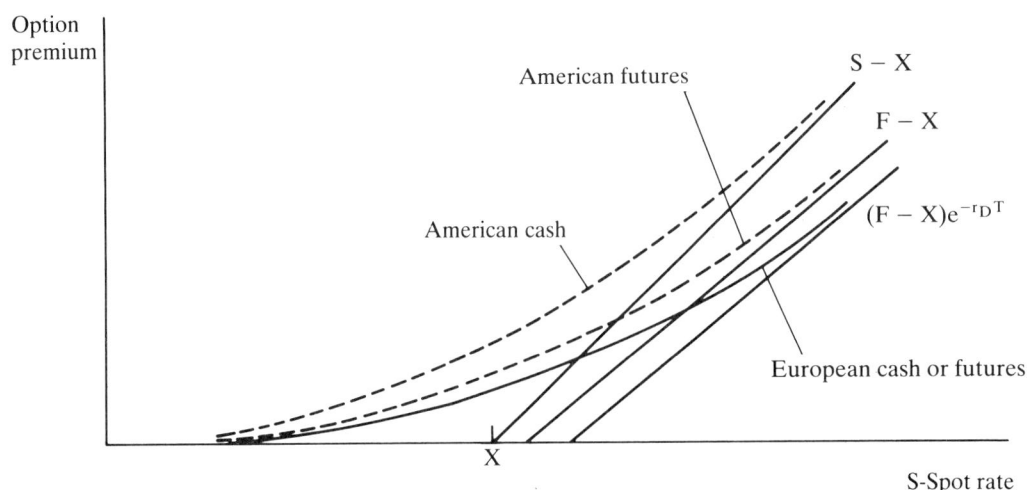

margin payment on which it is assumed interest is paid. Another way of looking at this consistent with Exhibit 7.5 is to consider the implications of the futures price being at a discount to spot. Since this could be taken to imply that the spot rate will fall, holding the call longer will reduce its value. The table below shows comparative call premiums for American options on futures and cash.

### American cash versus futures calls: premium paid

Sterling spot = $1.2500    U.S rate = 10%    UK rate = 12%

June (90-day) future      = 1.2439
September (180-day) future = 1.2382
December (270-day) future = 1.2328

| Exercise price | 90-day | | 180-day | | 270-day | |
|---|---|---|---|---|---|---|
| | Cash | Futures | Cash | Futures | Cash | Futures |
| 115 | 10.21 | 10.09 | 10.67 | 10.34 | 11.11 | 10.57 |
| 120 | 6.33 | 6.25 | 7.25 | 7.07 | 7.94 | 7.66 |
| 125 | 3.50 | 3.49 | 4.60 | 4.55 | 5.42 | 5.34 |
| 130 | 1.69 | 1.69 | 2.79 | 2.79 | 3.57 | 3.55 |
| 135 | 0.71 | 0.71 | 1.59 | 1.59 | 2.29 | 2.29 |

As expected, for call options the major discrepancies arise with the deep in-the-money calls, and become more extreme as the maturity of the options increases. Anyone using currency options markets for hedging or trading must be aware of these valuation differences between options, and be confident that the specific option valuation model being used will pick them up accurately.

### d. Currency volatilities

The importance of correct estimation of volatility for option valuation has already been stressed. The point is emphasized when examining the charts in Exhibit 7.6[5] covering the UK pound from January 1985 to January 1986. During this period the pound fell to $1.05, its lowest level ever against the dollar, before rising back to nearly $1.50 in November. Both implied and historical volatility moved very dramatically over the period – in the case of implied volatility from 14% at the beginning of the period to as high as 22% and back around 12% in December 1985. This highlights two points: first, any volatility estimation procedure using historical information needs to be adjustable rapidly to more recent information: second, any hedger or valuation trader would have considerable exposure to volatility risk in this sort of market. A comparison of the historical and implied volatilities suggests a tendency for historical volatility to lag behind changes in implied volatility, which is consistent with a view that traders use information other than simply historical exchange rate data when forecasting volatility over the life of an option.

Almost identical results can be seen for the DM, although the deviations between historical and implied volatilities can be larger. A trader should also explore whether deviations between implied and historical volatilities have any forecasting information about the subsequent evolution of option prices.

## 3. Trading and arbitrage with currency options

All the basic trading techniques for options described in Chapter 4 can be applied to currency options. However, some relationships specific to currency options can be used for arbitrage or semi-arbitrage trading.[6]

---

[5] These charts were prepared by Donaldson, Lufkin and Jenrette for the 1986 Euromoney conference on Interest Rate and Currency Options.

[6] The first consistent discussion of arbitrage relationships with foreign exchange options was contained in J. H. Giddy, "Foreign exchange options", *Journal of Futures Markets*, 1983, Vol. 3, No. 2, 143–66.

## Exhibit 7.6: Historical volatilities

**British pound implied/Historical volatility**
**January 1985–January 1986**

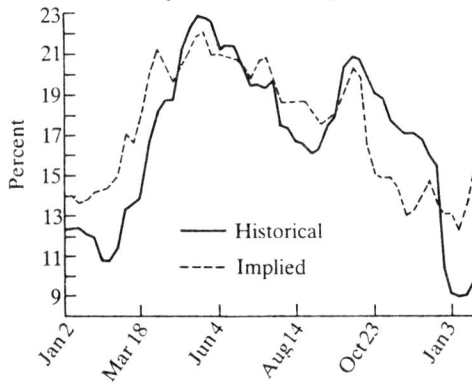

**British pound implied volatility**
**January 1985–January 1986**

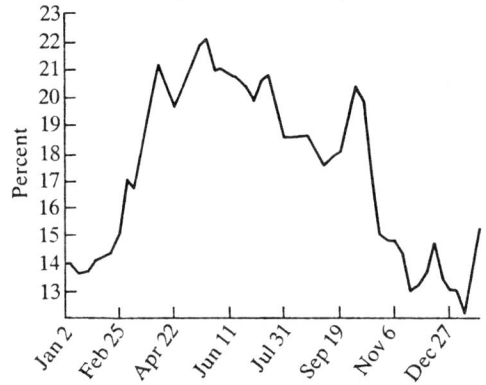

**British pound implied/Historical volatility**
**January 1985–January 1986**

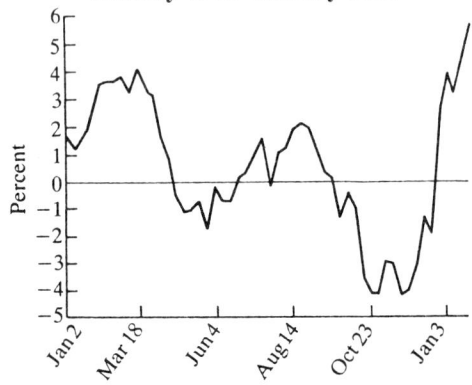

**British pound historical volatility**
**January 1985–January 1986**

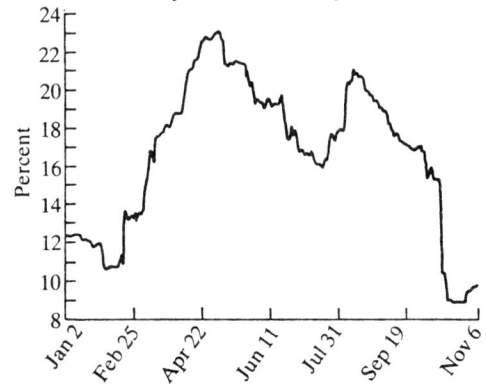

**Deutschmark implied/Historical volatility**
**January 1985–January 1986**

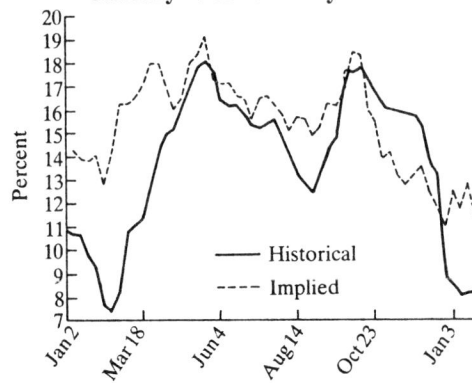

**Deutschmark implied volatility**
**January 1985–January 1986**

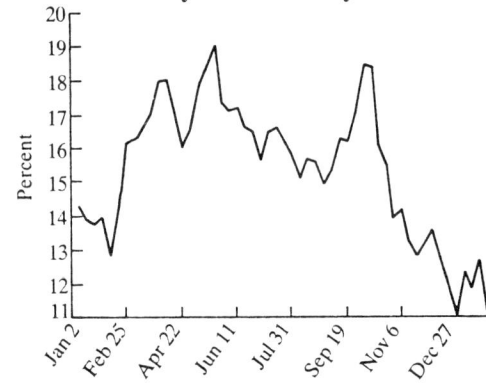

**Deutschmark implied/Historical volatility**
**January 1985–January 1986**

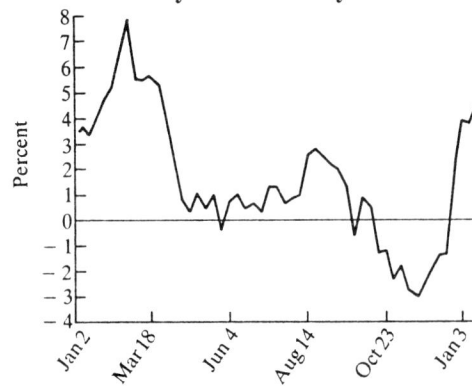

**Deutschmark historical volatility**
**January 1985–January 1986**

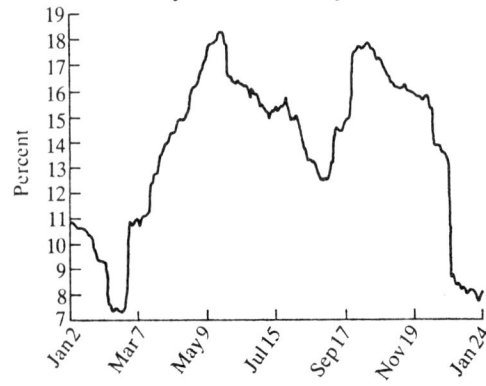

Source: Donaldson, Lufkin and Jenrette.

## a. Put-call parity

This was discussed briefly in Chapter 3 when explaining how to price put options when the fair price of the call option is determined.

$$\text{Call} - \text{put} = (\text{Forward rate} - \text{Exercise price})\, e^{-r_D T}$$

For arbitrage purposes, it is more usual to use a simple add-on interest rate rather than a continuously compounded rate.

### Example: March

A June 125 sterling call option is priced at 2.7 cents and a June 125 put is priced at 3.00 cents. The current three-month dollar interest rate is 10%, and the three-month sterling forward rate is $1.2465.

*Equilibrium relationship*

$$\text{Fair put premium} = 2.70 - \frac{(124.65 - 125)}{1.025}$$

$$= 3.0425\cancel{c}$$

Since the put appears undervalued relative to the value of the call, an arbitrage opportunity appears to exist.

Buy the put option      Cash outflow 3.00¢
Sell the call option      Cash inflow 2.70¢

Buy sterling forward at $1.2465

$$\text{Net investment} = 0.30\cancel{c}$$

$$\text{Cost of borrowing at } 10\% \text{ for 3 months} = (0.30)(0.025)$$
$$= 0.0075\cancel{c}$$

*At expiration:*

|  | Rate < 125 | Rate = 125 | Rate > 125 |
|---|---|---|---|
| Put | 125 − X | 0 | 0 |
| Call | 0 | 0 | −(125 − X) |
| Forward | X − 124.65 | 125 − 124.65 | X − 124.65 |
| Interest + Principal | −(0.3075) | −(0.3075) | −(0.3075) |
| New value | 0.0425¢ | 0.0425¢ | 0.0425¢ |

Arbitrage profit = 0.0425¢ per £

The trader, however, should remember that this arbitrage is guaranteed only at expiration, and since the trader will be short call options, he is at risk to a disadvantageous early exercise.

## b. Differential quotations

The price of a foreign exchange put option in one currency should be identical to that of a call option in the other currency at the same exercise price. This applies only if the options are identical in condition apart from the method of foreign exchange quotation.

### Example: March – spot $/DM rate 2.48

Consider a call option giving the right to buy US $ for DM. The June 2.50 call is priced at 3.00 pfennig per dollar.
A put option giving the right to deliver DM for US $ with exercise price 0.40 and June maturity should be

$$P(0.40) = \frac{(3.00)(0.40)}{2.48} = 0.48\cancel{c}$$

i.e. 0.48¢ per DM

This arbitrage could be of considerable interest as the number of options priced using European as opposed to American FX quotation methods begins to increase. To illustrate the arbitrage further, let us suppose the call option is the LIFFE DM call on $50,000, and the put option is the right to sell DM 125,000 at $0.40 for 0.52 cents per DM.
Thus, the put option appears relatively overpriced.

$$\text{Sell put option at } 0.52\cancel{c} \quad \text{Cash outflow} = 125,000 \times \$0.0052$$
$$= \$650$$

$$\text{Buy call option at 3.00pf} \quad \text{Cash inflow} = \$50,000 \times \text{DM } 0.03$$
$$= \text{DM } 1500$$

$$\text{Dollar equivalent at } 2.48 = \$604.84$$

$$\text{Net cash inflow} = \$45.16$$

This can be invested to gain interest over three months.

*At expiration:*

|  | Rate < 2.50 | Rate = 2.50 | Rate > 2.50 |
|---|---|---|---|
| Put | 0 | 0 | $-0.40 - 1/R$ |
| Call | 0 | 0 | $R - 2.50$ |
| Principal + Interest at 10% | 46.29 | 46.29 | 46.29 |

Assume the rate ends up at 2.60 and translate all cash flows into US $:

$$-(0.40 - 1/2.60)(125,000) + \frac{(2.60 - 2.50)(50,000)}{2.60} + 46.29 = \$46.29$$

### c. International options price parity

This relationship is described in Giddy (*op. cit.*). He shows that a relationship exists between the spot exchange rate and options prices defined on domestic and foreign currency rates.

$$S = \left[ C(X) + \frac{X}{(1 + r_D)^T} \right] \left[ XC^*(1/X) + \frac{1}{(1 + r_F)^T} \right]^{-1}$$

$$S = \left[ P(X) - \frac{X}{(1 + r_D)^T} \right] \left[ XP^*(1/X) - \frac{1}{(1 + r_F)^T} \right]^{-1}$$

where $C(X)$ and $P(X)$ are option prices for calls and puts for domestic currency per foreign currency unit. $C^*(1/X)$ and $P^*(1/X)$ are options prices for calls and puts for foreign currency per domestic currency unit.

### d. Box arbitrage

The concept of debit and credit boxes was described in Chapter 4. For foreign currency options, it can be shown, as an extension of the arbitrages defined above, that for calls and puts with two different exercise prices $X_1$ and $X_2$ but with the same maturity

$$C(X_1) - P(X_1) + P(X_2) - C(X_2) = \frac{X_1 - X_2}{(1 + r_D)^T}$$

If this condition is violated, arbitrage profits can be realized.

## 4. Hedging with currency options

As with other types of options, currency options are particularly useful in hedging uncertain assets or liabilities, i.e. cash flows which are expected but not certain at the time the hedge is put on. The most typical example of this is the contract for tender, where the hedger bids for a contract on a specific day but will not know until later whether the contract will be awarded to him, and may not receive any funds until an even later date. Currency options can also be used as a substitute for normal forward exchange hedging, for the hedger to retain some of the benefit of a favourable exchange rate movement. However, currency option hedging of this type seems generally inferior to straightforward forward currency hedging.

In this section, various types of currency option hedges and their important features are discussed.

### a. A simple option hedge

**Example**

A UK importer is expecting to pay $1.5 million in September for a shipment of goods. The current sterling-dollar spot rate in June 1987 is $1.1050, the three-month forward rate is 1.1000, and the Philadelphia sterling put option with a $1.1000 strike price is selling for 4.50 cents.

The first step for the hedger is to work out how many contracts to purchase. An appropriate hedge will call for the purchase of put options, for these enable the importer to hand over sterling in exchange for dollars at a fixed exchange rate.

$$\text{Option contract size} = £12,500$$

$$\text{Equivalent at } \$1.1000 \text{ to } \$13,750$$

$$\text{Number of contracts for total hedge} = \frac{\$1,500,000}{\$13,750}$$

$$= 109 \text{ contracts}$$

Buy 109 September put options.

The hedger then calculates the total cost of the options hedge.

$$\text{Total cost} = 109 \times \$0.045 \times £12,500$$
$$= \$61,312.50$$

The total cost amounts to 4.1% of the $1.5 million hedged, as compared with a cost of the forward cover of a discount of only 0.45%. This is the main reason why currency option hedges are not attractive compared with straightforward cover. The cost of the option of 4.5 cents means that the best exchange rate that the option buyer can absolutely guarantee is only £1.0550 ($1.10 minus $0.045).

The outcome of the options hedge for two extreme values of the sterling-dollar exchange rate can be examined.

## Alternative 1: September 5

Dollar-sterling spot rate 1.00     Option premium 10.25¢

(a) Importer purchases $1,500,000 at spot rate of $1.00

$$\text{Cost} = £1,500,000$$

(b) Importer sells 109 September put options at 10.25¢

$$\text{Profit} = 109 \times £12,500 \times (\$0.1025 - \$0.045)$$
$$= \$78,343.75^7$$

$$\text{Equivalent at } \$1.00 \text{ to } £78,343.75$$

The hedger can then calculate the effective exchange rate obtained by dividing the amount of currency purchased by the effective amount of sterling paid.

$$\text{Effective exchange rate} = \frac{\$1,500,000}{£1,500,000 - £78,343.75}$$

$$= \$1.05511$$

This can be compared with the forward exchange rate of $1.10 that could have been obtained back in June. The exchange rate actually obtained is slightly better than the best guaranteed rate of $1.055 because the option had a small amount of time value left just before maturity in September.

## Alternative 2: September 5

Dollar-sterling rate $1.20     Option premium $0.01¢

(a) Importer purchases $1,500,000 at spot rate of $1.20

$$\text{Cost} = \$1,250,000$$

(b) Importer sells 109 September put options at 0.01¢

$$\text{Loss} = 109 \times £12,500 \times (\$0.045 - \$0.0001)$$
$$= \$61,176.25$$

$$\text{Equivalent at } \$1.20 \text{ to } £50,980.21$$

---

[7] The profit would not be as high as this, because the original cost of $61,312.50 would be borrowed for three months. If the interest rate were 10%, that would constitute an additional cost of $1,532.81.

Again the hedger calculates the effective exchange rate

$$\text{Effective exchange rate} = \frac{\$1,500,000}{£1,250,000 + £50,980.21}$$

$$= \$1.1530$$

If this effective exchange rate is compared with the forward rate back in June of $1.10, it is apparent that the option hedge has preserved some of the benefits of the favourable exchange rate movement. The problem, however, is the cost of achieving this. Even if the exchange rate had moved in favour of the hedger by as much as 4 cents to $1.14, the option hedge would still have been inferior to the forward hedge at an option premium of 4.5 cents. The benefit of preserving the favourable impact of sterling appreciation is only obtainable at a relatively high cost.

## b. Constructing non-dollar currency options

One of the problems with the traded currency options market is that, with very few exceptions, it is not possible to buy and sell options between pairs of non-dollar currencies. Even in the OTC options market, most options granted tend to be in terms of the dollar against some other major currency. However, artificial or proxy currency options can be constructed from traded dollar-based options which give a wide choice of options hedges to the importer or exporter.

### Example

A German importer expects to pay £1 million in September 1986 for a shipment of goods. The current DM spot rate in June is 3.645 and the three-month forward rate is 3.635. The current DM-dollar spot rate is 32 cents and the sterling-dollar rate $1.1664. Philadelphia DM and sterling options for September are priced as follows:

| Deutschmark | | Sterling | |
|---|---|---|---|
| Strike price | Put premium | Strike price | Call premium |
| 30 | 0.20 | 110 | 7.50 |
| 31 | 0.80 | 115 | 3.40 |
| 32 | 1.20 | 120 | 0.90 |
| 33 | 2.40 | 125 | 0.02 |

Since the Deutschmark put options give the right to hand over Deutschmarks for dollars at a fixed rate, and the sterling call options give the right to hand over dollars for sterling at a fixed rate, the combination of a DM put and a sterling call is equivalent to an option to hand over Deutschmarks for sterling at a fixed rate. However, the different combinations of DM put strike prices and sterling call strike prices create a whole array of different DM-sterling exchange rates, each of which can be obtained at a different dollar cost.

The importer, therefore, examines the different cross rates available and their costs.

| | Sterling rate | | | |
|---|---|---|---|---|
| DM rate | 110 | 115 | 120 | 125 |
| 30 | 3.667 | 3.833 | 4.000 | 4.167 |
| | (82,375) | (41,625) | (17,000) | (8,575) |
| 31 | 3.548 | 3.710 | 3.871 | 4.032 |
| | (103,500) | (63,500) | (40,000) | (32,700) |
| 32 | 3.438 | 3.594 | 3.750 | 3.906 |
| | (116,250) | (76,750) | (54,000) | (47,450) |
| 33 | 3.333 | 3.485 | 3.636 | 3.788 |
| | (154,500) | (116,500) | (96,000) | (91,700) |

Figures in brackets represent costs of options hedges to obtain specific cross-rates.

It is difficult to see which of these combinations is the best. Much will depend on the degree of risk aversion of the hedger. However, the hedger should draw up a table of the best guaranteed DM-sterling exchange rates, assuming that the dollar cost of the options is converted into Deutschmarks at the current spot rate of 32 cents.

*Best guaranteed cross-rate*

| | Sterling rate | | | |
|---|---|---|---|---|
| DM rate | 110 | 115 | 120 | 125 |
| 30 | 3.924 | 3.963 | 4.053 | 4.194 |
| 31 | 3.871 | 3.908 | 3.996 | 4.134 |
| 32 | 3.801 | 3.834 | 3.919 | 4.054 |
| 33 | 3.816 | 3.849 | 3.936 | 4.075 |

Although, as expected, none of the options hedges guarantees a better rate than the forward rate, substantial differences exist between the best guaranteed rates using different combinations of DM puts and sterling calls. This is because the ability to benefit from favourable exchange rate changes varies from one position to another. Below is a complete table of options hedge costs, best guaranteed rates, and the cross-rate beyond which the options hedge gives a more favourable result than the simple forward hedge.

| Option strategy | | Best guaranteed rate | Break even rate | Cost ($) |
|---|---|---|---|---|
| DM | Sterling | | | |
| 30 | 110 | 3.924 | 3.378 | 82,375 |
| 30 | 115 | 3.963 | 3.505 | 41,625 |
| 30 | 120 | 4.053 | 3.582 | 17,000 |
| 30 | 125 | 4.194 | 3.608 | 8,575 |
| 31 | 110 | 3.871 | 3.312 | 103,500 |
| 31 | 115 | 3.908 | 3.437 | 63,500 |
| 31 | 120 | 3.996 | 3.510 | 40,000 |
| 31 | 125 | 4.134 | 3.533 | 32,700 |
| 32 | 110 | 3.801 | 3.272 | 116,250 |
| 32 | 115 | 3.834 | 3.395 | 76,750 |
| 32 | 120 | 3.919 | 3.466 | 54,000 |
| 32 | 125 | 4.054 | 3.487 | 47,450 |
| 33 | 110 | 3.816 | 3.152 | 154,500 |
| 33 | 115 | 3.849 | 3.271 | 116,500 |
| 33 | 120 | 3.936 | 3.335 | 96,000 |
| 33 | 125 | 4.075 | 3.348 | 91,700 |

Having established the different combinations of best guaranteed rates and breakeven rates, the next task for the hedger is to establish which combination, if any, looks the most favourable. The final choice will not be easy, and will depend upon the degree of risk aversion of the hedger. In this case, it is highly probable that the hedger would decide to use the forward market. If he did not, the DM 32 put and sterling 115 call represent the best compromise between a low best guaranteed rate and a high breakeven rate.

$$\text{Number of sterling calls} = \frac{£1,000,000}{£12,500} = 80 \text{ contracts}$$

$$\text{Cost} = 80 \times £12,500 \times \$0.034 = \$34,000$$

$$\text{Number of DM puts} = \frac{£1,000,000 \times \$1.15}{\text{DM } 62,500 \times \$0.32} = 57 \text{ contracts}$$

$$\text{Cost} = 57 \times \text{DM } 62,500 \times \$0.012 = \$42,750$$

$$\text{Total cost} = \$76,750$$

The hedger has guaranteed a sterling-Deutschmark exchange rate for September of no worse than 3.594 for a total cost of $76,750.

Come September, however, the position evaluation will be more complex than for the simple sterling-dollar options hedge discussed earlier, since the effective exchange rate will be influenced by the actual DM-dollar and sterling-dollar spot exchange rates which will be controlling the level of option premiums. To illustrate, a couple of alternative results are examined.

*Alternative 1*

DM-dollar spot rate   $0.3315
£-dollar spot rate      $1.1900
£-DM spot rate        DM 3.5900

       DM put premium = 0.01¢     Sterling call premium = 4.20¢

(a) Hedger buys £1,000,000 at spot rate of DM 3.5900

$$\text{Cost} = \text{DM } 3,590,000$$

(b) DM put option loss = 57 × DM 62,500 × ($0.012 − $0.0001)
                       = $42,393.75

Equivalent at $0.3315 to DM 127,884.62

Sterling call option gain = 80 × £12,500 × ($0.042 − $0.034)
                          = $8,000.00

Equivalent at $0.3315 to DM 24,132.73

Net DM loss = DM 103,751.89

$$\text{Effective exchange rate} = \frac{\text{DM } 3,590,000 + \text{DM } 103,751.89}{£1,000,000}$$

$$= \text{DM } 3.6938$$

*Alternative 2*

DM-dollar spot rate    $0.3092
£-dollar spot rate     $1.11
£-DM spot rate         DM 3.5900

DM put premium 1.22¢    Sterling call premium = 0.01¢

(a) Hedger buys £1,000,000 at spot rate of DM 3.5900

Cost = DM 3,590,000

(b) DM put option gain = 57 × DM 62,500 × ($0.0122 − $0.012)
                       = $712.50

Sterling call option loss = 80 × £12,500 × ($0.034 − $0.0001)
                          = $33,900

Net dollar loss = $33,187.50

Equivalent at $0.3092 to DM 107,333.44

$$\text{Effective exchange rate} = \frac{\text{DM } 3,590.000 + \text{DM } 107,333.44}{£1,000,000}$$

$$= \text{DM } 3.6973$$

Thus when constructing a cross exchange rate hedge with currency options, the pattern of currency changes which results in a specific DM-sterling cross rate can have an effect on the effective exchange rate obtained, because the profits and losses to the currency options positions are not necessarily symmetrical across currencies. Nonetheless, the fact that traded options on dollar exchange rates can be combined to produce cross-rate options is a useful feature.

Even so, one should beware of making too much of this. The fair price of a DM-sterling cross-rate option considered as an individual option will invariably be significantly less than the price of the artificial option set up by combining a dollar-DM option and a dollar-sterling option. This is because the combination does not take into account any lack of correlation between dollar-DM and dollar-sterling rates in pricing the option. In effect the rates are assumed to be perfectly correlated, and hence the volatility will be the weighted sum of the two volatilities. If there is any lack of perfect correlation, which will certainly be the case, using the DM-sterling rate volatility will inevitably produce a lower fair option price.

---

**Cross-rate options**

1. **The fair price of a cross-rate option will be less than that of a combination of two options. Hence it is better to hedge with an OTC cross-rate option than through the traded options market when hedging cross rates.**
2. **When hedging OTC cross-rate options written, it may be better on the grounds of cost to hedge with cash or forward rather than traded options combinations, though hedge performance may suffer thereby.**

---

The main point is that cross-rate options activity in the absence of equivalent traded cross-rate options involves additional costs and risks that need to be monitored carefully by both writers and buyers.

## c. Hedging in a contract for a tender

This is the classic case when an options hedge can provide insurance cover for a potential foreign exchange exposure which cannot be obtained in the forward market.

**Example**

A UK firm is bidding for a $2 million contract. The date is July 1987. The firm will be informed if it is successful in November 1987 and payment will be made in February 1988. The current sterling-dollar spot exchange rate is $1.10 and the February 1988 forward rate is $1.1025. The March 1988 Philadelphia call option with a strike price of $1.10 is selling for 2.75 cents.

The hedger's initial reaction is probably to sell $2 million forward for February delivery at the current forward exchange rate of $1.1025. However, difficulties may arise if the firm does not win the contract. If sterling has appreciated against the dollar, there is no problem since the forward position will be showing a profit. However, if sterling has depreciated sharply against the dollar, the hedger will be the proud possessor of an uncovered forward position showing a substantial loss. In a period of volatile exchange rates, this latter risk will almost certainly be too great for the tendering firm to undertake.

Currency options provide an ideal means for hedging this type of risk. The hedger decides to buy sterling calls[8] to enable him to exchange dollars for sterling at a fixed rate.

$$\text{Number of March sterling calls} = \frac{\$2,000,000}{£12,500 \times \$1.10}$$

$$= 145.5 \text{ contracts}$$

Hedger buys 146 March sterling calls at $0.0275

$$\text{Cost of hedge} = 146 \times £12,500 \times \$0.0275$$

$$= \$50,187.50$$

Several points should be made. First, the hedger has guaranteed an exchange rate of at least $1.10 at a maximum cost of $50,187.50. In fact, the net cost and consequently the actually realized exchange rate will in all likelihood, be more favourable than this because the options contracts are likely to still possess substantial time value in November, when the hedger will learn whether he has obtained the contract. In November, if the contract is won, the hedger would normally sell $2 million forward at the prevailing February forward rate and sell the sterling call options in the market.

The second point concerns the possible use of the *delta hedge ratio*. At first sight, since the hedger is not planning to use the options to obtain physical currency at a later date, but to sell them in the market in November, it might be argued that the delta of the option should be used in deciding how many contracts will adequately hedge a $2 million cash position. In fact the delta of the March sterling $1.10 call is only 0.53 which would suggest a hedge of 146/0.53 or 276 contracts.

However, consider the situation in November. If the hedger wins the contract, he can keep the options to ensure exchange for cash currency in March or sell them and do a forward transaction, whichever is more profitable. If the hedger does not win the contract, then if the exchange has moved against him, the call options will make money anyway. If the exchange moves in his favour and he fails to win the contract, the fewer the contracts he holds, the lower the cash loss. Thus in general a hedger who is long calls will tend to ignore delta when determining his hedge.

To illustrate the variety of possibilities with this type of hedge, four alternative scenarios in November are examined.

*Alternative 1: Firm fails to win contract*

*Sterling rate $1.05*

$$\text{March 110 call premium} = 0.02¢$$

$$\text{Value of options position} = 146 \times £12,500 \times \$0.0002 = \$365.00$$

---

[8] An equivalent currency options hedging strategy would involve selling the $2,000,000 forward for February delivery and protecting the forward position by buying March sterling puts. The hedger will follow the strategy which achieves the best exchange rate at the lowest cost.

The value of the options position is so small that the hedger will probably keep them as a speculation against subsequent exchange rate movements.

*Sterling rate $1.15*

$$\text{March 110 call premium} = 5.90\text{¢}$$

$$\text{Value of options position} = 146 \times £12,500 \times \$0.059$$
$$= \$107,675$$

The hedger is able to liquidate his options position for a net profit of $57,487.50.

## *Alternative 2: Firm wins contract*

*Sterling rate $1.05*

Forward rate for February = $1.0510
March call premium = 0.02¢
Sell $2,000,000 forward at $1.0510 = £1,902,949.60
Option loss = $50,187.50 − $365 = $49,822.50
Equivalent at $1.105 to £47,450

$$\text{Effective exchange rate} = \frac{\$2,000,000}{£1,902,949.50 - £47,450}$$

$$= \$1.0779$$

*Sterling rate $1.15*

Forward rate for February = $1.1515
March call premium = 5.90¢
Sell $2,000,000 forward at $1.1515 = £1,736,865.00
Option gain = $57,487.50
Equivalent at $1.15 to £49.989.13

$$\text{Effective exchange rate} = \frac{\$2,000,000}{£1,736,865 + £49,989.13}$$

$$= \$1.1193$$

It is now possible to summarize this type of hedging.

1. If the firm does not win the contract, the maximum loss is $50,187.50, and there is the chance of substantial gain if the sterling exchange rate appreciates.
2. If the contract is won and the exchange rate has moved in the hedger's favour, the effective exchange rate will frequently be better than the forward rate back in July.
3. If the contract is won and the exchange rate has moved against the hedger, the effective exchange rate will be generally worse than the forward rate back in July. The cost will not, however, be the full option premium because the option will still have time value in November. A rise in implied volatility which could increase time value would reduce the hedge cost even further.[9]
4. Other hedging strategies are available to the hedger in November. He could simply keep the March 110 calls and not deal in the forward market. He could sell the March 110 calls and buy March 105 or March 115 calls, or follow many other strategies.

Currency option hedges are an excellent form of insurance in the contract for tenders. The only problem that has concerned the corporates is the cost of the insurance. In the example above, the total cost of the currency options hedge amounted to some 2.5% of the value of the underlying contract. This is a sizeable payment, but perhaps worthwhile when compared with the risks attached in volatile markets with either not hedging at all or hedging what is only a potential cash flow with a forward sale of currency.[10]

---

[9] In this case where the contract was won, a delta hedge would have locked in an exchange rate closer to the forward rate of $1.1025 back in July. However, the dangers of the delta hedge when the contract is not won have been described previously.

[10] The net cost to the hedger would be much less if the option premiums could be treated as insurance premiums and hence tax-deductible. See Chapter 10 on accounting and taxation of options for a further discussion of this point.

There are ways of reducing the cost of contract-for-tender currency option hedges. First, if a group of contractors operating within a single currency are bidding for a contract, they could form a consortium to purchase a currency option hedge, with only the successful contractor (if any) allowed to exercise the option. This would substantially reduce the cost of the hedge to any one bidder. If none of the consortium won the contract, option hedge losses or gains could be divided up *pari passu*. Agencies such as the Export Credit Guarantee Department in the United Kingdom or EximBank in the United States could co-ordinate such activity for bidders within a single country.

Another alternative would be for a bank or financial institution to put together a group of investors plus a contract bidder to buy an appropriate number of currency options, with the premium cost divided up between the two in some agreed manner. If the contractor fails to win the contract, the losses are shared but all profits go to the speculator group. If the contractor wins the contract, the option losses are shared but all profits go to the contracting firm. Many variants of this type of hedge structure could be envisaged, but in each case the aim would be to reduce the net cost of currency option hedging to the bidder for a contract.

The concept of options as an expensive form of hedging, which is common among many corporates, can be misleading since it tends to focus on a specific hedge transaction rather than a stream of such transactions. A more interesting question is whether, if a corporation hedged with currency options all the time, substituting them for all forward transactions, the net exchange achieved over a substantial period would be better or worse. In some periods the option premium would be lost, and the hedge would be more expensive; in others, the option would show windfall profits benefiting the hedger. The question is: what would the overall result be? This can be answered theoretically: if all the options are purchased at a fair price, then with sufficient transactions the effective exchange rate achieved through continuous option hedging should be the same as that achieved from continuous forward hedging.

The charts and summary tables in Exhibits 7.7a and 7.7b[11] show results of this in two cases: a US corporation hedging payables in various currencies; and US and German investors investing in each other's bonds. In both sets of results, in highly volatile currency markets, the continuous option hedging strategy can frequently outperform the standard forward hedging strategy. Options are a cheap rather than expensive way of hedging foreign exchange exposure.

## Exhibit 7.7a: Comparison of forward and options hedges

|  | Forward hedge better than options hedge | | Options hedge better than forward hedge | |
| --- | --- | --- | --- | --- |
|  | % of time | By % of foreign exchange payable | % of time | By % of foreign exchange payable |
| British pound | 64 | 2.17 | 35 | 4.36 |
| Deutschmark | 49 | 1.01 | 51 | 4.26 |
| Japanese yen | 49 | 1.36 | 51 | 4.24 |
| Weighted average | 54 | 1.51 | 46 | 4.29 |

(See the three alternatives on p. 162.)

---

[11] This material was provided by Salomon Brothers International.

**(i) British pound three-month hedging alternatives – a historical comparison (April 1978–April 1983)**

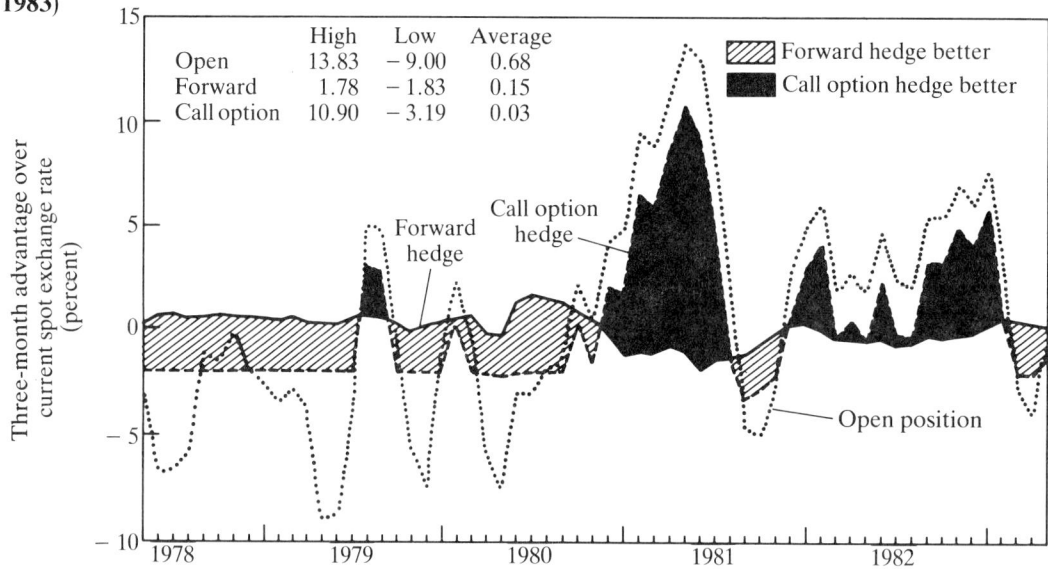

| | High | Low | Average |
|---|---|---|---|
| Open | 13.83 | − 9.00 | 0.68 |
| Forward | 1.78 | − 1.83 | 0.15 |
| Call option | 10.90 | − 3.19 | 0.03 |

*Forward hedge better*
*Call option hedge better*

Forward hedge

Call option hedge

Open position

**(ii) Deutschmark three-month hedging alternatives – a historical comparison (April 1978–April 1983)**

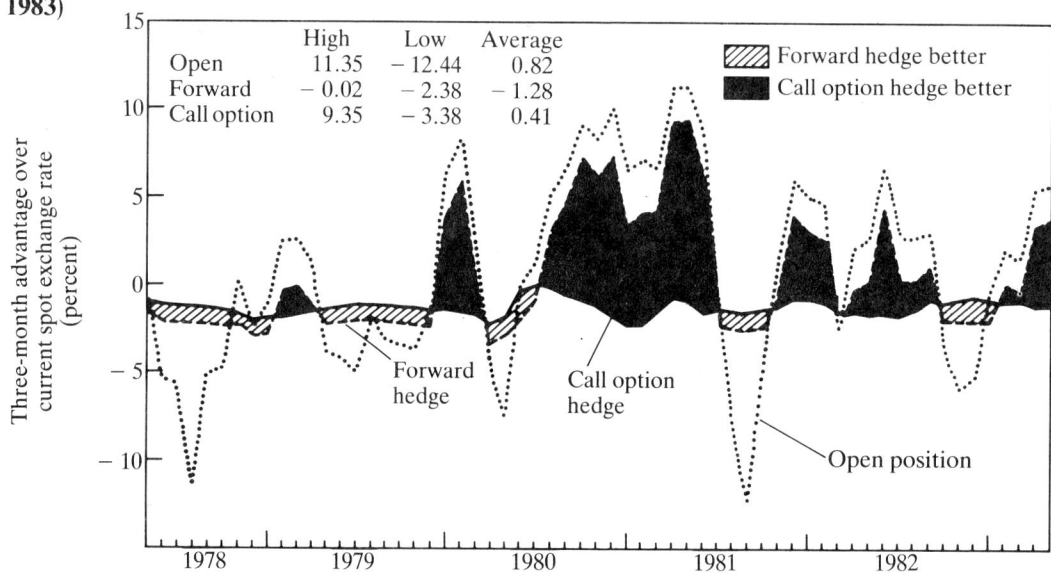

| | High | Low | Average |
|---|---|---|---|
| Open | 11.35 | − 12.44 | 0.82 |
| Forward | − 0.02 | − 2.38 | − 1.28 |
| Call option | 9.35 | − 3.38 | 0.41 |

*Forward hedge better*
*Call option hedge better*

Forward hedge

Call option hedge

Open position

**(iii) Japanese yen three-month hedging alternatives – a historical comparison (April 1978 – April 1983)**

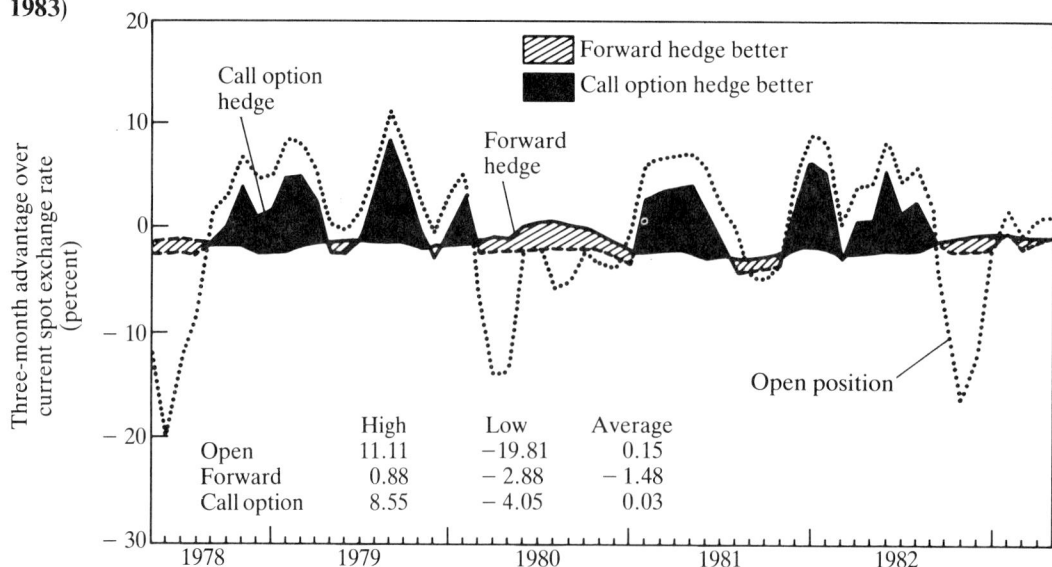

Call option hedge

Forward hedge

Open position

*Forward hedge better*
*Call option hedge better*

| | High | Low | Average |
|---|---|---|---|
| Open | 11.11 | −19.81 | 0.15 |
| Forward | 0.88 | − 2.88 | − 1.48 |
| Call option | 8.55 | − 4.05 | 0.03 |

**Exhibit 7.7b: Summary of the quarterly returns for alternative currency investors** (%)

|  | High | Low | Average |
|---|---|---|---|
| *Deutschmark return on investment in US government bonds* | | | |
| Open position | 17.70 | −9.50 | 2.31 |
| Forward hedge | 18.39 | −12.48 | 0.50 |
| Options hedge | 17.39 | −8.93 | 2.49 |
| *US dollar return on investment in West German government bonds* | | | |
| Open position | 23.04 | −21.33 | 0.44 |
| Forward hedge | 15.88 | −7.10 | 2.79 |
| Options hedge | 21.04 | −10.70 | 1.19 |

**(i) Three-month hedging alternatives for a US dollar investor in West German government bonds**

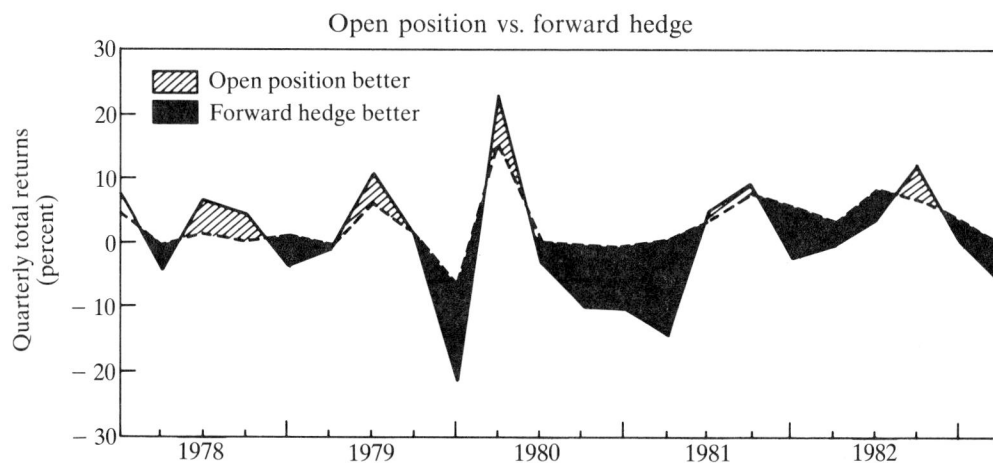

Open position vs. forward hedge

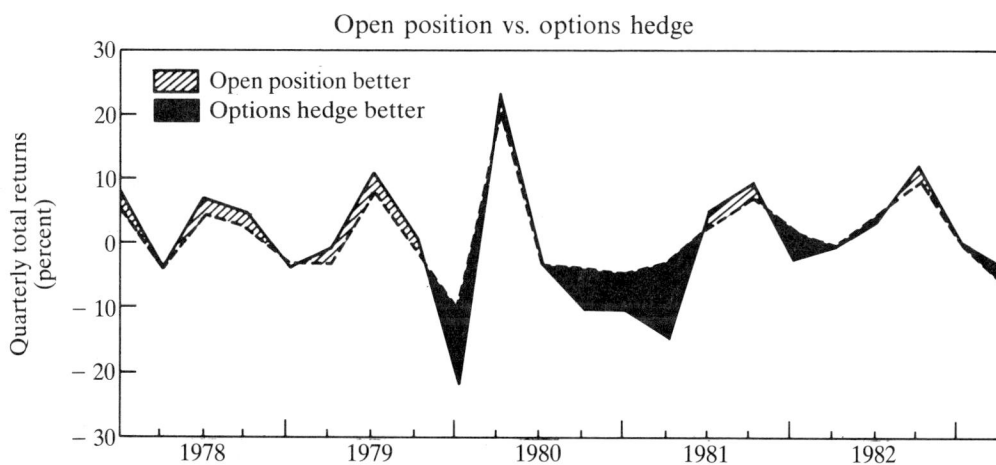

Open position vs. options hedge

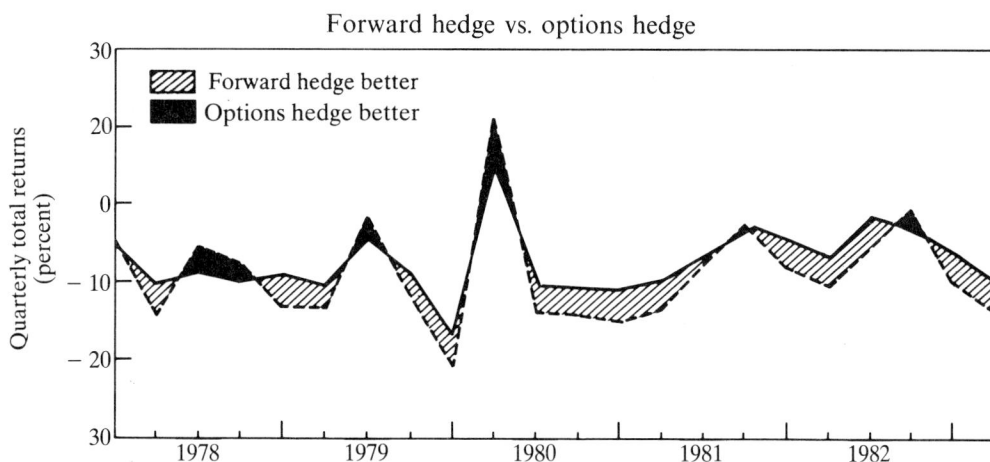

Forward hedge vs. options hedge

163

**(ii) Three-month hedging alternatives for a deutschmark investor in US government bonds**

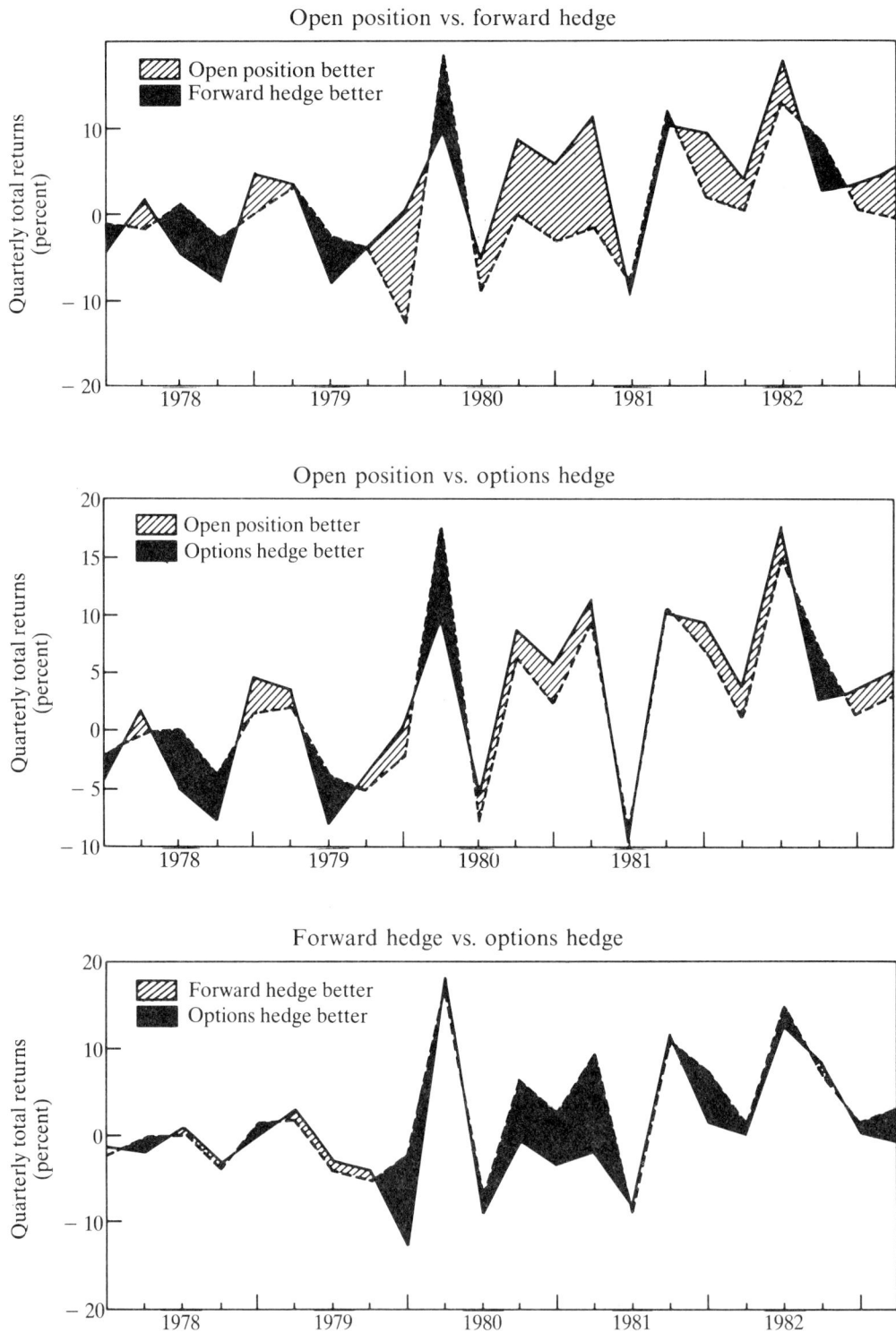

Open position vs. forward hedge

Open position vs. options hedge

Forward hedge vs. options hedge

So far we have been concerned with currency options hedges where the hedge was put on for the full amount of the currency exposure. In many cases, however, delta hedging strategies are more appropriate, particularly in short-term hedging, or where American options have been written by investors or financial institutions. In these circumstances, the number of options contracts is determined in the usual manner for a delta hedge.

$$\text{Number of currency options contracts} = \frac{\text{Face value of currency exposure}}{\text{Face value of currency option}} \times \frac{1}{\text{Delta of option}}$$

## Exhibit 7.8: Returns on selling three-month call options (weekly data)

|  | 1973–76 | | 1977–80 | | 1981–83 | |
|---|---|---|---|---|---|---|
| Number of observations | 153 | | 172 | | 110 | |
| Observations for volatility estimate | 20 | | 20 | | 20 | |
|  | $/£m | % | $/£m | % | $/£m | % |
| Average profit per option | −1,380 | (−0.06) | −184 | (−0.02) | 4,274 | (0.23) |
| Standard deviation | 18,086 | (0.82) | 11,594 | (0.56) | 12,285 | (0.69) |
| Maximum profit | 47,909 | | 25,869 | | 37,055 | |
| Minimum profit | −55.266 | | −38,922 | | −34,012 | |

Source: Haldem Securities Ltd.

Options hedges using delta need to be rebalanced regularly as inputs into the option delta change. Empirical testing will indicate how frequently option hedge rebalancing needs to be carried out with currency exposures. However, Exhibit 7.8 gives an idea of the risk in options hedges during the period 1973–83. Even with weekly rebalancing, losses on individual hedges were as high as $55,000 per £1 million in the 1973–76 period, and $34,000–39,000 per £1 million in the 1977–83 period.

More frequent rebalancing than weekly is necessary for adequate hedging of currency options positions, with all the attendant implications for transactions costs.

### d. Hedging a written currency option position

One of the obvious instances where a delta currency option hedge is appropriate is that of a bank or money centre institution writing or selling an OTC currency option. The ramifications of such a transaction will be examined.[12]

### Example

The current sterling-dollar spot rate is $1.1500. A corporate customer of a major money centre bank asks for a quote on a sterling call option in amount £1,000,000 with a maturity of 180 days and a strike price of $1.16.

The current US six-month rate is 10% and the UK six-month rate is 11%. The bank estimates that a reasonable forecast of sterling volatility over the life of the option is 10% per annum.

There are two tasks for the bank: first, to decide on a fair price for the OTC option; and second, the construction of an appropriate hedging strategy to reduce the risk of its overall position.

*Step 1*
The bank decides to use the previously discussed Garman-Kohlhagen currency option pricing model to value the OTC option.

Assuming an annual volatility of 10%, the fair price of the option is determined as $24,000 and its implied delta is 0.4372. The bank then successfully quotes a price of $30,000 to the corporate customer, and hence its expected profit is $6,000.

*Step 2*
The first alternative that is examined is hedging the currency option position with a cash currency position.

Day 1    The bank hedges the option position by establishing a long spot position in sterling of £437,200.

Day 5    The exchange rate has moved to $1.16. Interest rates and expected volatility have not changed.

$$\text{Fair price of option} = \$28,600$$

$$\text{Implied delta} = 0.4864$$

$$\text{Profit on sterling spot position} = £437,200 \times (\$1.16 - \$1.15)$$

$$= \$4,372.00$$

$$\text{Loss on options position} = \$4,600.00$$

$$\text{Net loss} = \$228$$

---

[12] This example is deliberately simplified to bring out the essential points. A much fuller case study of hedging an OTC options position is presented later in this chapter.

At this point, the bank should increase the spot sterling position to £486,400. The small net loss of $228 has arisen because no rebalancing of the option hedge took place within the five-day period. Since the implied delta of the option at the beginning of the period was 0.4372 and at the end was 0.4864, it is apparent that, taking into account the average delta over the five-day period, the bank was underhedged. To achieve a perfect hedge over the five-day period would have required a long sterling currency position of £460,000, somewhere between the original hedge of £437,200 and the £486,400 required at the end of the period.

Two other points emerge from this cash hedge. First, the cash currency hedge is exposed to changes in market implied volatilities. For instance, a sharp increase in the volatility being used by the market to value currency options would increase the price of the option without a corresponding change in the sterling exchange rate. This would make the spot currency position created by using the implied delta from the historical volatility estimate far too low. The risk would be much diminished if the bank had decided to hedge the OTC call it had written by buying other sterling call options. Any abrupt change in implied volatility would then have a similar effect on the written option, and on the call options purchased, and the hedge performance would be much improved.

---

**The safest way to hedge a currency option position written is by buying a similar currency option position. Hedge options with options for better hedge effectiveness.**

---

The options position loss of $4,600 is not a true cash loss for the bank. The exercise value of the OTC sterling call is only

$$\text{Exercise value} = £1,000,000 \times (\$1.16 - \$1.15)$$
$$= \$10,000$$

This compares with a total income originally received by the bank of $30,000 plus the $4,372 earned on the spot position. The net option position value of $28,600 can only be obtained immediately by the corporate customer if the bank has to repurchase the OTC option at the fair price – and who is to decide what is a fair price and what volatility estimate should be used to construct the price.[13]

There are various techniques of hedging this written OTC sterling call with traded options. The bank could examine the Philadelphia currency options market and see that the following June call options have reasonable liquidity:

| Strike price | Premium | Implied delta |
|---|---|---|
| 110 | 5.90¢ | 0.8140 |
| 115 | 2.82¢ | 0.4840 |
| 120 | 0.40¢ | 0.2100 |

The obvious hedge would be to use only the June 115 calls.

$$\text{Number of contracts} = \frac{£1,000,000}{£12,500} = 80 \text{ calls}$$

However, this does not take into account the deltas of the options, which is necessary for short-term options hedging, nor the likelihood that there may be insufficient volume in the 115 calls to carry out the hedge quickly. In this case the bank might decide to buy a mixture of all three options, weighting the amount of each one by the implied deltas.

---

[13] The question of a fair price for OTC options is an interesting one. In calculating the fair price, the crucial input is the volatility estimate, and the bank could use one of several. It is in the interests of the bank to use the highest estimate in setting the selling price and the lowest estimate in setting the buying price. It is in the interests of the corporation to insist on a formal procedure indicating which valuation model will be adopted and which volatility estimate will be used before purchasing the OTC option.

1. Buy 15 June 110 calls

$$\text{Amount of OTC call hedged} = 15 \times £12,500 \times \frac{0.8140}{0.4372}$$

$$= £349,096.52$$

2. Buy 40 June 115 calls

$$\text{Amount of OTC hedged} = 40 \times £12,500 \times \frac{0.4840}{0.4372}$$

$$= £553,552.42$$

3. Buy June 120 calls to match remaining £97,381.06

$$\text{Number} = \frac{£97,381.06}{£12,500} \times \frac{0.4372}{0.2100} = 16.2 \text{ (or 16) contracts}$$

Buy   15 June 110 calls at 5.90¢
      40 June 115 calls at 2.82¢
      16 June 120 calls at 0.40¢

$$\begin{aligned}
\text{Total cost} = \ & 15 \times £12,500 \times \$0.059 \\
+ \ & 40 \times £12,500 \times \$0.0282 \\
+ \ & 16 \times £12,500 \times \$0.004 \\
= \ & \$25,962.50
\end{aligned}$$

Assuming the hedge works perfectly, the locked-in profit for the bank is, therefore, \$4,037.50. Five days later the position is examined again. The new set of traded option premiums is shown below:

| Strike price | Premium | Implied delta |
|---|---|---|
| 110 | 6.72¢ | 0.8500 |
| 115 | 3.33¢ | 0.5351 |
| 120 | 0.63¢ | 0.2400 |

$$\begin{aligned}
\text{Profit on 110 calls} &= 15 \times £12,500 \times (\$0.0672 - \$0.059) \\
&= \$1,537.50
\end{aligned}$$

$$\begin{aligned}
\text{Profit on 115 calls} &= 40 \times £12,500 \times (\$0.0333 - \$0.0282) \\
&= \$2,550.00
\end{aligned}$$

$$\begin{aligned}
\text{Profit on 120 calls} &= 16 \times £12,500 \times (\$0.0063 - \$0.0040) \\
&= \$460.00
\end{aligned}$$

$$\text{Total profit} = \$4,547.50$$

$$\text{Net loss} = \$52.50$$

As was to be expected, the options hedge did significantly better than the cash hedge. Although all the deltas altered over five days, making the original deltas inappropriate when describing the response of the option premiums to movements in the underlying currency rate, errors were mutually offsetting, ensuring a good hedge result. This will almost invariably be the case. From the bank's point of view, however, the major problem is the lack of liquidity in the traded currency options market, which makes it difficult to hedge large OTC options in this manner. The choice then is to try and purchase a matching OTC option from another bank, or to hedge in the cash market with the attendant risks discussed previously. Nonetheless the OTC currency option market is growing rapidly, and banks have to hedge their positions.[14]

---

[14] Given current margining systems at the time this book is being written, banks hedging OTC options may find LIFFE options more attractive than Philadelphia or Chicago, since they will receive the full use of the premium from the customer but will only have to pay an initial margin on buying LIFFE options.

The underlying exchange rate must also be taken into account if options are to be used to exchange physical currency. This is particularly the case with cylinder hedges of currency positions (see Chapter 5).

### Example

Suppose an investor is long £1,000,000 sterling at $1.50 and decides to set up a cylinder hedge by buying a 145 put option and selling a 155 call. This sets up the classic cylinder hedge described in Chapter 5.

$$\text{Long position at 150} \quad (1, 1, 1, 1)\,(145, 150, 155)$$
$$\text{Long 145 put} \quad (-1, 0, 0, 0)\,(145, 150, 155)$$
$$\text{Short 155 call} \quad (0, 0, 0, -1)\,(145, 150, 155)$$
$$\text{Net cylinder} \quad (0, 1, 1, 0)\,(145, 150, 155)$$

How many of each option should be bought and sold? This will depend upon the exercise price. The long put position at 145 enables the investor to sell his £1,000,000 for dollars at a fixed exchange rate if the pound falls.

$$\text{Number of 145 puts required} = \frac{\pounds1,000,000}{\pounds25,000} = 40 \text{ contracts}$$

By selling the calls, the investor is allowing someone to call away the £1,000,000 at a fixed rate of $1.55.

$$\text{Number of 155 calls sold} = \frac{\pounds1,000,000}{\pounds25,000} = 40 \text{ contracts}$$

Now suppose an investor is long $1,000,000 at $1.50

$$\text{Long \$ position at 150} \quad (-1, -1, -1, -1)\,(145, 150, 155)$$
$$\text{Short 145 put} \quad (1, 0, 0, 0)\,(145, 150, 155)$$
$$\text{Long 155 call} \quad (0, 0, 0, 1)\,(145, 150, 155)$$
$$\text{Net cylinder} \quad (0, -1, -1, 0)\,(145, 150, 155)$$

The long 155 call allows the investor to exchange his long dollar position for sterling at a rate of $1.55.

$$\text{Number of 155 calls required} = \frac{\$1,000,000}{\pounds25,000 \times \$1.55} = 26 \text{ contracts}$$

The short 145 put allows the purchaser to buy the $1,000,000 from the investor at a fixed rate of $1.45.

$$\text{Number of 145 puts sold} = \frac{\pounds1,000,000}{\pounds25,000 \times \$1.45} = 28 \text{ contracts}$$

There is an asymmetry in the number of contracts required for a cylinder hedge when the underlying position is dollar-denominated rather than sterling-denominated.


## e. Hedging the value of an offshore portfolio

A final and obvious use of currency options is hedging offshore portfolios against an appreciation of the domestic currency. This is difficult through the forward market because the dollar value, say, of a US stock portfolio changes through time because of changing stock prices. Currency options are a possible solution to this problem.


### Example

**December 1987**

Buy 20,000 IBM shares at $150      Cost = $3,000,000
Sterling spot rate = $1.20      1-month forward rate = $1.20
Sterling value of shares = £2,500,000
120 June Philadelphia call premium = 3¢
Implied delta = 0.50

Consider two alternatives: the hedger sells $3,000,000 forward at $1.20, or he buys an appropriate number of 120 calls.

$$\text{Number of options for ratio hedge} = \frac{\pounds2,500,000}{\pounds12,500} \times \frac{1}{0.50}$$

$$= 400 \text{ contracts}$$

$$\text{Cost} = 400 \times \pounds12,500 \times \$0.03 = \$150,000 \text{ (or } \pounds125,000 \text{ at } \$1.20)$$

Hence the total sterling investment is £2,625,000. Examine three possible alternatives one month later, assuming option implied volatilities do not change.

*Alternative 1*

$$\text{IBM price} = \$160$$
$$\text{Sterling spot rate} = \$1.25$$
$$\text{June 120 call premium} = 6.5¢$$
$$\text{Delta} = 0.90$$

$$\text{Sterling value of IBM stock} = \frac{\$3,200,000}{\$1.25} = £2,560,000$$

$$\text{Call option value} = 400 \times £12,500 \times \$0.065$$
$$= \$325,000 \ (£260,000 \text{ at } \$1.25)$$

$$\text{Sterling portfolio value} = £2,560,000 + £260,000$$
$$= £2,820,000 \ (+7.4\%)$$

*Alternative 2*

$$\text{IBM price} = \$160$$
$$\text{Sterling spot rate} = \$1.15$$
$$\text{June 120 call premium} = 1.25¢$$
$$\text{Delta} = 0.20$$

$$\text{Sterling value of IBM stock} = £2,782,608.70$$

$$\text{Call option value} = 400 \times £12,500 \times \$0.0125$$
$$= \$62,500 \ (£54,347.83 \text{ at } \$1.15)$$

$$\text{Sterling portfolio value} = £2,782,608.70 + £54,347.83$$
$$= £2,836,956.50 \ (+8.1\%)$$

*Alternative 3*

$$\text{IBM price} = \$1.60$$
$$\text{Sterling spot rate} = \$1.20$$
$$\text{June 120 call premium} = 2.74¢$$
$$\text{Delta} = 0.50$$

$$\text{Sterling value of IBM stock} = \frac{\$3,200,000}{1.20} = £2,666,666.70$$

$$\text{Call option value} = 400 \times £12,500 \times \$0.0274$$
$$= \$137,000 \ (£114,166.67)$$

$$\text{Sterling portfolio value} = £2,666,666.70 + £114,166.67$$
$$= £2,780,833.40 \ (+5.9\%)$$

|  | *$1.15* | *$1.20* | *$1.25* |
|---|---|---|---|
| No hedge | +11.3% | +6.7% | +2.4% |
| 1-month forward hedge | +6.7% | +6.7% | +6.7% |
| Option hedge | +8.1% | +5.9% | +7.4% |

One of the additional merits of the option hedge is the less frequent rebalancing as delta changes; but the hedger would not have rebalanced, anyway, as the price changes were in his favour. Nevertheless, it illustrates the possibilities of using currency options to hedge stock portfolio performance. Options are ideal for this type of hedging because the period of the hedge is often completely undetermined in advance, and the degree of currency exposure at future dates is unknown since asset values in foreign currency vary through time.

## 5. Over-the-counter hedging case study

This section explores the hedging performance of the traded option market in currencies in protecting the commercial margin on an OTC option issued by a bank. To keep the example simple, assume the OTC option is a three-month option written at the current sterling spot exchange rate. The techniques used to design the hedge are described in Chapter 5.

**Day 1**
A money centre bank is asked to quote on a 90-day sterling £1 million call option with the exercise price equal to the current spot exchange rate of $1.2200. The following set of Philadelphia sterling call option premiums are observed.

| Exercise price | June (65 days) | September (156 days) | December (247 days) |
|---|---|---|---|
| 115 | 7.92 (0.78) | 9.24 (0.68) | 10.24 (0.64) |
| 120 | 4.74 (0.57) | 6.40 (0.53) | 7.56 (0.54) |
| 125 | 2.54 (0.38) | 4.23 (0.41) | 5.46 (0.41) |
| 130 | 1.22 (0.22) | 2.78 (0.30) | 3.90 (0.33) |
| 135 | 0.52 (0.11) | 1.72 (0.21) | 2.72 (0.25) |
| Futures price | 121.57 | 120.99 | 120.45 |

The first task for the bank is to price the OTC option. It can approach this in two ways. First, it could apply the Garman-Kohlhagen model discussed earlier, adjusted for the possibility of premature exercise. To do this it will need to choose a volatility figure. This could be derived from historical data; more likely, the bank will use the implied volatility consistent with the set of traded premiums shown above.

The composite implied volatility in fact is 19.50%. Thus, the bank uses this implied volatility to estimate the fair price of the option.

$$\text{Volatility} = 19.50\%$$
$$\text{Dollar interest rate} = 10.00\%$$
$$\text{Sterling interest rate} = 12.00\% \quad \text{Fair price of 90-day \$1.2200 call} = 4.33\text{¢}$$
$$\text{Sterling spot rate} = \$1.2200 \quad \text{Delta} = 0.49$$
$$\text{Days to expiration} = 65 \text{ days}$$

The problem for the bank, however, is that it cannot purchase a 122 exercise price option as a hedge. Following the principles outlined in Chapter 5, the most likely hedge would involve the bank buying a mixture of 120 and 125 exercise price calls to create an artificial option that would be expected to behave similarly to the OTC option sold. Because the 90-day maturity of the option does not correspond to the expiration dates of the traded options, the bank will also probably adopt an extrapolative hedge strategy. Following the simple linear interpolation principles of Chapter 5, the hedge would involve:

*Exercise price mismatch*

$$(\text{Total contracts} = £1,000,000/£12.500 = 80)$$

Linear interpolation of prices

$$X(1.2000) + (1 - X)(1.2500) = 1.2200$$
$$X = 0.60$$

Hence

$$\text{Buy } 0.60 \, (80) \, 120 \text{ calls} = 48 \text{ contracts}$$
$$\text{Buy } 0.40 \, (80) \, 125 \text{ calls} = 32 \text{ contracts}$$

*Time mismatch*

The June contracts have 65 days to expiration, the OTC has 90 days and the September contracts have 156 days. An interpolative hedge would therefore fulfil the equation

$$Y(65) + (1 - Y)(156) = 90$$
$$Y = 0.725$$

Thus the interpolative hedge would involve buying (0.725 (80) or 58 June contracts and (0.275) (0.80) or 22 September contracts. However, since it was argued in Chapter 5 that it is generally easier to put on an extrapolative hedge straight away, because the June contracts will have to be rolled into September at some point anyway, the appropriate hedge would be

$$\text{Buy } 138 \, (80 + 58) \quad \text{September contracts}$$
$$\text{Sell } 58 \quad \text{December contracts}$$

This will be done in the proportions developed to cover the exercise price mismatch. So the final suggested option hedge would consist of

$$\text{Buy } 138 \, (0.6) \text{ September } 120 \text{ calls} = 83 \text{ contracts}$$
$$\text{Buy } 138 \, (0.4) \text{ September } 125 \text{ calls} = 55 \text{ contracts}$$
$$\text{Sell } 58 \, (0.6) \quad \text{December } 120 \text{ calls} = 35 \text{ contracts}$$
$$\text{Sell } 58 \, (0.4) \quad \text{December } 125 \text{ calls} = 23 \text{ contracts}$$

Finally, it is useful to check the delta neutrality of the overall position including the OTC 122 call option.

$$\text{Position delta} = -80(0.49) + 83(0.53) + 55(0.41)$$
$$-35(0.54) - 23(0.41)$$
$$= -0.99$$

This is close enough to delta neutrality to be acceptable to the bank.

The bank should also compare the fair cost of the option with the cost of the options position being used to hedge it, since if the sterling exchange rate were to fall dramatically, all the options could become essentially worthless.

$$\text{Fair price of OTC option} = £1,000,000 \times \$0.0433 = \$43,300$$

$$\text{Cost of hedge} = 83(£12,500)(\$0.0640) + 55(£12,500)(\$0.0432)$$
$$-35(£12,500)(\$0.0756) - 23(£12,500)(\$0.0546)$$
$$= \$47,327.50$$

The cost of the hedge is thus $4,027.50 more than the fair price of the option. It would be sensible for the bank to attempt to charge the customer at least the cost of the hedge. And since the hedging of time mismatching is rarely perfect, the bank may try to cover some of this risk by changing a further premium. Let us assume that the bank is able to charge the customer $50,000 for the option. The ability to charge such a hefty premium over the fair cost of the option according to the standard model will depend on the state of the OTC market at the time. However, the precise price charged for the option is less important than the ability of the traded option hedge to protect the commercial margin assumed here to be $6,700 ($50,000 − $43,300).

A simple hedge with IMM futures contracts is also worth examining, to compare it with the option hedge described above.

$$\text{Number of contracts} = \frac{£1,000,000}{£25,000} \times 0.49 \text{ (delta of OTC)}$$

$$= 20 \text{ contracts}$$

To reduce basis risk, an extrapolative hedge is also adopted.

$$\text{Buy } (20) (1.725) \text{ September futures at } 1.2099 = 35 \text{ contracts}$$

$$\text{Sell } (20) (0.725) \text{ December futures at } 1.2045 = 15 \text{ contracts}$$

Hedge performance is measured by assuming potential rebalancing and profit appraisal every five days until the expiration of the OTC option. If the OTC option is an American option it may be sold back to the bank or exercised at any time before expiration. Different hedging strategies may also be adopted, depending on whether the bank runs a two-way book in OTC options and hence is prepared to buy the option back at a fair price depending on the implied volatility in the traded options market at the time, or whether it only allows the client the right to exercise the option. In this example we assume the former, so that the aim of the hedge is to match profits and losses to the OTC option exactly through time, to maintain the value of the commercial margin to the bank.

In the case of the option hedge, theoretically no rebalancing through time is required although delta neutrality will be checked every five days. By contrast the futures hedge will require continuous rebalancing as the delta of the OTC option changes through time. The assumption here is that the round-trip commission on both options and futures is $15 per contract.

The set of data below illustrates the progress of the two alternative hedges at five-day intervals up to the expiration date of the OTC option. It is assumed that the original option hedge is held throughout the hedge period while the futures hedge is rebalanced at five-day intervals in line with the changes in the delta of the OTC option. The option hedge maintains the commercial margin on the OTC sale in a range of $856 to $13,202 round the anticipated level of $6,700. Even taking into account commissions, the maximum loss to the OTC option writer if the option were sold back at the most disadvantageous time would be just over $2,000. Given the size of the overall exchange rate movements, and the volatility changes and interest rate changes that occurred during the hedge period, this is an adequate hedge performance.

Given a reasonably large OTC option portfolio, the type of option hedges described in Chapter 5 will adequately protect commercial margins on such a portfolio. However, hedge performance could have been improved in practice by rebalancing slightly as the overall position delta drifted away from neutrality over the life of the hedge. By the latter part of the hedge period, the position delta was heavily negative, which could have been adjusted by increasing the net size of the long traded option position. The profit pattern of the extrapolative hedge at expiration corresponds to the patterns discussed earlier in Chapter 5, with abnormal profits being achieved when the final exchange rate is not too far removed from the exercise price of the OTC option.

By contrast, although in this case the futures hedge achieved substantial windfall profits compared with the options hedge, the size of the deviations of achieved commercial margins from the expected level of $6,700 should actually serve as a warning. Hedge performance was not good, and if prices and volatilities had moved differently the deviations from the expected commercial margin could easily have been as large in the opposite direction. In general, hedging an option position with another option position will produce a less risky overall hedged portfolio than a hedge with a futures position.

**Day 6**

| | |
|---|---|
| Spot rate | = 1.2360 |
| Implied volatility | = 20.20% |
| Dollar interest rate | = 9.75% |
| Sterling interest rate | = 11.50% |

Fair price of OTC option = 5.27

Delta = 0.54

| Exercise price | September | December |
|---|---|---|
| 120 | 7.48 (0.57) | 8.70 (0.57) |
| 125 | 5.18 (0.45) | 6.44 (0.45) |
| Future | 122.73 | 122.25 |

| Option hedge | | |
|---|---|---|
| | OTC profit/loss | − $9,400.00 |
| | Hedge profit/loss | + $7,450.00 |
| | Net commercial margin | + $4,750.00 |
| | Position delta | − 1.44 |

| Futures hedge | | |
|---|---|---|
| | OTC profit/loss | − $9,400.00 |
| | Hedge profit/loss | + $8,700.00 |
| | Net commercial margin | + $6,000 |

Contracts bought/sold   2 Sept bought at 122.73

**Day 10**

| | |
|---|---|
| Spot rate | = 1.2450 |
| Implied volatility | = 20.60% |
| Dollar interest rate | = 9.75 |
| Sterling interest rate | = 11.25 |

Fair price of OTC option = 5.81

Delta = 0.57

| Exercise price | September | December |
|---|---|---|
| 120 | 8.13 (0.59) | 9.36 (0.59) |
| 125 | 5.70 (0.48) | 7.03 (0.47) |
| Future | 123.77 | 123.35 |

| Option hedge | | |
|---|---|---|
| | OTC profit/loss | − $14,800 |
| | Hedge profit/loss | − $12,038 |
| | Net commercial margin | + $3,938 |
| | Position delta | − 1.69 |

| Futures hedge | | |
|---|---|---|
| | OTC profit/loss | − $14,800 |
| | Hedge profit/loss | + $14,420 |
| | Net commercial margin | + $6,320 |

Contracts bought/sold   1 Sept bought at 123.77

**Day 16**

Spot rate          = 1.2240
Implied volatility   = 21.20%   Fair price of OTC option = 4.65
Dollar interest rate  = 10.00                      Delta = 0.51
Sterling interest rate = 11.50

| Exercise price | September | December |
|---|---|---|
| 120 | 7.01 (0.55) | 8.31 (0.53) |
| 125 | 4.82 (0.43) | 6.23 (0.44) |
| Future | 121.71 | 121.30 |

| Option hedge | OTC profit/loss | −$3,200 |
|---|---|---|
| | Hedge profit/loss | +$3,417 |
| | Net commercial margin | +$6,917 |
| | Position delta | −0.17 |

| Futures hedge | OTC profit/loss | −$3,200 |
|---|---|---|
| | Hedge profit/loss | +$2,575 |
| | Net commercial margin | +$6,075 |

Contracts bought/sold   3 Sept sold at 121.71

**Day 21**

Spot rate          = 1.2465
Implied volatility   = 21.00%   Fair price of OTC option = 5.80
Dollar interest rate  = 11.00                      Delta = 0.59
Sterling interest rate = 11.75

| Exercise price | September | December |
|---|---|---|
| 120 | 8.33 (0.61) | 9.65 (0.57) |
| 125 | 5.83 (0.49) | 7.32 (0.48) |
| Future | 124.31 | 124.10 |

| Option hedge | OTC profit/loss | −$14,700 |
|---|---|---|
| | Hedge profit/loss | +$12,731 |
| | Net commercial margin | +$4,731 |
| | Position delta | −0.61 |

| Futures hedge | OTC profit/loss | −$14,700 |
|---|---|---|
| | Hedge profit/loss | +$14,550 |
| | Net commercial margin | +$6,550 |

Contracts bought/sold   4 Sept bought at 124.31

**Day 27**

Spot rate          = 1.2684
Implied volatility   = 22.60%   Fair price of OTC option = 7.45
Dollar interest rate  = 12.00                      Delta = 0.66
Sterling interest rate = 11.75

| Exercise price | September | December |
|---|---|---|
| 120 | 10.28 (0.66) | 11.80 (0.61) |
| 125 | 7.51 (0.55) | 9.26 (0.53) |
| Future | 126.95 | 127.02 |

| Option hedge | OTC profit/loss | −$31,200 |
| | Hedge profit/loss | +$26,169 |
| | Net commercial margin | +$1,669 |
| | Position delta | −1.31 |

| Futures hedge | OTC profit/loss | −$31,200 |
| | Hedge profit/loss | +$30,390 |
| | Net commercial margin | +$5,890 |

Contracts bought/sold   2 Sept bought at 126.95

## Day 31

Spot rate           = 1.2740
Implied volatility  = 22.00%   Fair price of OTC option = 7.59
Dollar interest rate = 12.00                        Delta = 0.69
Sterling interest rate = 11.75

| Exercise price | September | December |
|---|---|---|
| 120 | 10.42 (0.67) | 11.89 (0.63) |
| 125 | 7.56 (0.56) | 9.28 (0.54) |
| Future | 127.51 | 127.58 |

| Option hedge | OTC profit/loss | −$32,600 |
| | Hedge profit/loss | +$27,245 |
| | Net commercial margin | +$1,345 |
| | Position delta | −3.26 |

| Futures hedge | OTC profit/loss | −$32,600 |
| | Hedge profit/loss | +$35,055 |
| | Net commercial margin | +$9,155 |

Contracts bought/sold   2 Sept bought at 127.51

## Day 36

Spot rate           = 1.2622
Implied volatility  = 22.40%   Fair price of OTC option = 6.77
Dollar interest rate = 12.00                        Delta = 0.66
Sterling interest rate = 11.25

| Exercise price | September | December |
|---|---|---|
| 120 | 9.77 (0.66) | 11.44 (0.61) |
| 125 | 7.02 (0.54) | 8.89 (0.53) |
| Future | 126.53 | 126.74 |

| Option hedge | OTC profit/loss | −$24,400 |
| | Hedge profit/loss | +$21,352 |
| | Net commercial margin | +$3,652 |
| | Position delta | −1.86 |

| Futures hedge | OTC profit/loss | −$24,400 |
| | Hedge profit/loss | +$28,195 |
| | Net commercial margin | +$10,495 |

Contracts bought/sold   2 Sept sold at 126.53

**Day 41**

Spot rate = 1.2530
Implied volatility = 23.00%    Fair price of OTC option = 6.02
Dollar interest rate = 11.50                              Delta = 0.63
Sterling interest rate = 11.50

| Exercise price | September | December |
|---|---|---|
| 120 | 9.04 (0.63) | 10.72 (0.59) |
| 125 | 6.42 (0.51) | 8.30 (0.51) |
| Future | 125.30 | 125.30 |

*Option hedge*          OTC profit/loss          − $16,900
                        Hedge profit/loss        + $15,870
                        Net commercial margin    + $5,670
                        Position delta           − 2.44

*Futures hedge*         OTC profit/loss          − $16,900
                        Hedge profit/loss        + $20,200
                        Net commercial margin    + $10,000

Contracts bought/sold   1 Sept sold at 125.30

**Day 45**

Spot rate = 1.2785    Fair price of OTC option = 7.71
Implied volatility = 24.50%                    Delta = 0.70
Dollar interest rate = 10.75
Sterling interest rate = 11.75

| Exercise price | September | December |
|---|---|---|
| 120 | 10.76 (0.67) | 12.34 (0.62) |
| 125 | 7.92 (0.56) | 9.78 (0.54) |
| Future | 127.47 | 127.17 |

*Option hedge*          OTC profit/loss          − $33,800
                        Hedge profit/loss        + $29,322
                        Net commercial margin    + $2,222
                        Position delta           − 5.36

*Futures hedge*         OTC profit/loss          − $33,800
                        Hedge profit/loss        + $33,762.50
                        Net commercial margin    + $6,662.50

Contracts bought/sold   3 Sept bought at 127.47

**Day 51**

Spot rate = 1.2850
Implied volatility = 23.00%    Fair price of OTC option = 7.73
Dollar interest rate = 10.50                              Delta = 0.75
Sterling interest rate = 11.75

| Exercise price | September | December |
|---|---|---|
| 120 | 10.68 (0.70) | 12.14 (0.67) |
| 125 | 7.70 (0.58) | 9.43 (0.55) |
| Future | 128.04 | 127.67 |

| Option hedge | OTC profit/loss | − $34,000 |
| | Hedge profit/loss | + $28,953 |
| | Net commercial margin | + $1,653 |
| | Position delta | − 6.10 |
| | | |
| Futures hedge | OTC profit/loss | − $34,000 |
| | Hedge profit/loss | + $37,752.50 |
| | Net commercial margin | + $10,452.50 |

Contracts bought/sold   2 Sept purchased at 128.04

## Day 56

Spot rate          = 1.2912
Implied volatility    = 22.15%   Fair price of OTC option = 7.97
Dollar interest rate  = 10.50                    Delta = 0.79
Sterling interest rate = 11.50

| Exercise price | September | December |
|---|---|---|
| 120 | 10.90 (0.72) | 12.29 (0.69) |
| 125 | 7.78 (0.60) | 9.49 (0.57) |
| Future | 128.77 | 128.47 |

| Option hedge | OTC profit/loss | − $36,400 |
| | Hedge profit/loss | + $30,556 |
| | Net commercial margin | + $856 |
| | Position delta | − 7.70 |
| | | |
| Futures hedge | OTC profit/loss | − $36,400 |
| | Hedge profit/loss | + $43,227.50 |
| | Net commercial margin | + $13,527.50 |

Contracts bought/sold   2 Sept bought at 128.77

## Day 62

Spot rate          = 1.2872
Implied volatility    = 22.00%   Fair price of OTC option = 7.47
Dollar interest rate  = 10.75                    Delta = 0.80
Sterling interest rate = 11.50

| Exercise price | September | December |
|---|---|---|
| 120 | 10.52 (0.72) | 11.96 (0.65) |
| 125 | 7.40 (0.60) | 9.20 (0.56) |
| Future | 128.47 | 128.25 |

| Option hedge | OTC profit/loss | − $31,400 |
| | Hedge profit/loss | + $27,134 |
| | Net commercial margin | + $2,434 |
| | Position delta | − 6.87 |
| | | |
| Futures hedge | OTC profit/loss | − $31,400 |
| | Hedge profit/loss | + $40,827.50 |
| | Net commercial margin | + $16,127.50 |

Contracts bought/sold   None

**Day 66**

Spot rate = 1.2842
Implied volatility = 20.85%   Fair price of OTC option = 6.98
Dollar interest rate = 10.75                              Delta = 0.82
Sterling interest rate = 11.63

| Exercise price | September | December |
|---|---|---|
| 120 | 9.97 (0.73) | 11.32 (0.69) |
| 125 | 6.82 (0.60) | 8.54 (0.56) |
| Future | 128.14 | 127.88 |

| *Option hedge* | OTC profit/loss | −$26,500 |
|---|---|---|
| | Hedge profit/loss | +$23,137 |
| | Net commercial margin | +$3,437 |
| | Position delta | −9.04 |

| *Futures hedge* | OTC profit/loss | −$26,500 |
|---|---|---|
| | Hedge profit/loss | +$38,187.50 |
| | Net commercial margin | +$18,387.50 |

Contracts bought/sold   1 Sept bought at 128.14

**Day 71**

Spot rate = 1.2863
Implied volatility = 20.15%   Fair price of OTC option = 6.95
Dollar interest rate = 10.50                              Delta = 0.86
Sterling interest rate = 11.50

| Exercise price | September | December |
|---|---|---|
| 120 | 9.88 (0.75) | 11.19 (0.70) |
| 125 | 6.65 (0.61) | 8.31 (0.57) |
| Future | 128.83 | 128.03 |

| *Option hedge* | OTC profit/loss | −$26,200 |
|---|---|---|
| | Hedge profit/loss | +$22,439 |
| | Net commercial margin | +$2,939 |
| | Position delta | −10.61 |

| *Futures hedge* | OTC profit/loss | −$26,200 |
|---|---|---|
| | Hedge profit/loss | +$39,755 |
| | Net commercial margin | +$20,255 |

Contracts bought/sold   1 Sept bought at 128.33

**Day 76**

Spot rate = 1.2750
Implied volatility = 20.85%   Fair price of OTC option = 5.88
Dollar interest rate = 10.50                              Delta = 0.84
Sterling interest rate = 11.50

| Exercise price | September | December |
|---|---|---|
| 120 | 9.10 (0.72) | 10.55 (0.65) |
| 125 | 6.02 (0.58) | 7.84 (0.54) |
| Future | 127.22 | 126.92 |

| Option hedge | OTC profit/loss | − $15,500 |
| | Hedge profit/loss | + $15,821 |
| | Net commercial margin | + $7,021 |
| | Position delta | − 10.71 |

| Futures hedge | OTC profit/loss | − $15,500 |
| | Hedge profit/loss | + $30,320 |
| | Net commercial margin | + $21,520 |

Contracts bought/sold    None

## Day 80

Spot rate           = 1.2622
Implied volatility    = 20.10%    Fair price of OTC option = 4.61
Dollar interest rate  = 10.50                         Delta = 0.82
Sterling interest rate = 11.38

| Exercise price | September | December |
|---|---|---|
| 120 | 7.99 (0.70) | 9.51 (0.63) |
| 125 | 5.05 (0.54) | 6.89 (0.52) |
| Future | 125.99 | 125.73 |

| Option hedge | OTC profit/loss | − $2.800 |
| | Hedge profit/loss | + $7,098 |
| | Net commercial margin | + $10,998 |
| | Position delta | − 11.81 |

| Futures hedge | OTC profit/loss | − $2,800 |
| | Hedge profit/loss | + $19,865 |
| | Net commercial margin | + $23,765 |

Contracts bought/sold   1 Sept sold at 125.99

## Day 86

Spot rate           = 1.2610
Implied volatility    = 19.74%    Fair price of OTC option = 4.22
Dollar interest rate  = 10.50                         Delta = 0.90
Sterling interest rate = 11.38

| Exercise price | September | December |
|---|---|---|
| 120 | 7.71 (0.71) | 9.24 (0.63) |
| 125 | 4.74 (0.54) | 6.62 (0.52) |
| Future | 125.89 | 125.62 |

| Option hedge | OTC profit/loss | + $1,100 |
| | Hedge profit/loss | + $4,635 |
| | Net commercial margin | + $12,435 |
| | Position delta | − 17.38 |

| Futures hedge | OTC profit/loss | + $1,100 |
| | Hedge profit/loss | + $19,040 |
| | Net commercial margin | + $26,840 |

Contracts bought/sold   3 Sept bought at 125.89

178

**Day 91**

Spot rate = 1.2595
Implied volatility = 20.20%   Fair price of OTC option = 3.95
Dollar interest rate = 10.50                         Delta = 1.00
Sterling interest rate = 11.50

| Exercise price | September | December |
|---|---|---|
| 120 | 7.53 (0.71) | 9.16 (0.63) |
| 125 | 4.58 (0.53) | 6.55 (0.51) |
| Future | 125.73 | 125.43 |

*Option hedge*

| | |
|---|---|
| OTC profit/loss | +$3,800 |
| Hedge profit/loss | +$2,702 |
| Net commercial margin | +$13,202 |
| Position delta | n/a |

*Futures hedge*

| | |
|---|---|
| OTC profit/loss | +$3,800 |
| Hedge profit/loss | +$16,445 |
| Net commercial margin | +$26,945 |

Contracts bought/sold   36 Sept sold at 125.73

Commercial margin

| | Maximum | Minimum | Average | Final | Final after commissions |
|---|---|---|---|---|---|
| Option hedge | 13,202 | 856 | 5,987 | 13,202 | 10,262 |
| Futures hedge | 26,945 | 5,890 | 13,609 | 26,945 | 26,300 |

# Chapter 8
# Interest rate options

## 1. The basics

Traded options on interest rates can be divided on two different criteria: first, whether they are options on cash or options on futures contracts; second, whether they are options on short-term rates or options on long-term rates. Currently the only short-term interest rate option which shows reasonable liquidity is the Eurodollar futures option traded on the Index and Options Market of the CME and LIFFE. The Chicago option demands the full premium to be paid by the buyer, while the London option is margined futures style.[1]

A *Eurodollar futures option* is the right to buy or sell a Eurodollar futures contract at a specific price at or before a specific date in the future.

### Example

Buy a CME June Eurodollar call option at an exercise price of 90.00 for a premium of 0.50.

You are buying the right between now and June to establish a long Eurodollar futures position at an original price of 90.00.

$$\text{Cost of right} = 50 \text{ ticks} \times \$25 \text{ per tick} = \$1,250$$

If the option is exercised, a long futures position will be established for the trader at 90.00 which will be immediately marked to market.

*Exercise*[2]

Futures price = 91.50
Holder: Long futures at 90.00
Margin account: $\$25 \times (91.50 - 90.00) \times 100 = \$3,750.00$
$$\text{Net profit} = \$3,750.00 - \$1,250.00 = \$2,500.00$$

Options on long-term interest rate instruments follow similar principles. The most liquid long-term interest rate option is the Chicago Board of Trade option on its Treasury bond futures contract, which in turn is the most liquid futures contract worldwide. The holder of an option has the right – as with the Eurodollar futures options – to buy or sell a CBT Treasury bond futures contract at a specific price on or before a specific date.

### Example

Buy a CBT June Treasury bond call option at an exercise price of 100-00 for a premium of 3-48[3]

$$\text{Cost of right: } 240 \text{ ticks} \times \$15.625 \text{ per tick}[4]$$
$$= \$3,750.00$$

---

[1] Cash Treasury bill options are traded on the American Stock Exchange, but with very limited volume.

[2] LIFFE exercise procedures are more complex because of the LIFFE margining system. See Chapter 7 on currency options for an illustration.

[3] Although CBT Treasury bond futures are priced in 32nds (98-12 is equivalent to 98 and $\frac{12}{32}$nd), Treasury bond options are priced in 64ths (3-48 is equivalent to 3 and $\frac{48}{64}$th).

[4] $\frac{1}{64}$ of 1% of a $100,000 T-bond futures contract is $15.625.

*Exercise*

T-bond futures price = 104-16
Holder: Long future at 100-00

Margin account: $31.25 × 144 ticks (4-16 is equivalent to 144/32nd) = $4,500.00
Net profit = $4,500.00 − $3,750.00 = $750.00

In addition to the Chicago Board of Trade T-bond futures options, other reasonably liquid futures options contracts include the LIFFE long gilt and T-bond options, the CBT 10-year Treasury note options, and the Canadian Treasury bond option.

Options on cash long-term interest rates are traded on the Chicago Board Options Exchange (T-bond options) and on the London Stock Exchange (short and long gilt options). On the London Stock Exchange, the short gilt option is a cash option on £50,000 nominal of the Treasury $11\frac{3}{4}\%$ 1991.

**Example**

Buy a May stock exchange Treasury $11\frac{3}{4}\%$ 1991 call option exercise price 102-00 for a premium of 2-22 (priced in 32nds).

Cost of option = 86 ticks × £15.625 per tick
= £1,343.75

*At exercise*  Holder will be required to pay £51,000 (500 × £102) and will take delivery of £50,000 nominal of Treasury $11\frac{3}{4}\%$ 1991.

One of the disadvantages of American options on cash long-term instruments for the trader is immediately apparent. If a trader is short futures options and is exercised against, his only liability will be to cover his margin account when the new futures position is marked to market. With cash options, the call option writer is required to come up with the actual cash gilt which, if he does not hold it already, will have to be purchased in the market place, with credit lines necessary to finance such purchases maintained.

## 2. Pricing of interest rate options

### a. Short-term interest rate options

The simple Black-Scholes model for a premium paid European option on a Eurodollar future is

$$e^{-rT}[FN(d_1) - XN(d_2)]$$

where $F$ = current Eurodollar futures price
$X$ = exercise price
$N(.)$ = cumulative standard normal distribution
$$d_1 = \frac{\ln(F/X) + (\sigma^2/2)T}{\sigma\sqrt{T}}$$
$d_2 = d_1 - \sigma\sqrt{T}$
$\sigma$ = volatility of futures price
$T$ = time to maturity

Using standard put-call parity, the similar formula for a put option can be derived as

$$P(F, X, T) = e^{-rT}[XN(-d_2) - FN(-d_1)]$$

The usual structures concerning early exercise of American options will apply.

The formulae for LIFFE options differ somewhat because of the margining system. Prices have to be higher to compensate the seller for the fact that he does not receive the premium at the beginning and consequently it is not available for investment. If it is assumed initially that the premium is paid over to the seller of the option only at maturity, the premium will have to be increased by the additional interest that could have been earned over the life of the option if the premium was available for investment. Hence the value of the call will become

$$e^{-rT}[FN(d_1) - XN(d_2)]e^{rT} = FN(d_1) - XN(d_2)$$

In addition the value of the LIFFE put option will be found from the put-call parity relationship

Call premium = Put premium + Futures price − Exercise price

$$P(F, X, T) = C(F, X, T) + X - F$$

In practice it will not be so simple,[5] because if nothing changes, part of the premium will be paid over to the writer of the option as the time value decays to zero over the option maturity. Since the time value falls in line with the square root of time, other things being equal, the average amount of the time value held over the life of the option will be

$$C(F, X, T)\left\{\frac{\sqrt{T} - \sqrt{T/2}}{\sqrt{T}}\right\} = C(F, X, T)[1 - \sqrt{\tfrac{1}{2}}]$$
$$= C(F, X, T)(0.2929)$$

Hence, in estimating the fair price of a LIFFE call option on the Eurodollar future, a small adjustment has to be made. The fair price will be

Intrinsic value + [Time value assuming no premium paid $\times e^{-(0.2929)rT}$]

Exhibit 8.1 gives comparison figures for CME and LIFFE options.

## Exhibit 8.1: Eurodollar call option contracts

Volatility = 2.5%   Futures price = 89.00   Short-term interest rate = 10%

| Exercise price | CME options | | LIFFE option (no premium assumption) | | LIFFE option (with adjustment) | |
|---|---|---|---|---|---|---|
| | 3-month | 9-month | 3-month | 9-month | 3-month | 9-month |
| 88.00 | 1.08 | 1.26 | 1.11 | 1.36 | 1.11 | 1.35 |
| 88.50 | 0.72 | 0.97 | 0.74 | 1.04 | 0.74 | 1.03 |
| 89.00 | 0.43 | 0.71 | 0.44 | 0.76 | 0.44 | 0.74 |
| 89.50 | 0.23 | 0.50 | 0.24 | 0.54 | 0.24 | 0.53 |
| 90.00 | 0.11 | 0.33 | 0.11 | 0.36 | 0.11 | 0.35 |

The adjustment makes comparatively little difference at short maturities, but could result in discrepancies of one or two ticks at the longer maturities.

Another problem with the models for Eurodollar options is that the assumption of a log-normal distribution may be out of keeping with the properties of futures prices. In essence, the distribution is skewed towards high values, and is therefore more in keeping with empirical distributions for interest rates rather than for Eurodollar futures prices, which are based on an index of (100 − Libor). A simple alternative often used in the Eurodollar options market is to reverse the scale, so that options are valued not relative to the futures price, but relative to $(K - F)$ where $K$ is a constant – taken normally to be 100. Volatilities are then calculated on the $(100 - F)$ scale, and option values calculated accordingly remembering that a call option on the $F$ scale is a put option on the $(100 - F)$ scale and vice versa.

It is interesting to examine the impact such a change of scale may have on option values. Consider the 20 weekly ED3 futures prices shown below:

| No. | Date | Price | No. | Date | Price |
|---|---|---|---|---|---|
| 1 | 19.09.84 | 88.4400 | 11 | 28.11.84 | 90.2500 |
| 2 | 26.09.84 | 88.2100 | 12 | 5.12.84 | 90.1000 |
| 3 | 3.10.84 | 87.9900 | 13 | 12.12.84 | 90.1900 |
| 4 | 10.10.84 | 88.3300 | 14 | 19.12.84 | 90.6200 |
| 5 | 17.10.84 | 88.6200 | 15 | 27.12.84 | 90.5900 |
| 6 | 24.10.84 | 89.1900 | 16 | 2.01.85 | 90.4700 |
| 7 | 31.10.84 | 89.2700 | 17 | 9.01.85 | 90.8900 |
| 8 | 7.11.84 | 89.6100 | 18 | 16.01.85 | 90.8700 |
| 9 | 14.11.84 | 89.5100 | 19 | 23.01.95 | 91.2300 |
| 10 | 21.11.84 | 90.1300 | 20 | 30.01.85 | 91.1800 |

Volatility $\sigma = 0.0217$.
Note: On a price of 90.00, this volatility corresponds to a price change of $90.00 \times 0.0217 = 1.95$.

---

[5] I am indebted to Dr. Gordon Gemmill of the City University Business School and Mr. Hamish Raw of Amsterdam Option Traders for discussions on this point.

The volatility $\sigma = 0.0217$ applied to the evaluation of fair prices of LIFFE options with exercise price of 90.00 and 180 days to expiry gives:

| Futures price | Call premium | Put premium |
|---|---|---|
| 88.00 | 0.04 | 2.04 |
| 88.50 | 0.09 | 1.59 |
| 89.00 | 0.19 | 1.19 |
| 89.50 | 0.33 | 0.83 |
| 90.00 | 0.55 | 0.55 |
| 90.50 | 0.84 | 0.34 |
| 91.00 | 1.19 | 0.19 |
| 91.50 | 1.60 | 0.10 |
| 92.00 | 2.05 | 0.05 |

Now suppose the scale is changed to Libor $= 100 -$ Futures price. The equivalent annual volatility is calculated to be 18.80%. On an interest rate of 10%, this volatility corresponds to a variation of $10 \times 0.1880 = 1.88$.

On an ED3 90.00 call with 180 days to expiry:

*Call premium*

| Futures price | Interest rate scale $\sigma = 0.1880$ | Futures price scale $\sigma = 0.0217$ | Difference (ticks) |
|---|---|---|---|
| 88.00 | 0.06 | 0.04 | +2 |
| 88.50 | 0.11 | 0.09 | +2 |
| 89.00 | 0.19 | 0.19 | +0 |
| 89.50 | 0.33 | 0.33 | +0 |
| 90.00 | 0.53 | 0.55 | −2 |
| 90.50 | 0.80 | 0.84 | −4 |
| 91.00 | 1.15 | 1.19 | −4 |
| 91.50 | 1.57 | 1.60 | −3 |
| 92.00 | 2.02 | 2.05 | −3 |

The differences in options values produced by altering the scale can be significant: the interest rate scale tends to produce higher values for out-of-the-money options and lower values for at-the-money and in-the-money options. It will be up to the individual trader to decide which scale is the most appropriate to use for his needs, although most participants in the market prefer to calculate Eurodollar options premiums on an interest rate scale basis.

In practice, the incidence of early exercise in Eurodollar futures options in both London and Chicago is comparatively rare, and valuation using the formulae above should give good results.[6] The volume of trading in other short-term interest rate options is too small to merit much attention, although trading in Treasury bill futures options has commenced in Chicago. For this reason it is worth discussing the valuation of options on discount instruments. Cash Treasury bill options also trade on the American Stock Exchange, though in relatively limited volume.

Under reasonable assumptions,[7] it appears that a Black-Scholes type option valuation formula can be derived for options on cash Treasury bills. The model takes the form

$$C(X, T) = P(t, M)N(d_1) - P(t, T)\frac{X}{P*}N(d_2)$$

---

[6] One specific institutional detail which could lead to early exercise of a Eurodollar option is the possibility of exercising the option after trading on the exchange has ceased. For example, suppose an investor holds a long ED call position on LIFFE at 90.00. After the close, the price in Chicago rises sharply to 91.00. The option holder may choose to exercise his option to buy the LIFFE future at 90.00 and simultaneously sell the Chicago future at 91.00, locking in a profit of approximately 100 basis points while LIFFE is closed.

[7] See C. A. Ball and W. N. Torous, "Bond price dynamics and options", *Journal of Financial and Quantitative Analysis*, Dec. 1983, vol. 18, no. 4.

where $P(t, M) = $ current price of a T-bill maturing in period M,
the bill on which the option is written

$P(t, T) = $ current price of a T-bill maturing in period T,
the expiry date of the option

$P^* = $ price of T-bill maturing in period $M$ in period M
(normally \$1,000)

$$d_1 = \frac{\ln(P(t, m)/E) - \ln(P(t, T)) + \left(\frac{V_T^2}{2}\right)T}{V_T\sqrt{T}}$$

$d_2 = d_1 - V_T\sqrt{T}$

$V_T^2 = \sigma_m^2 + \sigma_T^2 - 2\rho\sigma_m\sigma_T$

$\sigma_M = $ volatility of the M-maturity T-bill

$\sigma_T = $ volatility of the T-maturity T-bill

$\rho = $ correlation coefficient between the two T-bills

Ball and Torous (*op. cit.*) suggest that if $r$ daily returns to the two T-bills are available, a suitable well-behaved statistic for $V_T^2$ is

$$\hat{V}^2 = r^{-1} \sum_{i=1}^{r} (x_i - w_i)^2$$

where $x_i$ and $w_i$ are the daily returns to the M-maturity bill and the T-maturity bill respectively.

There has been little empirical testing of this kind of model, but it seems to be no more computationally difficult than the Black-Scholes model. A suitable adaptation of it could be used for valuing the new CME Treasury bill futures options.

## b. Long-term interest rate options

A wide range of options on long-term bonds trade on options and future exchanges around the world. In this section we will concentrate on pricing models applicable to the Treasury bond futures option which trades on the Chicago Board of Trade and the London International Financial Futures Exchange, and the options on cash gilt-edged stock which trade on the London Stock Exchange. The models developed will be applicable with minor modifications to other options on cash bonds and bond futures.

The CBT Treasury bond option is an option on the underlying Treasury bond future, as described earlier, with full payment of the premium at the time of purchase. On the usual assumptions of no early exercise, a log-normal distribution of the bond price at expiry, and a constant discount rate, the usual Black model for options on futures will apply to CBT bond options.

$$C(S, X, T) = e^{-rt}[F.N(d_1) - X.N(d_2)]$$

where $F = $ T-bond futures price

$X = $ exercise price

$r = $ discount price

$T = $ time to expiration

$d_1 = [\ln(S/X) + \sigma^2 T]/\sigma\sqrt{T}$

$d_2 = d_1 - \sigma\sqrt{T}$

$\sigma = $ volatility

All the problems concerning early exercise apply to T-bond options. Because of the discounting factor in the option valuation model, it may be advantageous to exercise puts and calls that are deeply in-the-money. Thus the simple Black model will undervalue these options. The only way to handle this problem will be by numerical methods modelling the evolution of bond futures prices over the intermediate periods between the current date and the expiration date of the option. Traders will need to study the early exercise behaviour of Treasury bond options to determine the degree of extra sophistication they need to add to the standard model. It appears, however, that a binomial model may be preferable to the Black model for Treasury bond options.[8]

The binomial model assumes that the underlying asset price $S$ will move in the next period to $\alpha S$ or $\gamma S$ where $\gamma < 1$ and $\alpha > 1$. Given values for $\alpha$ and $\gamma$ it is possible to find the current value of the option by splitting the period to maturity into many smaller sub-periods, and then following the value of the option back through the tree. The American nature of the option is handled by imposing the immediate exercise value whenever this is higher than the fair value.

The appropriate formula for a margined option on an interest rate future is

$$C(S, X, T) = M \cdot C_\alpha + \left\{ \left[ \frac{1}{1 + R} \right] - M \right\} C_\gamma$$
$$M = (1 - \gamma)/[(\alpha - \gamma)(1 + R)]$$

$$\text{where } C_\alpha = \alpha S - X$$
$$C_\gamma = \gamma S - X$$
$$R = \text{short-term interest rate}$$

Jarrow and Rudd suggest values of $\alpha$, $\gamma$ and the number of time periods to divide up the period of

$$\alpha = e^{(R - 0.5\sigma 2)T/I + \sigma\sqrt{(T/I)}}$$
$$\gamma = e^{(R - 0.5\sigma 2)T/I - \sigma\sqrt{(T/I)}}$$
$$I = 150$$

Gemmill suggests that using $I = 30$ gives satisfactory results. Suppose we have $\alpha = 1.1$ and $\gamma = 0.90$, with a current price for the bond future of 70.00 and the short-term one-period interest rate equal to 5%. The call exercise price is 70-00.

| Bond futures price | | Call price | |
|---|---|---|---|
| | 77-00 | | 7-00 |
| 70-00 | | C | |
| | 63-00 | | 0 |

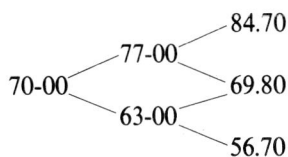

$$M = (1 - 0.90)/(1.10 - 0.90)(1.05) = 0.4762$$
$$C(S, X, 1) = 0.4762\ (7\text{-}00) + \left[ \frac{1}{1.05} - 0.4762 \right](0)$$
$$= 3.33$$

To get an accurate picture of the value of the option, the period of the option must be split into different sub-periods.

Below is an example of a two-period call option, exercise price 66-00.

| Bond futures price | | | Call price | | |
|---|---|---|---|---|---|
| | | 84.70 | | | 18.70 |
| | 77-00 | | | C' | |
| 70-00 | | 69.80 | C | | 3.30 |
| | 63-00 | | | C'' | |
| | | 56.70 | | | 0 |

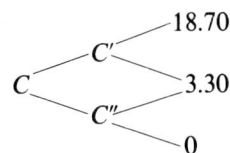

First we solve for C' and C''

$$C' = 0.4762(18.70) + \left[ \frac{1}{1.05} - 0.4762 \right](3.30)$$
$$= 10.48$$
$$C'' = 0.4762(3.30) = 1.57$$

Treating those payoffs as a one-period option, we would obtain

$$C(S, X, 2) = 0.4762(10.48) + \left[ \frac{1}{1.05} - 0.4762 \right](1.57)$$
$$= 5.74$$

---

[8] The binomial model is described in Cox and Rubinstein (*op. cit.*). The application to currencies and interest rate options is covered in G. Gemmill, "A primer on the pricing of options on currencies and short-term interest rates", City University Business School (1985).

However, this is the value of a European option. The value of $C'$ is found to be 10.48, but the option is immediately exerciseable to yield a profit of 11.00 (the difference between the bond futures price of 77.00 and the option exercise price of 66.00). If we replace 10.48 with 11.00, the value of the call at time 0 is

$$C(S, E, 2) = 0.4762(11) + \left[ \frac{1}{1.05} - 0.4762 \right](1.57)$$
$$= 5.99$$

In this instance, the European option value turns out to be lower than the American value. The binomial approach is a useful and quick approach to handling the problems of American options. Chapter 6 on stock options discusses how it can be applied to the question of dividends. Below, however, are the appropriate binomial formulae for currency options derived by Gemmill (*op. cit.*).

*Cash currency options: premiums paid*

$$C = M \cdot C_\alpha + \left[ \left( \frac{1}{1 + R_D} \right) - M \right] C_\gamma$$
$$M = [(1 + R_D) - (1 + R_F)\gamma]/[(1 + R_D)(1 + R_F)(\alpha - \gamma)]$$

*Cash currency options: premiums margined*

$$C = M \cdot C_\alpha + (1 - M)C_\gamma$$
$$M = [(1 + R_D) - (1 - R_F)\gamma]/[(1 + R_D)(\alpha - \gamma)]$$

where $R_D$ = domestic interest rate
$R_F$ = foreign interest rate

Binomial models of this kind can be applied to the Eurodollar futures options discussed earlier. They provide a viable alternative to the Black-Scholes model.

The problem of short-term rate uncertainty was mentioned earlier. In most approaches to option valuation, it is assumed that there is no correlation between movements in short-term interest rates and underlying asset prices. While this may be a reasonable assumption for stocks and commodities, it is an unlikely one for Treasury bond options, where there is likely to be some positive correlation of long-term and short-term interest rate movements. This in turn means a negative correlation between the underlying bond futures prices and short-term interest rates. This will have some effect on option values. If we look at the simple Black model for bond options

$$C(S, X, T) = e^{-rT}[SN(d_1) - X \cdot N(d_2)]$$

The impact of a rise in long-term rates will be to push down Treasury bond futures prices and consequently fair call prices. At the same time, however, short-term rates are likely to rise, which will increase the discount factor $e^{-rT}$ and push down prices even further. The easiest way to handle this effect is to increase the volatility used in calculating fair option values by a factor related to short- and long-term interest rate correlation. The table below shows typical adjustments using correlation estimates established in the first half of 1985.

| Historical period (in trading days) | Bond price volatility | | Interest rate adjusted volatility | |
|---|---|---|---|---|
| | Daily | Weekly | Daily | Weekly |
| 96 | 11.53 | 11.48 | 11.94 | 11.94 |
| 64 | 10.64 | 9.33 | 10.92 | 9.61 |
| 32 | 8.67 | 6.73 | 8.90 | 6.91 |

Allowance for interest rate correlation pushes up volatility estimates by between $\frac{1}{4}$ and $\frac{1}{2}$ of 1%. The effect, in fact, is not as large as that of using daily as opposed to weekly price changes in calculating volatility.

For options on cash bonds, the appropriate valuation formula must take into account the coupon yield on the underlying asset which will be paid to the holder of the asset and not to the holder of a futures position. Since accrued interest is added to the bond on a daily basis through standard clean price plus accrued interest, price calculation for an option is analogous to a model developed by Merton[9] for an option on a stock which pays known dividends continuously.

This takes the form

$$C(S, X, T) = e^{-\delta T} S . N(d_1) - X e^{-rT} N(d_2)$$

where $\delta$ = interest yield on the gilt
$r$ = short-term interest rate

$$d_1 = \frac{\ln(S/X) + [r - \delta + (\sigma^2/2)] \, T}{\sigma \sqrt{T}}$$

$$d_2 = d_1 - \sigma \sqrt{T}$$

This is a simple variant of the Black-Scholes formula which can be applied readily since the coupon yield on the gilt is known.

## 3. Trading and arbitrage with interest rate options

### a. Short-term rate contracts

All the basic trading techniques discussed in Chapter 4 are directly applicable to Eurodollar futures options. In addition, because of the simple nature of contracts, arbitrage operations are also relatively simple, and *conversions* and *reversals* are particularly easy to perform.

*Put-call parity*

It was shown in Chapter 3 on pricing that the following would hold for premium paid options:

$$P(F, X, T) = e^{-rT}(X . N(-d_2) - F . N . (-d_1))$$

which boils down to

$$P(F, X, T) = C(F, X, T) + (X - F) e^{-rt}$$

If this is violated, an arbitrage profit should be ensured.

**Example**

Futures price = 90.25      3-month rate = 10%
90.00 June call (3 months) premium = 0.50
90.00 June put (3 months) premium = 0.28

$$\text{Fair put price} = 0.50 - \frac{0.25}{1.025} = 0.256$$

|  | *Cash flow* |
|---|---|
| Sell 90 put | 0.28 |
| Buy 90 call | −0.50 |
| Sell future | 0 |
|  | −0.22 |

Borrow 0.22 at 10% for three months.

*Expiry*

|  | *Futures price* | | |
|---|---|---|---|
|  | *F < 90.00* | *F = 90.00* | *F > 90.00* |
| Call | 0 | 0 | F − 90.00 |
| Put | −(90.00 − F) | 0 | 0 |
| Future | 90.25 − F | 0.25 | −(F − 90.25) |
| Repayment of borrowing | −0.226 | −0.226 | −0.226 |
| Net profit | 0.024 | 0.024 | 0.024 |

The net profit is precisely the difference between the fair put price of 0.256 and the actual put price of 0.28.

---

[9] R. Merton, "Theory of rational option pricing," *Bell Journal of Economics and Management Science*, Spring 1973, pp. 141–83.

The arbitrage would work slightly differently with a LIFFE Eurodollar option, because the premium would not be paid out or received initially.

$$P(F, X, T) = C(F, X, T) + (F - X)$$
$$\text{Fair put price} = 0.50 - 0.25 = 0.25$$

This means that since the net implied cash outflow of 0.22 does not need to be paid and hence borrowed, the net expected profit is 0.03 rather than 0.024 – the difference is the 0.006 of interest.

## b. Long-term rate contracts

With LIFFE and CBT long-term interest rate options, which are also options on futures, the same simple put-call parity conditions will apply. With options on cash, however, the position will be more complex.

To explain this, we will look at arbitrage possibilities with the London Stock Exchange gilt options, although the principles will apply equally to other cash bond options.

The first major arbitrage restriction on a cash gilt option is that the value of a call option should be at least as high as the current price of the underlying gilt minus the discounted value of all interest payments and accrued interest on the gilt between now and expiry and minus the discounted value of the exercise price.

$$C(S, X, T) \geqslant S - D_{0,T} - X/(1 + R_T)$$

where $D_{0,T}$ = discounted value of dividends paid
between now and time $T$.

If this is not the case, buy call and sell underlying gilt at current price S.

|  | | Cash flow at expiration | |
| Transaction | Now | $S^* < X$ | $S^* \geqslant X$ |
|---|---|---|---|
| Buy call | $-C$ | 0 | $S^* - X$ |
| Sell gilt | $S$ | $-(S^* + D_{TT})$ | $-(S^* + D_{TT})$ |
| Invest balance | $-(S - C)$ | $(S - C)(1 + R_T)$ | $(S - C)(1 + R_T)$ |
| Net | 0 | $(S - C)(1 + R_T)$ | $(S - C)(1 + R_T)$ |
|  |  | $-S^* - D_{TT}$ | $-X - D_{TT}$ |

$D_{TT}$ = Value at time T of dividends paid between now and time T

Hence the minimum arbitrage profit is $(S - C)(1 + R_T) - X - D_{TT}$.

This is positive when

$$(S - C) > \frac{X + D_{TT}}{1 + R_T}$$

$$S - D_{0,T} - \frac{X}{(1 + R_T)} > C$$

## Example
### 9 April 1986

Treasury $11\frac{3}{4}\%$ 2003-07 price = 124-16
Short sterling interest rate = 11%
August 120 call = 4–28 (141 days to expiry)

Is there an arbitrage between the gilt stock and the August 120 call?
Examine the arbitrage relationship:

$$S - D_{0,T} - \frac{X}{(1 + R_T)}$$

$$124.50 - \frac{(11.75 \times \frac{141}{365})}{(1 + (0.11 \times \frac{141}{365}))} - \frac{120.00}{(1 + (0.11 \times \frac{141}{365}))} = 5.037$$

Since this is higher than the price of the call option, an arbitrage opportunity exists. In practice, the cash flows are somewhat more complicated because of the pattern of accrued interest payments on the gilt.

| 77 days accrued | Half-yearly coupon | 37 days accrued |
|---|---|---|
| April 9 | July 22 | August 28 |
| $A_0$ | $H_t$ | $A_T$ |

Assuming that all the interest payments can be discounted at the flat short-term rate of 11% the cash flows will be

$$(S + A_0 - C)(1 + R_T) - H_T(1 + R_{T-t}) - X - A_T$$

or

$$S + A_0 - \frac{H_T(1 + R_{T-t})}{(1 + R_T)} - \frac{X}{(1 + R_T)} - \frac{A_T}{(1 + R_T)} > C$$

Putting all this into the numbers used in the example

$$124.50 + (11.75 \times \tfrac{77}{365}) - 5.875 \frac{(1 + 0.11 \times \tfrac{37}{365})}{(1 + 0.11 \times \tfrac{141}{365})} - \frac{120.00}{(1 + 0.11 \times \tfrac{141}{365})} - \frac{(11.75 \times \tfrac{37}{365})}{(1 + 0.11 \times \tfrac{141}{365})}$$

which is calculated to equal 5.029. Hence an arbitrage opportunity still exists.

Now let us look at the actual cash flows.

**April 9**   Sell cash gilt   Receive £124.50 + £2.479
Buy call option   Pay £4.875
Invest net £122.104 for 141 days at 11%

**August 28**
*Case 1*   Gilt price £115.00
Call expires worthless
Receive £127.293 from investment
Repurchase gilt   Cost £115.00 + £1.191
Net cash gain = £11.102

*Case 2*   Gilt price £125.00
Call worth intrinsic value of £5.00
Receive £127.293 from investment
Repurchase gilt   Cost £125.00 + £1.191
Net cash gain = £6.102

Compare this with the cash gain that would occur in each case if the cash gilt had been held throughout. Make a negative assumption for the arbitrage potential by assuming that the half-yearly interest payment can be reinvested at a higher rate than 11%, say 15%. Since the option buyer now again holds the gilt, the comparison is with

$$£5.875(1 + 0.15 \times \tfrac{37}{365}) = £5.964.$$

Thus there is still an arbitrage profit of £0.138. In fact the reinvestment rate would need to rise to around 38% to eliminate the arbitrage entirely. This is a true arbitrage because, since the call is purchased, any exercise procedure is under the control of the buyer.

A similar arbitrage condition will apply for put options.

$$P(S, X, T) \geqslant X/(1 + R_T) - S - D_{0,T}$$

If this is not true, the put should be purchased and the cash gilt purchased with borrowed funds. The precise pattern of interest payments will be taken into account in determining the arbitrage potential.

Next, we shall look at put-call parity conditions. These are more difficult to establish for London Stock Exchange options because not only the pattern of dividend or interest payments needs to be considered, but also the possibility of early exercise.

Take European options first.

|  |  | *Cash flow at expiry* |  |
|---|---|---|---|
| *Transaction* | *Now* | $S^* < X$ | $S^* \geqslant X$ |
| Sell call | $C$ | $0$ | $-(S^* - X)$ |
| Buy put | $-P$ | $X - S^*$ | $0$ |
| Buy cash gilt | $-S$ | $S^* + D_{TT}$ | $S^* + D_{TT}$ |
| Borrow funds | $S + P - C$ | $-(S + P - C)(1 + R_T)$ | $-(S + P - C)(1 + R_T)$ |
| Net | $0$ | $(C - P - S)(1 + R_T)$ | $+E + D_{TT}$ |

Hence, to avoid arbitrage

$$C - P = S - \frac{D_{TT}}{(1 + R_T)} - \frac{X}{(1 + R_T)}$$

In practice the actual cash flows must be taken into account. There is also the question of premature exercise. The above arbitrage condition only holds at expiration. Before expiration less tight arbitrage bounds will hold

$$S - D_{0,T} - X \leqslant C - P \leqslant S - X/(1 + R_T)$$

These bounds can be tightened if conditions in the market suggest early exercise of particular options is unlikely. Thus if the coupon yield on the gilt is lower than the short-term rate, calls are not likely to be exercised and the arbitrage bounds will be

$$S - D_{0,T} - X/(1 + R_T) \leqslant C - P \leqslant S - X/(1 + R_T)$$

**Arbitrage example**

Treasury $11\frac{3}{4}\%$ 2003-07 cash options

| | Calls | | Puts | |
|---|---|---|---|---|
| Exercise price | 3-month | 6-month | 3-month | 6-month |
| 120 | 5.00 | 5.60 | 0.10 | 0.35 |
| 122 | 3.30 | 4.10 | 0.40 | 0.75 |
| 124 | 1.95 | 2.80 | 1.00 | 1.45 |

Current gilt price = 124–16        3 + 6-month rates = 11%

Do any arbitrage possibilities exist? It is reasonable to anticipate no early exercise for the calls. We also assume accrued interest is payable at delivery.

$$\text{3-month options} \quad D_{0,T} = (11.75/4)/(1 + 0.11/4) = 2.86$$
$$S - D_{0,T} = 124.50 - 2.86 = 121.64$$

| Exercise price | $S - D_{0,T} - X$ | $\leqslant$ | $C - P$ | $\leqslant$ | $S - D_{0,T} - X/(1 + R_T)$ |
|---|---|---|---|---|---|
| 120 | 1.64 | | 4.90 | | 4.85 |
| 122 | −0.32 | | 2.90 | | 2.91 |
| 124 | −2.32 | | 0.95 | | 0.96 |

$$\text{6-month options} \quad D_{0,T} = (11.75/2)/(1 + 0.11/2) = 5.57$$
$$S - D_{0,T} = 124.50 - 5.57 = 118.93$$

| Exercise price | $S - D_{0,T} - X$ | $\leqslant$ | $C - P$ | $\leqslant$ | $S - D_{0,T} - X/(1 + R_T)$ |
|---|---|---|---|---|---|
| 120 | −1.07 | | 5.25 | | 5.19 |
| 122 | −3.07 | | 3.35 | | 3.29 |
| 124 | −5.07 | | 1.35 | | 1.40 |

Three call-put combination options appear to violate the arbitrage bounds: the three-month 120 and the six-month 120 and 122 options. However, it is unlikely that the difference in any of the cases would be enough to justify an arbitrage operation after taking into account dealing costs, margin financing costs and possible taxes. If larger deviations were observed, the gain could be rechecked taking the precise timing of gilt interest payments into account. The impact of early exercise should be examined, to see how tight are the upper bounds on the option prices compared with the very loose lower bounds which arise because the puts may be exercised early. Early exercise possibilities would cause even bigger problems with more complex arbitrage strategies such as the box spread arbitrages discussed in Chapter 4.

## 4. Hedging with interest rate options

### a. Short-term rate contracts

Hedging with the Eurodollar contract was discussed in detail as the central feature of Chapter 5 on hedging techniques. One other specific area of short-term interest rate hedging that is worth discussing is the provision of so-called caps and collars on interest rate loans.

A *cap* is a loan agreement whereby a floating rate loan is guaranteed never to have an interest rate exceeding a certain level. A *collar* is a loan agreement whereby the interest rate on a floating rate loan is not allowed to move outside a certain band.

### (i) Interest rate caps

In issuing a cap loan agreement, the banker effectively sells a Eurodollar rate put option to the borrower, i.e. the borrower will make profits if interest rates fall but the loss is limited if interest rates rise; if the option is expressed in the futures index terms of (100 − Libor), the banker sells the borrower a Eurodollar futures call option, i.e. the borrower will make profits if interest rates fall and futures prices rise but will have limited losses if futures prices decline. The appropriate hedge is for the bank to purchase offsetting Eurodollar futures call options in the market. Since the loan rollover dates are fixed, so that continuous option hedging is not required, simple option hedges rather than ratio hedges will be sufficient.

**Case study**
**February 15**
A bank makes a cap loan of $10 million to a corporation on a basis of three-month rollovers with the interest rate guaranteed not to exceed 10%.

Current spot rate = 9%

| Exercise price | March futures = 91.20 | | June futures = 91.00 | | September futures = 90.75 | |
|---|---|---|---|---|---|---|
| | Calls | Puts | Calls | Puts | Calls | Puts |
| 90.00 | 1.34 | 0.12 | 1.41 | 0.41 | 1.35 | 0.60 |
| 90.50 | 0.85 | 0.15 | 0.95 | 0.45 | 0.90 | 0.65 |
| 91.00 | 0.40 | 0.20 | 0.55 | 0.55 | 0.56 | 0.81 |
| 91.50 | 0.10 | 0.40 | 0.25 | 0.75 | 0.28 | 1.04 |
| 92.00 | 0.02 | 0.82 | 0.08 | 1.08 | 0.12 | 1.37 |

Suppose the bank felt able to charge an additional 50bp for the cap facility. The profit-loss profile for the borrower at the next rollover date compared with the current spot rate would be as shown in Exhibit 8.2. The solution is for the bank to buy a Eurodollar 90.00 call. Looking at the

**Exhibit 8.2: Cap loan profile**

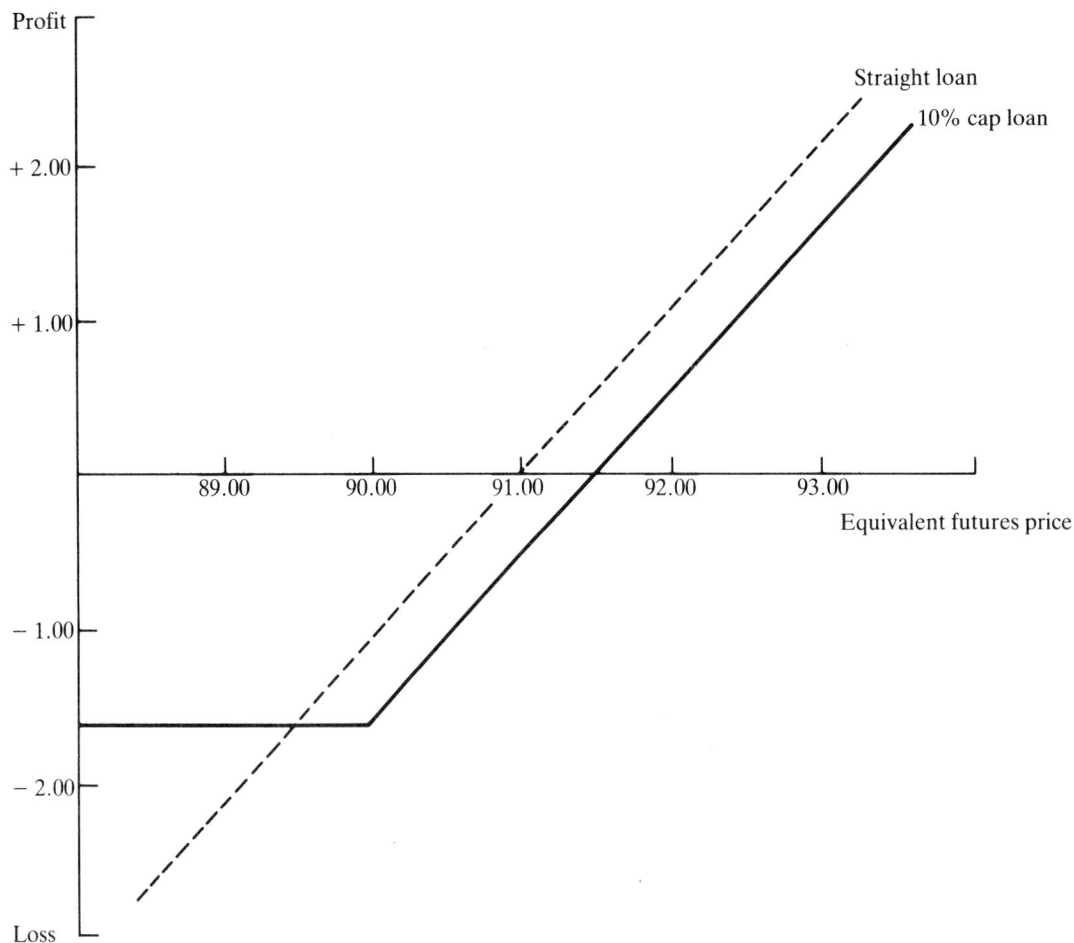

192

next rollover, it will have to be an extrapolative hedge.[10] Using the June and September contracts, this would involve buying 13 June 90.00 calls and selling 3 September 90.00 calls.

$$\text{Net cash flow} = [-(13 \times 1.41) + (3 \times 1.35)] \times \$25 \times 100$$
$$= -14.28 \times \$25 \times 100 = \$35,700.00$$

This effectively breaks down to a cost of 1.43% on an annual basis. Now consider alternative interest rate scenarios in May.

| Option cost | Option value | Profit/loss | Libor rate | Loan rate | Effective loan rate |
|---|---|---|---|---|---|
| −1.43 | 2.00 | 1.57 | 7 | 7.5 | 9.07 |
| −1.43 | 2.00 | 0.57 | 8 | 8.5 | 9.07 |
| −1.43 | 1.00 | −0.43 | 9 | 9.5 | 9.07 |
| −1.43 | 0 | −1.43 | 10 | 10.5 | 9.07 |
| −1.43 | 0 | −1.43 | 11 | 10.5 | 9.07 |
| −1.43 | 0 | −1.43 | 12 | 10.5 | 9.07 |

The bank has turned the expected profit/loss profile into a flat rate seven basis points above the current spot rate of 9%. As we saw in Chapter 5, there is always some risk with extrapolative hedges using different expiration date options. The bank could have decided to sell put options rather than buy call options. At the prices shown that would have given the following profit-loss profile, which is effectively that of an option straddle.

| Option cost | Option value | Profit/ loss | Libor rate | Loan rate | Effective loan rate |
|---|---|---|---|---|---|
| +0.34 | 0 | 0.34 | 7 | 7.5 | 7.84 |
| +0.34 | 0 | 0.34 | 8 | 8.5 | 8.84 |
| +0.34 | 0 | 0.34 | 9 | 9.5 | 9.84 |
| +0.34 | 0 | 0.34 | 10 | 10.5 | 10.84 |
| +0.34 | −1.00 | −0.66 | 11 | 10.5 | 9.84 |
| +0.34 | −2.00 | −1.66 | 12 | 10.5 | 8.84 |

Whether either of these positions suits the bank will depend on whether a fixed rate loan fits in with interest rate expectations. If the bank expects rates to decline or stay around current levels, the hedges will be suitable. However, the bank is still exposed to risk on the funding side. Since an effective fixed rate loan has been created with the call hedge, the bank may have to fund the position at a higher rate than the fixed one if interest rates rise. The bank can lock in the funding rate by a simple futures hedge: selling Eurodollar futures which will give compensating gains if rates rise and futures prices fall. However, there is a simpler solution. The effective positions in symbolic notation are:

| | |
|---|---|
| Borrower has bought a 90.00 call | (0, 1)(90) |
| Bank has sold a 90.00 call | (0, −1)(90) |

So, by buying an equivalent option (0, 1)(90) the bank creates a neutral position on the lending side (0, 0)(90) but is running a risk position on the funding side.

*Net position if call is not purchased*
Assume implicit futures price for May 15 is

$$91.20(\tfrac{1}{3}) + 91.00(\tfrac{2}{3}) = 91.07$$

| | |
|---|---|
| Call sold | (0, −1, −1)(90, 91.07) |
| Funding risk | (1, 1, 1)(90, 91.07) |
| Net | (+1, 0, 0)(90, 91.07) |

Effectively the bank has a short 90.00 put position, which can be offset by buying an appropriate extrapolative put hedge consisting of buying 13 June 90 puts and selling 3 September 90 puts.

$$\text{Net cash flow} = -(13 \times 0.41) + (3 \times 0.65)$$
$$= 3.38$$

---

[10] See Chapter 5 for details of option hedging techniques.

This corresponds to a cost of 0.34% on an annual basis. The alternative interest rate scenarios in May are:

| Option cost | Option value | Profit/ loss | Libor rate | Loan rate | Effective loan rate | Spread over Libor |
|---|---|---|---|---|---|---|
| −0.34 | 0 | −0.34 | 7 | 7.5 | 7.16 | 0.16 |
| −0.34 | 0 | −0.34 | 8 | 8.5 | 8.16 | 0.16 |
| −0.34 | 0 | −0.34 | 9 | 9.5 | 9.16 | 0.16 |
| −0.34 | 0 | −0.34 | 10 | 10.5 | 10.16 | 0.16 |
| −0.34 | 1.00 | 0.66 | 11 | 10.5 | 11.16 | 0.16 |
| −0.34 | 2.00 | 1.66 | 12 | 10.5 | 12.16 | 0.16 |

The bank has locked in a fixed spread of 16 basis points on the loan, i.e. by charging a margin of 50 basis points compared with the put option cost of 34 basis points, it has added 16 basis points to whatever commercial margin is being charged. In other words, the bank has a choice with hedging cap loans: it can buy calls and fix the loan rate running the funding exposure, or it can buy puts and fix the spread. It can also construct any other hedge.

## (ii) Interest rate collars

The collar loan is more difficult to analyse. By giving the borrower the advantage of an interest rate ceiling but forcing him to accept the disadvantage of an interest rate floor, the lender has effectively bought and sold an equivalent Eurodollar futures option.

**Example**
**February 15**
A bank makes a collar loan of $10 million to a corporation on the basis of three-month rollovers with the interest rate guaranteed not to exceed 10% nor to fall below 8%.

$$\text{Current spot rate} = 9\%$$

Call and put prices are as in the previous cap example.

The profit/loss profile for the borrower assuming a 25 basis point margin is shown in Exhibit 8.3. The lender has effectively sold the borrower a 90.00–92.00 vertical spread at a premium of 125 basis points. The first alternative for the lender is to simply buy an equivalent spread. Because the hedge is for May, an extrapolated hedge is appropriate.

Buy 13 90 June calls at 1.41
Sell 3 90 Sept. calls at 1.35
Sell 13 92 June calls at 0.08
Buy 3 92 Sept. calls at 0.12

$$\text{Net cost} = 13.6 \times \$25 \times 100$$
$$= \$34,000$$

This breaks down to a cost of 1.36% on an annual basis. Various rate alternatives can be considered.

| Option position cost | Option position value | Profit/ loss | Libor rate | Loan rate | Effective loan rate |
|---|---|---|---|---|---|
| −1.36 | 2.00 | 0.64 | 7 | 8.25 | 8.89 |
| −1.36 | 2.00 | 0.64 | 8 | 8.35 | 8.89 |
| −1.36 | 1.00 | −0.36 | 9 | 9.25 | 8.89 |
| −1.36 | 0.00 | −1.36 | 10 | 10.25 | 8.89 |
| −1.36 | 0.00 | −1.36 | 11 | 10.25 | 8.89 |
| −1.36 | 0.00 | −1.36 | 12 | 10.25 | 8.89 |

Once again the bank has fixed in a fixed rate, although this time at 8.89%, some 11 basis points below the current spot Libor of 9.00%. In other words it is necessary to charge the borrower a premium of 36 basis points rather than 25 basis points for the collar loan to ensure a fixed rate of 9% equal to the current Libor rate. The bank also has to remember that the extrapolative loan will not necessarily yield the exact same profile as a true May expiry 90.00–92.00 vertical spread.

**Exhibit 8.3: Collar loan profile**

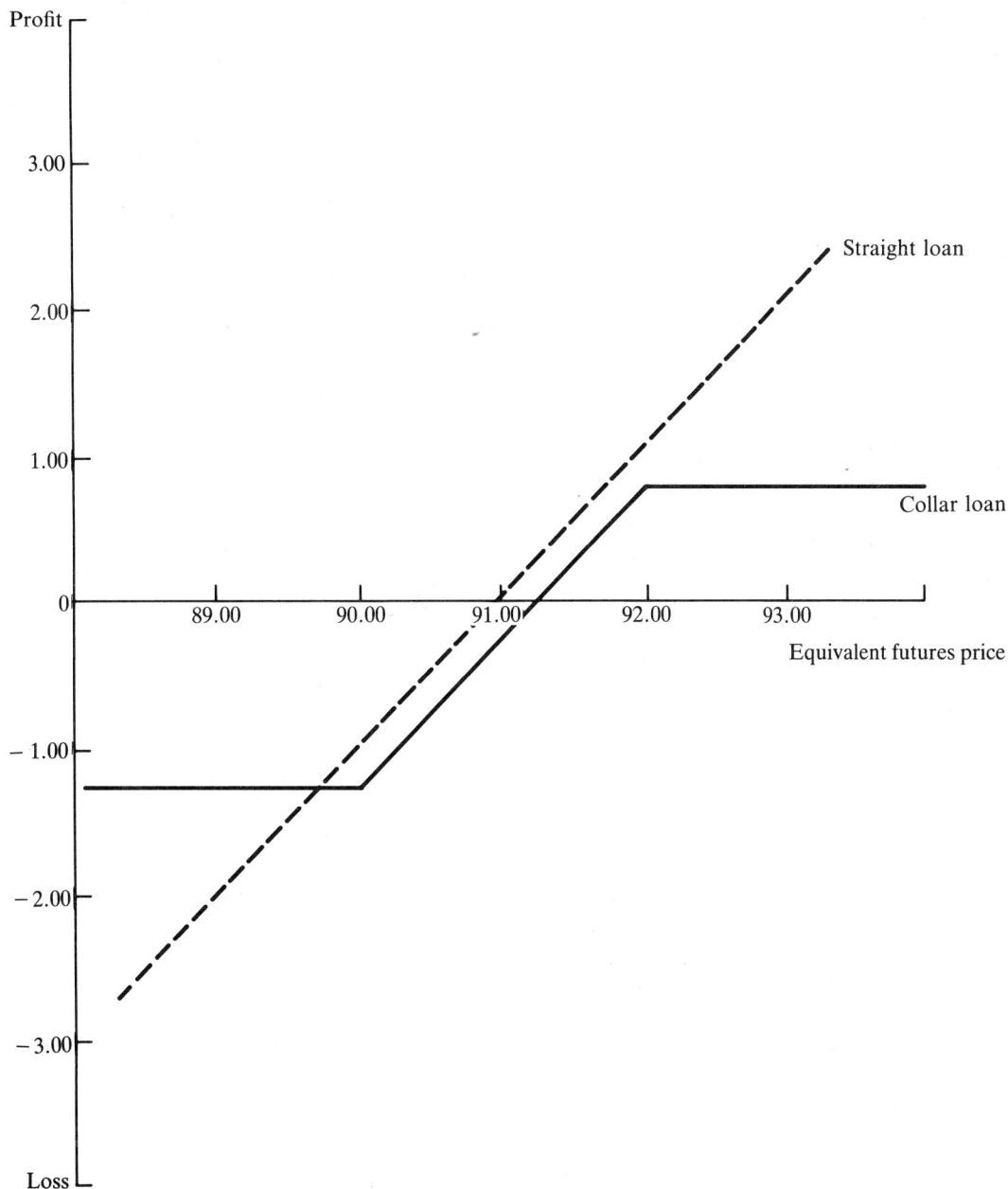

The banker could also experiment with other profit profiles – perhaps by buying the 90.00 to 92.00 put spread, or decreasing the cost by selling the 91.50 options in the vertical call spread rather than the 92.00 calls. The profit profiles of each are shown below.

*(i) Vertical put spread*

| Option cost | Option value | Profit/ loss | Loan rate | Effective loan rate |
|---|---|---|---|---|
| +0.58 | 0 | 0.58 | 8.25 | 8.83 |
| +0.58 | 0 | 0.58 | 8.25 | 8.83 |
| +0.58 | −1.00 | −0.42 | 9.25 | 8.83 |
| +0.58 | −2.00 | −1.42 | 10.25 | 8.83 |
| +0.58 | −2.00 | −1.42 | 10.25 | 8.83 |
| +0.58 | −2.00 | −1.42 | 10.25 | 8.83 |

This approach is inferior to the call strategy by six basis points.

## (ii) Vertical 90.00 to 91.50 call spread

| Option cost | Option value | Profit/ loss | Loan rate | Effective loan rate |
|---|---|---|---|---|
| −1.19 | 1.50 | 0.31 | 8.25 | 8.56 |
| −1.19 | 1.50 | 0.31 | 8.25 | 8.56 |
| −1.19 | 1.00 | −0.19 | 9.25 | 9.06 |
| −1.19 | 0 | −1.19 | 10.25 | 9.06 |
| −1.19 | 0 | −1.19 | 10.25 | 9.06 |
| −1.19 | 0 | −1.19 | 10.25 | 9.06 |

Here the banker has given up interest rate gains, if the rates fall, to secure higher than current rates if rates do rise. In practice there are numerous strategies that could be adopted, including the cylinder and rotated cylinder hedges discussed in Chapter 5. It is important to realise that by offering a collar loan, the bank has sold a particular profit-loss profile to the borrower. For the instance above, using the symbolic algebra for options, it could be written in futures terms as

$$(0, 1, 0)(90.00, 92.00) \text{ for borrower}$$
$$(0, -1, 0)(90.00, 92.00) \text{ for lender}$$

The collar loan seller (the bank) then has to decide what profit/loss profile he would like to convert this into, and secondly what fair premium he can charge for offering the loan. He will attempt to charge a premium that will at least cover the cost of converting the option profit-loss profile to the desired one. Competitive pressures may, however, prevent this. He will also want to look at the volatility risk of the position, given that the hedge date is not a traded option expiration date.

As in the previous case, this more or less fixes the rate on the lending leaving the funding risk. Let us look at the position including the funding risk.

$$\text{Vertical spread sold} \quad (0, -1, -1, 0)(90, 91.07, 92)$$
$$\text{Funding risk} \quad (1, 1, 1, 1)(90, 91.07, 92)$$
$$\text{Net} \quad (1, 0, 0, 1)(90, 91.07, 92)$$

The banker, in fact, is creating the position usually achieved in the rotated cylinder hedge described in Chapter 5. If he is happy with this, there is nothing to be done; if he wants an overall flat position on the spread, he needs to buy a 90 put option and sell a 92 call option.

$$\text{Net} \quad (1, 0, 0, 1)(90, 91.07, 92)$$
$$\text{90 put bought} \quad (-1, 0, 0, 0)(90, 91.07, 92)$$
$$\text{90 call sold} \quad (0, 0, 0, -1)(90, 91.07, 92)$$
$$\text{Final position} \quad (0, 0, 0, 0)(90, 91.07, 92)$$

Thus the hedge is to buy 13 90 June puts, sell 3 90 Sept puts, and sell 13 June calls, buy 3 Sept 92 calls.

$$\text{Net cash flow} = -(13 \times 0.41) + (3 \times 0.65) + (13 \times 0.08) - (3 \times 0.12)$$
$$= 2.7$$

This corresponds to a cost of 0.27% on an annual basis. Once again let us look at the rate alternatives.

| Option cost | Option value | Profit/ loss | Libor | Loan rate | Effective loan rate | Spread |
|---|---|---|---|---|---|---|
| −0.27 | −1.00 | −1.27 | 7 | 8.25 | 6.98 | −0.02 |
| −0.27 | 0 | −0.27 | 8 | 8.25 | 7.98 | −0.02 |
| −0.27 | 0 | −0.27 | 9 | 9.25 | 8.98 | −0.02 |
| −0.27 | 0 | −0.27 | 10 | 10.25 | 9.98 | −0.02 |
| −0.27 | 1.00 | 0.73 | 11 | 10.25 | 10.98 | −0.02 |
| −0.27 | 2.00 | 1.73 | 12 | 10.25 | 11.98 | −0.02 |

Once again a flat spread is guaranteed, but the banker has slightly undercharged for the collar. If a premium of 27 basis points was charged, any commercial margin on the loan would be guaranteed. The collar lender has the choice of fixing the loan rate and running the funding risk or fixing the spread.

**Caps and collars**

1. A cap loan is the effective sale to the borrower of a Eurodollar futures call option, exercise price equal to the cap rate implied futures price.
2. A collar loan is the effective sale to the borrower of a Eurodollar futures vertical call spread, with the lower exercise price equal to the cap rate implied futures price and the higher exercise price equal to the floor rate implied futures price.
3. Hedging such loans can be achieved by taking opposite (or complementary) positions in the Eurodollar traded options market.
4. The bank always has the choice of fixing the loan rate and running the funding risk, or fixing the spread, with options positions.
5. Any premium for a cap or a collar should equal or exceed the net cost of the (options) hedge.

Similar techniques could be envisaged for depositors. Banks could offer, say, fixed one-year deposits with the interest rate changing every three months but with the rate guaranteed not to decline below a certain level. Or perhaps the banks could offer a one-year deposit rate, with the option to switch to a three-month rate basis after each quarter. This is effectively selling various types of options to the investor which could be hedged in the traded options market.

## b. Long-term rate contracts

In Chapter 5, general principles of hedging with options contracts were discussed. Before analysing options hedging with Treasury bond options, however, some analysis of the underlying Treasury bond contract is needed.[11]

### (i) The Treasury bond futures contract

The Chicago Board of Trade Treasury-bond contract[12] is based on a notional $100,000 8% Treasury bond. At delivery actual Treasury bonds have to be delivered against the Treasury bond futures contract; all Treasury bonds with call dates further than 15 years from the current date can be delivered against the contract. The price for these deliverable bonds is determined by a *conversion factor* or *price factor*. The price factor is the price per $1 nominal value at which each deliverable Treasury bond will yield 8% at its current time to maturity rounded down to the nearest three months.

Thus, if a specific bond is delivered against a futures contract

Invoice payment = [Futures settlement price × Conversion factor × $1,000] + Accrued interest

**Example of delivery**
Contract   September 1985
Exchange delivery settlement price   September 5   77-16
Bond to be delivered   $8\frac{3}{4}\%$ 2003-08
Conversion factor   1.0709

$$\text{Invoice amount} = (77\text{-}16 \times 1.0709 \times \$1{,}000) + \text{Accrued interest}$$

$$\text{Accrued interest} = \text{May 15} - \text{September 9}$$

$$= \$4{,}375 \times \frac{117}{184} = \$2{,}781.93$$

$$\text{Invoice amount} = \$82{,}994.75 + \$2{,}781.93$$

$$= \$85{,}776.68$$

The important question is precisely which Treasury bond is most likely to be delivered. The answer is the one that can be delivered with maximum profit or minimum loss to the deliverer. This is what is termed the *cheapest to deliver bond* (CTD). This concept is bound up with a type of arbitrage called *cash and carry* arbitrage. The idea of this is simple: buy a cash Treasury bond

---

[11] The discussion of Treasury bond futures here is limited to what is required for an understanding of Treasury bond option hedging. For a full discussion, see M. D. Fitzgerald, *Financial Futures*, Euromoney Publications (1983).
[12] The LIFFE contract is almost identical to the CBT contract.

deliverable against the T-bond futures contract with borrowed funds; simultaneously sell a T-bond futures contract, fixing the price at which the cash bond will be delivered, and when the bond is delivered, use the invoice payment received to repay the loan and, hopefully, keep the balance left over.

### Evaluating a T-bond futures cash and carry transation

Initial investment:   Bond price quote + Accrued interest + Discounted borrowing cost

*Total proceeds*
Bond sale:   (Futures price × Conversion factor) + Accrued interest
Coupon (if any):   Compounded value of coupon at delivery

$$\text{Rate of return:} \frac{\text{Total proceeds} - \text{Initial investment}}{\text{Initial investment}} \times \text{Annualizing factor}$$

The table below shows a typical table for evaluating cash and carry returns.

| Bond coupon (%) | Date of maturity | Cash price | Conversion factor | Delivery price | Rate of return (%) |
|---|---|---|---|---|---|
| 12.00 | 15 Aug 2013 | 95-10 | 1.4239 | 93-27 | 3.57 |
| 10.375 | 15 Nov 2012 | 83-00 | 1.6487 | 82-09 | 7.38 |
| 14.00 | 15 Nov 1012 | 110-10 | 1.6187 | 106-22 | −5.49 |
| 8.75 | 15 Nov 2008 | 71-08 | 1.0728 | 70-22 | 7.61 |

The cheapest deliverable bond is that bond which yields the highest return to a *cash and carry arbitrage*; for the bonds quoted above, this is the $8\frac{3}{4}\%$ 15 Nov 2008 bond.

The important point is that since arbitrage will closely link the price of the cheapest to deliver bond to that of the Treasury bond futures contract, it is normally assumed that the Treasury bond future will behave as if it is a futures contract written on the cheapest to deliver bond, with the prices being linked through the conversion factor.

Price change of futures contract = Price change of cheapest to deliver bond/Conversion factor

This forms the basis for determining the appropriate number of contracts for a Treasury bond hedge.

### (ii) Hedging with the T-bond futures contract

This will be considered in three stages.

1. hedging the cheapest to deliver bond,
2. hedging other Treasury bonds; and
3. hedging other dollar bonds such as Eurobonds.

It has already been explained how arbitrage between cash and futures links the price of the Treasury bond future to the price of the cheapest to deliver bond. Since the prices are linked through the *conversion factor*, the appropriate hedge ratio is the cheapest to deliver bond's conversion or price factor.[13]

$$\text{Number of futures contracts} = \frac{\text{Par value of bond position}}{\$100,000} \times \text{Conversion factor}$$

**Example**
Assume on 15 December 1984 the cheapest to deliver Treasury bond against the CBT March 1985 bond future is the 8.75% 2003–08 Treasury bond.

Conversion factor = 1.0718

Investor holds $10,000,000 nominal of bond
Bond price = 67-14   Futures price = 61-23

$$\text{Number of contracts} = \frac{\$10,000,000}{\$100,000} \times 1.0718 = 107 \text{ contracts}$$

---

[13] Our discussion of hedging with Treasury bond options is exclusively concerned with options on Treasury bond futures. Although cash Treasury bond options are traded on the CBOE, volume is so small there that use for true commercial hedging purposes is very limited. Hedging with gilt options is covered later in this chapter.

Since the investor will wish to protect against falling bond prices caused by rising interest rates, he will sell 107 March Treasury bond futures contracts to benefit from price falls if rates rise. It is interesting to determine what bond price is being guaranteed. Assuming the bond futures go to delivery at the last possible date in the month because bond yields are higher than short-term interest rates, the locked-in bond price on 29 March 1985 can be found from the relationship.

$$\text{Guaranteed price March 29} = \text{Futures price} \times \text{Conversion factor} = 61\text{-}23 \times 1.0718$$
$$= 66.15 \text{ (or } 66\text{-}05) \text{ for the } 8.75\% \text{ } 2003\text{-}08$$

If, by contrast, the hedge period were expected to only extend to February 15, the anticipated price would be different, and would normally be found by linear interpolation between the 8.75% 2003-08 price òn December 15 and the price suggested by the futures market for 29 March 1985.

*Anticipated February 15 price*

$$\text{Dec. 15–Feb. 15} \quad 62 \text{ days}$$
$$\text{Feb. 16–Mar. 29} \quad 42 \text{ days}$$

$$\text{Expected price} = [67\text{-}14 \times 42/104] + [66.15 \times 62/104]$$
$$= 66.67 \text{ (or } 66\text{-}21)$$

As with all futures hedges for dates other than delivery dates on the futures contracts, this price is not a guaranteed price but is subject to basis risk, i.e. that the relationship between futures prices and the cash price of the cheapest to deliver bond will not have behaved exactly in line with predictions by February 15.

Treasury bond futures basis can be defined as

$$\text{Basis} = \text{Cash price} - \text{Futures price} = \frac{\text{Cheapest to deliver price}}{\text{Conversion factor}} - \text{Futures price}$$

*On December 15*

$$\text{Basis} = \frac{67\text{-}14}{1.0718} - 61\text{-}23 = 1.20$$

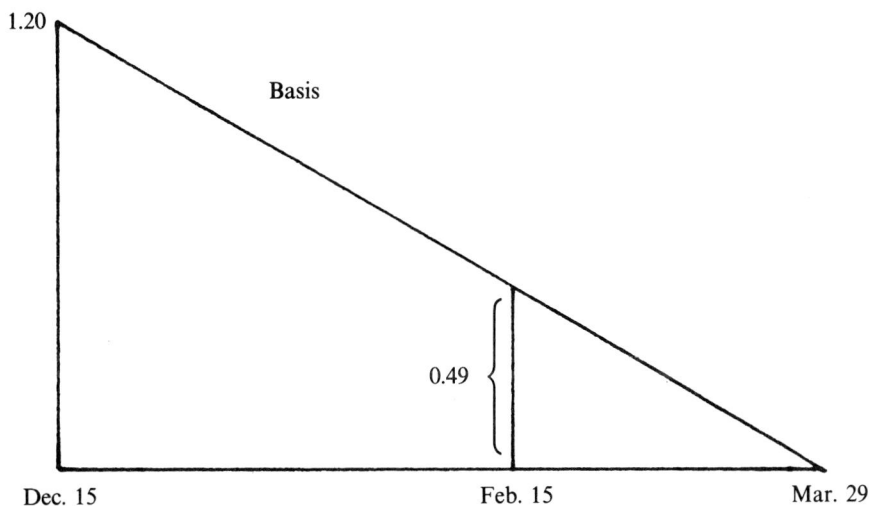

This tells us that the expected futures price on February 15 will be

$$61\text{-}23 + 0.49 = 62.20$$

$$\text{Expected cash price February 15} = 62.20 \times 1.0718$$
$$= 66.67$$

By moving ahead to 15 February 1985 it is possible to see what actually happened. At the time the hedge is unwound, the cash price for the 8.75% 2003-08 bond is 65-29 and the Treasury bond March futures price has fallen to 61-08.

$$\text{Futures profit} = \$31.25 \times 107 \text{ contracts} \times [61\text{-}23 - 61\text{-}08]$$
$$= \$50,156.25$$

$$\text{Effective price of cash bond} = \frac{\$6,590,625 + \$50,156.25}{\$100,000}$$
$$= 66.41$$

199

The reason for the discrepancy between the expected 66.67 and the realized 66.41 is an unexpected change in the basis.

$$\text{Expected basis} \quad \text{Feb. } 15 = 0.49$$

$$\text{Actual basis} \quad \text{Feb. } 15 = \frac{65\text{-}29}{1.0718} - 61\text{-}08 = 0.24$$

This is a difference of 0.25 or $\frac{8}{32}$nd, and is responsible for the apparent inefficiency of the Treasury bond hedge.

Apart from basis risk which is a feature of most futures hedges, the design of futures hedges of the cheapest to deliver bond is relatively simple. Hedging Treasury bonds other than the cheapest to deliver is a more complicated matter, since the different volatility or interest rate risk of different bonds as interest rates change must be taken into account. Prices of long maturity, low coupon bonds are more volatile than prices of short maturity, high coupon bonds. Hence the relative volatility of the bond to be hedged and the cheapest to deliver bond must be used in calculating hedge ratios.

$$\text{Number of contracts} = \frac{\text{Face value of bond position}}{\$100,000} \times \begin{array}{l}\text{Relative volatility of bond to be hedged}\\ \text{and cheapest to deliver bond}\end{array}$$

$$\times \text{ Cheapest to deliver bond conversion factor}$$

The two most common methods used for determining relative volatility are *perturbation analysis* and *duration analysis*.[14] We will examine examples of these two approaches in turn.

### Perturbation analysis

This approach relies on examining the impact of a specific change in redemption yield on the price of the bond to be hedged and the cheapest to deliver bond. It is common to look at the impact of a 1% yield change, though if an interest forecast is available, the forecast rate change may be applied to both bonds.

### Example
**15 Dec. 1984**
Bond to be hedged    $10,000,000 of 10.375% 2007–12    Price = 78-09
Cheapest-to-deliver bond 8.75% 2003–08    Price = 67-14
Conversion factor of CTD March 1985    1.0718
Conversion factor of 10.375% 2007–12    1.2461

We now examine the impact of a 1% increase in redemption yield on both bonds.

$$\$ \text{ value of a } 1\% \text{ increase in yield} = \$546,875 \text{ for } 10.375\% \text{ } 2007\text{-}12$$

$$\$ \text{ value of a } 1\% \text{ increase in yield for } 8.75\% \text{ } 2003\text{–}08 = \$478,125$$

$$\text{Relative volatility} = \frac{\$546,875}{\$478,125} = 1.144$$

$$\text{Number of contracts for hedge} = \frac{\$10,000,000}{\$100,000} \times 1.144 \times 1.0718$$

$$= 123 \text{ contracts}$$

### Duration analysis

Rather than look at the direct price impact of a specific interest rate change, this approach looks at the relative duration of the two bonds. Duration is the *weighted average maturity* of a bond, the weights being the relative contribution of each period's cash flow to the total present value or price of the bond.

$$\text{Duration} = \sum_{t=1}^{N} \frac{C_t(t)}{(1+R)^t} \bigg/ P_B$$

where $C_t$ = cash flow to bond in period $t$
$N$ = number of periods to maturity
$R$ = redemption yield
$P_B$ = market price of bond

---

[14] For a fuller discussion on perturbation and duration, see M. D. Fitzgerald, *Financial Futures*, Euromoney Publications (1983).

**Example**

A two-year bond with a 10% coupon currently has a redemption yield of 12%. Interest is paid semi-annually.

$$\text{Bond price} = \frac{5}{(1.06)} + \frac{5}{(1.06)^2} + \frac{5}{(1.06)^3} + \frac{105}{(1.06)^4}$$

$$= 96.54$$

$$\text{Duration} = \frac{\dfrac{5(1)}{(1.06)} + \dfrac{5(2)}{(1.06)^2} + \dfrac{5(3)}{(1.06)^3} + \dfrac{105(4)}{(1.06)^4}}{96.54}$$

$$= 3.72 \text{ periods or } 1.86 \text{ years}$$

The importance of duration is that it is a common measure of the interest rate sensitivity or volatility of a bond. The following relationship is a fundamental one.

% change in bond price $= (-\text{Duration}) \times$ % change in (1 + Redemption yield)

Thus if, using the previous example, we wished to examine the price impact of a change in the redemption yield from, say, 12% to 13%.

$$\frac{\Delta P}{P} = (-3.72) \times \frac{0.005}{1.06} = -0.0176$$

Change in bond price $= -[96.54 \times 0.0176] = -1.70$
New bond price $= 96.54 - 1.70 = 94.84$

Since relative volatility is measured as the ratio of the price change in the bond to be hedged to that of the cheapest to deliver in response to an identical change in yield, the following relationship for hedge ratios can be written:

$$\text{Relative volatility} = \frac{\text{Duration of hedge bond}}{\text{Duration of CTD}} \times \frac{\text{Clean price of hedge bond}}{\text{Clean price of CTD}}$$
$$\times \frac{1 + \text{Redemption yield of CTD}}{1 + \text{Redemption yield of hedge bond}}$$

**Example**

**December 1984**

Bond to be hedged: $10,000,000 of 11.75% 2001    Price = 88-27
Redemption yield = 13.44%    Duration 7.22 years

Cheapest to deliver bond 8.75% 2003-08    Price = 67-14
Redemption yield = 13.26%    Duration 8.03 yrs

Conversion factor CTD March 1985 = 1.0718

$$\text{Relative volatility} = \frac{7.22}{8.03} \times \frac{88\text{-}27}{67\text{-}14} \times \frac{1.1326}{1.1344}$$
$$= 1.18$$

$$\text{Number of contracts for hedge} = \frac{\$10,000,000}{\$100,000} \times 1.18 \times 1.0718 = 126.5 \text{ contracts}$$

An appropriate futures hedge is therefore 127 contracts.

What bond price is being promised by this particular hedge? We have already calculated that the expected price change for the cheapest to deliver bond is (67-14 minus 66.15) or 1.2875. Using the relative volatility just calculated, the equivalent price change for the 11.75% 2001 will be (1.18 × 1.2875) or 1.5193.

$$\text{Expected price 11.75\% 2001 29 March 1985} = 88\text{-}27 - 1.5193$$
$$= 87.32 \text{ (or 87-10)}$$

And if we wanted the expected price on February 15, we would obtain it by linear interpolation.

$$[87.32 \times \tfrac{62}{104}] + [88\text{-}27 \times \tfrac{42}{104}] = 87.94 \text{ (or 87-30)}$$

The basis risk involved in hedging other Treasury bonds is substantially greater than in hedges of cheapest to deliver bond positions. For non-CTD hedges, the basis consists of two components:

(a) the difference between the futures equivalent price of the cheapest to deliver bond and the current futures price; and
(b) the difference between the futures equivalent price of the hedged Treasury bond and the adjusted clean price of the cheapest to deliver bond.

$$\text{Basis} = \frac{\text{Hedge bond price}}{\text{Conversion factor of hedge bond}} - \text{Futures price}$$

$$= \underbrace{\left[ \frac{\text{Hedge bond price}}{\text{Conversion factor of hedge bond}} - \frac{\text{CTD price}}{\text{Conversion factor of CTD}} \right]}_{(B)} + \underbrace{\left[ \frac{\text{CTD price}}{\text{Conversion factor of CTD}} - \text{Futures price} \right]}_{(A)}$$

Arbitrage should ensure that basis (A) will steadily and predictably reduce to near zero at delivery. Basis (A) will generally reflect the interest rate differential between short-term money market interest rates and bond yields, normally known as the cost of carry. Basis (B) by contrast can alter substantially through time, especially with changes in the shape of the long-term yield curve, and adds additional risks to hedging Treasury bonds other than the cheapest to deliver bond.

If we consider hedging bonds other than Treasury bonds such as Eurobonds or US corporate bonds, a further element of basis will be introduced: the credit or quality spread between the actual bond and a Treasury bond of equivalent maturity and coupon. Unpredictable movements in quality spreads can affect hedge performance substantially.

### (iii) Hedging with T-bond futures options

Having discussed the basics of hedging with T-bond futures, it is now possible to discuss hedging with T-bond futures options. The basic principles are the same as with other options.

---

1. **If your cash position will be adversely affected by higher long-term interest rates, buy T-bond put options or sell T-bond call options.**
2. **If the cash position will be adversely affected by lower interest rates, buy T-bond call options or sell T-bond put options.**

---

Options hedging with T-bond futures/options can be thought of in two steps.

1. A T-bond futures contract locks in (almost) a specific price for the cheapest to deliver bond.
2. A T-bond futures option insures against the cheapest to deliver bond price moving against the hedger by more than a certain amount for payment of a premium.

A comparison of options and futures T-bond hedges is shown in Exhibit 8.4, with the assumption that the instrument being hedged is an amount of the cheapest to deliver of $100,000/conversion factor.

As discussed in Chapter 5, hedging with options is particularly suitable for hedging uncertain and/or asymmetric exposures. For Treasury bonds, the following applies:

|  | Symmetrical | Asymmetrical |
| --- | --- | --- |
| Known: | Specific cash T-bond portfolio | Offering T-bond portfolio insurance |
| Uncertain: | Investment of future cash flow in T-bonds | Offering T-bond portfolio insurance facility |

A numerical example of a T-bond options hedge can be developed by considering the cheapest to deliver hedge analysed earlier.

Hedge $10,000,000 of 8.75% 2003–08   Price 67-14

Treasury bond futures price = 61-23

**Exhibit 8.4: T-bond futures and options hedges**

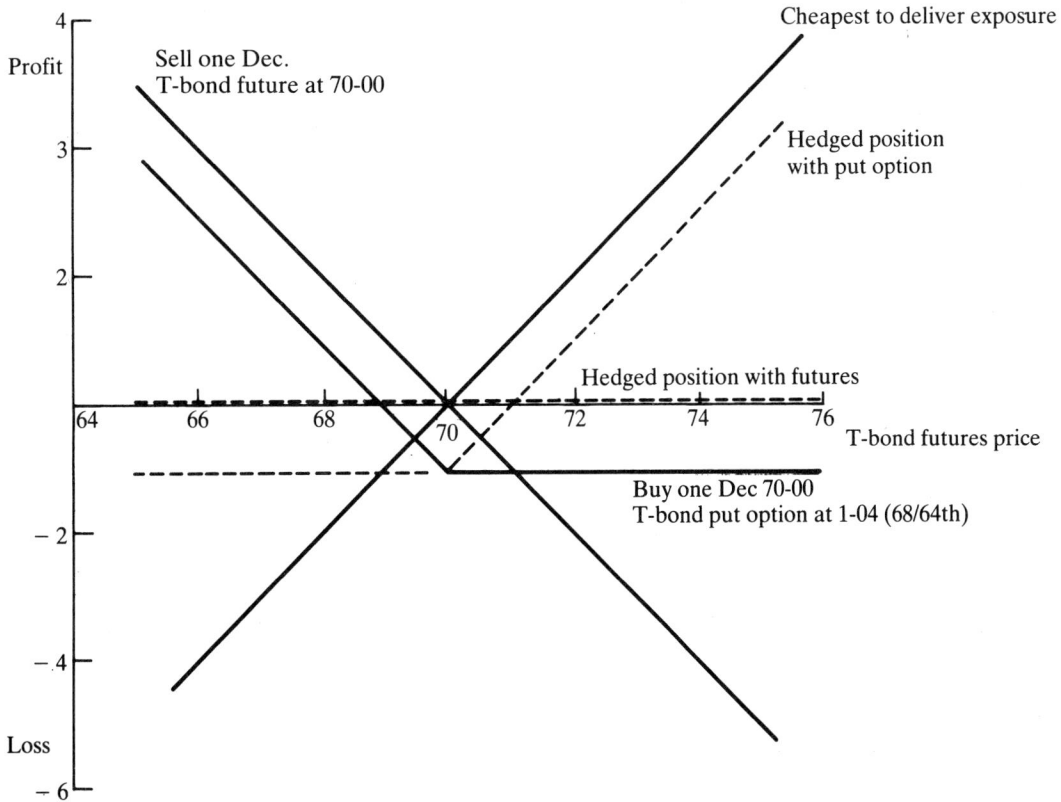

$$\text{Number of contracts} = \frac{\$10,000,000}{\$100,000} \times 1.0718 = 107 \text{ contracts}$$

Buy 107 March T-bond put options   Exercise price 62-00   Premium 1-32.[15]

Best guaranteed cheapest to deliver price in March = (62-00 minus 1-32) × 1.0718
= 64.84 (or 64-27)

This expected price of 64.84 compares with the expected price of 66.15 locked in through the future hedge. The difference of 1.31 is accounted for by the net cost of the premium taking into account the difference between the exercise price of 62-00 and the actual futures price of 61-23.

$$(1.50 - [62.00 - 61.71875]) \times 1.0718 = 1.31$$

If we lift the hedge on February 15, the precise result will depend on movements in futures prices and volatility between December 15 and February 15.

*Result: February 15*
8.75% 2003-08 = 65-29
Treasury bond futures price = 61-08
March T-bond 62-00 put premium = 1-16

Options loss = $15.625 × 107 × [1-32 minus 1-16]
= $26,750

$$\text{Effective price of cash bond} = \frac{\$6,590,625 - \$26,750}{\$100,000} = 65.64$$

An alternative would have been to sell 62-00 call options on December 15 at a call option premium of 1-14.

With other bond hedges, the step remains the same: calculate the number of Treasury bond futures contracts for a good hedge, then replace the futures hedge with long or short options positions if the options hedge appears more favourable to the hedger. In hedging bond portfolios

---

[15] T-bond futures are priced in 32nds and T-bond options in 64ths.

on a short-term basis, the hedger may wish to employ a delta hedge. The ideal number of T-bond futures contracts is divided by the delta of the T-bond option position being used in the hedge.

---

## Hedging a bond portfolio with options

1. **Work out the best futures hedge using perturbation or duration analysis.**
2. **Replace the futures hedge with an identical number of long or short bond options.**
3. **If using a ratio hedge**

$$\text{Number of contracts} = \frac{\textbf{Futures hedge number}}{\textbf{Option delta}}$$

---

Basis risk in all its forms applies to options hedges as well as futures hedges, because the option is priced off the futures contracts. Options hedges also add volatility: if the volatility of T-bond prices changes, the expected option value line for February 15 will not be valid. In the case of the put option hedge, a decline in implied volatility will reduce hedge performance, although the best guaranteed bond price will still be assured.

The discussion has so far been concerned with Treasury bond options on the Chicago Board of Trade. The trading of options on the long T-bond contract and the long gilt contract was introduced on the London International Financial Futures Exchange in 1986. The basics of these options was discussed earlier. Because both are options on futures, the same hedging principles as discussed with CBT Treasury bond options apply. In fact, the LIFFE T-bond option is identical with the Chicago T-bond option. The other options trading in the United Kingdom with reasonable liquidity are the cash gilt options on the London Stock Exchange, mentioned earlier. The introduction of options on cash bonds introduces only small differences to hedging strategies.

Because the option is written on a specific gilt, its price will move directly in line with movements in the cash gilt price, and hence the conversion factor relationship with the cheapest to deliver gilt will not be necessary in calculating hedge ratios. Assuming a duration hedging approach is adopted then for, say, the option on the Treasury $11\frac{3}{4}\%$ 1991, the number of contracts would be

$$\frac{\text{Face value of hedged gilt}}{£50,000} \times \frac{\text{Duration of hedged gilt}}{\text{Duration of Treasury } 11\frac{3}{4}\%} \times \frac{\text{Price of hedged gilt}}{\text{Price of Treasury } 11\frac{3}{4}\%}$$

$$\times \frac{1 + \text{Redemption yield of hedged gilt}}{1 + \text{Redemption yield of Treasury } 11\frac{3}{4}\%}$$

Volatility rather than duration is often used with UK gilt hedging as a measure of the interest rate sensitivity of a gilt-edged stock.

$$\text{Volatility} = -\frac{1}{P} \frac{dP}{dY}$$

$$\text{where } P = \text{gilt price}$$
$$Y = \text{redemption yield}$$
$$dP = \text{first differential of the gilt price with respect to yield.}$$

The appropriate hedge ratio for option hedging with volatilities can be found by observing that

$$d(\text{Hedged gilt price}) = V_H . P_H . dY_H$$
$$d(\text{Treasury } 11\frac{3}{4}\% \text{ price}) = V_{11\frac{3}{4}} . P_{11\frac{3}{4}} . dY_{11\frac{3}{4}}$$

Assuming that the absolute yield change is the same in each case, the relative change in price is given by

$$\frac{V_H . P_H}{V_{11\frac{3}{4}} . P_{11\frac{3}{4}}}$$

There is a direct relationship between the duration of a specific bond and its volatility.

$$\text{Volatility} = \text{Duration}/1 + \text{Redemption yield}$$

In the United States, volatility is often called modified duration. However, with the exception of the use of the conversion factor of the cheapest to deliver gilt, all the standard hedging techniques apply with options on cash bonds. Similar hedging techniques will apply to bond options trading on other exchanges in Sydney, Tokyo, Amsterdam and Montreal.

# Chapter 9
# Integrating options into portfolios

## 1. Introduction

So far this book has discussed the general principles of hedging and trading with options, and examined how to price and use the various types of options. In all instances the discussion was of options either by themselves or in combination with a single underlying asset. Option strategies are frequently more complex than this. A stock portfolio manager may have hundreds of stocks in his portfolio, and may have written options against many of them; a London gilt portfolio manager may have written a combination of LIFFE gilt futures options and London Stock Exchange cash gilt options against a cash gilt portfolio, and so on. Such complex combined portfolios of the underlying assets, options and perhaps futures as well are not as easy to characterize in terms of risk and return. This is particularly so because the introduction of options into asset portfolios with their asymmetric return distributions produces complex expected return distributions which are impossible to classify by the usual measures of risk and return.

It is worth examining a two-asset portfolio of $1,000,000, half invested in IBM stock price $100 and half in General Motors at $50.

**Portfolio**
$500,000 = 5,000 IBM shares
$500,000 = 10,000 GM shares

The trader decides to write calls against the portfolio.

Sell 50 IBM calls   $100 strike price   Premium = $6
Sell 100 GM calls   $50 strike price   Premium = $4

Consider two alternative final positions.

*Alternative 1*
Final price IBM   $108
Final price GM   $51

$$\text{Value of stock portfolio} = \$1,050,000$$
$$\text{Loss on 50 IBM calls} = (\$6-\$8)\,(5,000)$$
$$= -\$10,000$$
$$\text{Gain on 100 GM calls} = (\$4-\$1)\,(10,000)$$
$$= \$10,000$$
$$\text{Net portfolio value} = \$1,050,000$$

*Alternative 2*
Final price IBM   $106
Final price GM   $54

$$\text{Value of stock portfolio} = \$1,070,000$$
$$\text{Position on IBM calls} = (\$6-\$6)\,(5,000) = 0$$
$$\text{Position on GM calls} = (\$4-\$4)\,(10,000) = 0$$
$$\text{Net portfolio value} = \$1,070,000$$

The point is obvious: the expected returns to the portfolio depend upon the expected values of all the stocks in the portfolio. An interesting example would be alternative purchases of a portfolio on individual stocks and a stock index put at the same effective price.

**Example**

$500.000    5,000 IBM at $100
$500,000   10,000 GM at $50
S & P 500 level = 200.00

For the sake of simplicity, assume the betas of both IBM and GM are 1.0.

*Either*   Buy 50 IBM 100 puts   Premium = $5
+
Buy 100 GM 50 puts   Premium = $3.50

*Or*   Buy $\dfrac{\$1,000,000}{200 \times \$500}$ S & P 500 puts = 10 puts

Premium = 12

**Final 1**

IBM price = $95
GM price = $40
S & P value = 175.00
Portfolio value = $875,000
% fall = 12.5
% fall in S & P 500 index = 12.5
Loss on IBM put = ($5 − $5) (5,000) = 0
Gain on GM put = ($10 − $3.50)(10,000) = $65,000
Net gain = $65,000
Net portfolio value = $940,000
Gain on S & P put = (25 − 12) ($500) (10)
= $65,000
Net portfolio value = $940,000

**Final 2**

IBM price = $70
GM price = $52.50
S & P value = 175.00
Portfolio value = $875,000
% fall = 12.5
% fall in S & P 500 index = 12.5
Gain on IBM put = ($30 − $5) (5,000) = $125,000
Gain on GM put = ($0.00 − $3.50) (10,000) = −$35,000
Net gain = $90,000
Net portfolio value = $965,000
Gain on S & P put = (25 − 12) ($500) (10)
= $65,000
Net portfolio value = $940,000

This example brings out a major point: the way in which a specific change in a cash portfolio occurs, i.e. by what combination of individual asset price changes, will affect the profit/loss profile of the combined options-assets position.

## 2. The characterization of complex portfolios

The simplest characterization of a combined option-asset portfolio is to use the concept of share equivalents. The delta of an option defines exactly that in terms of short-term risk and return.

**Example**
**Portfolio**

| | |
|---|---|
| Long 2,000 shares ICI | 600p |
| Long 5 ICI 575 calls | Premium 40p |
| | Delta 0.65 |
| Long 4 ICI 600 calls | Premium 22p |
| | Delta 0.50 |
| Long 10,000 shares Marks and Spencer | 225p |
| Long 5 M & S 200 puts | Premium 10p |
| | Delta 0.30 |

$$\text{ICI share equivalent} = 2{,}000 + (5{,}000)(0.65) + 4{,}000(0.50)$$
$$= 7{,}250$$
$$\text{ICI position investment} = £14{,}880.00$$
$$\text{M \& S share equivalent} = 10{,}000 - (5{,}000)(0.30)$$
$$= 8{,}500$$
$$\text{M \& S position investment} = £22{,}000$$

Thus the portfolio manager owns a portfolio of value £36,880.00 invested 59.7% in M & S and 40.3% in ICI. This has risk equivalent to a holding of 7,250 shares of ICI and 8,500 shares of M & S. To hold the cash equivalent portfolio would entail a net investment of £62,625.00.

The problem with the share equivalent approach is that technically it only determines the absolute risk for very short periods, since it will alter continuously as the share price and the volatility of the share price alter, and as the time to expiration changes. Over a longer period, the information set needed to calculate risks and returns will be the share equivalent for each underlying asset associated with each possible terminal asset price, and conditional on all other possible terminal asset prices.

There have been several approaches to handling this problem, but none of the analyses currently available is completely satisfactory. However, this is a rapidly developing field, and new and improved approaches will undoubtedly be developed over the next year or two. This section will briefly discuss three approaches.

1. The certainty equivalent approach: Cox and Rubinstein;[1]
2. Index and dispersion algorithms: Bookstaber and Clarke;[2] and
3. Multiple factor risk models: Evnine and Rudd.[3]

### a. Certainty equivalent method

Consider a situation where an investor is indifferent between a portfolio with a specific risk and return, and another investment with no risk and a specific return. The latter return is known as the *certainty equivalent return*, and the investor will want to choose the portfolio with the highest such return. With a combined options-assets portfolio the two measures of risk are the volatility, or variance, of return and the skewness of the return.

**Example**

| Event | Probability | Expected return |
|-------|-------------|-----------------|
| 1 | 0.2 | 5 |
| 2 | 0.6 | 10 |
| 3 | 0.2 | 15 |

$$\text{Mean return} = (0.2)(5) + (0.6)(10) + (0.2)(15)$$
$$= 10\%$$
$$\text{Standard deviation} = \sqrt{(0.2)(5 - 10)^2 + (0.6)(10 - 10)^2 + (0.2)(15 - 10)^2}$$
$$= \sqrt{10} = 3.16$$
$$\text{Skewness} = \sqrt[3]{(0.2)(5 - 10)^3 + (0.6)(10 - 10)^3 + (0.2)(15 - 10)^3}$$
$$= \sqrt[3]{0} = 0$$

Cox and Rubinstein suggest a useful approximation for calculating the certainty equivalent return of a portfolio when its mean return, standard deviation and skewness are known.

$$E\left(\frac{1}{1 - b} \hat{R}^{1 - b}\right) = \frac{1}{1 - b} m^{1 - b} - \tfrac{1}{2}bm^{-b-1}\sigma^2 + \tfrac{1}{6}b(b + 1)m^{-b-2}S^3$$

where $\hat{R} = (1 + \text{expected rate of return on the portfolio})$

$$E\left(\frac{1}{1 - b} \hat{R}^{1 - b}\right) = \text{expected utility}$$

$b = $ degree of risk aversion

$m = (1 + \text{mean portfolio rate of return})$

$\sigma^2 = $ variance of portfolio return

$S = $ skewness of return

[1] J. C. Cox and M. Rubinstein, *Options Markets*, Prentice-Hall (1985).
[2] R. M. Bookstaber and R. G. Clarke, *Option Strategies for Institutional Investment Management*, Addison-Wesley (1983).
[3] J. Evnine and A. Rudd, "Option portfolio risk analysis," *Journal of Portfolio Management*, 10, Winter 1984, 23–27.

Then the certainty equivalent return is found by solving

$$E\left[\frac{1}{1-b}\,\hat{R}^{1-b}\right] = \frac{1}{1-b}\,\bar{R}^{1-b}$$

where $\bar{R} - 1$ = certainty equivalent return.

### Example
Consider two portfolios

$$\begin{array}{llll} \text{A:} & m = 1.20 & \sigma = 10\% & S = 15\% \\ \text{B:} & m = 1.18 & \sigma = 5\% & S = 10\% \end{array}$$

**Portfolio A**

$$E\left(\frac{1}{1-b}\,\hat{R}^{1-b}\right) = \frac{1}{0.2}(1.20)^{0.2} - \tfrac{1}{2}(0.8)(1.20)^{-1.8}(0.10)^2 + \tfrac{1}{6}(0.8)(1.8)(1.20)^{-2.8}(0.15)^3$$

$$= 5.183292$$

$$\text{Certainty equivalent return} = [(5.183292)(0.20)]^5 - 1$$

$$= 19.73\%$$

**Portfolio B**

$$E\left(\frac{1}{1-b}\,\hat{R}^{1-b}\right) = \frac{1}{0.2}(1.18)^{0.2} - \tfrac{1}{2}(0.8)(1.18)^{-1.8}(0.05)^2 + \tfrac{1}{6}(0.8)(1.8)(1.18)^{-2.8}(0.10)^3$$

$$= 5.167693$$

$$\text{Certainty equivalent return} = [(5.167693)(0.20)]^5 - 1$$

$$= 17.93\%$$

The investor will clearly prefer portfolio A to portfolio B.

Cox and Rubinstein show that where investors and the market agree about the stock volatility,[4] the option's expected annual return over any holding period will be approximately the same, and equal to that implied by the elasticity of the option.

The annual return $r_c$ can be found from

$$\ln(1 + r_c) - \ln(1 + r_f) = \frac{S}{C}\Delta(\ln(1 + r_s) - \ln(1 + r_f))$$

where
$r_c$ = annual option return  $\quad C$ = option price
$r_f$ = *riskless rate*  $\quad\quad\quad \Delta$ = option delta
$S$ = stock price  $\quad\quad\quad\quad r_s$ = stock return

### Example
IBM stock price $150
150 call premium = $7   Delta = 0.50

Expected stock return = 15%
Riskless rate = 10%

$$\ln(1 + r_c) = \frac{150}{7}(0.5)[0.1397619 - 0.0953101] + 0.0953101$$

$$= 0.4762692 + 0.0953101$$

$$1 + r_c = 1.77106$$

$$\text{Expected option annual return} = 77\%$$

The expected annual return of the whole portfolio of stocks and options is then

$$r_p = \left[\sum_{j=1}^{n} w_j E(r_j)\right]$$

where  $w_j$ = proportion of portfolio in asset $j$
$E(r_j)$ = expected return on asset $j$

### Example
**Portfolio**
2,000 shares ICI 500p
Long 1 ICI 525 call   Premium = 30p
                      Delta    = 0.40

---

[4] See Cox and Rubinstein (*op. cit.*) for a description of expected returns when the investor has differing views to the market both on expected volatility and the under- or over-valuation of stock and option.

ICI beta = 1.1
3,000 shares M & S 220p
Short 2 M & S 225 puts   Premium = 20p
                          Delta    = −0.53

M & S beta = 0.90
Expected market return = 15%   Riskless rate = 8%

$$\text{Expected return ICI} = 8 + (1.1)(15 - 8) = 15.7\%$$

$$\text{Expected return ICI call} = \ln(1 + r_c) = \frac{500}{30}(0.40)[0.1458304 - 0.076961] + 0.076961$$

$$= 0.53609$$

$$r_c = 70.9\%$$

$$\text{Expected return M \& S} \quad 8 + 0.9(15 - 8) = 14.3\%$$

$$\text{Expected return M \& S put} = \ln(1 + r_p) = \frac{220}{20}(-0.53)[0.1336563 - 0.076961] + 0.076961$$

$$= -0.2535726$$

$$rp = -22.4\%$$

$$\text{Portfolio value} = (2,000)(5) + (1,000)(0.30)$$
$$+ (3,000)(2.20) - (2,000)(0.20)$$
$$= £16,500$$

$$\text{Expected portfolio return} = \left(\frac{10,000}{16,500}\right)(15.7) + \left(\frac{300}{16,500}\right)(70.9)$$
$$+ \left(\frac{6,600}{16,500}\right)(14.3) - \left(\frac{400}{16,500}\right)(-22.4)$$
$$= 17.1\%$$

What about the portfolio volatility and skewness? Cox and Rubinstein suggest the following approximations:

$$\sigma_\rho = \sqrt{\sum_{j=1}^{n} w_j^2(1 - \rho_j^2)\sigma_j^2 + \left[\sum_{j=1}^{N} w_j \rho_j \sigma_j\right]^2}$$

$$S = 3\sqrt{\left[\sum_{j=1}^{n} w_j^3\left\{1 - \left[\rho_j\left(\frac{\sigma_j}{\sigma_m}\right)\left(\frac{S_m}{S_j}\right)\right]^3\right\}S_j^3 + \left[\sum_{j=1}^{n} w_j\rho_j\left(\frac{\sigma_j}{\sigma_m}\right)\left(\frac{S_m}{S_j}\right)S_j\right]^3\right]}$$

where $w_j$ = portfolio weight of asset $j$
  $p_j$ = correlation of $j^{\text{th}}$ asset with market
  $\sigma_j$ = standard deviation of return asset $j$
  $S_j$ = skewness of return of asset $j$
  $\sigma_m$ = standard deviation of market return
  $S_m$ = skewness of market return

Consider a simple portfolio.

## Example
Riskless rate = 8%
Market risk = 10%        Market skewness = 2%
5,000 shares IBM         Expected return = 15%
                         Standard deviation = 8%
                         Skewness = 2%
                         Price = $150
Correlation with market = 0.70
Short 90 IBM options     Expected return = 60%
                         Standard deviation = 90%
                         Skewness = 15%
Premium = $7     Correlation with market = 0.5

$$\text{Expected return} = \frac{750,000(0.15) - 63,000(0.60)}{687,000}$$

$$= 0.1087 \ (10.87\%)$$

209

$$\text{Standard deviation} = \sqrt{\begin{array}{l}\left[\dfrac{750,000}{687,000}\right]^2 [1-(0.7)^2][0.08]^2 \\[2mm] +\left[\dfrac{63,000}{687,000}\right]^2 [1-(0.5)^2][0.90]^2 \\[2mm] +\left[\left(\dfrac{750,000}{687,000}\right)(0.7)(0.08)-\left(\dfrac{63,000}{687,000}\right)(0.5)(0.90)\right]^2\end{array}}$$

$$= 0.097 \ (9.7\%)$$

$$\text{Skewness} = \sqrt[3]{\begin{array}{l}\left[\dfrac{750,000}{687,000}\right]^3\left\{1-\left[0.7\left(\dfrac{0.08}{0.10}\right)\left(\dfrac{0.02}{0.02}\right)\right]^3\right\}(0.08)^3 \\[3mm] -\left[\dfrac{63,000}{687,000}\right]^3\left\{1-\left[0.5\left(\dfrac{0.90}{0.10}\right)\left(\dfrac{0.02}{0.15}\right)\right]^3\right\}(0.90)^3 \\[3mm] +\left[\left(\dfrac{750,000}{687,000}\right)(0.7)\left(\dfrac{0.08}{0.10}\right)\left(\dfrac{0.02}{0.02}\right)(0.02)-\left(\dfrac{63,000}{687,000}\right)(0.5)\left(\dfrac{0.90}{0.10}\right)\left(\dfrac{0.02}{0.15}\right)(0.15)\right]^3\end{array}}$$

$$= 0.0816 \ (8.2\%)$$

This is thus a reasonably complete description of the assets-option portfolio.

$$\text{Return} = 10.87\% \qquad \text{Risk} = 9.7\% \qquad \text{Skewness} = 8.2\%$$

As before, if the degree of risk aversion of the investor is known, the certainty equivalent of the portfolio can be determined. Assume $b = 0.5$

$$E\frac{1}{1-b}\hat{R}^{1-b} = \frac{1}{0.5}(1.1087)^{0.5} - \tfrac{1}{2}(0.5)(1.1087)^{-1.5}(0.097)^2 + \tfrac{1}{6}(0.5)(1.5)(1.1087)^{-2.5}(0.082)^3$$

$$= 2.103935$$

$$\text{Certainty equivalent return} = [(2.103935)(0.5)]^2 - 1$$

$$= 10.66\%$$

Although full of approximations, the method just discussed provides a quick way to characterize a complex portfolio, and it will probably be used increasingly in the future.

### b. Index and dispersion algorithms

The approach taken by Bookstaber and Clarke is along similar lines, but involves the use of computer simulation algorithms to determine the complete return distribution of the complex portfolio. They explore two algorithms: what they call the *index algorithm* and a slightly more complex *dispersion algorithm*.

The index algorithm, like the Cox and Rubinstein approach, depends on the single index market model.

$$R_j = R_f(1 - \beta_j) + \beta_j R_m + u_t$$

where $R_j =$ expected return on the stock
$\qquad R_f =$ riskless rate
$\qquad \beta_j =$ systematic risk (beta) of the stock
$\qquad R_m =$ expected return to market
$\qquad u_t =$ random error term

The method determines the return on the stocks on which options have been purchased or written by a weighted average of the return, given exercise of the option, and the return if the option is not exercised. As shown in Bookstaber and Clarke (*op. cit.*) the procedure is:

*Step 1:* Compute the expected return on the portfolio conditional on a specific market return.

*Step 2*: Assign a cumulative probability to the portfolio return equal to the probability of the market return.

*Step 3*: Repeat for all possible market returns.

The dispersion algorithm broadens the assumptions by dropping the market model assumption that the random error terms are independent across securities. In this case, the return distribution of the optioned portfolio depends on two distributions – the distribution of returns to the individual stocks, and the distribution measuring the dispersion of stock returns, both assumed to be normal distributions.

The actual computer algorithms will not be discussed here (the interested reader should consult Bookstaber and Clarke, *op. cit.*). The method, however, provides a means of presenting investors with the complete return distributions of different complex portfolios to allow him to choose the portfolio that best suits him. As Bookstaber and Clarke point out, portfolios with the same mean, standard deviation and skewness can have profit-loss profiles that look very different.

## c. Multiple factor risk models

This approach (see Evnine and Rudd, *op. cit.*) tries to extend the factor approach to modelling asset and asset portfolio returns (the market model mentioned above is a typical example of a single factor model) to complex portfolios including options and assets.

Evnine and Rudd suggest the following basic structure for such a model:

$$r_c - r_f = W(r_s - r_f) + \sum_{i=1}^{n} X_i . F_i^* + u_{ct}$$

where

$r_c$ = return on call option

$r_f$ = riskless rate

$W$ = elasticity of option $= \dfrac{S}{C} . \Delta$

$\Delta$ = option delta

$r_s$ = return on stock

$F_1^*, ..., F_n^*$ = common factors that account for the non-equity nature of options

$u_{ct}$ = random error term

Then $(rs - rf)$ can be substituted by any multi-factor model for asset returns themselves. The model suggested by Evnine and Rudd is

$$r_c - r_f = (\hat{r}_c - r_f) + W(r_s - r_f) + \alpha_1 . \beta_s^2 \, MKTSQR$$
$$+ \alpha_2 . DELR + \alpha_3 . DELVAR + CONS$$
$$+ \alpha_4 . DURG + \alpha_1 . \sigma_s^2 RES\, 2$$
$$+ b_1 . OTM + b_2 . SHRT + b_3 . LONG + \varepsilon_c$$

This looks – and is – complicated. Consider the terms:

$\hat{r}_c$ = the return the option would achieve if all the other factors realized zero return.

$\beta_s^2 MKTSQR$ = square of stock's systematic return.

$\sigma_s^2 . RES\, 2$ = adjusted non-systematic risk of the stock return.

$DELR$ = proportional prediction error in the interest rate, i.e. actual realized rate minus forward rate.

$DELVAR$ = proportional change in market implied variance.

$DURG$ = measures extent to which option price biases are self-correcting.

$CONS$ = autonomous option market factor.

$OTM$ = out-of-the-money factor, $\quad b_1 = 0$ or $1$

$SHRT$ = short maturity factor $\quad\quad b_2 = 0$ or $1$

$LONG$ = long maturity factor $\quad\quad b_3 = 0$ or $1$

The model could be redefined for puts and calls as appropriate.

Models of this kind allow the investor to compare the risk and returns of portfolios along the different factors. Thus, a stock portfolio might be characterized by its expected return, its standard deviation and its beta. A portfolio with stocks and options might have additional exposure to $MKTSQR$, a measurement of skewness, $DELVAR$, a measure of volatility exposure, and $CONS$, a measure of general option market exposure. The system, like all factor models, allows the development of performance measurement statistics and possibly portfolio optimization rules to determine the single best portfolio. A typical example, as mentioned in Evnine and Rudd, would be the determination of optimal portfolio insurance: determining the factor characteristics of the desired portfolio put and then duplicating them with portfolios of actual stock index and individual stock options.

This section attempts to give an intuitive idea of the possible approaches to characterizing the risk and return of complex portfolios involving both assets and options. Most of these ideas are relatively new, not yet fully developed, and capable of further improvement and developments over the next few years. It is an important area because of the many types of portfolio management strategies that are increasingly being implemented (see the next section). There are serious dangers in such strategies if the basic risk-return characteristics are not fully identifiable.

## 3. Option portfolio strategies

There are innumerable ways in which options of all kinds can be combined with assets to build portfolios with different characteristics. This section discusses some of the more common approaches.

### a. Return enhancement strategies

These broadly involve call writing programmes against an existing asset portfolio. Various approaches can be adopted.

### (i) *Fully covered portfolio call writing strategies*

Perpetually write individual asset call options to the full extent of the holdings of the underlying assets, and let the options run through to expiration. This is usually done with a holding period corresponding to the normal option expiration cycle. It can be considered a conservative strategy, since it will reduce losses if asset prices fall at the expense of giving up potential asset gains since the asset will be called away if the call expires in-the-money.

### (ii) *Individual stock call writing*

Write individual asset call options to the full or partial extent of holdings of individual assets in line with the portfolio manager's view of the short-term price evolution of the individual stock. If there is an intention to repurchase options in the short-term this is *volatility trading*; if there is an intention to maintain the option positions to expiration, this is a *bearish to neutral price trade*. The risk characteristic of this type of trading will depend on the option writing programme decisions. The portfolio characteristics will be complex.

### (iii) *Writing index options*

Write asset index options against the full or partial value of the overall asset portfolio. This has the effect of retaining some of the non-systematic risk of the individual assets, while being a conservative strategy in terms of the systematic performance of the portfolio. The portfolio characteristics are simpler to assess because index options and the underlying portfolio systematic component can be analysed as options on a single asset. This strategy is becoming increasingly common.

### b. Cash-option strategies

### (i) *90–10 call portfolios*

This is one of the more famous option buying strategies and involves putting 90% of the portfolio into money market instruments and using the remaining 10% of the funds to buy a portfolio of individual asset call options. This should lower the downside risk of the overall portfolio, and has proved capable in the past of generating a higher return than an equivalent asset portfolio. Different proportions of cash and call options could be used, and there is a growing tendency with stock investment to look at 90% cash and 10% stock index call options. This effectively removes the non-systematic risk of the standard 90–10 strategy with individual stock call options.

### (ii) *Cash-put write portfolios*

An alternative cash-options strategy is to write a portfolio of put options, and invest enough in cash to always be able to purchase the underlying assets if the puts are exercised. This could be achieved with portfolios of individual stock puts or with stock index puts. With stock index options being subject to a cash settlement system, the cash requirements for the strategy may not be so severe. The investor can also experiment with different quantities of put writes for a specific amount of available cash. These strategies tend to be very conservative.

### c. Asset-option buy strategies

#### (i) Protective put strategies

An alternative to the 90–10 call buying strategy is the protective put strategy, where the original portfolio is divided into long asset positions and puts purchased to provide a guaranteed selling price. A full strategy would involve a cash portfolio and a complete set of put options purchased to cover all the asset holdings on a continuous basis. This will effectively create a portfolio of synthetic call options, and so should give similar risk-return results to the 90–10 call buying strategy. Some investors may buy only protective puts against a proportion of the portfolio assets, or may buy protective index put options to cover the whole value or partial value of the portfolio. An interesting strategy along these lines is the so-called *naked blue lightning bolt* (Exhibit 9.1), involving the regular purchase of insurance index puts in a rising market at increasing exercise prices, i.e. as the market or individual stocks advance, some of the profit is used on a regular basis to buy insurance.

**Exhibit 9.1: Naked blue lightning bolt**

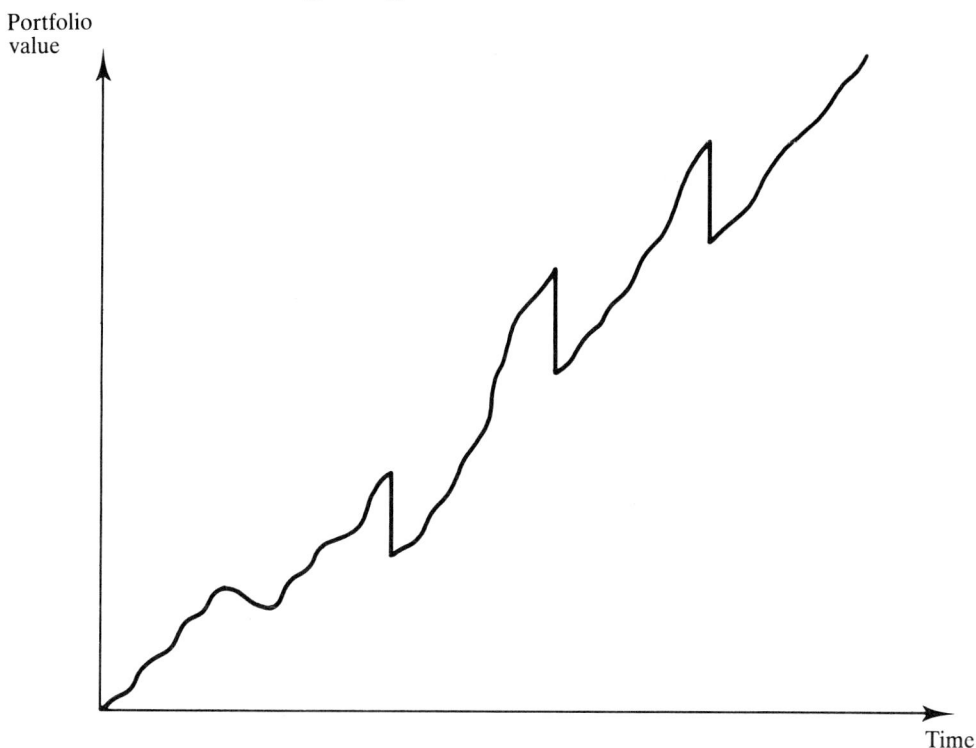

Overall portfolio insurance for a large portfolio of money assets and over a long period may be difficult to obtain directly. As mentioned earlier, it will then be the task of the portfolio manager to construct a portfolio of index and individual options which will behave as closely as possible like the required portfolio put. The willingness of several financial institutions to offer bond and stock portfolio insurance would indicate that they believe this can be achieved.

#### (ii) Synthetic put strategies

When listed put options are not available, protective portfolio strategies could involve synthetic puts constructed by selling shares short and buying call options. The principles are the same as in strategy 2.[5]

#### (iii) Asset-protective put-call write strategies

The combination of the long asset portfolio with protective puts creates artificial calls; one can further turn this into an artificial vertical bull spread by selling a listed call option at a higher effective exercise price. This reduces the cost of the protective put for the price of reducing the potential profit if the portfolio value rises further. An interesting use of this strategy would be if the investor believed the market had somewhat further to go but his individual stocks were going

---

[5] For an interesting discussion of synthetic puts, see J. C. Singleton and R. Grieves, "Synthetic puts and portfolio insurance strategies," *Journal of Portfolio Management*, .

to outperform the market comfortably. He could use the asset-protective put strategy with individual stock options, but use the call write with a higher exercise price stock index call option.

## d. Options-options and options-futures strategies

### (i) The relative performance portfolio

One way of preserving the relative performance of a cash portfolio and getting rid of the market-related performance is by trading stock index futures and options against it. But why use the cash market at all? Why not use the following strategies:

Relatively bullish    Buy individual stock call options.
Sell against them stock index futures or call options.
Relatively bearish    Buy individual stock put options.
Buy stock index futures or sell stock index puts.

Appropriately weighted this will give a net portfolio relative strength position.

### (ii) Futures – artificial cash arbitrage

Programmed trading involves arbitrage between the stock index futures market and the cash market. Instead of duplicating the index with a cash portfolio, it could be duplicated with a set of artificial stock positions created by buying calls and selling puts for a long position or selling calls and buying puts for a short position. Many arbitrageurs are now operating in this way as an alternative to using cash portfolios in arbitrage.

These are just a few of the option portfolio strategies that could be adopted. Although this section has concentrated on stock and stock index options, similar strategies can be adopted with all the other financial options. In more complex strategies, using the different types of options, the yield gap could be traded by buying or selling stock index options simultaneously with long bond options; currency options could be used by a UK investor, to remove currency risk from a US stock portfolio, and so on. The use of options greatly widens the number of strategies available to the financial manager.

## 4. Performance measurement with options

Much work has been done on methods of measuring the performance of cash portfolios, whether equities or fixed interest portfolios. One example is the so-called Fama decomposition[6] for equity portfolios. This attempts to break the excess return to a stock portfolio down into returns due to market timing, returns due to the taking on of additional diversifiable risk, and returns due to net selection of stocks.

Consider a stock portfolio:

Trustee's desired beta = 0.75

*Ex post performance*

| | | | |
|---|---|---|---|
| Riskless rate | = 10% | Portfolio average beta | = 0.90 |
| Market return | = 16% | Portfolio return | = 22% |
| Market standard deviation | = 10% | Portfolio standard deviation | = 12% |

### Step 1

Determine return to a portfolio consisting only of the market portfolio and the riskless asset using the trustee's desired beta.

$$Rp = (0.75)(16) + (0.25)(10) = 14.5\%$$

$$\text{Excess return} = 22\% - 14.5\% = 7.5\%$$

### Step 2: Return to market timing

Measure return to a portfolio consisting only of the market portfolio and the riskless asset with actual average beta of 0.90.

$$Rp = (0.90)(16) + (0.10)(10) = 15.4\%$$

$$\text{Market timing return} = 15.4\% - 14.5\% = 0.9\%$$

---

[6] E. F. Fama, "Components of investment performance", *Journal of Finance*, 27, June 1972, 551–67.

This is the additional return because the manager put more money in risky assets than his trustees would have done acting on their own.

## Step 3: Return to diversifiable risk

Measure return to a portfolio consisting only of the market portfolio and the riskless asset which has the same standard deviation as the actual portfolio.

To get standard deviation of 12%, you need 120% of your wealth in the market with a risk of 10% and minus 20% in the riskless asset (i.e. borrowing).

$$Rp = (1.20)(16) + (-0.20)(10) = 16.7\%$$

$$\text{Diversifiable risk return} = 16.7\% - 15.4\% = 1.3\%$$

The manager has earned an additional 1.3% from his willingness to purchase a less than fully diversified portfolio.

## Step 4: Return to stock selection

Any remaining excess return is the additional return from picking individual stocks which was not paid for with an increased risk to the portfolio.

$$\text{Stock selection return} = 22\% - 16.7\% = 5.3\%$$

Hence the complete performance breakdown can be written

Benchmark portfolio return = 14.5%
Actual portfolio return = 22.0%
Excess return = 7.5%
 of which, Market timing return    = 0.9%
      Return to diversifiable risk = 1.3%
      Return to net selection    = 5.3%

This is a favourable performance by the portfolio manager.

The problem with applying this type of portfolio performance assessment when options are included in the portfolio is that historic betas are not really applicable to portfolios containing options because the risk characteristics of the options change continuously through time as price, volatility and time to expiration changes.

For individual stock options, it is possible to measure the instantaneous beta of the option assuming the beta of the stock is known.

$$\text{Option beta} = \text{Stock beta} \times \text{Option delta} \times \frac{\text{Price of stock}}{\text{Price of option}}$$

The performance of the portfolio on a daily basis can then be assessed using the total beta of the portfolio relative to a daily capital asset pricing model security line.

### Example

*Day 1* Riskless rate = 10% per annum
   Market return = 12% per annum

*Portfolio* Long $1,000,000 IBM Price = $150
           Beta  = 1.10
    Short 4 $150 IBM  Options price = $7
           Delta = 0.50

$$\text{Overall option beta} = 1.10 \times 0.50 \times \frac{150}{7} = 11.8$$

$$\text{Portfolio investment value} = \$1,000,000 - \$28,000$$
$$= \$972,000$$

$$\text{Portfolio beta} = \frac{1,000,000}{972,000}(1.10) - \frac{36,000}{972,000}(11.8)$$
$$= 0.695$$

$$\text{Expected daily return} = \frac{10\%}{365} + 0.695\left(\frac{12-10}{365}\right)$$
$$= 0.0312\%$$

$$\text{Expected annual return} = 11.4\%$$

The difference between the actual return on the combined asset-option portfolio and the expected return is the measure of above or below average performance. The problem with this technique is that the excess returns will be composed partly of the returns to net option selection and partly of the result of not adjusting the expected return (i.e. the instantaneous beta) continuously but only at daily intervals. To solve this problem Galai (1984) has suggested a decomposition approach involving the use of the riskless option hedge. He shows that the rate of return on a call option can be decomposed through the following expression.

$$r_c = r_f + \varepsilon_{t-1}(r_{vt} - r_f) + u_t + r_{gt}$$

where   $r_f$ = short-term daily riskless rate

$\varepsilon_{t-1}$ = elasticity of option estimated at $t - 1$

$r_{vt}$ = actual return on underlying stock on day $t$

$u_t$ = random return due to non-continuous adjustment of hedge

$r_{gt}$ = return to net selectivity, i.e. from identifying undervalued and overvalued options

There is a close relationship between the two approaches.

Beta-adjustment model

$$E(r_{ct}) = r_f + h_t \frac{V_{t-1}}{C_{t-1}} (E(r_{vt}) - r_f)$$

where $E(.)$ = expectations operator

$C_t$ = price of call in period $t$

$V_t$ = price of stock in period $t$

$h_t$ = option delta

Decomposition model

$$r_{ct} = r_f + h_t \frac{V_{t-1}}{C_{t-1}} (R_{vt} - R_f) + C_{t-1}(\eta_t - r_{gt})$$

$$\eta_t = r_{ct} - E(r_{ct})$$

Hence excess return on the option in the beta model is composed of a time adjustment element; in the decomposition model, it is composed of a selectivity element.

Both these methods can be used to measure the performance of a combined option stock portfolio. The beta model can be used to measure the excess return of a stock option portfolio on a daily or weekly basis. The decomposition model can be used to distinguish how much the return to an option portfolio is due to the ability to buy undervalued options and sell overvalued options. For a combined stock options portfolio, the return is achieved because the proportion of stock was different to that necessary for a riskless hedge. In the example above, the delta of 0.5 suggests a ratio of one share of stock to two options. In fact the ratio was

$$\frac{\$1,000,000/\$150}{4,000} = 1.67 \text{ shares} - 1 \text{ option}$$

In other words, what is happening is the following return breakdown.

Portfolio return = Return to net asset position

+

Return to riskless hedge

+/−

Return because rebalancing is not
carried out continuously

+/−

Return to option selection

The return to the net asset position can be analysed further using the Fama decomposition. A similar approach could be used for interest rate options in conjunction with a bond or money market portfolio, with the net asset position being analysed through one of the bond portfolio performance measurement systems available. As the use of options in combination with

216

underlying cash portfolios widens, there will be further developments in option performance measurement. One example would be the development of performance measures for the type of cashless relative strength portfolio discussed earlier, where individual stock options are combined with stock index futures or options positions.

## 5. Empirical tests of option portfolio strategies

Despite the increasing use of options strategies, and the development of integrated cash and options strategies, there has been little formal study of how effective options strategies are in improving risk and returns, or how much better or worse they are than pure cash strategies. The most important studies to date have been two papers by Merton, Scholes and Gladstein (1978, 1982).[7] Both these studies use simulated options prices using the traditional Black-Scholes model rather than actual options prices. The first strategy they examine is that of fully covered writing of options against two portfolios of stock – the 136 listed stocks on which options were available as of December 1975, and the Dow Jones 30 stock market index. The assumption is that six-month options are written and the options are not exercised prior to maturity. The graphs in Exhibit 9.2, taken from the 1978 article, show the pattern of portfolio values with covered call writing for the two portfolios, and different degrees of in- or out-of-the-money levels for the option: $E = 1.20$ indicates an exercise price of 120% of the underlying stock price, $E = 0.90$ indicates 90%.

The basic conclusions are that the policy of writing covered calls substantially reduces the risk, or standard deviation, of returns to the portfolio by about 70% for the in-the-money strategy down to about 25% for the deep out-of-the-money strategy. There was a reduction in return compared to the stock portfolios of about the same magnitude as the reduction in risk. Because of the skewness properties of options portfolios, the impact upon returns was not symmetric – the lowest returns for options strategies lay above the lowest return for the stock portfolios by a much smaller margin than the best returns lay below the best stock portfolio returns.

The second call option strategy tested was the 90-10 buying strategy, i.e. 10% of the portfolio is allocated to call purchases and 90% to investment in prime commercial paper. Different stock portfolios are examined and different stock price-exercise price ratios used. The graphs in Exhibit 9.3 show the relative performance of the various portfolios. Here, the results are more favourable for the option buyer: for the in-the-money options, the overall portfolio returns are significantly higher than for the stock portfolios and the standard deviations of returns significantly less. A study of one period is hardly sufficient evidence on which to base a portfolio strategy, but the 90-10 strategy was extremely successful in the July 1963–December 1975 period.

The second paper looks at put options strategies in a similar way, examining in turn uncovered put writing strategies, insurance strategies of protecting a stock portfolio with put purchases, and conversion strategies. The simulation period was July 1963 to June 1977.

The put writing strategies involve a combination of written puts and sufficient cash invested in commercial paper to guarantee that the writer will be able to purchase all the shares if the puts are exercised. However, because of the frequency of early exercise of American puts, puts where the model indicates that early exercise would occur are repurchased at that point for their in-the-money value. Otherwise, all options positions are carried to expiration. The graphs in Exhibit 9.4 show the results of the put writing strategies. As expected the put writing results behave very much like the covered call writing strategies: option portfolio risks are substantially less than those of the stock portfolio at the expense of substantially lower returns. The degree of risk reduction is rather more than for the covered call writing programmes, because the lower degree of leverage and the early exercise assumption tends to push down the return variance.

Protective put buying strategies are equivalent to buying synthetic calls. The simulation was carried out along the lines discussed above. The return patterns are shown in the graphs in Exhibit 9.5. As expected, all strategies had lower risks than the underlying stock portfolio. In all cases, the reduction in risk was paid for with a significant reduction in overall return, though the compound growth of the portfolio was sometimes higher. Over the longer period, the option-paper buying programmes continued to outperform both the stock portfolios and the put buying programmes.

---

[7] R. C. Merton, M. S. Scholes and M. L. Gladstein, "The returns and risks of alternative call option portfolio investment strategies," *Journal of Business*, 1978, vol. 51, no. 2, 183–242; "The returns and risks of alternative put-option portfolio investment strategies," *Journal of Business*, 1982, vol. 55, no. 1, 1–55.

## Exhibit 9.2: Performance of fully covered writing strategies

**a. Growth of $1,000 in each of four fully covered strategies and stock (136-stock sample).**

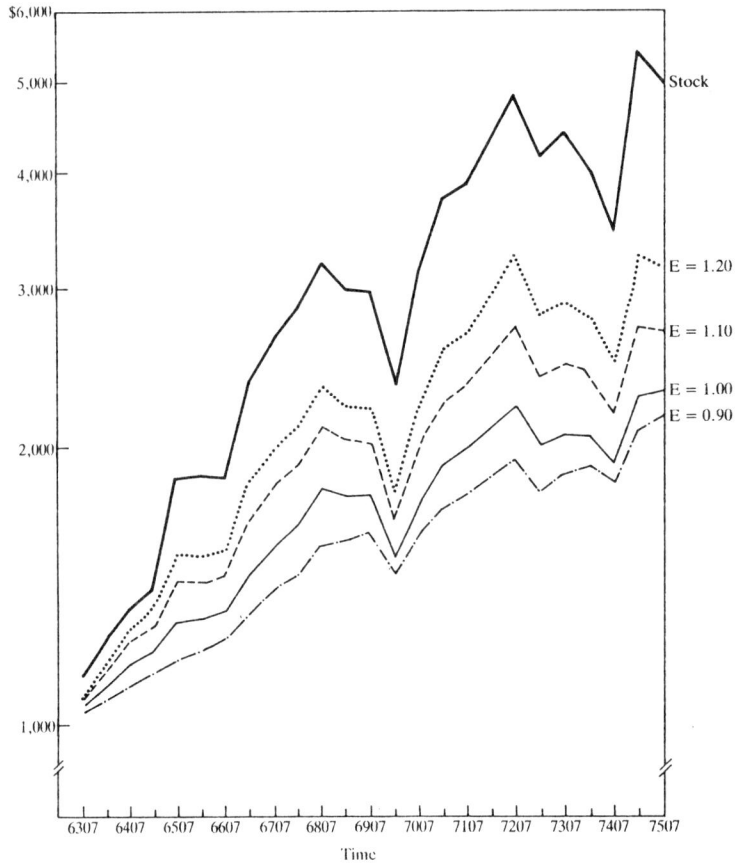

**b. Growth of $1,000 in each of four fully covered strategies and stock (DJ sample).**

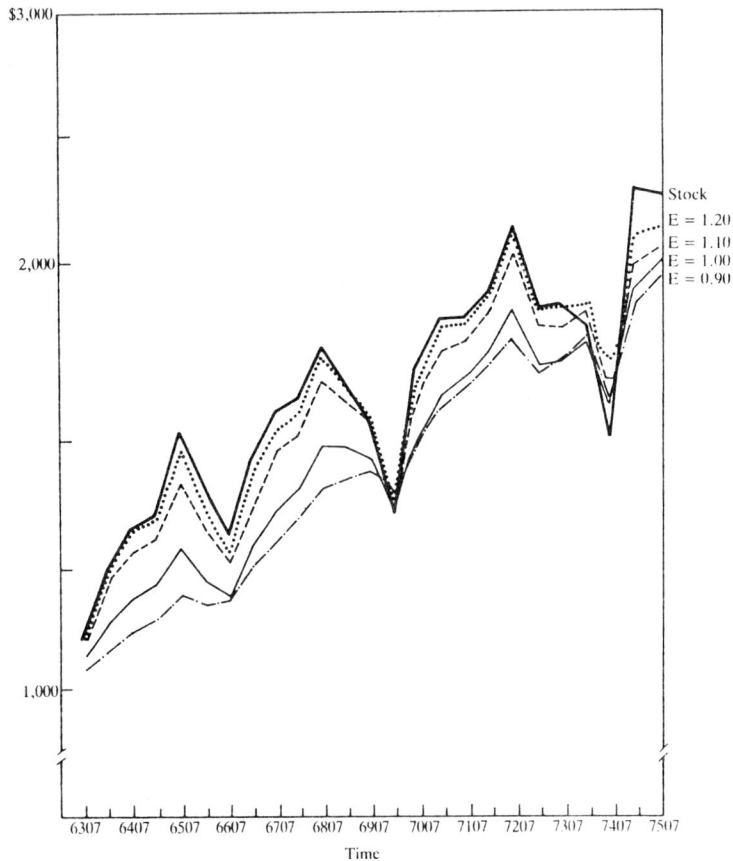

Merton, Sholes & Gladstein, "The Returns and Risks of Alternative Call-Option Portfolio Investment Strategies," *Journal of Business* 1978, vol. 51, no. 2, pp. 183–243, figs. 4, 5, 7, 8. © by The University of Chicago. All rights reserved. And by kind permission of the authors.

218

# Exhibit 9.3: Performance of 90–10 strategies

## a. Growth of $1,000 in each of four options/paper strategies and stock (136-stock sample).

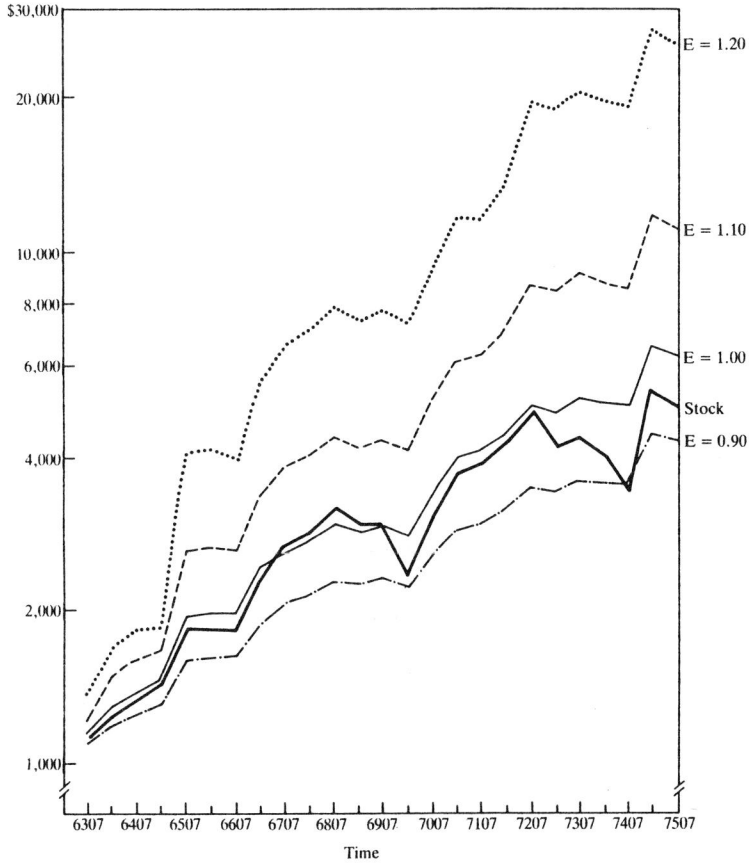

## b. Growth of $1,000 in each of four options/paper strategies and stock (DJ sample).

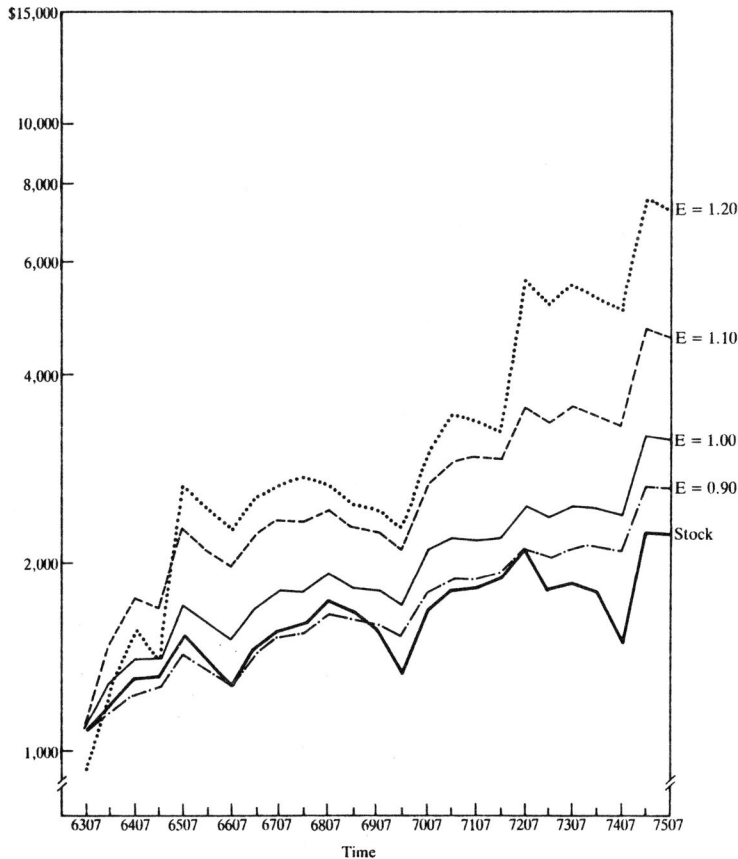

Merton, Sholes & Gladstein, "The Returns and Risks of Alternative Call-Option Portfolio Investment Strategies," *Journal of Business* 1978, vol. 51, no. 2, pp. 183–243, figs. 4, 5, 7, 8. © by The University of Chicago. All rights reserved. And by kind permission of the authors.

**Exhibit 9.4: Performance of uncovered put writing strategies**

a. Growth of $1,000 invested in each of three uncovered put strategies and stock (136-stock sample).

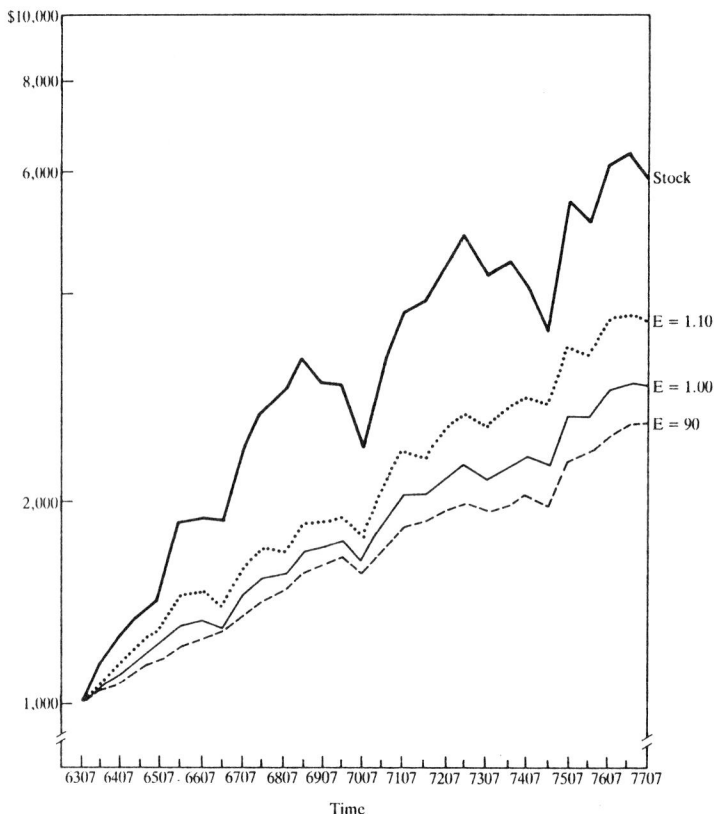

b. Growth of $1,000 invested in each of three uncovered put strategies and stock (DJ sample).

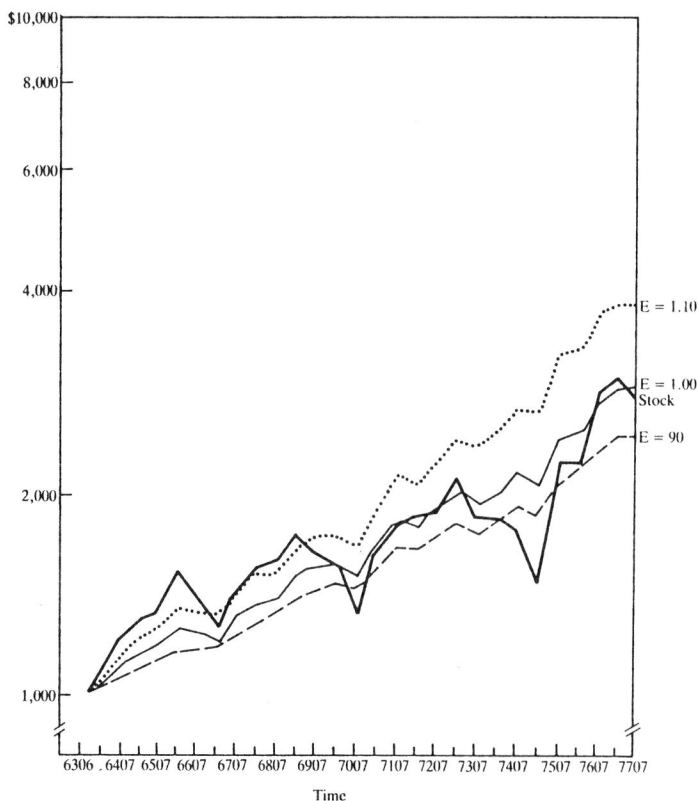

Merton, Sholes & Gladstein, "The Returns and Risks of Alternative Put-Option Portfolio Investment Strategies," *Journal of Business* 1982, vol. 55, no. 1, pp. 1–55, figs. 10, 11, 12, 13. © by The University of Chicago. All rights reserved. And by kind permission of the authors.

220

## Exhibit 9.5: Performance of protective put strategies

**a. Growth of $1,000 invested in each of three protective-put strategies and stock (136-stock sample).**

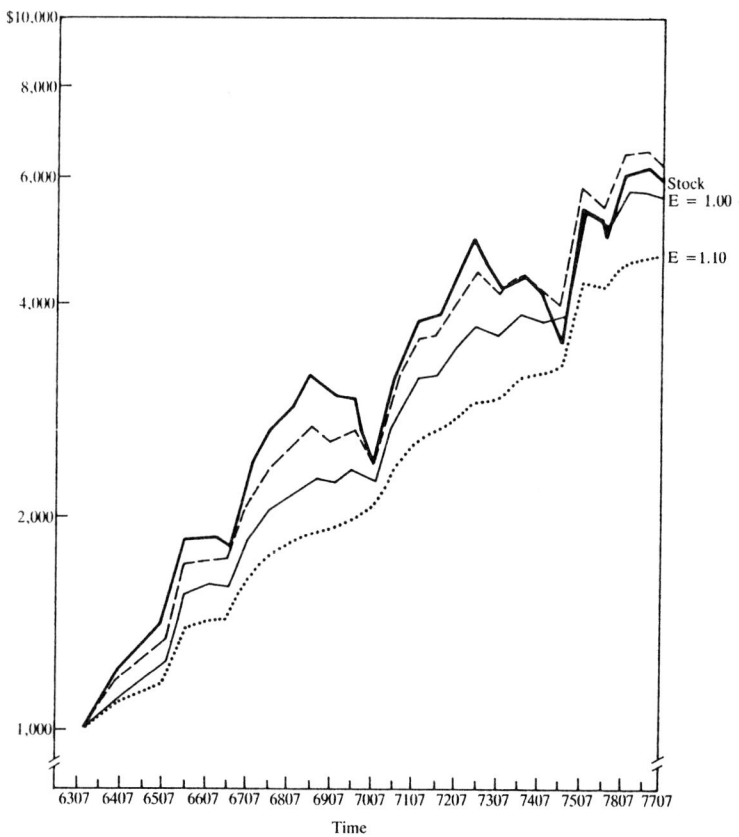

**b. Growth of $1,000 invested in each of three protective-put strategies and stock (DJ sample).**

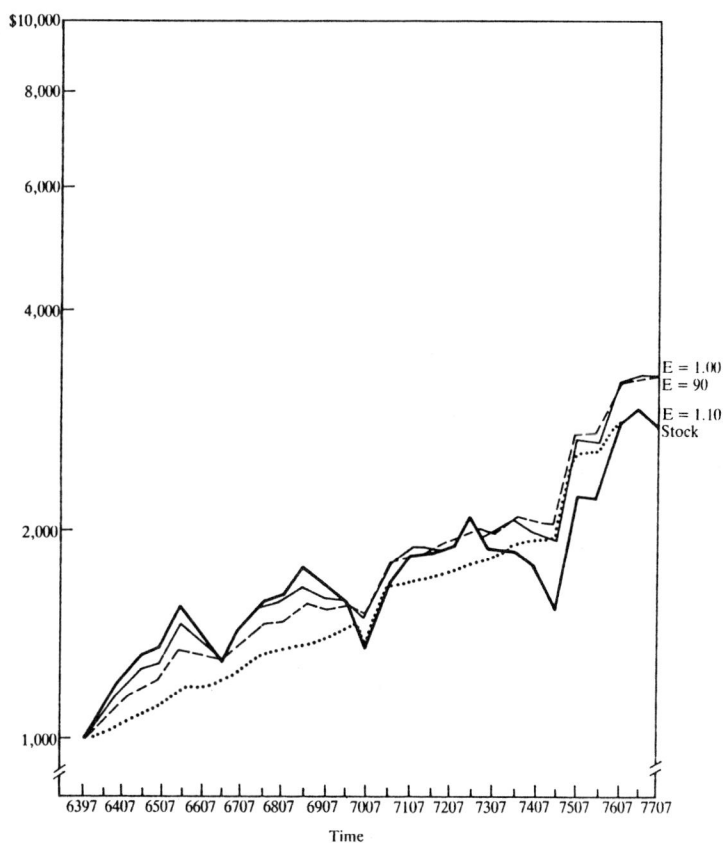

Merton, Sholes & Gladstein, "The Returns and Risks of Alternative Put-Option Portfolio Investment Strategies," *Journal of Business* 1982, vol. 55, no. 1, pp. 1–55, figs. 10, 11, 12, 13. © by the University of Chicago. All rights reserved. And by kind permission of the authors.

221

## Exhibit 9.6: Combined stock-option portfolio return distributions

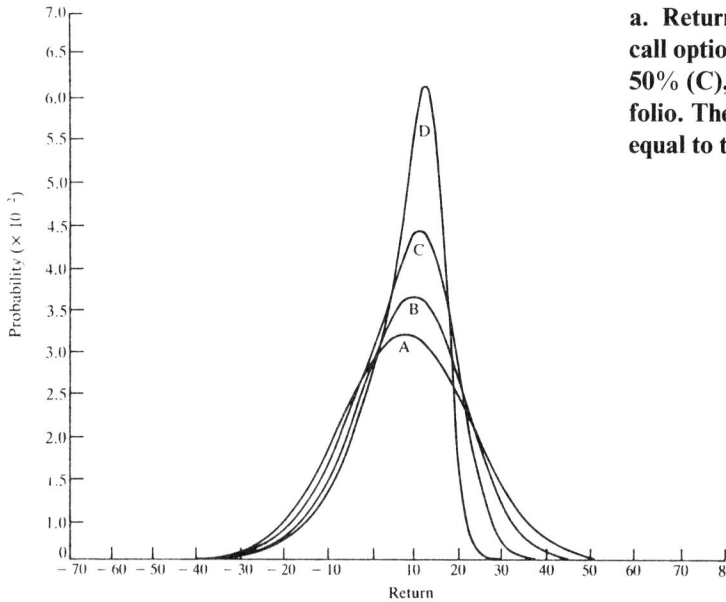

a. Return distribution of a portfolio with call options written on 0% (A), 25% (B), 50% (C), and 75% (D) of the stock portfolio. The exercise price of the options is equal to the current stock price.

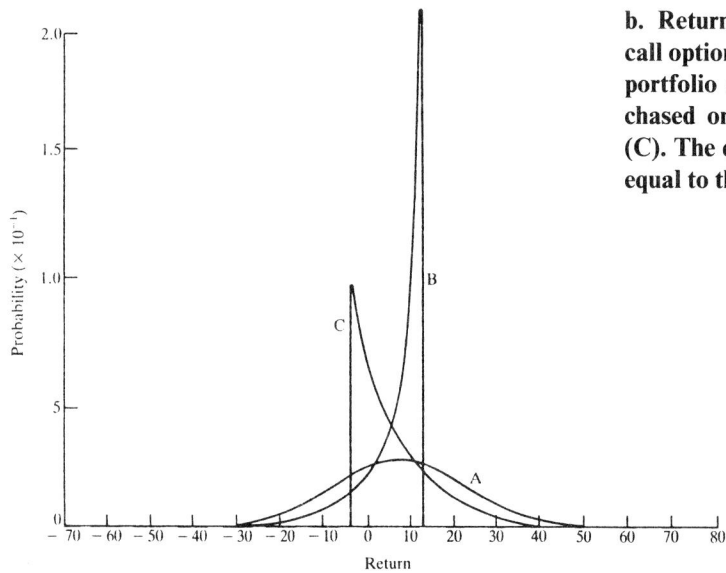

b. Return distribution of a portfolio with call options written on 100% of the stock portfolio (B), and with put options purchased on 100% of the stock portfolio (C). The exercise price of both options is equal to the current stock price.

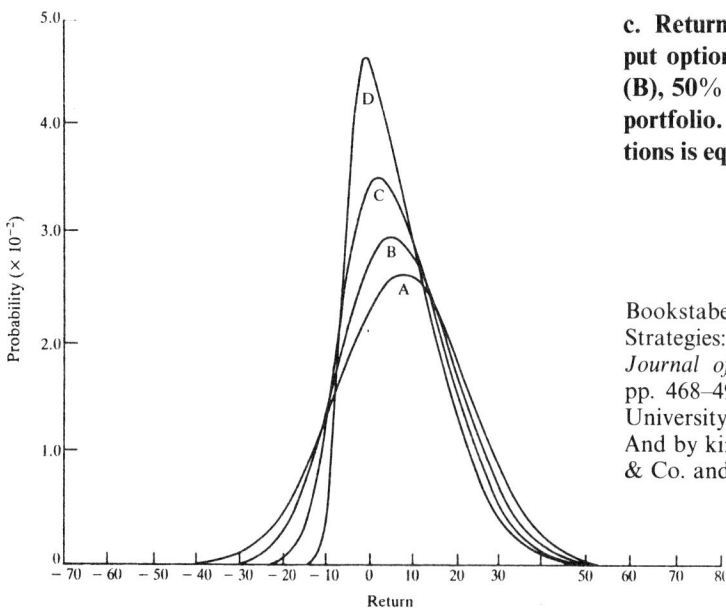

c. Return distribution of a portfolio with put options purchased on 0% (A), 25% (B), 50% (C), and 75% (D) of the stock portfolio. The exercise price of the options is equal to the current stock price.

## Exhibit 9.6: Combined stock-option portfolio return distributions

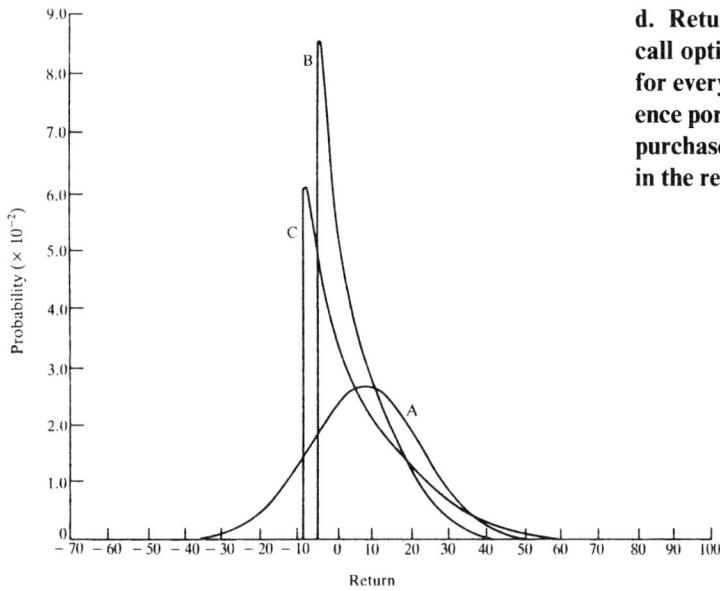

**d. Return distribution of a portfolio of call options, with 1.15 options purchased for every 100 shares of stock in the reference portfolio (B), and with 1.685 options purchased for every 100 shares of stock in the reference portfolio (C).**

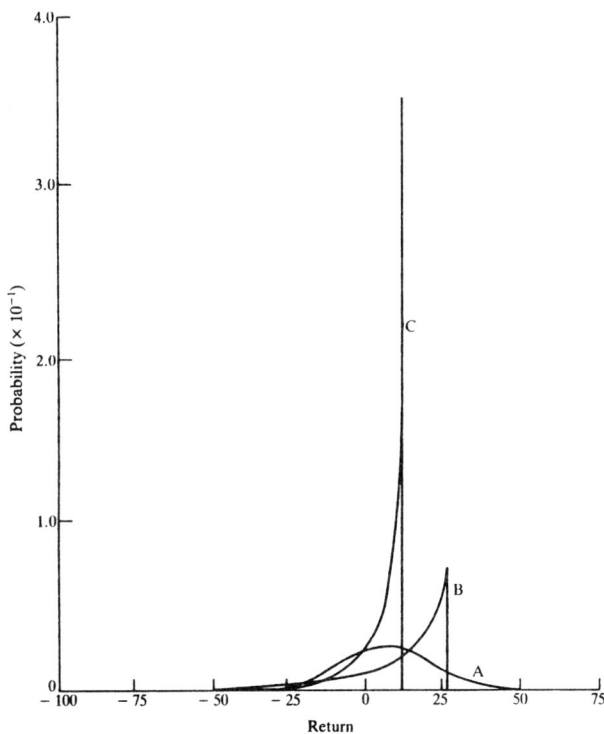

**e. Return distribution of a portfolio of uncovered puts, with 1.0 options sold for every 100 shares of stock in the reference portfolio (B), and with 2.46 options sold for every 100 shares of stock in the reference portfolio (C).**

Bookstaber & Clarke, "Option Portfolio Strategies: Measurement and Evaluation," *Journal of Business* 1984, vol. 57, no. 4, pp. 468–493, figs. 1, 2, 3, 4, 5. © by The University of Chicago. All rights reserved. And by kind permission of Morgan Stanley & Co. and the authors.

The following points may be noted:

1. Covered call writing programmes and put writing-paper programmes can substantially reduce the risk of stock portfolios at the expense of lower returns. The risk-returns will vary according to the stock price/exercise price ratios adopted. The put writing-paper programmes are more conservative than the covered call write programmes.
2. Call buying-paper programmes and put buying insurance programmes substantially reduce the risk of stock portfolios. Over the simulation period 1963–77, protective put programmes reduced both the return and risk of stock portfolios, and call buying-paper programmes were able to generate both lower risk and higher returns, especially with strategies using in-the-money options.
3. The skewness of the return distribution is significantly affected by the introduction of options, and hence a simple mean-variance analysis of return performance may not be appropriate.

Further work needs to be done in this area, particularly using actual options premiums, and taking transactions costs and taxes into account. Gastineau and Mandansky (1979) have been critical of the simulation approach, specifically because of the changes in the stock equivalent risk exposure over the simulation period. This problem with measuring performance of combined stock-option portfolios was referred to earlier. Nonetheless, the results provoke a good deal of thought.

A more recent article by Bookstaber and Clarke (1984) used a Monte Carlo simulation to look at the distribution of returns to various options strategies. The basic approach was discussed in the section on characterizing combined stock-option portfolios. The graphs in Exhibit 9.6 illustrate the Bookstaber-Clarke results, showing how option/stock portfolios generate portfolio return distributions which are too complex to be analysed in a mean-variance framework. This reinforces the earlier discussion of performance measurement.

# Chapter 10
# Accounting and taxation principles for options*

## 1. Accounting issues

Any deal involving options has accounting implications. This chapter highlights and discusses the various accounting matters which have to be resolved before accounts can be prepared. Legislation, accounting standards and taxation considerations are not internationally uniform and these all have a bearing on the accounting treatment which should be adopted. Markets in certain types of options, particularly commodities, have existed for a number of years while those for stock options and currency options are newer developments. Practice has thus developed at different rates in different countries. It is possible to come to some broad conclusions for options independent of the particular type involved; however some problems arise which may lead to different treatments for traded and non-traded options.

This chapter explores the types of accounting problems that have to be faced, and suggests some solutions. The resolution of these problems will depend upon the needs and characteristics of a particular enterprise and the environment in which it operates. Consideration is also given to the treatment of gains and losses arising on transactions, appropriate treatments for transactions for trading and hedging purposes, and what items should be disclosed in financial statements.

## 2. Accounting principles

There are no authoritative guidelines on accounting for options in the United Kingdom or in Europe. In the United States, the American Institute of Certified Public Accountants (AICPA) issued a paper on accounting for options in March 1986; the contents of this paper are open for discussion and, in due course recommendations may be made.

The circumstances of each user will be different and the commercial intentions and ramifications of individual transactions will vary. It is important that users should involve their auditors or financial advisers when considering appropriate accounting policies and accounting and reporting systems for options.

Before discussing any of the specific accounting issues arising from options transactions, it is useful to look at the background to accounting and reporting in the United Kingdom, North America and Europe – the principal operating options markets.

### a. United Kingdom

Accounting and reporting in the United Kingdom is governed by the Companies Acts which until recently were not prescriptive in terms of profit measurement but were concerned with disclosure and truth and fairness. The development of standards to regulate profit measurement has largely been left to the accounting profession. The Accounting Standards Committee of the Consultative Committee of Accountancy Bodies has promulgated a number of Statements of Standard Accounting Practices (SSAPs) which seek to standardize the treatment of the individual aspects they address. Many of these standards are similar to the International Accounting Standards (IASs) issued by the International Accounting Standards Committee.

The 1981 Companies Act which was later incorporated into the 1985 Companies Act

---

* This chapter has been contributed by Andrew Sutton and Philip Gillett of Price Waterhouse.

implemented the EEC Fourth Directive, and adds to the disclosure requirements particularly in terms of the prescribed format of company accounts; it also incorporated certain rules of profit measurement and embraced the concepts set out in IAS 1, 'Disclosure of Accounting Policies'. In particular the inclusion of unrealized profits in the distributable reserves of an entity (exluding banks) is prohibited. Realized profits are defined as those profits which fall to be treated as realized in accordance with generally accepted accounting principles, i.e. either in the form of cash or other assets, the ultimate cash realization of which can be assessed with reasonable certainty. This is particularly relevant, when considering the accounting and reporting of options transactions.

### b. United States

In the United States there is a considerable amount of literature concerned with generally accepted accounting principles (GAAP) in that country which are normally applicable to all published financial statements. In addition in March 1986, the AICPA submitted an issues paper to the Financial Accounting Standards Board (FASB) dealing with the accounting treatment of options.

Issues papers identify financial accounting issues which the AICPA believes need to be addressed or clarified by the FASB. They include discussions of the issues identified together with suggested solutions. The issues paper on options includes consideration of what the carrying amounts of options should be, whether exchange-traded options and non-exchange-traded options should be accounted for similarly, whether hedge accounting should be permitted for options transactions and, if permitted, to what kinds of options transactions it should be applied and how it should be applied. While this issues paper does not establish standards of financial accounting, it does provide an insight into the way in which the accountancy profession in the United States currently views options. Many of the suggested accounting practices discussed in this chapter are in accordance with the advisory conclusions shown in the issues paper.

### c. Canada

Practice in Canada on many accounting matters has tended to closely follow that of its neighbour, the United States. However, there are no formal pronouncements on options.

### d. Europe

Accounting and reporting requirements historically have varied considerably from one country to another within Europe. The implementation of the EEC Directive by the major countries on the continent of Europe has gone some way to standardize disclosure in accounts and also to lay down basic rules of measurement of profit. As a general rule European accounting has adopted a conservative approach by favouring asset valuations on a lower of cost and market value basis and by limiting items included in the profit and loss account to those realized.

## 3. Principles to be applied

In view of the limited specific guidance on accounting for options, some additional guidance may be obtained from the fundamental accounting concepts which are set out in IAS 1.

1. The going concern concept, which assumes that the entity will continue in business for the foreseeable future.
2. The accruals concept, under which revenue and costs are accrued, matched and dealt with in the accounting period to which they relate.
3. The consistency concept, whereby like items in the accounts and from period to period are treated consistently.
4. The prudence concept, which says that revenue and profits are not anticipated but are recognized only when realized and provision is made for all known liabilities.

The application of the going concern and consistency concepts is straightforward in relation to options transactions and warrants little attention. The most important concept in determining how to account for options is the accruals concept which permits the reality of any transaction to be reflected in the accounting policy adopted. This concept must, however, be tempered by the prudence concept where the outcome of a situation is uncertain. It is these generally accepted fundamental accounting concepts which provide the justification for the policies which follow.

In addition to the fundamental accounting concepts some further guidance may be obtained from accounting practice on forward foreign exchange transactions and financial futures markets as these have a number of similarities with options transactions. Although the accounting treatment for forward foreign exchange transactions and financial futures transactions is not completely uniform, the common practice is to revalue forward positions on a 'buy back' or liquidation basis (this has been given the name 'mark to market' in the United States). This approach recognizes the cost or benefit which would arise on closing out the position and hence recognizes unrealized profits and losses on open positions.

There are four main accounting issues that need to be addressed in accounting for options transactions. These are:

1. The valuation of open positions in options.
2. The recognition of profit and loss.
3. The consideration of the underlying asset/liability.
4. The treatment of margins and premiums.

## a. Valuation of open positions

The timing of recognition of profits and losses on options transactions is fundamental to accounting for open positions therein. Since an active and liquid market provides the opportunity for positions to be closed at any time, it follows that a decision to keep a position open is no different in principle from a decision to close out. It would be incongruous to recognise one type of decision and not the other.

This view leads to the conclusion that open positions in options should be revalued to market value (marked to market). The difference between the aggregate value thus obtained and the aggregate value of the positions at their contracted prices will be the profit and loss on open contracts at the valuation day. The treatment of this profit or loss in the accounts will depend on the nature of the transaction and is discussed in detail later.

The policy above clearly advocates the recognition of unrealized profits and, relating this to the fundamental accounting concepts discussed earlier, may appear to lean towards the accruals concept and away from that of prudence. This conflict is apparent rather than real as the overriding requirement is for accounts to show a true and fair view. The following arguments help to support a mark to market policy.

1. The liquidity of the market ensures that profits and losses are instantly realizable.
2. Because the opportunity exists for management to close out a transaction in the market, a profit or loss is effectively made when the market rate moves and does not depend on a formal decision to close out.
3. The mark to market approach is consistent with the predominant practice of banks and others in accounting for forward foreign exchange transactions, other types of dealing securities and financial futures.
4. In some circumstances since the profits or losses have been realized in the form of margins, it can be argued that these profits or losses have actually been realized.
5. Given the close connection between options and futures contracts, it could be misleading to adopt differing treatments for the two types of contract.
6. The mark to market basis prevents the possibility of manipulation which might otherwise result from management's flexibility either to leave open or to close out contracts on a selective basis.
7. Management can evaluate performance only by reference to the current market values of all open contracts.

The possibility of manipulation and the evaluation of performance can best be illustrated by looking at a simple example. Let us assume a trader had only two contracts open at his year end, one showing a profit and the other showing a loss. For the purposes of the example it does not matter what type of options contract these are. If the trader had an accounting policy other than to value the open contracts at market value then the results could be varied for the year simply by closing out, or leaving open, the profitable contract. Prudence requires provision for the loss-making contract whether or not it has been closed out. A difference would arise despite the fact that the trader had applied his particular accounting policy consistently. This would provide scope for manipulating the results; such manipulation will only be avoided by valuing open contracts at closing market prices.

|  | Results declared as a result of different accounting policies for open contracts | | |
|  | Provide all losses | Provide net losses | Value at market |
|  |  | (£) |  |
| Contract 1–loss £2,500 | (2,500) | (2,500) | (2,500) |
| Contract 2–gain £10,000 | — | 2,500 | 10,000 |
| *Accounting results* |  |  |  |
| If both contracts open | (2,500) |  | 7,500 |
| If contract 1 closed | (2,500) | (2,500) | 7,500 |
| If both contracts closed | 7,500 | 7,500 | 7,500 |

This example demonstrates how, by selectively closing out contracts, the accompanying results can be varied except when following a mark to market policy.

For traded options, market values are easily obtained as there is a clearly identified central market place with quoted market prices. In the case of dealer or over-the-counter (OTC) options, obtaining market values may be more difficult. However, it will usually be possible for an institution to close an open OTC position either by buying back similar OTC options or through the use of exchange traded options. A good approximation to the current value of an OTC option can be obtained by using a mathematical pricing model. The same model as was used for originally pricing the option should be used for revaluation (e.g. the same basis should be used for determining volatility.)

If no mathematical model exists to revalue OTC options, it may be necessary to seek an independent quotation from an OTC dealer.

## b. Recognition of profit/loss

Once the profit/loss on a futures or option contract has been determined it is necessary to decide in which accounting period it should be recognized. This will depend primarily on the underlying reason for the transaction. Accordingly, it is necessary to consider trading and hedging transactions separately.

### (i) Trading transactions

The accounting treatment for a trading transaction is relatively straightforward. Having determined the profit or loss on the trading transactions on a mark to market basis as described above, the whole of that profit or loss should be recognized immediately. This treatment reflects the fact that each day a trader effectively makes a decision either to keep a position open or to close it out. Taking profits or losses on a daily basis recognizes the effect of that decision in the period in which the decision was made.

Consider the following situation:

Day 1: A dealer writes a June 89.00 call option on a three-month Eurodollar future at a premium of 66.
Day 2: The price of the option falls to 61.
Day 3: The dealer closes out his position by purchasing a June 89.00 call option on a three-month Eurodollar contract at 61.

The dealer makes a profit due to the five point movement, which at say $25 per point will be a profit of $125. Suppose also that the organization's year end for accounting purposes in Day 2.

If the transaction described above were entered into as a trading transaction then the whole of the $125 profit would be recognized on Day 2 even though the position was not closed out until Day 3. This would have the effect of recognizing the whole of $125 profit before the accounting year end.

One advantage of this method is that no matter how complex the trading position constructed, the calculation of the profit and loss is easy. The mark to market method of valuations is simply applied to each contract individually and the resultant net profit or loss is recognized, together with any profits or losses on closed out contracts.

### (ii) Hedging transactions

The aim of a hedger is to reduce risk and protect against potentially adverse price changes.

Logically therefore the accounting treatment of hedging transactions should reflect this purpose. It would be appropriate therefore to defer profits and losses arising on the option transaction so that they can be recognized and offset against the effect of price changes on the asset or liability being hedged.

### (iii) Criteria for determining a hedge

To prevent possible abuses of the difference in treatment between trading and hedging, they must be clearly distinguished.

The intention of hedge transactions is to manage and limit the risks of an enterprise. As market conditions change, management's view of the risks which they are seeking to limit by means of an existing hedging transaction may also change. The management of a hedging programme should be considered as just one aspect of risk management, which is a dynamic process. These factors suggest that identification of, and accounting for, hedging transactions may in some circumstances be difficult and complex. Neither the accountant nor the auditor should expect to apply rigid and inflexible rules in meeting the challenge of providing useful information to management and of giving a true and fair view in published financial statements.

Nevertheless, there may be limits on the extent to which an accounting system can reflect all hedging transactions. Before undertaking hedging activities, the accounting implications should be carefully considered by management. It is important that the auditors of the enterprise should have been involved at an early stage to help agree the basic principles to be applied.

Ground rules should be set to identify hedging transactions which are most suitable to the activities of the business. The following three criteria might be considered:

(a) *Intent.* The transaction should be intended to be a hedge so that the accounting reflects the economic substance. This will also involve evidence of management's intention that the transaction is a hedge and identification of its exact purpose. Thus at the time the option transaction is entered into, its purpose should be specifically identified and documented, including the asset or liability being hedged and the period over which the hedge is intended to be effective.

(b) *Correlation.* The price of the option contract and the hedged asset or liability should show a high positive correlation so that they will move in the same direction and with similar magnitude. This will involve matching the option contract as closely as possible to the hedged asset or liability in terms of the sensitivity to interest and currency rate changes, principal amount and exercise period.

(c) *Certainty.* In the case of anticipatory hedges (transactions intended to occur at a future date) there should be a reasonable expectation that the cash transaction will be fulfilled. This will be demonstrated by experience.

The three criteria above are similar to those set out in the US Financial Accounting Standard on foreign currency translation (FAS 52) when it considers hedging of foreign currency positions. FAS 52 suggests that, to qualify as a hedge, a transaction should be both 'designated' and 'effective' as a hedge. These equate to the intent and to the correlation/certainty criteria set out above.

In this context, therefore, the first criterion of intent is fundamental. If the intention is that the transaction is a hedge, it should be possible to record that intention and the reasons for it, at the time the transaction is made. Furthermore, to establish internal control the nature and intent of the transaction must be recorded so that it can be subsequently monitored and reported to management in an appropriate manner.

The second criterion of correlation is more factual. Reasonable correlation, or a reasonable expectation of correlation, is a factor upon which management should have satisfied itself before entering a hedge transaction, by reference to information to which others, including the auditors, should similarly be able to refer.

The third criterion of certainty will not always be relevant. When it is relevant (in anticipated cash transactions) management will need to be clear about its plans for future cash transactions and it would not be unreasonable for the auditor to expect to see that management had established a good track record in planning effectively and in subsequently actioning its plans by entering into the cash transactions anticipated.

This criterion is particularly relevant to the hedging of uncertain future currency payments or receipts and, as we shall see later, has a fundamental effect on the way such transactions are accounted for. Nevertheless, even with the criteria established for treatment as a hedge, some difficult assessment may need to be made. A responsible approach would be to assume that a transaction is a trading transaction, rather than a hedge, unless it can be reasonably shown that the hedge criteria are satisfied, especially where the deferral of losses is in question.

The prudence concept suggests, it may be argued, that both losses and profits are immediately reflected in the profit and loss account; however, it may be evident that, to show a true and fair view, the matching concept should be followed and the loss or profit be deferred as a hedging item. This would seem to be consistent with the spirit of IAS 1.

The practical effects of this principle are best demonstrated by means of an example. Consider the same deal using traded options as described above, but instead of the transaction having been entered into as a trade, it has been done to hedge:

1. an OTC option; or
2. a six-month rollover on a Eurodollar borrowing.

In the first case, the $125 profit must be recognized at the same time as the profit or loss on the OTC option. In many cases the profit or loss on the OTC option will have been calculated using a variation of the mark to market method and this profit or loss will also be recognized immediately. Accordingly, the $125 profit on the traded options transactions will also be recognized immediately.

Thus, in practical terms, the $125 profit has been recognized in the same period as it was when the transaction was a trade. However, the reasons for it being recognized in this period are quite different. In the case of the hedges of the OTC option, the profit is recognized on Day 2 as this is when the profit or loss on the OTC option is also recognized.

For the second situation described above it is assumed that the Eurodollar borrowing rolls over on Day 3. The $125 profit on the option contract should be carried forward in the balance sheet and taken to the profit or loss account at a rate of $20.83 a month for the six months beginning on Day 3.

The rationale behind this treatment may be explained as follows: the fall in the price of the option contract on Day 2 reflects a fall in the price of underlying futures contracts which in turn is a result of higher interest rates. Thus the interest rate at which the loan rolls over is higher on Day 3 than it was on Day 1 and the extra cost resulting from this higher interest rate is recognized over the six-month period commencing on Day 3. The purpose of writing the traded option was to afford some protection against such rises in interest rate and it is therefore appropriate for the profit on the options transactions to be recognized over the same period as the extra interest costs on the Eurodollar loan.

The above example illustrates an interesting point. The matching of profits and losses on a hedge with the corresponding income and expenditure on the underlying transactions may involve carrying forward profits and losses in the balance sheet for recognition at a later date. To prevent profit manipulation, particularly where losses are being carried forward, it is vital that trades and hedges be differentiated. Thus in designating options transactions as a hedge, the three criteria for determining a hedge previously discussed must be satisfied.

The determination of the period over which the results of the hedge should be recognized may not be straightforward, particularly where the transaction is a general hedge (see below). Where there is any doubt as to the period over which the results of a hedge should be recognized, this should be specified at the inception of the hedge together with the rationale for such a treatment.

### (iv) Hedge accounting

In the light of the foregoing, the criteria for hedging transactions should be established by management, preferably in consultation with the auditors, and the risks and circumstances of the business recognized. A record should be maintained which will demonstrate that transactions comply with these criteria; the more complex the hedging activity, the more detailed these records may need to be.

Below are some of the practical problems that might arise.

### (v) General hedges

The consideration of hedging transactions has so far been based on hedges for single assets; however, there will be situations where hedges are part of general asset/liability management and based on aggregates of assets and liabilities rather than individual items. There is no reason why this should necessarily invalidate hedging treatment although the criteria may have to be refined to accommodate the identification of the aggregate assets and liabilities being hedged.

### (vi) Rolling hedges

In general hedging contracts would normally extend at least until the date of the anticipated cash market transaction, otherwise an exposure would exist between the time the options contracts are closed out or the option exercised and the time when the cash market transaction is made. This exposure can be avoided, particularly in the case of transactions well into the future, by the use of successive contracts; for example, by closing out a position for one delivery month and simultaneously opening an equivalent position for a subsequent delivery month, thereby 'rolling' the hedge forward to the later date. The use of this technique may be necessary because the date of the anticipated cash market transaction has been delayed; alternatively it may have been necessary to open the original hedge position in a delivery month earlier than the anticipated date of the cash transaction because no contract for the later delivery month was available.

Providing the rolling forward of the hedge can properly be viewed as an integral part of the hedge operation – and this will be a particularly relevant question where anticipated hedge transactions have been delayed – it should be appropriate for the relevant options transactions to be accounted for as part of the hedge. This may entail successive hedge transactions being deferred so that the total hedge profit or loss can be accounted for accordingly.

### (vii) Discontinued hedges

There will be occasions when hedges are discontinued. This may happen for a variety of reasons. For example, the anticipated cash market transaction may not take place. In this case it would be appropriate to treat the entire result of the hedge transaction as a trading transaction as soon as it becomes apparent that the anticipated cash market transaction will not take place.

A hedge may also be discontinued because management's view of the risks which the hedge was designed to give protection against has altered, e.g. their expectations of the trend in interest rates or currency rates has changed. This could arise when:

1. rates have moved in the direction anticipated so that the hedge shows a profit and management then considers that the remaining risk of further movement in rates does not warrant continuation of the hedge; or
2. rates have not moved significantly but, because of changes in external factors, management now considers that the original risk which was hedged has reduced to the point where continuation of the hedge is not warranted.

Discontinuation of the hedge in these circumstances is likely to present problems to the accountant in monitoring and recording these transactions and to the auditor in assessing management's intentions. However, it would seem appropriate to account for the result of such options transactions up to the time of management's decision on hedges, provided management's intentions can be clearly established.

In the case of a hedge transaction being left open after the point when the relevant cash transaction has taken place, or after the point when the hedge had been deemed to be discontinued, it would be appropriate for the result of the hedge which arose after that point to be treated as a trading profit or loss if it is material.

### (viii) More complex situations

As a general rule, it would seem appropriate to try to apply the criteria set out in the preceding section to determine whether or not an options transaction qualifies for treatment as a hedge. While general rules are useful in giving guidance, each situation must be viewed on its merits. As mentioned earlier, it is probably better to regard all transactions as trades unless there is positive evidence to the contrary. It is important that management has an understanding of the differences between this accounting treatment and the commercial intention of the transactions, and appreciates that accounts prepared on this basis may not reflect in an ideal manner the outcome of their decisions.

## c. Underlying assets and liabilities

Consideration of the balance sheet treatment of the asset or liability underlying an options contract depends on the legal nature of such contracts. The holder's rights in an option may cease because of three events:

1. the option may lapse as it passes its expiry date;

2. the option may be exercised by the holder; or

3. the right to the option may be sold in the market place.

Only in the case of (2) does title to any underlying asset or liability pass. It is therefore appropriate that the underlying assets and liabilities should not be recognised prior to any title passing. This treatment, reflecting the economic reality of the transaction, is consistent with that adopted for forward foreign exchange and futures transactions.

A far more important matter is the valuation of hedged assets and liabilities. In cases where the hedge is to protect an asset value, valuation of the asset either at cost, the lower of cost and market value, or market value may affect the recognition of the hedge result. In cases where the hedge is intended to protect the value of an underlying asset, the resulting net book amount, comprising the cost or carrying value of the asset plus its hedge result, should be reviewed. It may be appropriate to compare this combined amount with the market value, or realizable value, of the underlying asset being hedged.

The original book amount for the hedged asset should not be compared to its market value in isolation since this could indicate the need for an amount to be written off to the profit and loss account in circumstances where a hedging profit has been received which partly or wholly offsets such a write off.

## d. Treatment of margins

The balance sheet of a holder or writer of options will include the cost of the option itself as reflected by the premium associated there together with the balances of any margin monies that may have been paid to an exchange or other person in relation to the options written or granted.

Deposit margins are a form of collateral and will be assets in the balance sheet of the depositer; they are unlikely to be other than current in nature. They may be payable in respect of traded or other options for all contracts taken out and may allow for the reduction in deposit margins where offsetting positions are held in different contracts.

Variation margins reflecting profits and losses on open contracts may also be required. The adoption of a mark to market policy as described above will require the immediate recognition of these profits and losses in the case of trading transactions. For hedging transactions a mark to market policy will still have been applied but the resultant profits and losses may be carried in the balance sheet. In such cases these profits and losses will again reflect the variation margins paid or received.

The margin paid or received each day will represent the net movement in deposit and variation margins for the previous day. In addition, the variation margin itself may well be the net effect of profits and losses for the day on open trading and hedging positions.

## e. Disclosure in financial statements

As already discussed at the beginning of this chapter, there are no relevant statutory or accounting standard requirements in any of the major countries to give guidance on the types of disclosure required. In addition current best practice on disclosure of options transactions and in other areas such as forward foreign exchange and financial futures still shows a wide variation in standards of disclosure. The purpose of disclosure is to enable the reader of a set of financial statements to assess the impact on the business of the item disclosed. Materiality is obviously a fundamental consideration. There will be a wide range of possible disclosures and in the absence of authoritative guidance and until an accepted market practice evolves this must be a matter of judgement by management and their auditors.

Wherever there is a material involvement in options transactions the disclosure of an accounting policy for those transactions must be an initial step. The policy should cover methods of valuation, treatment of profits and losses and whether hedging rules are applied. A possible accounting policy which might be appropriate would be as follows:

> 'The company is using options contracts as part of its overall risk management strategy. Gains and losses on contracts used in trading operations are recognized currently using the mark to market method of accounting and are included in trading results. Gains and losses on contracts used in asset/liability management are deferred and amortized over the lives of the hedged liabilities.'

The other common area of disclosure in options is in the note to the financial statements detailing contingent liabilities. Some organizations attempt to disclose the gross value for their open contracts under this heading although this would seem to be only of limited benefit to the reader of the accounts. Financial statements do not generally provide a comprehensive summary of the various risks to which an enterprise is exposed. A more common disclosure under the contingent liability note is a statement to the effect that open options contracts exist.

Apart from the above areas, it is not common practice to disclose any other information in the financial statements on options. However, the concepts of truth and fairness and materiality must clearly remain paramount. If options dealing constituted a material part of an organization's business, then further disclosure would be necessary.

# 4. Taxation issues

This section considers the taxation treatment of options transactions undertaken by businesses in major countries with significant experience of options.

The taxation regulations in each country are different, but in most countries the same issues have to be addressed. The treatment of options transactions will be most complex in countries with inherent mismatches in their tax systems. Complexities may arise where:

1. there are fundamental differences between the taxation of transactions on capital or revenue account (or short- or long-term capital gains), and/or
2. gains and losses are taxed on a realized rather than an unrealized basis, and/or
3. particular persons have a special tax status.

The United States and the United Kingdom are extreme examples of countries in which the mismatches within their tax systems mean that taxation of options transactions is not a simple matter. The additional legislation introduced in both territories to close avoidance opportunities or introduce specific reliefs adds to the complexities and makes it difficult to summarize the tax treatment.

This section therefore places particular emphasis on the United Kingdom and the United States, though it also summarizes the tax treatment in other territories. Tax law and/or practice is not certain or constant. The development in the use of financial or treasury products frequently leads to changes in tax systems and advice must be taken before entering into transactions.

## a. United Kingdom

It takes time for the products of sophisticated new markets to develop their taxation characteristics in detail. There have been some significant changes to the UK tax system in recent years as a result of the various traded options markets' activities. There is, however, little specific published guidance from case law or the Inland Revenue and these comments are merely an interpretation of existing legislation as adapted to the options market. The tax treatment of any particular transaction will depend on the specific circumstances of each case.

### (i) Possible methods of taxation of options transactions

There are two principal types of tax treatment which might apply to a taxpayer, depending on the circumstances in which transactions are carried out:

1. Assessment under Schedule D Case I as a trading transaction – for companies this will involve taxation at the normal rate of corporation tax (currently 35%). Companies with a sufficiently small level of profits may be taxed on trading income at a rate of only 29% (for year to 31 March 1987). For an individual, trading income may be taxed at rates up to the top marginal rate of 60%. Losses incurred in a trade may, broadly speaking, be offset against other income of the same year and, depending on the circumstances, against any income of the previous year and trading income of subsequent years.
2. Assessment under the capital gains rules – both companies and individuals are generally subject to an effective 30% rate of tax on chargeable capital gains. However there is a small annual exemption for gains made by individuals. While capital gains tax rates are lower than income rates there is a restriction on the use made of losses. Capital losses can only be offset against capital gains of the same or subsequent years. This means that care must be exercised in arranging the timing of transactions.

Assessment under Schedule D Case VI as income for speculating is still a possibility for options not traded on a recognized stock or futures exchange. In the past it has been much less frequently encountered than Schedule D Case I or capital gains tax treatment but did nevertheless arise where neither of the other treatments was considered appropriate, for example where the transactions were not related to any other transaction on capital account and yet did not bear all the hallmarks of a trading activity.

Where Case VI treatment applies, both companies and individuals were taxed at the same rates as for Case I. The principal distinction between Case VI and Case I treatment is the restricted offset available for losses arising from Case VI activities. The difference is that Case VI losses can only be offset against Case VI profits of the same or subsequent years. The more generous offset rules available for trading losses did not therefore apply.

## (ii) Application of methods of taxation to different types of taxpayer

### 1. Banks and similar financial sector companies

The results of options transactions undertaken by banks and similar financially based companies will normally be taxed under Schedule D Case I as trading transactions unless, unusually, the transaction represents a specific hedge relating to a capital asset of that company. The strict method for computing results from option trading for tax purposes is by reference to realized profits but the Inland Revenue is likely, as in other areas, to accept a measure of taxable profits including unrealized items if these are drawn up using established and even-handed accounting policies consistently applied.

### 2. Investment trusts and authorized unit trusts

It is unlikely that either investment trusts or authorized unit trusts would be taxable on transactions in options since both have been exempt from tax on capital gains since 31 March 1980. Transactions by such bodies in options are unlikely in practice to be regarded as trading and therefore taxable activities in normal circumstances; however, this area is under close scrutiny from the Inland Revenue and the position may change.

### 3. Pension funds

The general exemption from capital gains tax on investments available to pension funds was extended by the 1984 Finance Act to include traded options as investments for pension funds, so that any profits now made are tax-free.

### 4. Insurance companies

In non-life, non-pension business the results of options transactions are likely to be taxed as trading income with capital gains treatment only accorded to transactions linked to the fixed capital of the business. For transactions on their life funds, capital treatment will probably be granted, and for pension business Case VI will remain the case of charge, which means that any profits will be tax-free to the extent that they are reserved for policy-holders.

### 5. Individuals

Changes introduced in 1985 were of greatest assistance to individuals who have been the class of taxpayer most susceptible to assessment under Schedule D Case VI. The position now is that individuals should only be assessed either as traders or under the capital gains rules.

Trading status will normally only apply where the individual displays a number of what are termed 'the badges of trade'. The Inland Revenue will tend to view options transactions as forming part of a trade if, *inter alia*, they are significant in number, if the individual concerned has financial experience and exploits this in completing transactions with a clear profit motive displayed, and if the individual spends a reasonable amount of time involved in such option buying and selling. Trading status brings with it taxation at rates of up to 60%, but also the benefits of deductions for trading expenses and relief for trading losses against other general income of the individual. It is perhaps more likely that individuals will be obliged to adopt a stricter realization basis of taxation than other more sophisticated traders such as banks.

Capital gains tax is the more common basis of assessment with a flat rate of tax of 30% and an annual exemption for net gains of up to £6,300 for the year commencing 6 April 1986. One-off transactions by individuals and transactions intended to enhance income from existing investments should fall within the capital gains tax rules.

### 6. Non-financial companies

Capital gains treatment will apply only where the financial result of the underlying transaction that is being hedged does not fall to be included as part of the company's Schedule D Case I profit. Thus if the company can demonstrate as a matter of fact that the transaction being hedged was a capital transaction, then the Inland Revenue should normally be prepared to accept capital gains treatment. Agreement to this treatment will depend on the detailed circumstances of the transaction and documentary evidence available if necessary to support the capital motive, e.g. appropriate internal memoranda or board minutes on accounting treatment.

If, on the other hand, options are used to protect a company from exposure in the course of normal trading activities, the results of these transactions are likely to be taxed in the same way as the ordinary income or expenditure of the trade that gave rise to the option activity. In these circumstances options might be used to hedge the cost of a significant purchase of trading stock from overseas, or alternatively the receipt of substantial overseas trade debts. An option transaction will also usually be considered to be part of a trading activity for tax purposes if it is incidental to the central trading activity, e.g. if a manufacturing company uses options to hedge borrowing costs, although premiums paid to fix the interest rate payable on surplus funds will not necessarily attract tax relief.

Options may also be used in conjunction with futures contracts, e.g. to lock in a profit on an existing futures position while still retaining the opportunity for additional futures profits. Where this happens, the results of the options contract are likely to be taxed or relieved in the same manner as the futures contract and its related underlying transaction.

### 7. Non-residents

If a non-resident company enters into options transactions in the United Kingdom, it will not be chargeable to tax there unless it is trading in the country through a branch or agency. The same would apply to an individual who is neither resident nor ordinarily resident in the United Kingdom.

### (iii) *The tax effects of options transactions*

Once it has been decided whether the transaction is trading or capital, the tax effects must be considered.

The consequences of trading treatment are relatively straightforward. The net result of the option transaction and any related transaction will fall to be included as profits or losses of the overall trading activity and will therefore be taxed or relieved at the appropriate rate of tax.

If capital gains tax applies, the computational rules become more complicated and are best illustrated by the following table:

### *Capital gains treatment of options transactions*

| | |
|---|---|
| 1. Options in gilts or qualifying sterling corporate bonds | Exempt. |
| 2. Other options transactions | |
|    (i) Exercising call option | Option price added to exercise price to arrive at base cost of asset. Separate components of expenditure qualify for indexation relief on ultimate disposal. |
|    (ii) Buying and selling a put or call option | Proceeds less 'adjusted' costs brought into calculation of capital gain/loss. Cost of non-traded option is adjusted for write-off of expenditure over its life on a straight line basis. No relief is given for this write-off and cost of lapsed non-traded option is wasted. Cost of trading option is wholly deductible for capital gains purposes. Indexation relief applies to adjusted costs. |
|    (iii) Buying and exercising a put option | Capital gain/loss will be calculated as the proceeds from the sale of the asset less the capital gains base cost of the asset less the costs of the option premium. Indexation relief applies to the separate components. |
|    (iv) Writing an option | Capital gain on proceeds. |

---

1. For UK tax purposes the exercise of an option to acquire or sell sterling should be analysed as an option to sell or acquire foreign currency.
2. Traded option means an option which at the time of the abandonment is quoted on a stock exchange or a futures exchange designated by the Board of Inland Revenue as a recognized exchange. Over-the-counter options written by banks are not traded options, which has the disadvantage for UK taxpayers that expenditure on lapsed options is not an allowable capital loss.

The table is only a general summary and care is needed when considering options transactions within the wider context of the taxation of profits as a whole. The realization basis and mismatches in the treatment of foreign currency transactions can frequently result in a hedged transaction at the pre-tax level giving an unhedged position after tax. Accordingly not only the tax treatment of the option transaction but also the tax treatment of the transaction which is being hedged has to be examined. For example exercise of a call option to acquire dollars to repay a dollar loan may give a capital gain on the currency which cannot be offset against the non-allowable loss on borrowing.

### (iv) Value-added tax

The sale as principal of an option for a premium is treated as the granting of a right for a consideration and so is a supply for VAT purposes. The supply of options in currency contracts is treated as dealing in money and is consequently exempt as falling within Item 1, Group 5, Schedule 6 VATA 1983. Hence when these options are supplied to a person belonging in the United Kingdom, Isle of Man or the European Economic Community they are exempt. However, if the contract is supplied to someone who belongs outside the EEC, such a supply is zero-rated.

Interest rate options are treated in the same way as currency contracts, though where the option is a secondary security (as defined in the Exchange Control Act 1947), which will include gilts and Treasury bond contracts, the supply of the option is within Item 6 not Item 1 of Group 5 Schedule 6 VATA 1983. This does not affect the liability of the supply itself, but brokerage commission or other fees may be standard rated rather than exempt.

It is important to identify what record keeping of options transactions is required for VAT purposes, as well as the impact of exempt outputs on the VAT status of the person entering into options transactions. This is a complex matter and specific advice may be required. The VAT status of options on physical commodities is subject to different rules which are not considered here.

## b. United States

The aim of this section is to provide a brief overview of the current status of US legislation pertaining to the taxation of options transactions. This is a complex area of US tax law.

1. For US taxpayers rules regarding tax straddles and/or the special rules relating to Section 1256 contracts (defined below) are often imposed on transactions. These rules operate to affect the amount and character of taxable income reported from such transactions. Principally, this is done by requiring the deferral of recognized losses and the conversion of long-term capital gains to short-term capital gains and short-term capital losses to long-term capital losses. There are certain exceptions to these rules, principally for those taxpayers who enter into such transactions as part of their normal course of business and for whom such gains and losses are treated as ordinary, not capital items.
2. Non-resident aliens (the US tax term for non-US citizens) are generally not subject to US tax on capital gains from passive security investments. If such transactions are entered into as part of a non-resident alien's trade or business and such income is effectively connected with a US trade or business, then such income generally would be ordinary income, as noted above, and subject to the tax at graduated rates (the discussion below assumes that the taxpayer is a US citizen or resident alien).
3. Currently, the tax laws surrounding the taxation of options transactions are not entirely clear, and taxpayers are advised to consult with their US tax advisers on the current state of the law when contemplating entering into such transactions.

In short, the US tax position is dependent upon whether the person carrying out the transaction is a US citizen, the reason for the transaction and the state in which the transaction is carried out, and may even then be subject to some uncertainty.

### (i) Section 1256 contracts

Certain financial instruments are subject to the mark to market rules (i.e. they are treated as sold on the last day of the taxpayer's taxable year) and to the 60/40 rule (which treats 60% of any gain or loss from such deemed sale or an actual sale as long-term, and 40% as short-term, regardless of how long the instrument has been held). These instruments may also be subject to the straddle rules (discussed below).

The instruments subject to these rules, which are referred to as Section 1256 contracts, include non-equity options (NEO) and dealer equity options (DEO).

*Non-equity option.* A NEO is any listed option which is not an equity option. A listed option is any option (other than a right to acquire stock from the issuer) which is traded on (or subject to the rules of) a qualified board or exchange.

An equity option is any option to buy or sell stock, the value of which is determined directly or indirectly by reference to any stock (or group of stocks) or stock index. An equity option, however, does not include any option if there is in effect a designation by the Commodities Future Trading Commission (CFTC) of if the Secretary of the Treasury determines that such option meets the requirements for such designation of a contract market for a contract based on such a group of stocks or index.

Thus, generally, NEO's are options which are traded on or subject to the rules of a qualified board or exchange, except for options to buy or sell stock or options on specific stock indices. But options on specific stock groups or stock indices will be NEOs if the CFTC has in effect a designation of a contract market for such items, or the Treasury determines that such options meet the requirements for such a designation.

For example, the following options will be considered non-equity options which will be marked to market and eligible for 60/40 treatment:
- options on regulated futures;
- options on stock index futures (such as S & P 500 or S & P 100 index futures);
- options on US government securities futures;
- options on stock indices for which a designation has been made by the CFTC (such as the S & P 500 or S & P 100 indexes); and
- options on debt securities.

*Dealer equity options.* A DEO is generally defined as an equity sold by an options dealers in the course of his business.

## (ii) Equity options and non-listed non-equity options

*Purchased options.* If a put or call is sold or lapses, any gain or loss is long-term or short-term depending on the holding period of the option. If a call option is exercised, its cost is added to the taxpayer's basis cost of the securities purchased. If a put option is exercised, its cost reduces the amount of the proceeds received upon sale of the underlying stock. If, however, the put is acquired at a time when the underlying stock has been held for six months or less, then any gain upon termination of the put is a short-term capital gain and the holding period of the underlying stock is forfeited through the date of termination of the put.

*Written options.* If a put or call is closed out or lapses, any gain or loss is a short-term capital gain or loss. If a call is exercised, the premium received is added to the sale proceeds and a capital gain or loss is calculated based on the holding period of the stock. If a put is exercised, the premium received decreases the writer's basis in the stock acquired. The holding period of the stock begins on the date of its purchase, not the date the put was written.

Purchased and written options may be subject to the straddle rules.

## (iii) Tax straddles

*General.* The term straddle generally describes offsetting positions in personal property in which the value of each (gain or loss) position is expected to fluctuate inversely to that of the other. The term position means an interest (including a futures or forward contract or option) in personal property. An offsetting position occurs whenever risk or loss has been substantially minimized as a result of holding one or more other positions, e.g. although being at very little risk, a taxpayer could close a large loss position in year 1 (recognizing the tax loss) and close out the offsetting gain position in year 2.

*Restrictions.* The law generally defers realized losses from any position to the extent of unrealized gains from an offsetting position. Deferred losses are carried forward to the succeeding year and are subject to the deferral rules in that year as well. Losses in excess of unrealized gains are deductible.

Additionally, complicated rules exist for continuing to defer losses when offsetting positions are replaced during the year by other similar positions (the wash sales rules). Complex rules also exist which prevent taxpayers from converting short-term capital gains into long-term capital gains when they are not fully at risk for the required six-month holding period. Certain rules prevent taxpayers from creating short-term capital losses in circumstances where offsetting positions to the loss position disposed of have been held for over six months (the short sales rules).

No deduction is allowed for interest and carrying charges (e.g. storage, insurance, transportation) allocable to personal property which is part of a straddle. Any such non-deductible expenses are chargeable to the capital account of the personal property to which such expenses relate. Interest and carrying charges are those in excess of income includable in the taxable year.

*Types of straddle.* There are considered to be three types of straddles: regular, Section 1256 contract only, and mixed.

Regular straddles consisting of offsetting positions, such as a put option and related stock or a non-qualified covered call option and the related stock, are subject to the overall tax straddle rules previously discussed.

Straddles consisting solely of Section 1256 contracts (for example, offsetting positions consisting solely of combinations of non-equity options) are not subject to the straddle rule. This is because all open positions must be marked to market at year end, and all gains and losses (deferred and actual) will be recognized as 60/40 gains and losses. Thus, there is no perceived potential for abuse of the taxation system.

Mixed straddles are straddles in which at least one (but not all) of the positions is a Section 1256 contract. For example, writing a covered call option on a debt security constitutes a mixed straddle, as would selling a futures contract on a debt security when the security is held in the portfolio. Taxpayers currently have four choices as to how they may account for mixed straddles for US tax purposes:

1. make no election;
2. make a mixed straddle election under Section 1256(d);
3. make an identified mixed straddle election under Section 1092(b); or
4. make an election to use a mixed straddle account under Section 1092(b).

These elections are not mutually exclusive: i.e. a taxpayer may make different elections for different straddles during the course of the tax year.

The choices will affect the amount of long- and short-term capital gains/losses being reported by taxpayers in a given year. The recommended choice for a particular taxpayer depends upon the specific investment strategy being undertaken. All of the elections require contemporaneous indentification of the positions of a straddle which necessitates detailed record keeping.

*Exceptions to the rules.* There are certain exceptions to the straddle rules outlined above.

1. Hedging transactions: If a straddle meets the Internal Revenue Code definition of a hedging transaction, it will not be subject to any of the rules above. Not all economic hedges are recognized as hedges for tax purposes. The term as it has been used is a term of art. Only hedges within the statutory definition meet the exemptions outlined above.

    The Code defines a hedge as a transaction which is entered into in the normal course of a taxpayer's trade or business, as contrasted to an infrequent activity. The business must be an active business rather than an investment activity. The primary purpose of the transaction must be: (a) to reduce the risk of price change or currency fluctuations with respect to property which is held or to be held by the taxpayer, or (b) to reduce the risk of interest rate or price changes or currency fluctuations with respect to borrowings made or to be made, or obligations incurred or to be incurred by the taxpayer.

    The taxpayer must clearly identify the transaction as a hedge on the books before the close of the day in which it was entered. Gain or loss on disposition of the hedged property and the hedge itself must be ordinary income.

    Finally, no transaction entered into by a syndicate can qualify as a hedge.
2. Identified straddles: If a straddle meets the Code definition of an identified straddle, its positions are exempt from the loss deferral rules. To be an identified straddle, the straddle must be clearly designated on a taxpayer's records before the end of the day as an identified straddle; the straddle's positions must be acquired on the same day; the straddle must either have all of its positions closed on the same day during the taxable year or none of its positions disposed of as of the close of the taxable year; and the straddle must not be part of larger straddles.
3. Qualified covered call options: In recognition of the fact that investors use covered call writing as a means of protecting investment positions, an exception to the straddle provisions is provided for certain call options on equities which are not deep in-the-money. The covered

calls qualifying for the exception must be options traded on a national exchange, must cover stock held by the writer and granted more than 30 days before expiration, and must generate capital gain or loss. The law provides detailed rules, using strike price benchmark intervals, to determine whether an option is deep in-the-money. Under certain limited circumstances, however, the loss deferral rules may apply to qualified covered call options. The short sales rules described previously may apply to in-the-money qualified covered call options.

## c. Other user countries

There is significantly less specific tax legislation on options transactions in most other major countries. This is not simply because taxpayers and the authorities in these countries have less experience in dealing with options. More generally it is because of the relative absence of the mismatches and perceived avoidance opportunities in the tax systems of these countries when compared with the United States or the United Kingdom. A particular factor which simplifies the tax treatment of options transactions in many territories is the absence of the key UK distinction between income and capital gains. This is especially relevant in the European context, though the capital/revenue distinction continues to apply in certain other areas, notably in many countries where the tax systems were originally based on English law.

In the absence of a capital/revenue distinction for options transactions the questions to concentrate on are:

1. when are gains/losses realized for tax purposes; and
2. whether, in a hedging transaction, unrealized gains can be or must be netted against unrealized losses.

On (1) the question of the treatment of options transactions can, to a certain extent, be answered from general rules relating to the realization of profits and losses. However, in a number of countries the treatment of foreign exchange items is not always clear, particularly where hedging transactions have been entered into. On (2) the impact of accounting practice may be important though at times tax legislation will differ from the accounting treatment.

Once questions (1) and (2) are resolved, the taxation treatment of options will normally be relatively straightforward, in that profits and losses are treated as ordinary income and subject to standard rates of tax. However, because of the possible pitfalls, specific advice should be taken before entering into transactions in any territory. The corporate tax position for individual countries is briefly summarized below. The possible impact of other taxes is not examined here but should not be ignored.

### (i) Germany

Profits and losses on options will in normal circumstances be treated as normal trading income when carried out by normal business entities. However while the authorities will always seek to tax profits arising on such transactions, losses may only be recognized where it can be demonstrated that options were purchased in the normal course of business. While in the case of public companies this will almost always be the case, companies in which the shareholders are also the management would usually be asked to provide a greater measure of substantiation to show that losses were incurred in the pursuit of a trade.

### (ii) France

Profits and losses from options transactions will generally be taxable/allowable as ordinary income. The timing of realization of such profits and losses and the treatment of unrealized gains or losses is not entirely clear.

### (iii) The Netherlands

There are no specific tax regulations dealing with options transactions, but the results should fall to be taxable/allowable as ordinary income. In general the tax authorities will accept the profit figure determined for accounting purposes (after certain adjustments) as long as the accounting follows good commercial practice. Accordingly it may be possible to take a deduction for any losses while deferring tax on unrealized gains.

### (iv) Italy

The results of options transactions will generally fall to be taxable as income.

### (v) Switzerland

Profits and losses from options transactions of a business nature are subject to ordinary Swiss income taxes or allowed as a deduction from taxable income respectively. These rates will vary from canton to canton.

### (vi) Canada

The tax treatment of options transactions is dependent on whether the gain or loss is treated as being on income or capital account. Speculative transactions are generally treated as being on income account although the speculator may be able to elect for capital treatment if it is applied consistently. Transactions on both income and capital account will generally be dealt with on a realized basis.

### (vii) Hong Kong

Profits from options transactions will be taxable as income if the taxpayer is engaged in speculative dealing or in hedging an underlying transaction which is taxable on revenue account.

### (viii) Singapore

Profits should be taxed as income in the hands of financial institutions. For other taxpayers the transactions may be treated as capital in which case profits/losses are not taxable/allowable.

## 5. Conclusions

The development of the use of financial instruments such as options demonstrates the principle that new products may not fit into old law. The tax mismatches in certain tax systems create problems and/or opportunities which may be overcome only by complex specific legislation. Significant tax exposures may arise if transactions are not analysed in advance and advice taken where appropriate.

# Appendix 1: Glossary of options terms

| | |
|---|---|
| Adjusted exercise price | When a dividend is paid on a stock subject to a conventional option, or when any capital change such as a stock split occurs to a stock subject to a listed or conventional option, the exercise price is adjusted to reflect the change. |
| American option | An option that can be exercised at any time before expiration. |
| Arbitrage | The simultaneous purchase and sale of similar financial instruments to benefit from an expected change in relative prices. |
| Assignment | Notice to an option writer that an option has been exercised by an option holder. An assignment notice is generally issued by the clearing house for exchange-traded options. |
| Automatic exercise | A procedure for exchange-listed options whereby the clearing house automatically exercises in-the-money options at expiration. |
| At-the-money | An option where the exercise price of the option is equal to the market price of the underlying asset. |
| Basis | The difference between the spot price of a commodity or financial instrument and the price of a futures contract on that commodity or instrument. |
| Bear call spread | A spread designed to take advantage of falling asset prices by purchasing a call option with a high exercise price and selling one with a low exercise price. |
| Bear put spread | A spread also designed to take advantage of falling asset prices by purchasing a put option with a high exercise price and selling one with a low exercise price. |
| Beta | A measure of the relative volatility of stock price returns and market returns. |
| Box spread | A combination of a horizontal, or calendar, call spread (q.v.) and a horizontal put spread. Both spreads have the same expiration dates on their long and short positions. A bull call spread (q.v.) with a bear put spread (q.v.) is a debit box. A bear call spread (q.v.) with a bull put spread (q.v.) is a credit box. |
| Break | A sudden or rapid fall in asset prices. |
| Break-out | Undoing a conversion or a reversal to restore the option buyer's original position. |
| Bull call spread | A spread designed to take advantage of rising asset prices by selling a call option with a high exercise price and buying one with a low exercise price. |
| Bull put spread | A spread designed to take advantage of rising assets prices by selling a put option with a high exercise price and buying one with a low exercise price. |
| Butterfly spread | A combination of a bull and bear spread, either put or call, using three different exercise prices. Thus a typical butterfly spread might be short an option with an exercise price of 40, long two options at 45, and short another option at 50. |
| Buy-in | If an option writer does not hold enough assets to deliver to the option buyer at exercise, he will "buy in" the assets in the market. |

| | |
|---|---|
| Buyer | The purchaser of an option, either a call option (*q.v.*) or a put option (*q.v.*). |
| Calendar spread | A spread involving the simultaneous sale of an option with a nearby expiration date and the purchase of an option with a more deferred expiration date. Both options have the same exercise price. |
| Call option | An option giving the buyer the right to purchase the underlying asset at a fixed exercise price at or before expiration. |
| Cash option | An option written on an underlying cash instrument rather than a futures contract. |
| Cash settlement | A procedure for the settlement of a futures contract where, at delivery, instead of the physical transfer of the underlying asset, there is a final marking to market at the existing cash price and the positions are closed. |
| CBOE | Chicago Board Options Exchange. |
| CBT | Chicago Board of Trade. |
| CFTC | Commodity Futures Trading Commission. |
| Class of options | All call options or put options on the same underlying asset. |
| Closing purchase transaction | The purchase of an option identical in exercise price and expiration date to an option originally sold to liquidate an open option position. |
| CME | Chicago Mercantile Exchange. |
| Collateral | The loan value for margin of specific securities. |
| Combination | A position created either by purchasing a put and a call, or writing a put and a call, on the same underlying asset, i.e. not a straddle. |
| Conversion arbitrage | A transaction in which the arbitrageur buys an asset, buys a put option and sells a call option. The options have the same exercise price (*q.v.*) and expiration date (*q.v.*). |
| Conversion factor | A factor used to determine the invoice amount to be paid at delivery for a cash bond delivered against a futures contract. |
| Covered call write | A strategy of writing call options against a long position of the underlying asset. |
| Covered put write | A strategy of writing put options while simultaneously shorting an identical amount of the underlying asset. |
| Covered option | A written option is covered if it is matched by an opposing cash or futures position in the underlying asset, or by an opposing option position of specific characteristics. |
| Cycle | The set of expiration dates applicable to different classes of options. |
| Delta | A measure of the amount the option price will change for a one-unit change in the underlying asset (technically the first derivative of the option price with respect to the asset price). |
| Delta spread | A ratio spread of options established as a neutral position by using the deltas of the options concerned to determine the hedge ratio. |
| Diagonal bear spread | The purchase of a longer maturity option and the sale of a shorter maturity, lower exercise price option. The options can be either puts or calls. |
| Diagonal bull spread | The sale of a shorter maturity option and the purchase of a longer maturity, lower exercise price option. The options can either be puts or calls. |
| Discount | An option is trading at a discount if it is trading for less than its intrinsic value. |
| Double option | An option to buy or sell but not both. Exercise of the right to buy causes the right to sell to expire and vice-versa. |
| Down-and-out call | A call option that expires if the asset price falls below a predetermined level. |
| Epsilon | The change in the price of an option associated with a 1% change in implied volatility (technically the first derivative of the option price with respect to volatility). Also referred to as eta, vega, omega and kappa. |

| | |
|---|---|
| European option | A call or put option that can be exercised only on the expiration date. |
| Exercise | The action taken by the holder of an option contract to exercise his right. When a call is exercised, the holder acquires the underlying asset at the option exercise price. When a put is exercised, the holder sells the underlying asset at the option exercise price. |
| Exercise limit | A limit on the number of option contracts a holder may exercise within a specific period. |
| Exercise price | The price at which the option holder may buy or sell the underlying asset, as defined in the option contract. |
| Expiration date | The date after which an option can no longer be exercised. |
| Fair value | The option value derived from a mathematical option valuation model. |
| Futures contract | A contract traded on a futures exchange for the delivery of a specified quantity of a specified commodity or financial instrument at a future time. |
| Futures option | An option written on a futures contract rather than a cash or spot instrument. |
| Gamma | The amount by which the delta (*q.v.*) of an option changes for a one unit change in the price of the underlying asset (technically the second derivative of the option price with respect to the asset price). |
| Hedge | To protect a specific position against price risk by buying or selling offsetting positions. |
| Hedge ratio | The delta (*q.v.*) of an option derived from an option valuation model. It tells the proportion of options and underlying assets that will create a theoretically riskless hedge. |
| Holder | Same as buyer. |
| Horizontal spread | Same as a calendar spread (*q.v.*). |
| ICCH | International Commodities Clearing House |
| Implied volatility | The value of asset price volatility that will equate the market price of an option with the fair value of an option. |
| Index option | An option written on an underlying stock or commodity index as opposed to a specific asset. |
| In-the-money | An option is said to be "in-the-money" if it has intrinsic value. A call is in-the-money if the asset price is above the exercise price (*q.v.*); a put is in-the-money if the asset price is below the exercise price. |
| Intrinsic value | The amount of profit that would be realized if the option were immediately exercised. |
| Long | The position which is established by the purchase of an asset or option if there is no offsetting position. |
| Margin | The sum of money which must be deposited – and maintained – to provide protection to both parties to a trade. Buyers of options do not need to post margin, except on the London International Financial Futures Exchange. |
| Margin calls | Additional funds which a person with an asset position, or who has written an option, may be called upon to deposit if there is an adverse price change or if margin requirements alter. |
| Mark to market | The process of evaluating a position relative to the settlement price of the asset, and ensuring the interim payment of profits and losses to maintain the margin at required levels. |
| Naked writing | Writing a call or a put on an underlying asset which is not owned by the writer. |
| OCC | Options Clearing Corporation. |
| Opening transaction | The purchase or writing of a put or call option which establishes a new position. |
| Open interest | The net total of outstanding contracts for a particular options or futures class. |
| Option | The right to buy or sell a specific quantity of a specific asset at a fixed price at or before a future date. |

| | |
|---|---|
| Out-of-the-money | An option that has no intrinsic value – because for a call the exercise price is above the asset price, and for a put the excercise price is below the asset price. |
| Over-the-counter option | An option traded over-the-counter as opposed to on a listed exchange. There is a direct link between buyer and seller, and no standardization of striking prices and expiration dates. |
| Position limit | The maximum number of puts and calls on the same side of the market (e.g. long calls and short puts) that can be held in a single account. |
| Premium | The price of an option – the sum of money which the option buyer pays and the option writer receives for the rights granted by the option. |
| Profit graph | A graphical representation of the profits to a given options strategy for different underlying asset prices. |
| Put option | An option which gives the buyer the right to sell the underlying asset at a fixed price at or before the expiration date. |
| Ratio spread | Buying a specific quantity of options and selling a larger quantity of out-of-the-money options; either puts or calls can be used. |
| Ratio calendar spread | Selling more near-term options than longer maturity options at the same strike price. |
| Ratio write | Buying stock and selling options on a larger amount of stock. |
| Reversal | The process of changing a call into a put. |
| Reversal arbitrage | Selling an asset short, writing a put and buying a call on the asset with the same terms. |
| Rolling over | Substituting an option with a different expiration date and for a different striking price for a previously established position. |
| Sandwich spread | Same as a butterfly spread (q.v.). |
| SEC | Securities and Exchange Commission. |
| Seller | Equivalent to an option writer. |
| Series | All options of the same class having the same exercise price and expiration date. |
| Short | The position created by the sale of an asset or option if there is no offsetting position. |
| Spread | A position involving the purchase and sale of options on the same underlying asset but with different striking prices and/or expiration dates. |
| Straddle | A combination of a put and a call on the same underlying asset, each with the same exercise price and expiration date. |
| Strap | A combination of two calls and one put. |
| Strike price | Same as exercise price (q.v.). |
| Strip | A combination of two puts and one call. |
| Synthetic stock | A combination of a put and a call option which is equivalent to the stock. |
| Theta | The change in the price of the option associated with a one-period reduction in the time to expiration (technically the first derivative of the option price with respect to time). |
| Time value | The amount by which an option's premium exceeds its intrinsic value. |
| Vertical bear spread | The purchase of an option with a high exercise price and the sale of an option with a lower exercise price. Both options will have the same expiration date and could be puts or calls. |
| Vertical bull spread | The sale of an option with a high exercise price and the purchase of an option with a lower exercise price. Both options will have the same expiration date and could be puts or calls. |
| Volatility | A measure of the amount by which an asset price is expected to fluctuate over a given period. Normally measured by the annual standard deviation of daily price changes. |
| Writer | The seller of a call or a put option in connection with an opening transaction. |

# Appendix 2: Contract specifications

This appendix contains the specifications, at the time of writing, for the most important and/or heavily traded options contracts on the world's futures exchange. Although believed to be correct at the time of going to press, neither the author nor Euromoney Publications take responsibility for these descriptions. Exchanges often change contract specifications, particularly in terms of price limits, margin requirements, etc. at short notice. Anyone wishing to trade options should contact his broker or the relevant exchange to determine the up-to-date contract specifications.

## 1. Individual stock options

It is unnecessary to give details of each individual stock option. The following section gives broad details of stock options traded on various exchanges.

### London Stock Exchange (approximately 40 stocks)

| | |
|---|---|
| Contract size | 1,000 shares (Vaal Reef – 100 shares) |
| Contract months | Three different cycles: |
| | January/April/July/October |
| | February/May/August/November |
| | March/June/September/December |
| Last trading day | Varies year to year, contact exchange |
| Trading hours | 09.35–15.30 |
| Premium quote | Pence per share 5p = £50 |
| Minimum price movement | $\frac{1}{2}$p = £5 |
| Exercise price interval | Specific to individual shares and prices |

### American Stock Exchange / Chicago Stock Exchange / Pacific Stock Exchange / Philadelphia Stock Exchange / New York Stock Exchange / NASDAQ (approximately 450 stocks)

| | |
|---|---|
| Contract size | 100 shares |
| Contract months | Three different cycles:[1] |
| | January/April/July/October |
| | February/May/August/November |
| | March/June/September/December |
| Last trading day | Third Friday of delivery month |

---

[1] Many shares now trade on a near three-month cycle in addition to the normal cycle.

245

| Trading hours (local times) | AMEX 09.30–16.00 |
| | Chicago 08.30–15.00 |
| | Pacific 06.30–13.00 |
| | Philadelphia 09.30–16.00 |
| | NYSE 09.30–16.00 |
| | NASDAQ 09.30–16.00 |
| Premium quote | $ and fractions per share |
| Minimum price movement | $\frac{1}{16} = \$6.25$ |
| Exercise price interval | Specific to individual shares and prices |

## European Options Exchange (Amsterdam) (16 stocks)

| | |
| --- | --- |
| Contract size | 100 shares (Petrofina 10 shares) |
| Contract months | January, April, July, October |
| Last trading day | Third Friday of delivery months |
| Trading hours | 10.00–16.30 |
| | (Petrofina 12.30–14.30) |
| Premium quote | Guilders per share |
| | (Petrofina: Belgian francs per share) |
| Minimum price movement | 0.10 florins |
| Exercise price interval | Specific to individual shares and prices |

## Sydney Stock Exchange (13 stocks)

| | |
| --- | --- |
| Contract size | 1,000 shares |
| Contract months | Three different cycles: |
| | January/April/July/October |
| | February/May/August/November |
| | March/June/September/December |
| Last trading day | Thursday preceding last Friday of delivery months |
| Trading hours | 10.00–12.30 |
| | 14.00–15.00 |
| Premium quote | Australian dollars and cents per share |
| Exercise price interval | Specific to individual shares and prices |

## Montreal Exchange
## Toronto Stock Exchange
## Vancouver Stock Exchange } (53 stocks)

| | |
| --- | --- |
| Contract size | 100 shares |
| Contract months | Three different cycles: |
| | January/April/July/October |
| | February/May/August/November |
| | March/June/September/December |
| Last trading day | Third Friday of delivery month |
| Trading hours | Montreal 09.00–16.00 |
| | Toronto 10.00–16.00 |
| | Vancouver 09.00–13.00 |
| Premium quote | Canadian dollars and fractions per share |
| Minimum price movement | $\frac{1}{16} = \$6.25$ |
| Exercise price interval | Specific to individual shares and prices |

## 2. Currency options

| Exchange | Contract specification | Contract months | Last trading day | Expiration settlement day | Trading hours | Premium quote | Minimum price movement | Exercise price intervals |
|---|---|---|---|---|---|---|---|---|
| London Stock Exchange | £12,500 sterling cash | 1, 2, 3, 6, 9, 12 months out | Friday before third Wednesday of month | Third Wednesday of month | 09.00–15.30 | US cents per £ | 0.05¢ per £ or $6.25 | 5¢ |
| | Deutschmark 65,000 cash | 1, 2, 3, 6, 9, 12 months out | Friday before third Wednesday of month | Third Wednesday of month | 09.00–15.30 | US cents per per DM | 0.01¢ per DM or $6.25 | 1¢ |
| European Options Exchange | £5,000 sterling cash | March, June, Sept., Dec. | Third Friday of month | First business day after expiration | 10.00–16.30 | US cents per £ | 0.05¢ per £ or $2.50 | 5¢ |
| | £100,000 sterling cash | March, June, Sept., Dec. | Third Friday of month | First business day after expiration | 10.00–16.30. | US cents per £ | 0.01¢ per £ or $10 | 5¢ |
| | US$10,000 cash | March, June, Sept., Dec. | Third Friday of month | First business day after expiration | 10.00–16.30 | Pfennigs per US dollar | DM0.0005 per $ or DM5 | DM0.05 |
| | ECU 10,000 cash | March, June, Sept., Dec. | Third Friday of month | First business day after expiration | 10.00–16.30 | US cents per ECU | 0.01¢ per ECU or $1 | 2¢ |
| | US$10,000 cash | March, June, Sept., Dec. | Third Friday of month | First business day after expiration | 10.00–16.30 | Dutch florins per US dollar | Dfl0.0005 per $ or Dfl5 | Dfl0.05 |
| London International Financial Futures Exchange | £25,000 sterling cash | March, June, Sept., Dec. | Two business days before third Wednesday of delivery month | Third Wednesday of month | 08.32–16.02 | US cents per £ | 0.01¢ per £ or $2.50 | 5¢ |
| Philadelphia Stock Exchange | £12,500 sterling cash | Two near months, and March, June, Sept., Dec. | Friday before third Wednesday of month | Third Wednesday of month | 08.00–14.30 | US cents per £ | 0.05¢ per £ or $6.25 | 5¢ |
| | C$50,000 Canadian cash | Two near months, and March, June, Sept., Dec. | Friday before third Wednesday of month | Third Wednesday of month | 08.00–14.30 | US cents per C$ | 0.01¢ per C$ or $5.00 | 1¢ |
| | DM62,500 Deutschmark cash | Two near months and March, June, Sept., Dec. | Friday before third Wednesday of month | Third Wednesday of month | 08.00–14.30 | US cents per DM | 0.01¢ per DM or $6.25 | 1¢ |
| | FF125,000 French francs cash | Two near months, and March, June, Sept., Dec. | Friday before third Wednesday of month | Third Wednesday of month | 08.00–14.30 | US cents per Ffr10 | 0.005¢ per Ffr or $6.25 | ½¢ |
| | SF62,500 Swiss francs cash | Two near months, and March, June, Sept., Dec. | Friday before third Wednesday of month | Third Wednesday of month | 08.00–14.30 | US cents per SwFr | 0.01¢ per SwFr or $6.25 | 1¢ |

## 2. Currency options

| Exchange | Contract specification | Contract months | Last trading day | Expiration settlement day | Trading hours | Premium quote | Minimum price movement | Exercise price intervals |
|---|---|---|---|---|---|---|---|---|
|  | Y6,250,000 Yen cash | Two near months, and March, June Sept., Dec. | Friday before third Wednesday of month | Third Wednesday of month | 08.00–14.30 | US cents per Yen100 | 0.01¢ per Yen100 or $6.25 | 0.01¢ |
| Montreal Exchange | £100,000 sterling cash | Three near months and March, June, Sept., Dec. | Thursday preceding third Friday of month | Fourth business day after third Friday of month | 07.30–15.00 | US cents per £ | 0.01¢ per £ or $10 | 5¢ |
|  | US$100,000 cash | March, June, Sept., Dec. and three closest months | Thursday preceding third Friday of delivery month | Fourth business day after third Friday | 9.00–14.30 | Pfennigs per US dollar | DM0.0001 per $ or DM10 | DM0.05 |
| (Also Vancouver) | C$50,000 cash | March, June, Sept., Dec. | Thursday preceding third Friday of delivery month | Fourth business day after third Friday | 9.00–14.30 | US cents per C$ | 0.01¢ or C$5 | 1¢ |
|  | US$100,000 cash | March, June, Sept., Dec. | Thursday preceding third Friday of delivery month | Fourth business day after third Friday | 9.00–14.30 | Swiss francs per US dollar | SwFr0.0001 or SwFr10 | SwFr0.05 |
| Chicago Board Options Exchange | $100,000 cash European | March, June, Sept., Dec. | Third Friday of delivery month | Three business days after delivery day | 7.00–13.30 | US cents per C$ | 0.01¢ or $10.00 | 1¢ |
|  | DM125,000 cash European | March, June, Sept., Dec. | Third Friday of delivery month | Three business days after delivery day | 7.00–13.30 | US cents per DM | 0.01¢ or $12.50 | 1¢ |
|  | Ffr250,000 cash European | March, June, Sept., Dec. | Third Friday of delivery month | Three business days after delivery day | 7.00–13.30 | US cents per Ffr | 0.005¢ or $12.50 | 0.5¢ |
|  | Sterling £25,000 cash European | March, June, Sept., Dec. | Third Friday of delivery month | Three business days after delivery day | 7.00–13.30 | US cents per £ | 0.05¢ or $12.50 | $2\frac{1}{2}$ or 5¢ |
|  | Swfr125,000 cash European | March, June, Sept., Dec. | Third Friday of delivery month | Three business days after delivery day | 7.00–13.30 | US cents per Swfr | 0.01¢ or $12.50 | 1¢ |
|  | Yen12,500,000 cash American | March, June, Sept., Dec. | Third Friday of delivery month | Three business days after third Friday | 07.00–13.30 | US cents 0.01¢ per Yen100 | 0.0001¢ or $12.50 | 0.01¢ |
| Chicago Mercantile Exchange (IOM) | DM125,000 futures contract | March, June, Sept., Dec. | Two Fridays before third Wednesday of contract month | Business day following expiration day | 07.30–13.20 | US cents per DM | 0.01¢ per DM or $12.50 | 1¢ |

## 2. Currency options

| Exchange | Contract specification | Contract months | Last trading day | Expiration settlement day | Trading hours | Premium quote | Minimum price movement | Exercise price intervals |
|---|---|---|---|---|---|---|---|---|
| | Sterling $25,000 futures contract | March, June, Sept., Dec. | Two Fridays before third Wednesday of contract month | Business day following expiration day | 07.30–13.24 | US cents per £ | 0.05¢ per DM or $12.50 | 2.5¢ |
| | Swfr125,000 futures contract | March, June, Sept., Dec. | Two Fridays before third Wednesday of contract month | Business day following expiration day | 07.30–13.16 | US cents per Swfr | 0.01¢ per Swfr or $12.50 | 1¢ |
| Sydney Futures Exchange | US$100,000 futures contract | March, June, Sept., Dec. | Third Wednesday of contract month | Third Wednesday of contract month | 08.45–16.00 | Australian dollars per US dollar | A$0.0001 per US$ or A$10 | A$0.02 |

## 3. Interest rate options

| Exchange | Contract specification | Contract months | Last trading day | Expiration settlement day | Trading hours | Premium quote | Minimum price movement | Exercise price intervals |
|---|---|---|---|---|---|---|---|---|
| London Stock Exchange | Gilt £50,000 nominal Treasury $11\frac{3}{4}\%$ 1991 cash | Aug., Nov., Feb., May | Last business day of month | Second business day following exercise day | 09.35–15.30 | $\frac{1}{32}$ of a point | $\frac{1}{32}$ or £15.625 | 2 points |
| | £50,000 nominal Treasury $11\frac{3}{4}\%$ 2003/07 cash | Aug., Nov., Feb., May | Last business day of month | Second business day following exercise day | 09.35–15.30 | $\frac{1}{32}$ of a point | $\frac{1}{32}$ or £15.625 | 2 points |
| London International Financial Futures Exchange | Long gilt £50,000 12% long gilt future | March, June, Sept., Dec. | Six business days before first delivery day of gilt future | Business day following expiration day | 09.32–16.15 | $\frac{1}{64}$ of a point | $\frac{1}{64}$ or £7.8125 | 2 points |
| | T-bond $100,000 8% T-bond future | March, June, Sept., Dec. | First Friday preceding by at least six business days the first delivery day of T-bond future | Business day following expiration day | 08.17–16.10 | $\frac{1}{64}$ of a point | $\frac{1}{64}$ or $15.625 | 2 points |

## 3. Interest rate options

| Exchange | Contract specification | Contract months | Last trading day | Expiration settlement day | Trading hours | Premium quote | Minimum price movement | Exercise price intervals |
|---|---|---|---|---|---|---|---|---|
| Chicago Board Options Exchange | T-bond $100,000 nominal Various cash T-bonds recently auctioned | March, June, Sept., Dec. | Third Friday of delivery month | Business day after expiration day | 08.00–14.00 | $\frac{1}{32}$ of a point | $\frac{1}{32}$ or $31.25 | 2 points |
| Chicago Board of Trade | T-bond $100,000 8% T-bond future | March, June, Sept., Dec. | First Friday preceding by at least 5 days first notice day for futures contract | First Saturday following last day of trading | 08.00–14.00 | $\frac{1}{64}$ of a point | $\frac{1}{64}$ or $15.625 | 2 points |
| | T-note $100,000 8% T-note future | March, June, Sept., Dec. | First Friday preceding by at least 5 days first notice day for futures contract | First Saturday following last day of trading | 08.00–14.00 | $\frac{1}{64}$ of a point | $\frac{1}{64}$ or $15.625 | 2 points |
| Chicago Mercantile Exchange (IOM) | Eurodollar $1,000,000 face value 3-month ED futures contract | March, June, Sept., Dec. | Two business days before third Wednesday of month | Third Wednesday of month | 07.20–14.00 | Basis points or $\frac{1}{100}$ of 1% | 1 basis point or $25 | Below 91.00: 50bp Above 91.00: 25bp |
| | T-bill $1,000,000 face value 3-month T-bill future | March, June, Sept., Dec. | Friday before the Wednesday on which T-bill future goes to delivery | Delivery day of futures contract | 07.20–14.00 | Basis points or $\frac{1}{100}$ or 1% | 1 basis point or $25 | Below 91.00: 50bp Above 91.00: 25bp |
| Sydney Futures Exchange | Acceptances A$500,000 face value 90-day bank accepted bill futures contract | March, June, Sept., Dec. | Friday two weeks before futures settlement day | Day following last trading day | 09.00–12.30 14.00–16.30 | Basis points or $\frac{1}{100}$ of 1% | 1 basis point | 50 basis points |
| | T-bond A$100,000 face value T-bond futures contract | March, June, Sept., Dec. | 15th day (or next business day) of contract month | Delivery day of futures contract (15th of month) | 09.05–12.30 14.00–16.00 | Yield percent per annum | 1 basis point or about $A60; varies with prices | 25 points |

## 3. Interest rate options

| Exchange | Contract specification | Contract months | Last trading day | Expiration settlement day | Trading hours | Premium quote | Minimum price movement | Exercise price intervals |
|---|---|---|---|---|---|---|---|---|
| American Stock Exchange | Domestic CD $1,000,000 90-day CD cash | March, June, Sept., Dec. | Third Friday of delivery month | Two business days after expiration day | 09.00–15.00 | Yield points 1.50 = $3,750 | 1 basis point = $25 | 100 basis points |
| | 10-yr Treasury note $20,000 face value specific T-note cash | March, June, Sept., Dec. | Third Friday of delivery month | Two business days after expiration day | 09.00–15.00 | Points and 32nds 1–16 = $300 | $\frac{1}{32}$nd = $6.25 | 4 points |
| | 13-week T-Bill $20,000 face value current 13-week T-bill cash | March, June, Sept., Dec. | Third Friday of delivery month | Two business days after expiration day | 09.00–15.00 | Yield points 1.50 = $300 | 1 basis point = $25 | 100 basis points |
| | 26-week T-bill $20,000 face value, current 26-week T bill cash | March, June, Sept., Dec. | Third Friday of delivery month | Two business days after expiration day | 09.00–15.00 | Yield points 1.50 = $300 | 1 basis point = $25 | 100 basis points |

## 4. Stock index options

| Exchange | Contract specification | Contract months | Last trading day | Expiration settlement day | Trading hours | Premium quote | Minimum price movement | Exercise price intervals |
|---|---|---|---|---|---|---|---|---|
| London Stock Exchange | FTSE 100 £10 × FTSE-100 index level cash | Next one, two, three and four months | Last business day of month | First business day following expiration | 09.35–15.30 | Pence per index point | $\frac{1}{2}$p = £5 | 25 index points |
| Chicago Board Options Exchange | S & P 100 $100 × index level cash | Four nearest months | Third Friday of expiration month | First business day following expiration day | 09.00–15.10 | $ and cents per index point | Premium below $3: $\frac{1}{16}$ = $6.25 Premium above $3: $\frac{1}{8}$ = $12.50 | 2.5 index points |
| | S & P 500 $500 × index level cash | Four nearest months | Third Friday of expiration month | First business day following expiration day | 09.00–15.10 | $ and cents per index point | Premium below $3: $\frac{1}{16}$ = $31.25 Premium above $3: $\frac{1}{8}$ = $62.50 | 2.5 index points |

## 4. Stock index options

| Exchange | Contract specification | Contract months | Last trading day | Expiration settlement day | Trading hours | Premium quote | Minimum price movement | Exercise price intervals |
|---|---|---|---|---|---|---|---|---|
| | S&P OTC 250 index $100 × index level cash | Four nearest months | Third Friday of expiration month | First business day following expiration day | 09.00–15.10 | $ and cents per index point | Premium below $3: $\frac{1}{16}$ = $6.25 Premium above $3: $\frac{1}{8}$ = $12.50 | 2.5 index points |
| New York Stock Exchange | NYSE composite index $100 × index level cash | Three nearest months and next month of March, June, Sept., Dec. cycle | Third Friday of expiration month | First business day following expiration day | 09.30–16.10 | $ and cents per index point | $\frac{1}{16}$ = $6.25 1pt = $100 | 5 index points |
| American Stock Exchange | Major market index options $100 × index level cash | Three nearest months and next month of March, June, Sept., Dec. cycle | Third Friday of expiration month | First business day following expiration day | 09.30–16.10 | $ and cents per index point | Premium below $3: $\frac{1}{16}$ = $6.25 Premium above $3: $\frac{1}{2}$ = $12.50 | 5 points |
| | Airline index $100 × index level cash | March, June, Sept., Dec. | Third Friday of delivery month | First business day following expiration day | 09.30–16.10 | $ and cents per index point | Premiums below $3: $\frac{1}{16}$ = $6.25 Premiums above $3: $\frac{1}{8}$ = $12.50 | 5 index points |
| | Computer technology index $100 × index level cash | March, June, Sept., Dec. | Third Friday of delivery month | First business day following expiration day | 09.30–16.10 | $ and cents per index point | Premiums below $3: $\frac{1}{16}$ = $6.25 Premiums above $3: $\frac{1}{8}$ = $12.50 | 5 index points |
| | Oil index $100 × index level cash | Three nearest months and next month of Jan./April/July/Oct. cycle | Third Friday of delivery month | First business day following expiration day | 09.30–16.10 | $ and cents per index point | Premiums below $3: $\frac{1}{16}$ = $6.25 Premiums above $3: $\frac{1}{8}$ = $12.50 | 5 index points |

# 4. Stock index options

| Exchange | Contract specification | Contract months | Last trading day | Expiration settlement day | Trading hours | Premium quote | Minimum price movement | Exercise price intervals |
|---|---|---|---|---|---|---|---|---|
| | Market value index<br>$100 × index level cash | Three nearest months and next month of March/June/Sept./Dec. cycle | Third Friday of delivery month | First business day following expiration day | 09.30–16.10 | $ and cents per index point | Premiums below $3: $\frac{1}{16}$ = $6.25<br>Premiums above $3: $\frac{1}{8}$ = $12.50 | 5 index points |
| Philadelphia Stock Exchange | National OTC index<br>$100 × index level cash | Three nearest months and next month of March/June/Sept./Dec. cycle | Third Friday of delivery month | First business day following expiration day | 09.30–16.10 | $ and cents per index point | Premiums below $3: $\frac{1}{16}$ = $6.25<br>Premiums above $3: $\frac{1}{8}$ = $12.50 | 5 index points |
| | Gold and silver index<br>$100 × index level cash | Three nearest months and next month of March/June/Sept./Dec. cycle | Third Friday of delivery month | First business day following expiration day | 09.30–16.10 | $ and cents per index point | Premiums below $3: $\frac{1}{16}$ = $6.25<br>Premiums above $3: $\frac{1}{8}$ = $12.50 | 5 index points |
| | Value line index<br>$100 × index level cash | Three nearest months and next month of March/June/Sept. Dec. cycle | Third Friday of delivery month | First business day after expiration day | 09.30–16.10 | $ and cents per index point | Premium below $3: $\frac{1}{16}$ = $6.25<br>Premiums above $3: $\frac{1}{8}$ = $12.50 | 5 index points |
| NASDAQ System | NASDAQ 100 index<br>$100 × index level cash | Four nearest months | Third Friday of delivery month | First business day after expiration day | 09.30–16.10 | $ and cents per index point | $\frac{1}{16}$ = $6.25 | 5 index points |
| Toronto Stock Exchange | TSE-300 index<br>C$500 × index level cash | Three nearest months | Third Friday of delivery month | First business day after expiration day | 09.30–16.10 | Canadian $ and cents per index point | Premiums below C$5: 5¢<br>Premiums above C$5: 12.5¢ | 5 index points |

## 4. Stock index options

| Exchange | Contract specification | Contract months | Last trading day | Expiration settlement day | Trading hours | Premium quote | Minimum price movement | Exercise price intervals |
|---|---|---|---|---|---|---|---|---|
| Montreal Exchange | Canadian market Portfolio index C$100 × index level cash | Three nearest months | Third Friday of delivery month | First business day after expiration day | 09.30–16.00 | Canadian $ and cents per index point | C$0.05 = C$5 | 5 index points |
| Chicago Mercantile Exchange (IOM) | S & P 500 index $500 × index level futures contract | March, June, Sept., Dec. | Third Friday of delivery month | First business day after expiration day | 08.30–15.15 | Index points | 0.05pts = $25 | 5 index poir's |
| New York Futures Exchange | NYSE index $500 × index level futures contract | March, June, Sept., Dec. | Third Friday of delivery month | First business day after expiration day | 09.30–16.15 | Index points | 0.05pts = $25 | 2 index points |
| Sydney Futures Exchange | All ordinaries share price index A$100 × index level futures contract | March, June, Sept., Dec. | Second to last business day of delivery month | First business day after expiration day | 09.30–12.30 14.00–15.45 | Index points | 0.10pts = A$10 | 25 index points |
| Pacific Stock Exchange | Technology stock index $100 × index level cash | Three consecutive months and March, June, Sept., Dec. | Third Friday of contract month | First business day after expiration day | 06.30–13.10 | $ and cents per index point | Premiums under $3: $\frac{1}{16}$ = $6.25 Premiums above $3: $\frac{1}{8}$ = $12.50 | 5 index points |

# Appendix 3: Normal distribution table

| $(Y-\mu)/$ $\sigma = Z$ | 0.00 | 0.01 | 0.02 | 0.03 | 0.04 | 0.05 | 0.06 | 0.07 | 0.08 | 0.09 |
|---|---|---|---|---|---|---|---|---|---|---|
| 0.0 | 0.0000 | 0.0040 | 0.0080 | 0.0120 | 0.0160 | 0.0199 | 0.0239 | 0.0279 | 0.0319 | 0.0359 |
| 0.1 | 0.0398 | 0.0438 | 0.0478 | 0.0517 | 0.0557 | 0.0596 | 0.0636 | 0.0675 | 0.0714 | 0.0753 |
| 0.2 | 0.0793 | 0.0832 | 0.0871 | 0.0910 | 0.0948 | 0.0987 | 0.1026 | 0.1064 | 0.1103 | 0.1141 |
| 0.3 | 0.1179 | 0.1217 | 0.1255 | 0.1293 | 0.1331 | 0.1368 | 0.1406 | 0.1443 | 0.1480 | 0.1517 |
| 0.4 | 0.1554 | 0.1591 | 0.1628 | 0.1664 | 0.1700 | 0.1736 | 0.1772 | 0.1808 | 0.1844 | 0.1879 |
| 0.5 | 0.1915 | 0.1950 | 0.1985 | 0.2019 | 0.2054 | 0.2088 | 0.2123 | 0.2157 | 0.2190 | 0.2224 |
| 0.6 | 0.2257 | 0.2291 | 0.2324 | 0.2357 | 0.2389 | 0.2422 | 0.2454 | 0.2486 | 0.2517 | 0.2549 |
| 0.7 | 0.2580 | 0.2611 | 0.2642 | 0.2673 | 0.2704 | 0.2734 | 0.2764 | 0.2794 | 0.2823 | 0.2852 |
| 0.8 | 0.2881 | 0.2910 | 0.2939 | 0.2967 | 0.2995 | 0.3023 | 0.3051 | 0.3078 | 0.3106 | 0.3233 |
| 0.9 | 0.3159 | 0.3186 | 0.3212 | 0.3238 | 0.3264 | 0.3289 | 0.3315 | 0.3340 | 0.3365 | 0.3389 |
| 1.0 | 0.3413 | 0.3438 | 0.3461 | 0.3485 | 0.3508 | 0.3531 | 0.3554 | 0.3577 | 0.3599 | 0.3621 |
| 1.1 | 0.3643 | 0.3665 | 0.3686 | 0.3708 | 0.3729 | 0.3749 | 0.3770 | 0.3790 | 0.3810 | 0.3830 |
| 1.2 | 0.3849 | 0.3869 | 0.3888 | 0.3907 | 0.3925 | 0.3944 | 0.3962 | 0.3980 | 0.3997 | 0.4015 |
| 1.3 | 0.4032 | 0.4049 | 0.4066 | 0.4082 | 0.4099 | 0.4115 | 0.4131 | 0.4147 | 0.4162 | 0.4177 |
| 1.4 | 0.4192 | 0.4207 | 0.4222 | 0.4236 | 0.4251 | 0.4265 | 0.4279 | 0.4292 | 0.4306 | 0.4319 |
| 1.5 | 0.4332 | 0.4345 | 0.4357 | 0.4370 | 0.4382 | 0.4394 | 0.4406 | 0.4418 | 0.4429 | 0.4441 |
| 1.6 | 0.4452 | 0.4463 | 0.4474 | 0.4484 | 0.4495 | 0.4505 | 0.4515 | 0.4525 | 0.4535 | 0.4545 |
| 1.7 | 0.4554 | 0.4564 | 0.4573 | 0.4582 | 0.4591 | 0.4599 | 0.4608 | 0.4616 | 0.4625 | 0.4633 |
| 1.8 | 0.4641 | 0.4649 | 0.4656 | 0.4664 | 0.4671 | 0.4678 | 0.4686 | 0.4693 | 0.4699 | 0.4706 |
| 1.9 | 0.4713 | 0.4719 | 0.4726 | 0.4732 | 0.4738 | 0.4744 | 0.4750 | 0.4758 | 0.4761 | 0.4767 |
| 2.0 | 0.4772 | 0.4778 | 0.4783 | 0.4788 | 0.4793 | 0.4798 | 0.4803 | 0.4808 | 0.4812 | 0.4817 |
| 2.1 | 0.4821 | 0.4826 | 0.4830 | 0.4834 | 0.4838 | 0.4842 | 0.4846 | 0.4850 | 0.4854 | 0.4857 |
| 2.2 | 0.4861 | 0.4864 | 0.4868 | 0.4871 | 0.4875 | 0.4878 | 0.4881 | 0.4884 | 0.4887 | 0.4890 |
| 2.3 | 0.4893 | 0.4896 | 0.4898 | 0.4901 | 0.4904 | 0.4906 | 0.4909 | 0.4911 | 0.4913 | 0.4916 |
| 2.4 | 0.4918 | 0.4920 | 0.4922 | 0.4925 | 0.4927 | 0.4929 | 0.4931 | 0.4932 | 0.4934 | 0.4936 |
| 2.5 | 0.4938 | 0.4940 | 0.4941 | 0.4943 | 0.4945 | 0.4946 | 0.4948 | 0.4949 | 0.4951 | 0.4952 |
| 2.6 | 0.4953 | 0.4955 | 0.4956 | 0.4957 | 0.4959 | 0.4960 | 0.4961 | 0.4962 | 0.4963 | 0.4964 |
| 2.7 | 0.4965 | 0.4966 | 0.4967 | 0.4968 | 0.4969 | 0.4970 | 0.4971 | 0.4972 | 0.4973 | 0.4974 |
| 2.8 | 0.4974 | 0.4975 | 0.4976 | 0.4977 | 0.4977 | 0.4978 | 0.4979 | 0.4979 | 0.4980 | 0.4981 |
| 2.9 | 0.4981 | 0.4982 | 0.4982 | 0.4983 | 0.4984 | 0.4984 | 0.4985 | 0.4985 | 0.4986 | 0.4986 |
| 3.0 | 0.49865 | 0.4987 | 0.4987 | 0.4988 | 0.4989 | 0.4988 | 0.4989 | 0.4989 | 0.4989 | 0.4990 |

# Bibliography

**Books**

Bookstaber, Richard M., *Option Pricing and Strategies in Investing*, Addison-Wesley (1981).

Bookstaber, Richard M. and Roger G. Clarke, *Option Strategies for Institutional Investment Management*, Addison-Wesley (1983).

Brenner, Menachem, *Option Pricing: Theory and Applications*, Heath Lexington Books (1983).

Chamberlin, Geoffrey, *Trading in Options*, Woodhead-Faulkner, 2nd edition (1982).

Clasing, Henry K., Jr., *The Dow Jones-Irwin Guide to Put and Call Options*, Dow Jones-Irwin, revised edition (1978).

Cox, John C. and Mark Rubinstein, *Option Markets*, Prentice-Hall (1985).

Gastineau, Gary, *The Stock Options Manual*, McGraw-Hill, 2nd edition (1979).

Jarrow, Robert A. and Andrew Rudd, *Option Pricing*, Dow Jones-Irwin (1983).

Labuszewski, John and Jeanne Cairns Sinquefield, *Inside the Commodity Option Markets*, J. Wiley & Sons (1985).

McMillan, Lawrence G., *Options as a Strategic Investment*, New York Institute of Finance, 2nd edition (1986).

Nix, William and Susan Nix, *The Dow Jones-Irwin Guide to Stock Index Futures and Options*, Dow Jones-Irwin (1984).

**Articles**

No pretence is made here to construct a comprehensive options bibliography. Such a thing could contain hundreds, perhaps thousands, of articles. For a comprehensive bibliography, the reader should refer to Cox and Rubinstein (*op. cit.*). The list below is of seminal articles in various areas which should give the reader an overview of what is happening in options analysis.[1]

*1. General and survey articles*

a. Elementary

Beenstock, Michael, "The robustness of the Black-Scholes option pricing model," *The Investment Analyst*, no. 61, July 1981, 12–19.

Black, Fischer, "Fact and fantasy in the use of options," *Financial Analysts Journal*, 31, July–August 1975, 36–72.

Courtadon, Georges R. and John J. Merrick, "The option pricing model and the valuation of corporate securities," *Midland Bank Corporate Finance Journal*, vol. 1, no. 3, 43–57.

Fitzgerald, M. Desmond, "Traded options: a successful innovation," *The Banker*, May 1984, 103–107.

Galai, Dan, "Characterisation of options," *Journal of Banking and Finance*, 1, December 1977, 373–85.

Meisner, James F. and John Labuszewski, "Modifying the Black-Scholes option pricing model for alternative underlying instruments," *Financial Analysts Journal*, 40, Nov.–Dec. 1984.

Payne, A. F. T., "The market for options in London," *The Investment Analyst*, No. 60, April 1981, 12–18.

---

[1] My thanks are due to the London Stock Exchange traded options department who funded the preparation of an annotated options bibliography from which many of the titles are drawn. The complete version can be obtained from the London Stock Exchange.

b. Intermediate

Smith, Clifford W., "Option pricing: a review," *Journal of Financial Economics*, 3, Jan.–March 1976, 3–51.

c. Advanced

Merton, Robert C., "Theory of rational option pricing," *Bell Journal of Economics and Management Science*, 4, Spring 1973, 141–83.

*2. Stock and stock index options*

a. Elementary

Asay, Michael, "Stock index options: futures or physicals," *Market Perspectives*, Chicago Mercantile Exchange, vol. 1, no. 1, April 1983.

Dimson, Elroy, "Instant option valuation," *Financial Analysts Journal*, May–June 1977, 62–9; "Option valuation nomograms", *Financial Analysts Journal*, Nov.–Dec. 1977, 71–4.

b. Intermediate

Black, Fischer and Myron Scholes, "The pricing of options and corporate liabilities," *Journal of Political Economy*, May–June, 1973, 637–54.

Brennan, Michael J. and Eduardo S. Schwartz, "The valuation of American put options," *Journal of Finance*, 32, May 1977, 449–62.

Cox, John C., Stephen A. Ross and Mark Rubinstein, "Option pricing: a simplified approach," *Journal of Financial Economics*, 7, Sept. 1979, 229–63.

Roll, Richard, "An analytic valuation formula for unprotected American call options on stocks with known dividends," *Journal of Financial Economics*, 5, Nov. 1977, 251–58.

c. Advanced

Cox, John C. and Stephen A. Ross, "The valuation of options for alternative stochastic processes," *Journal of Financial Economics*, 3, Jan.–March 1976, 145–66; "A survey of some new results in financial option pricing theory," *Journal of Finance*, 31, May 1976, 383–402.

Geske, Robert, "The valuation of compound options," *Journal of Financial Economics*, 7, March 1979, 56–81.

Geske, Robert and H. E. Johnson, "The American put option valued analytically," *Journal of Finance*, 39, Dec. 1984, 1511–24.

Parkinson, Michael, "Option pricing: the American put," *Journal of Business*, Jan. 1977, 21–36.

*3. Currency options*

a. Elementary

*Euromoney supplement*, "Controlling risk with currency options," Feb. 1985.

Giddy, Ian H., "Foreign exchange options," *Journal of Futures Markets*, vol. 3, no. 2, 1983, 143–66.

Heywood, John, "Using currency options," *The Treasurer*, vol. 6, no. 2, Feb. 1984, 7–11.

b. Intermediate

Biger, Nahum and John Hall, "The valuation of currency options," *Financial Management*, 12, Spring 1983, 24–8.

Bodurtha, James N. and Georges R. Courtadon, "Efficiency tests of the foreign currency options market," *Journal of Finance*, vol. XLI, no. 1, March 1986, 151–62.

Garman, Mark B. and Steven W. Kohlhagen, "Foreign currency option values," *Journal of International Money and Finance*, 2, Dec. 1983, 231–37.

Grabbe, J. Orlin, "The pricing of call and put options on foreign exchange," *Journal of International Money and Finance*, 2, Dec. 1983, 239–53.

*4. Interest rate options*

a. Elementary

Goodman, Laurie S., "Put-call parity with coupon instruments," *Journal of Portfolio Management*, 11, Winter 1985, no. 2.

Parkinson, Michael, "The valuation of GNMA options," *Financial Analysts Journal*, 38, Sept.–Oct. 1982, 66–76.

Pitts, Mark, "The pricing of options on debt securities," *Journal of Portfolio Management*, 11, Winter 1985, no. 2, 41–50.

b. Intermediate

Ball, Clifford A. and Walter N. Torous, "Bond price dynamics and options," *Journal of Financial and Quantitative Analysis*, 18, Dec. 1983, 517–31.

c. Advanced

Courtadon, Georges, "The pricing of options on default-free bonds," *Journal of Financial and Quantitative Analysis*, 17, March 1982, 75–100.

Rendelman, Richard J. and Brit J. Bartter, "The pricing of options on debt securities," *Journal of Financial and Quantitative Analysis*, 15, March 1980, 11–24.

*5. Options on futures*

a. Elementary

Black, Fischer, "The pricing of commodity contracts," *Journal of Financial Economics*, Jan.–March 1976, 167–79.

Whaley, Robert E., "Valuation of American futures options, theory and empirical tests," *Journal of Finance*, vol. 41, no. 1, March 1986, 127–50.

b. Intermediate

Brenner, Menachem, Georges Courtadon and Marti Subrahmaniam, "Options on the spot and options on futures," *Journal of Finance* 40, Dec. 1985, 1303–17.

Ramaswamy, Krishna and Suresh M. Sundaresan, "The valuation of options on futures contracts," *Journal of Finance*, 40, Dec. 1985, 1319–40.

*6. Option trading techniques*

Dawson, Frederic, "Risk and returns in continuous option writing," *Journal of Portfolio Management*, 5, Winter 1979, 23–27.

Degler, W. H. and H. Phillip Becker, "19 option strategies and when to use them," *Futures*, June 1984.

Pounds, Henry M., "Covered call option writing: strategies and results," *Journal of Portfolio Management*, 4, Winter 1978, 31–42.

Ritchken, Peter H. and Harvey M. Salkin, "Safety first selection techniques for option spreads," *Journal of Portfolio Management*, 9, Spring 1983, 61–67.

Slivka, Ronald R., "Risk and return for option investment strategies," *Financial Analysts Journal*, 36, Sept.–Oct. 1980, 67–73.

Yates, James W., Jr. and Robert W. Kopprasch Jr., "Writing covered call options: profits and risks," *Journal of Portfolio Management*, 7, Fall 1980, 74–9.

*7. Options in portfolio management*

a. Elementary

Bookstaber, Richard M. and Roger G. Clarke, "Options can alter portfolio return distributions," *Journal of Portfolio Management*, 7, Spring 1981, 63–70.

Moriarty, Eugene, Susan Phillips and Paula Tosini, "A comparison of options and futures in the management of portfolio risk," *Financial Analysts Journal*, 37, Jan.–Feb. 1981, 61–7.

b. Intermediate

Bookstaber, Richard M. and Roger G. Clarke, "Option portfolio strategies: measurement and evaluation," *Journal of Business*, 57, 1984, 469–92.

Evnine, Jeremy and Andrew Rudd, "Option portfolio risk analysis," *Journal of Portfolio Management*, 10, Winter 1984, 23–7.

Merton, Robert C., Myron Scholes and Matthew L. Gladstein, "The returns and risks of alternative call-option portfolio investment strategies," *Journal of Business*, 51, April 1978, 183–242; "The returns and risks of alternative put-option portfolio investment strategies," *Journal of Business*, 55, Jan. 1982, 1–55.

## 8. Empirical tests of option models

Ball, Clifford A., Walter N. Torous and Adrian E. Tschoegl, "An empirical investigation of the European Exchange gold options market," *Journal of Banking and Finance*, 9, March 1985, 101–14.

Castagna, A. D. and Z. P. Matolesy, "The evaluation of a traded options pricing model in Australia," *Journal of Business Finance and Accounting*, 10, Summer 1983.

Chiras, Donald P. and Steven Manaster, "The information content of option prices and a test of market efficiency," *Journal of Financial Economics*, 6, June–Sept. 1978, 213–34.

Galai, Dan, "Tests of market efficiency of the Chicago Board Options Exchange," *Journal of Business*, 50, April 1977, 167–97.

Macbeth, James D. and Larry J. Merville, "Tests of Black-Scholes and Cox call option valuation models," *Journal of Finance*, 35, May 1980, 285–300.

Sterk, William E., "Comparative performance of the Black-Scholes and Roll-Geske-Whaley option pricing models," *Journal of Financial and Quantitative Analysis*, 18, Sept. 1983, 345–54.

## 9. Estimating volatilities

### a. Intermediate

Beckers, Stan, "Standard deviations implied in option prices as predictors of future stock price variability," *Journal of Banking and Finance*, 5, Sept. 1981, 363–82; "Variances of security price returns based on high, low and closing prices," *Journal of Business*, 56, Jan. 1983, 97–112.

Garman, Mark B. and Michael J. Klass, "On the estimation of security price volatility from historical data," *Journal of Business*, 53, Jan. 1980, 67–78.

Latane, Henry A. and Richard J. Rendleman Jr., "Standard deviations of stock price ratios implied in option prices," *Journal of Finance*, 31, May 1976, 369–82.

Parkinson, Michael, "The extreme value method for estimating the variance of the rate of return," *Journal of Business*, 53, Jan. 1980, 61–5.

### b. Advanced

Ball, Clifford A. and Walter N. Torous, "The maximum likelihood estimation of security price volatility: theory, evidence and application to option pricing," *Journal of Business*, 57, Jan. 1984, 97–112.

Beranek, William and Cyrus J. Mehta, "Tracking asset volatility by means of a Bayesian switching regression," *Journal of Financial and Quantitative Analysis*, 17, June 1982, 241–63.

## 10. Applications to other securities

Brennan, Michael J. and Eduardo S. Schwartz, "Convertible bonds: valuation and optimal strategies for call and conversion," *Journal of Finance*, 32, Dec. 1977, 1699–716; "The pricing of equity-linked life insurance with an asset value guarantee," *Journal of Financial Economics*, 3, June 1976, 195–213.

Emanuel, David C., "A theoretical model for valuing preferred stock," *Journal of Finance*, 38, Sept. 1983, 1133–55.

Galai, Dan and Ronald W. Masulis, "The option pricing model and the risk factor of stock," *Journal of Financial Economics*, 3, Jan.–March 1976, 55–81.

Geske, Robert, "The valuation of corporate liabilities as compound options," *Journal of Financial and Quantitative Analysis*, 12, Nov. 1977, 541–52.

Sharpe, William F., "Corporate pension funding policy," *Journal of Financial Economics*, 3, June 1976, 183–93.

Sosin, Howard W., "On the valuation of federal loan guarantees to corporations," *Journal of Finance*, 35, Dec. 1980, 1209–21.

## Other references
There are many other sources of information on options.

### a. The exchanges
All the exchanges publish numerous leaflets and booklets on options trading. Particularly good booklets have been published by the London International Financial Futures Exchange, the Chicago Board of Trade and the Chicago Mercantile Exchange.

*b. Journals*
Articles on options frequently appear in the following journals.

*The Banker*
*Euromoney*
*Euromoney Corporate Finance*
*Financial Analysts Journal*
*Futures and Options World*
*Futures*
*Intermarket*
*Investment Analyst*

*Journal of Business*
*Journal of Finance*
*Journal of Financial Economics*
*Journal of Financial and Quantitative Analysis*
*Journal of Futures Markets*
*Journal of Portfolio Management*
*Options and Futures*

# Index